"This Country is a hilarious and sometimes harrowing graphic memoir about the Mahdavians' quest to live self-sufficiently in rural Idaho. Learning how to cut down a tree to heat your own house and grow your own vegetables is only one part of it.... Wonderful drawings and beautiful writing make this book a great read."
—ROZ CHAST, cartoonist and author of Can't We Talk about Something More Pleasant?

"Why did urban, vegetarian, gun-wary Navied Mahdavian, of Iranian descent, have the big, bright idea to move with his wife to the frigid mountains of Idaho, months before Trump's inauguration? Riveting, searching, complex, and, oh, hilarious, this memoir ultimately is a quest for strength, wildness, and love, for a deeper vision of all things Earth. Surely this is my favorite graphic memoir I've read in years."
—DEB OLIN UNFERTH, author of Revolution: The Year I Fell in Love and Went to Join the War

"A charming, wise, and haunting book. [I've known] that town quite well for the last thirty years, [and Mahdavian has] captured it in all its complexity."
—CHRISTOPHER GUEST, actor, screenwriter, and director (Best in Show, Waiting for Guffman, This Is Spinal Tap)

"I knew Navied Mahdavian was one of the funniest cartoonists of his generation; This Country proves he is also one of its most subtle and sophisticated graphic storytellers. In Mahdavian's hands, comics feel like poetry. Perfect ink drawings bring land, beast, and humans, with all their delicacy and yearning, viscerally to life. This Country, a quintessential story of seeking a home in America and (maybe) finding it, made me want to grant my own surroundings the grace, humor, and dignity of Mahdavian's observant study."
—AMY KURZWEIL, cartoonist and author of Flying Couch: A Graphic Memoir

"Enamored of nature and dazzled by fantasies of the rugged West, a young mixed-race couple builds a tiny home in the wilds of Idaho—and must confront an America at odds with itself. In This Country, Mahdavian explores today's cultural divide with a keen eye and a graceful touch. The resulting portrait is by turns hilarious and heartbreaking, elegant and complex, brutal and tender. I dare you not to fall in love."
—ALIA VOLZ, author of Home Baked: My Mom, Marijuana, and the Stoning of San Francisco

"This Country is touching, personal, and frequently hilarious. Mahdavian weaves heavy themes of home and belonging with disarming moments of silliness and levity. It's a story specific to his experience, yet relatable to anyone who has ever searched for a place to be."
—REZA FARAZMAND, writer and illustrator of Poorly Drawn Lines

"Ostensibly, This Country is about a couple finding their place in the world and learning the true history of the land they're building a life on—a land that has seen both turmoil and awe—but amid the harsh truth, blatant racism, and struggles to fit in, there is so much beauty and humor and compassion. Mahdavian's drawings are deceptively simple, perfectly capturing the wonder of little everyday occurrences. Of time moving, a small family growing and changing, of an entire country still reckoning with past and present mistakes. This is a very important book for pretty much everyone."
—JULIA WERTZ, cartoonist and author of Impossible People and Tenements, Towers & Trash

This Country

Searching for Home in (Very) Rural America

NAVIED MAHDAVIAN

PA PRESS

PRINCETON ARCHITECTURAL PRESS · NEW YORK

To Emelie, for building me a home.

PROLOGUE

Rura mihi et rigui placeant in vallibus amnes,
Flumina amem sylvasque inglorius.

"Let my delight be the country, and the
running streams amid the dells—
may I love the waters and the woods,
though I be unknown to fame."
—Virgil, *Georgics*

SUMMER 2016

Listen to this:

"There is much confusion between land and country.

Country is the personality of land, the collective harmony of its soil, life, and weather."*

IN OUR FIRST SUMMER ON OUR LAND, ALL I KNEW WAS THAT IT WAS HOT IN JULY.

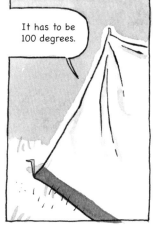

It has to be 100 degrees.

*ALDO LEOPOLD, "A SAND COUNTY ALMANAC"

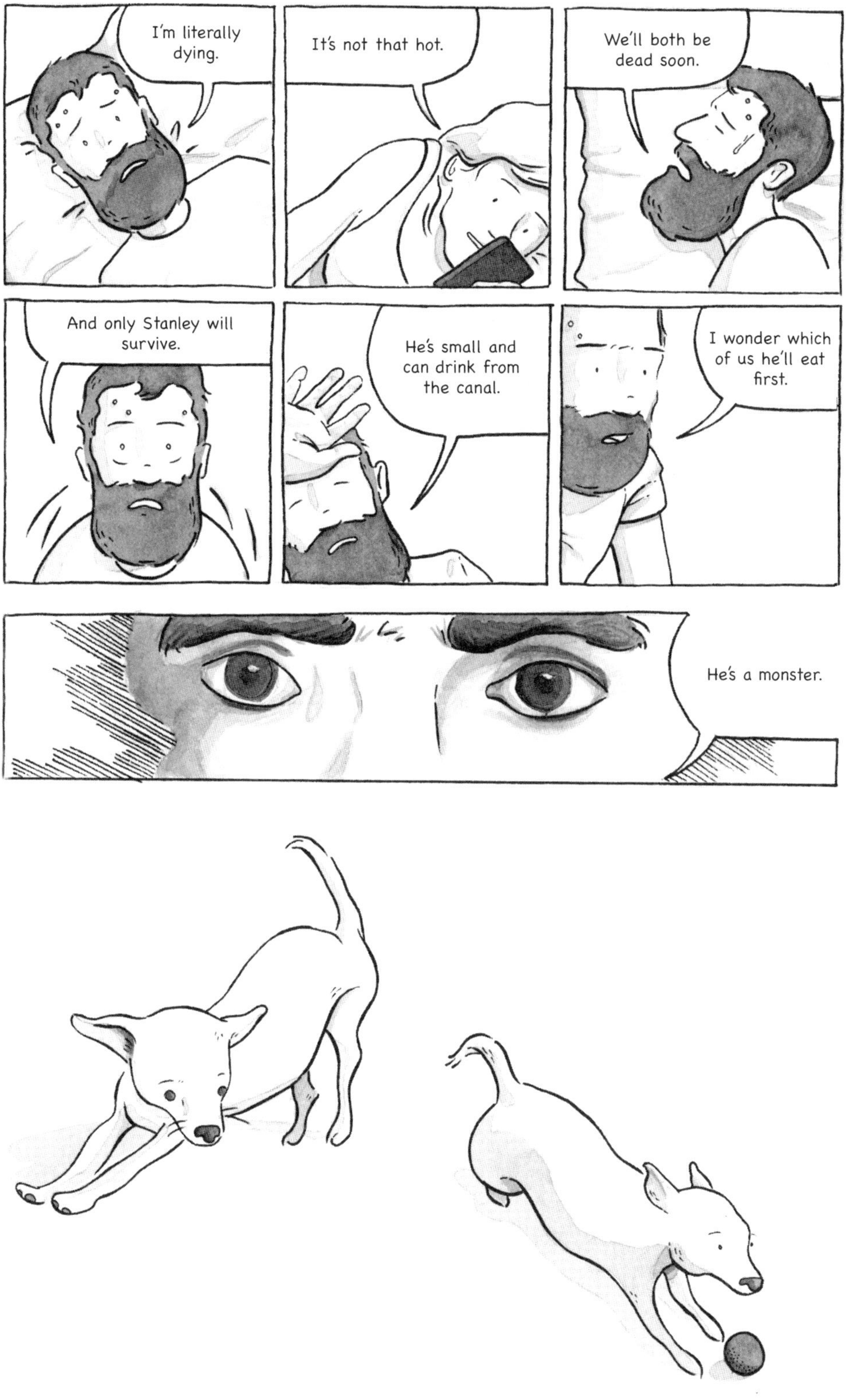
I'm literally dying.
It's not that hot.
We'll both be dead soon.
And only Stanley will survive.
He's small and can drink from the canal.
I wonder which of us he'll eat first.
He's a monster.

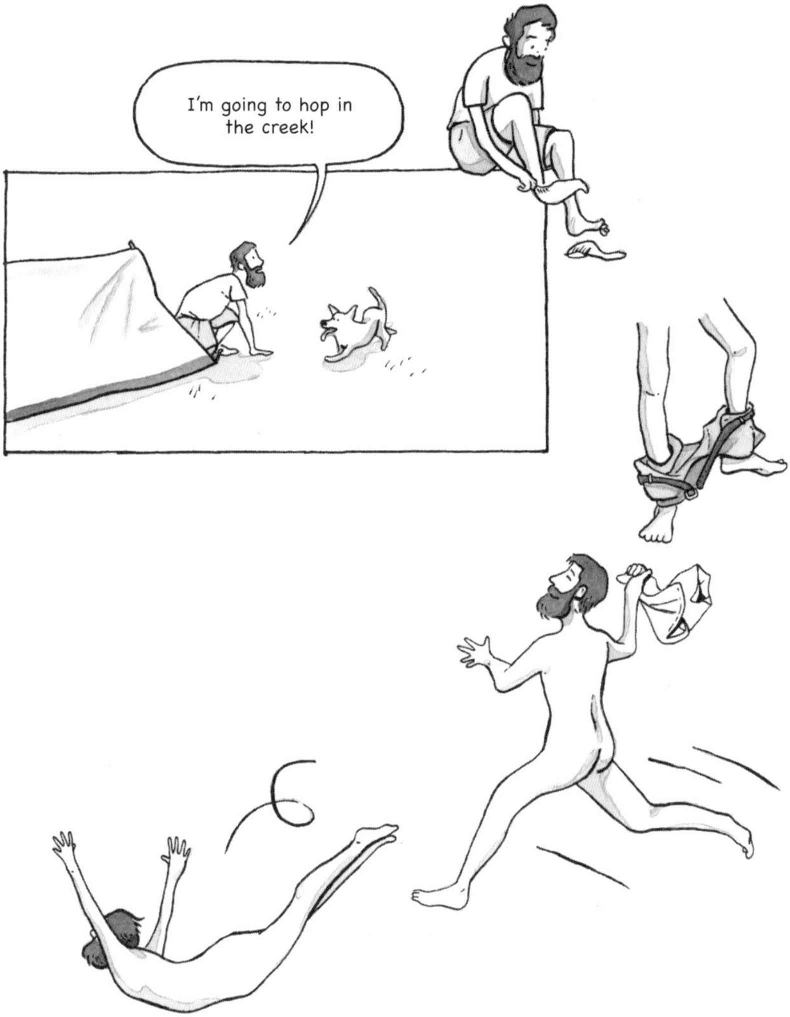
I'm going to hop in the creek!

AT THE TIME, MY WIFE, EMELIE, AND I WERE LIVING IN THE SAN FRANCISCO BAY AREA, BUT ON A TEACHER'S AND DOCUMENTARY FILMMAKER'S SALARIES WE HAD BEEN FORCED TO MOVE FARTHER AND FARTHER AWAY FROM THE CITY.

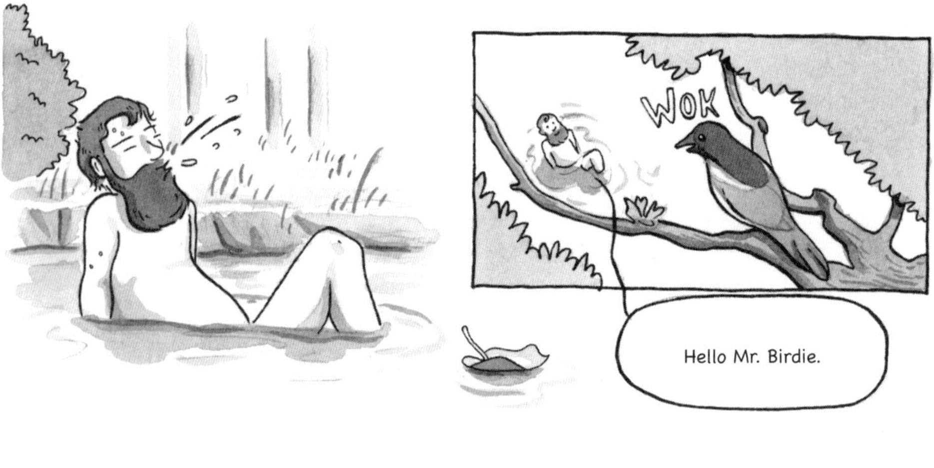
WOK
Hello Mr. Birdie.

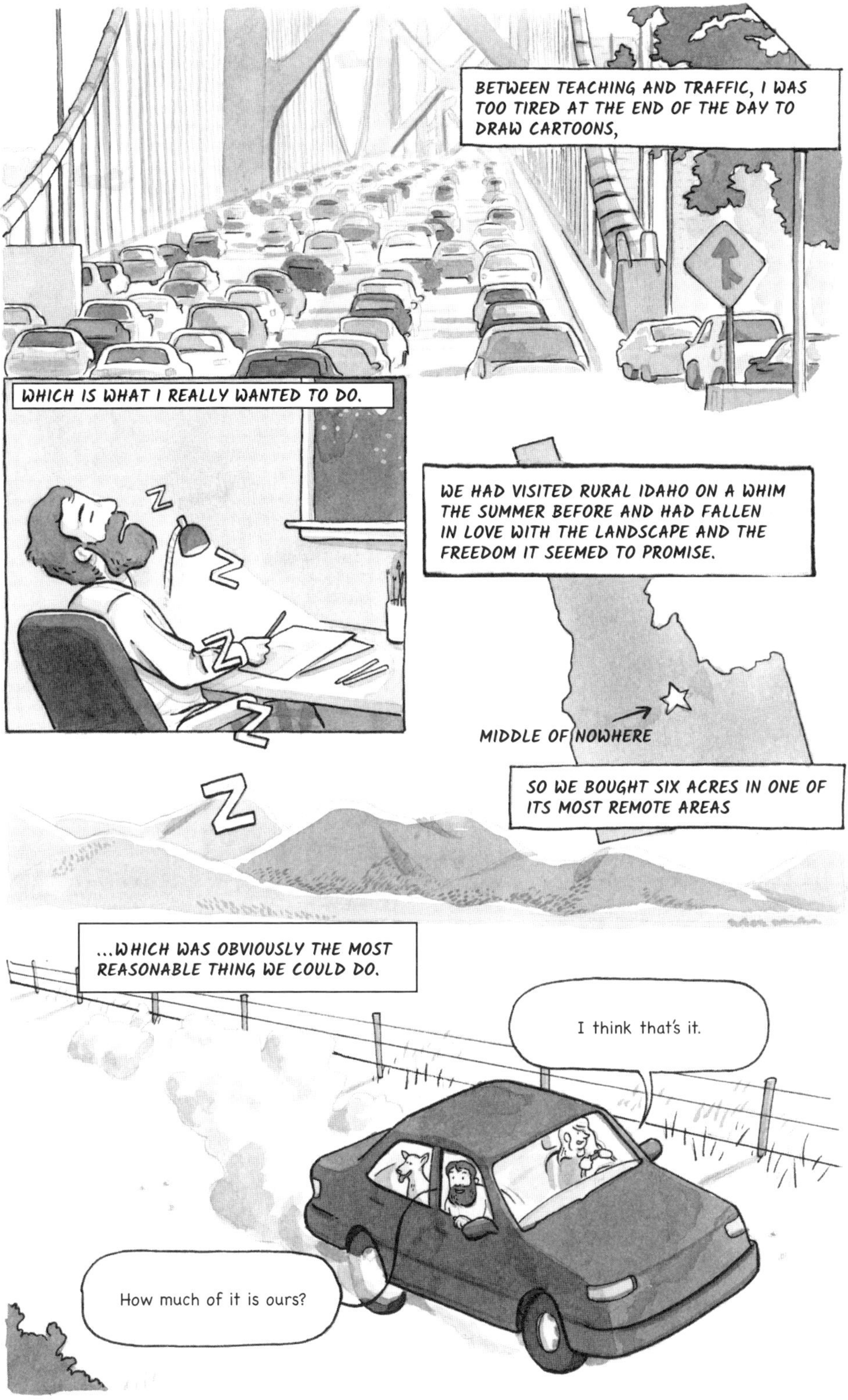
BETWEEN TEACHING AND TRAFFIC, I WAS TOO TIRED AT THE END OF THE DAY TO DRAW CARTOONS,
WHICH IS WHAT I REALLY WANTED TO DO.
WE HAD VISITED RURAL IDAHO ON A WHIM THE SUMMER BEFORE AND HAD FALLEN IN LOVE WITH THE LANDSCAPE AND THE FREEDOM IT SEEMED TO PROMISE.
MIDDLE OF NOWHERE
SO WE BOUGHT SIX ACRES IN ONE OF ITS MOST REMOTE AREAS
...WHICH WAS OBVIOUSLY THE MOST REASONABLE THING WE COULD DO.
I think that's it.
How much of it is ours?

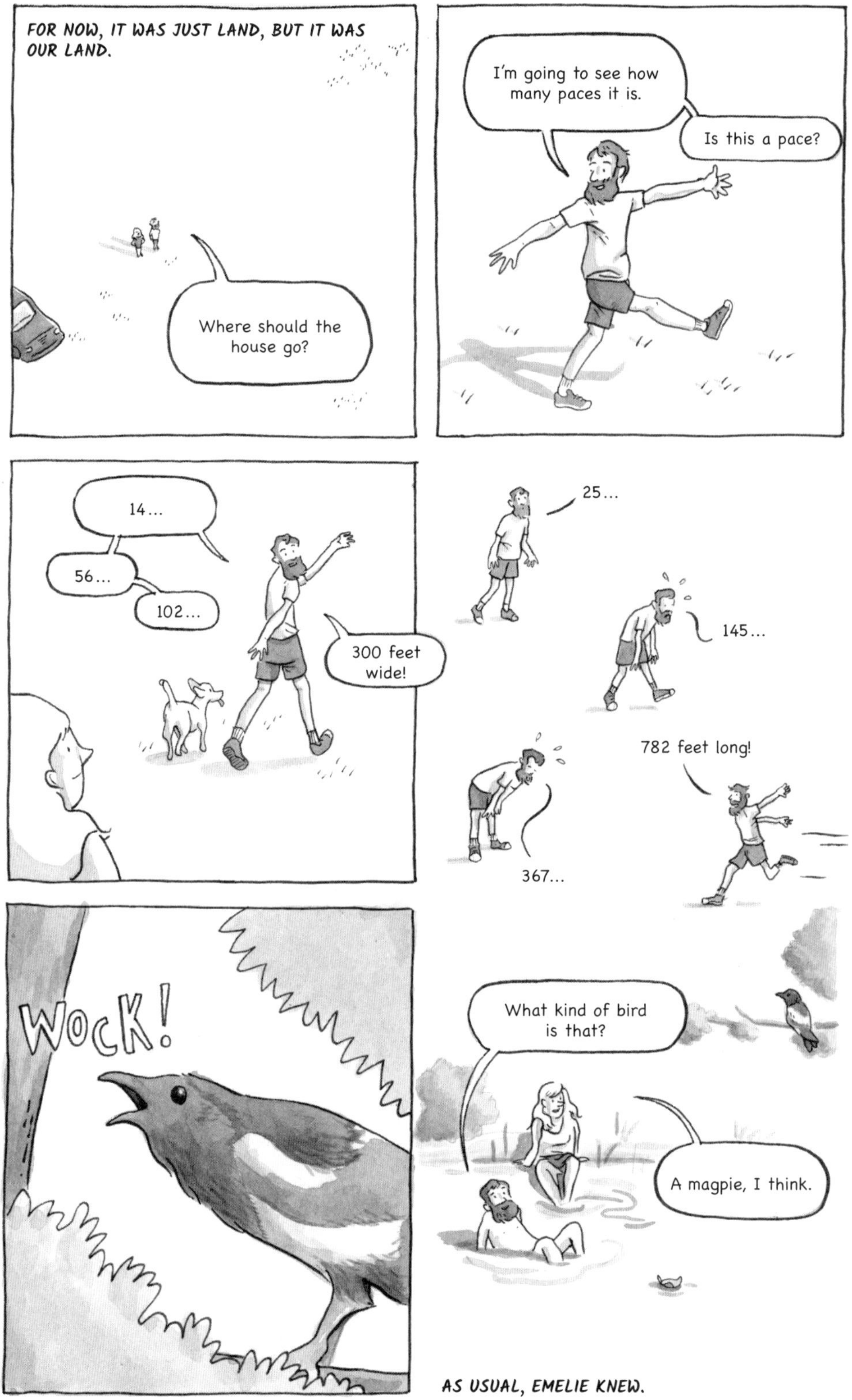
FOR NOW, IT WAS JUST LAND, BUT IT WAS OUR LAND.
Where should the house go?
I'm going to see how many paces it is.
Is this a pace?
14...
56...
102...
300 feet wide!
25...
145...
367...
782 feet long!
WOCK!
What kind of bird is that?
A magpie, I think.
AS USUAL, EMELIE KNEW.

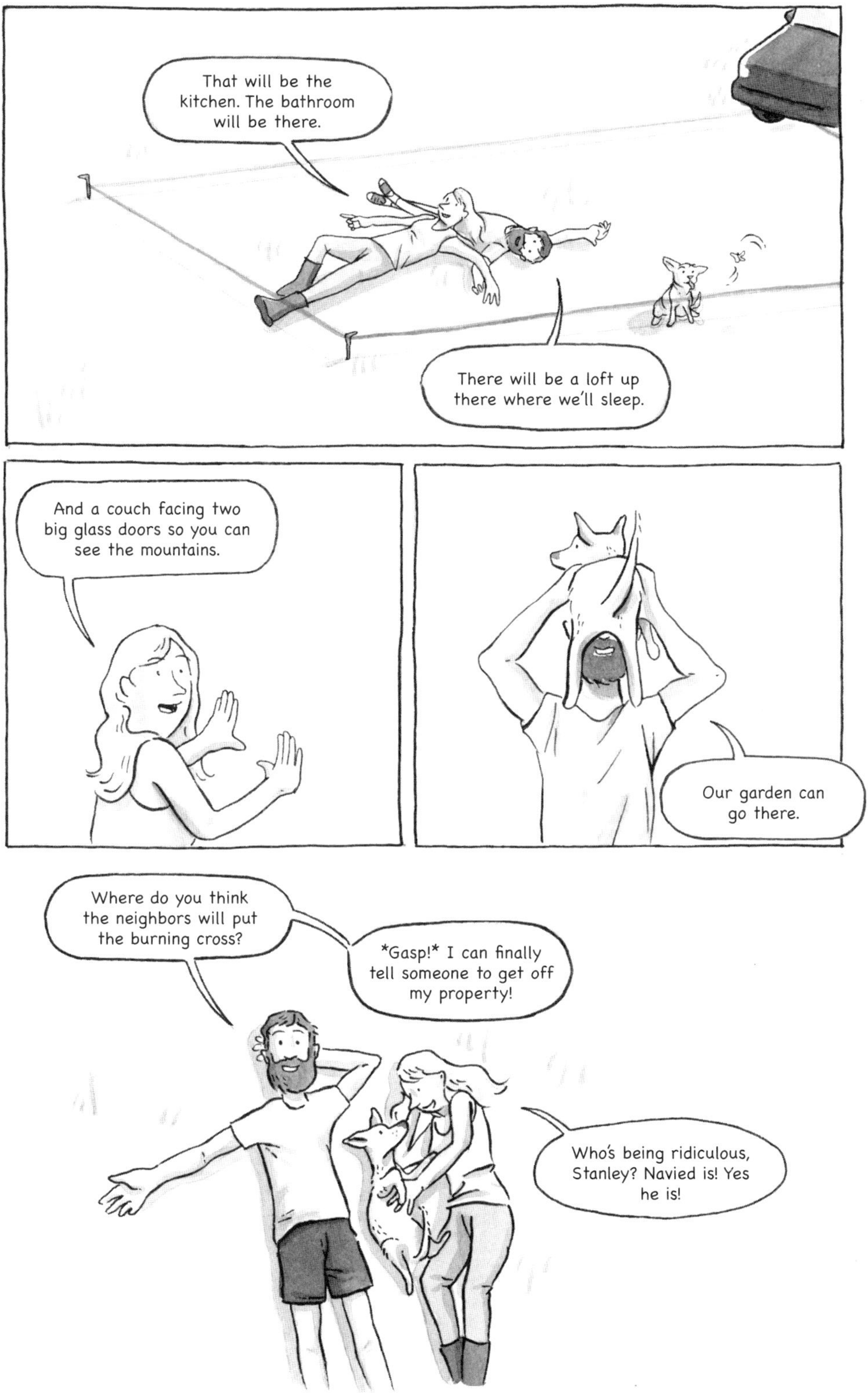
That will be the kitchen. The bathroom will be there.
There will be a loft up there where we'll sleep.
And a couch facing two big glass doors so you can see the mountains.
Our garden can go there.
Where do you think the neighbors will put the burning cross?
Gasp! I can finally tell someone to get off my property!
Who's being ridiculous, Stanley? Navied is! Yes he is!

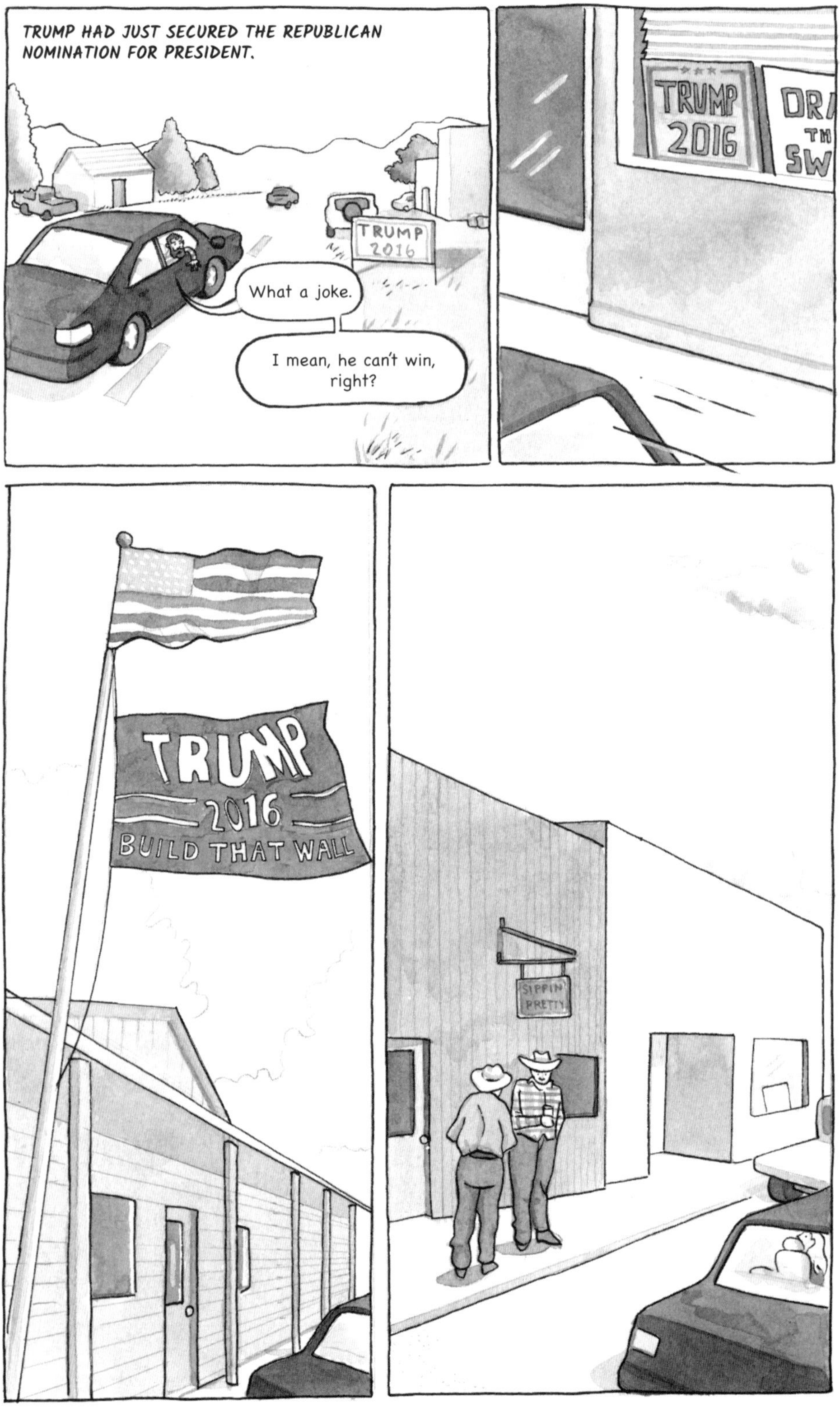
TRUMP HAD JUST SECURED THE REPUBLICAN NOMINATION FOR PRESIDENT.
TRUMP 2016
What a joke.
I mean, he can't win, right?
TRUMP 2016
TRUMP 2016 BUILD THAT WALL
SIPPIN' PRETTY

WE WERE IN SEARCH OF ADVENTURE.

A PLACE WE COULD OWN LAND AND START A FAMILY.

THE MILLENNIAL DREAM.

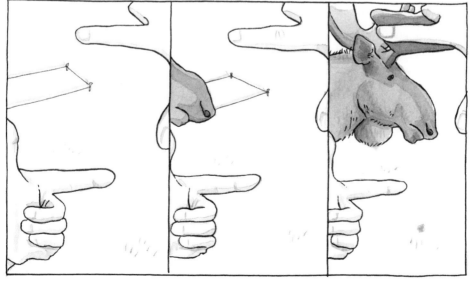

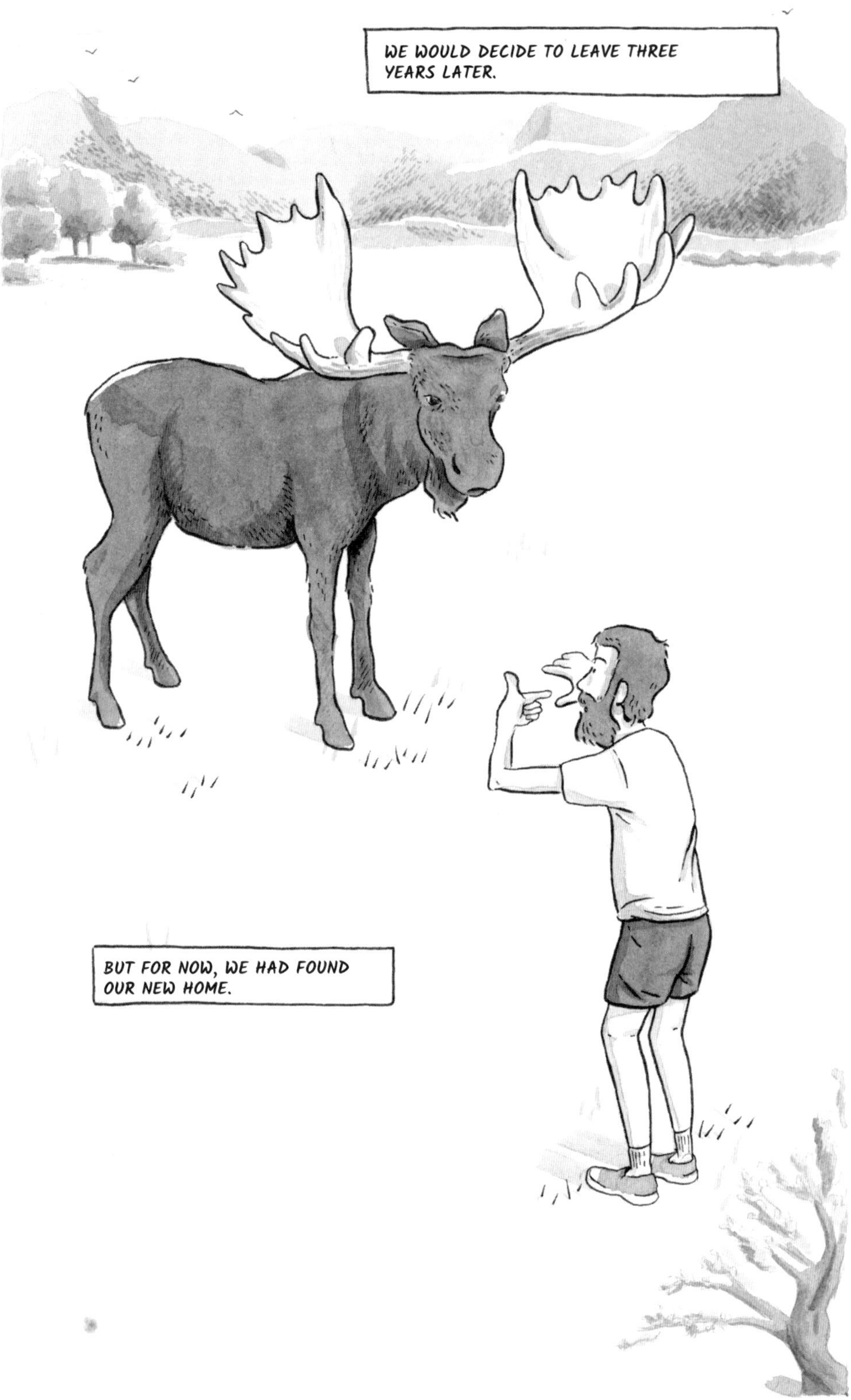
WE WOULD DECIDE TO LEAVE THREE YEARS LATER.
BUT FOR NOW, WE HAD FOUND OUR NEW HOME.

PART I

Winter 2016–Spring 2017

NOVEMBER 2016

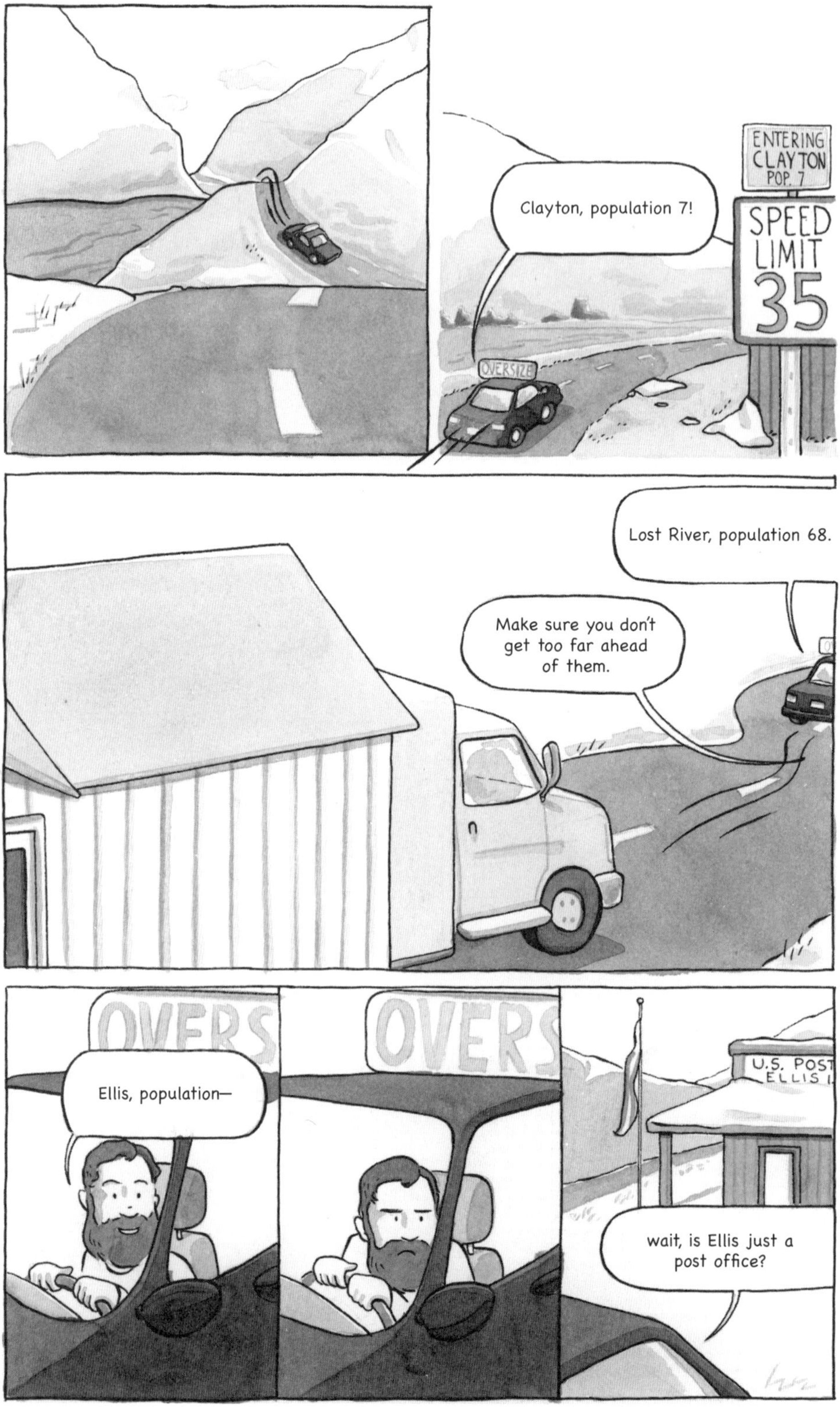
ENTERING
CLAYTON
POP. 7
SPEED
LIMIT
35
OVERSIZE
Clayton, population 7!
Lost River, population 68.
Make sure you don't get too far ahead of them.
OVERS
Ellis, population—
OVERS
U.S. POST
ELLIS
wait, is Ellis just a post office?

OUR HOUSE WAS BEING DELIVERED. WE WERE DRIVING A PILOT CAR FOR 98 MILES ALONG THE SNAKING SALMON RIVER.

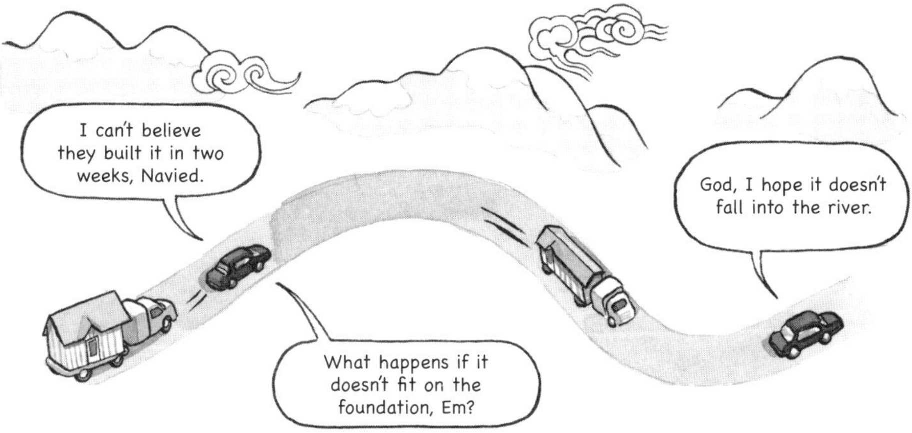
I can't believe they built it in two weeks, Navied.
What happens if it doesn't fit on the foundation, Em?
God, I hope it doesn't fall into the river.

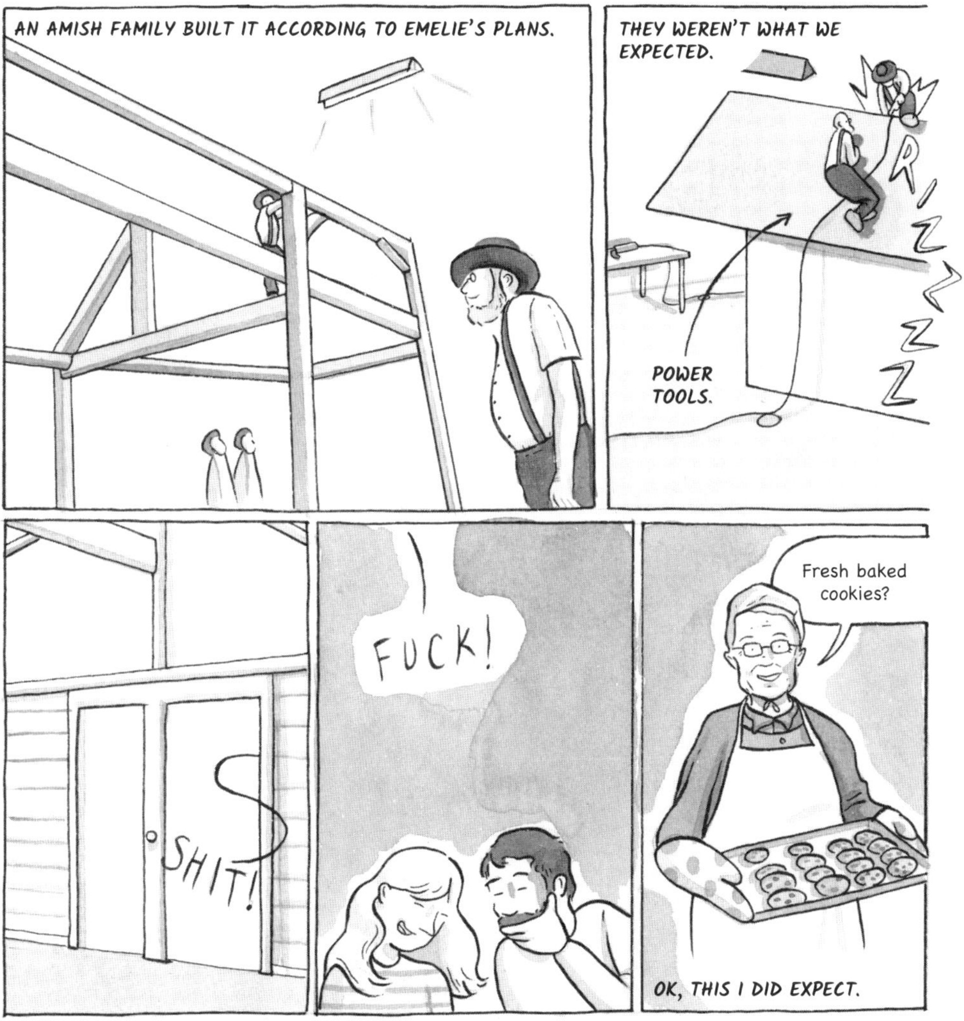
AN AMISH FAMILY BUILT IT ACCORDING TO EMELIE'S PLANS.
THEY WEREN'T WHAT WE EXPECTED.
RIZZZZ
POWER TOOLS.
SHIT!
FUCK!
Fresh baked cookies?
OK, THIS I DID EXPECT.

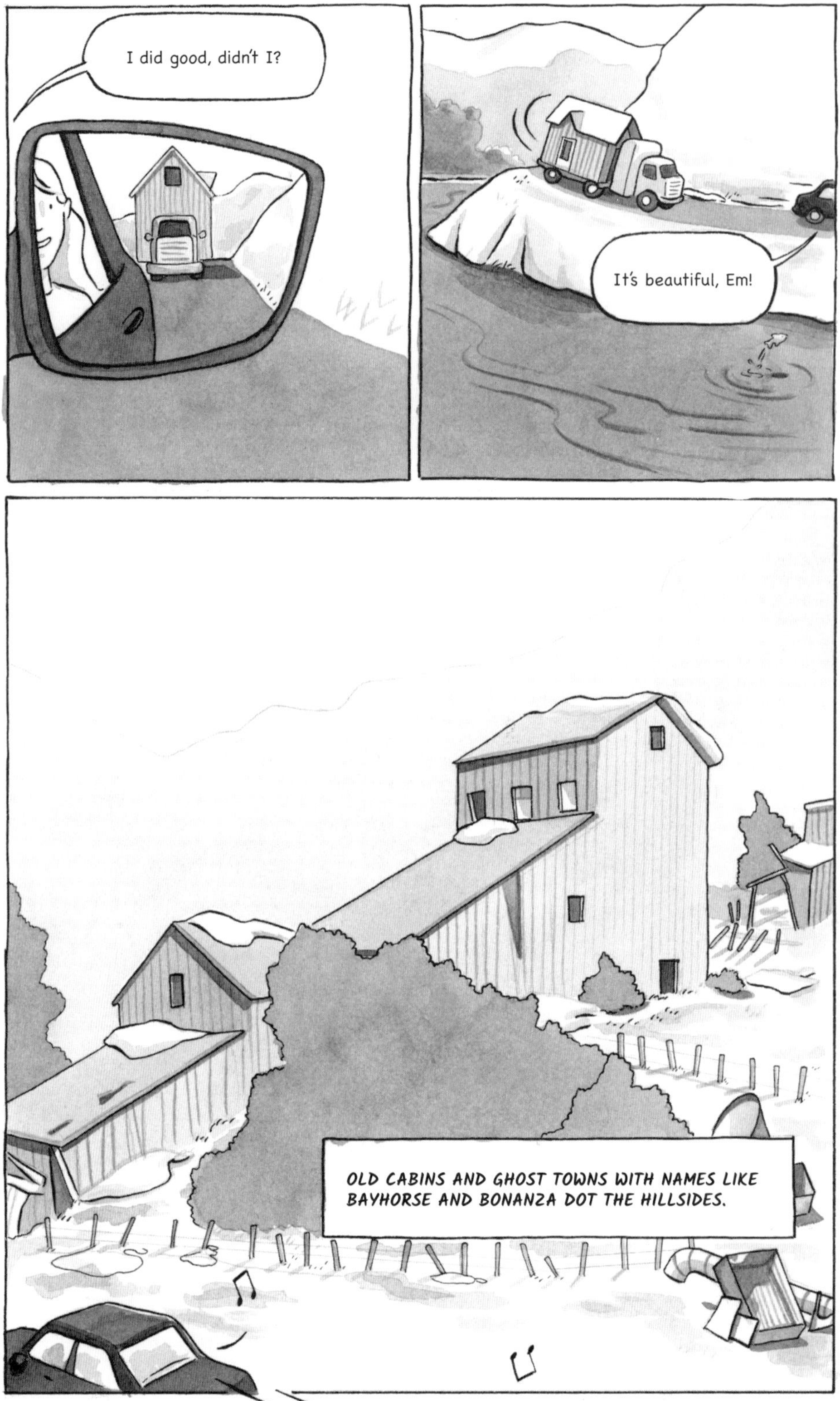
I did good, didn't I?
It's beautiful, Em!
OLD CABINS AND GHOST TOWNS WITH NAMES LIKE BAYHORSE AND BONANZA DOT THE HILLSIDES.

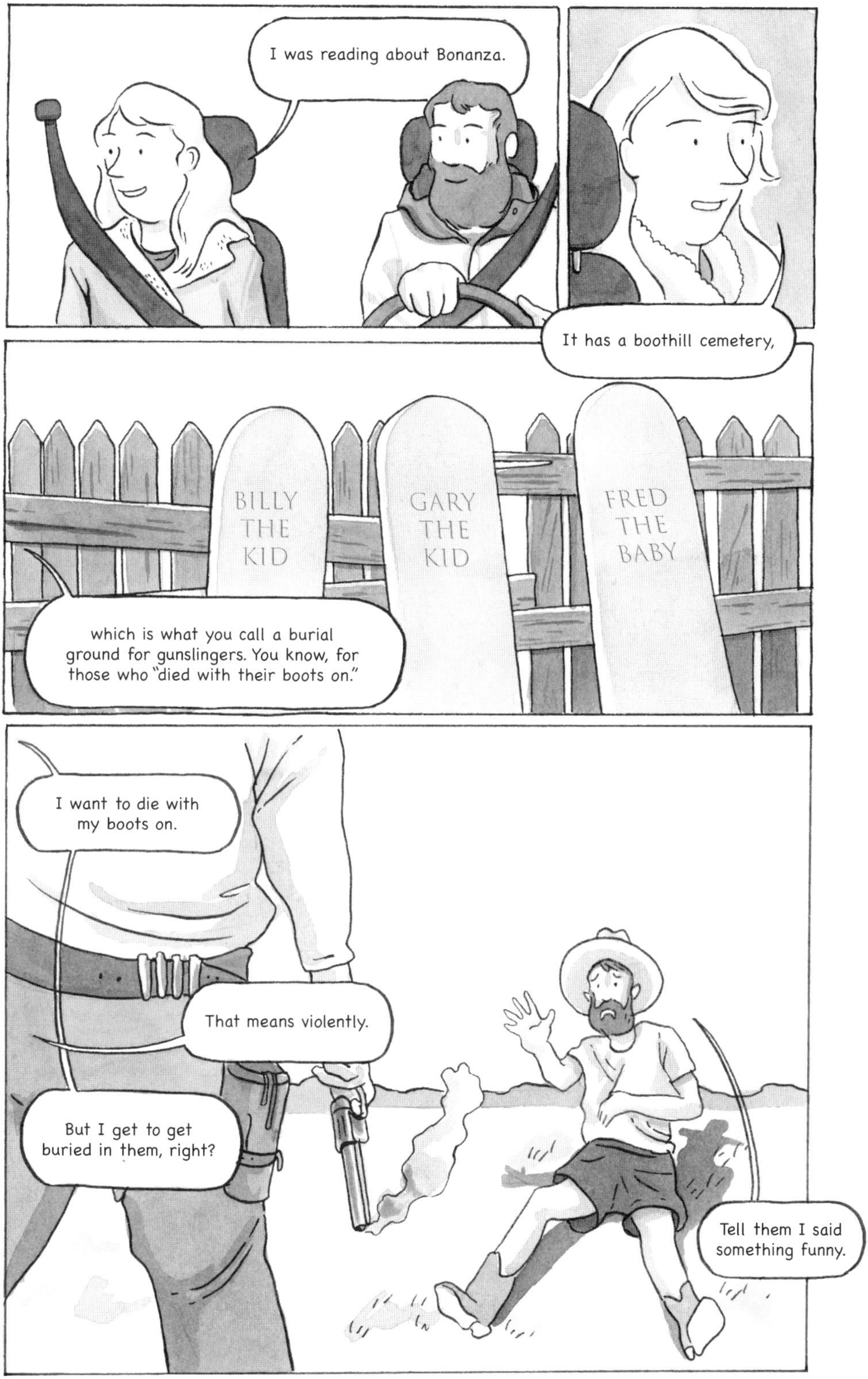
I was reading about Bonanza.
It has a boothill cemetery,
BILLY THE KID
GARY THE KID
FRED THE BABY
which is what you call a burial ground for gunslingers. You know, for those who "died with their boots on."
I want to die with my boots on.
That means violently.
But I get to get buried in them, right?
Tell them I said something funny.

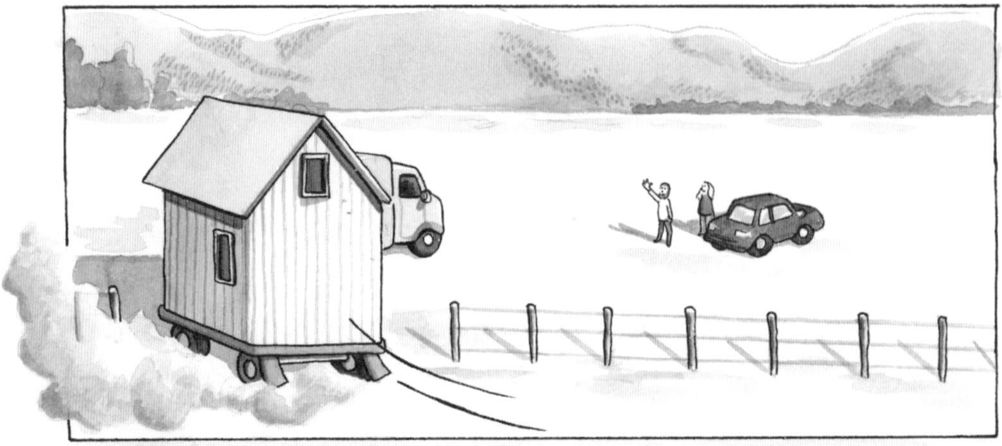

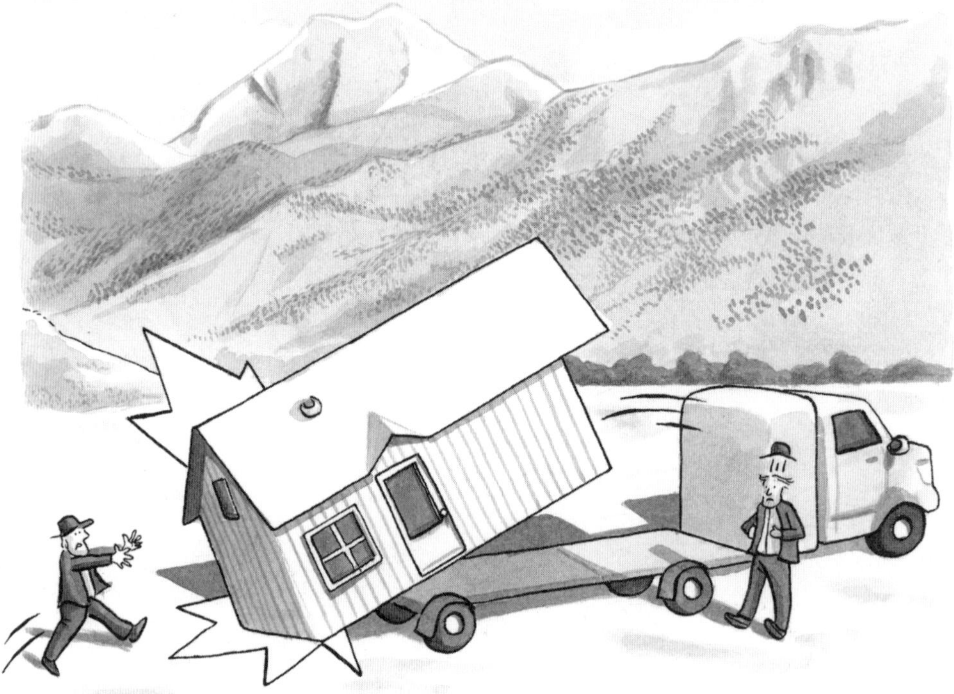

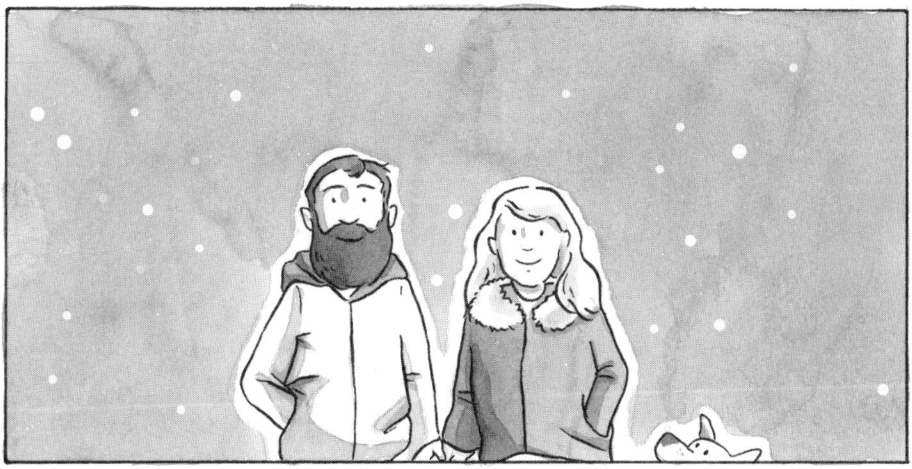

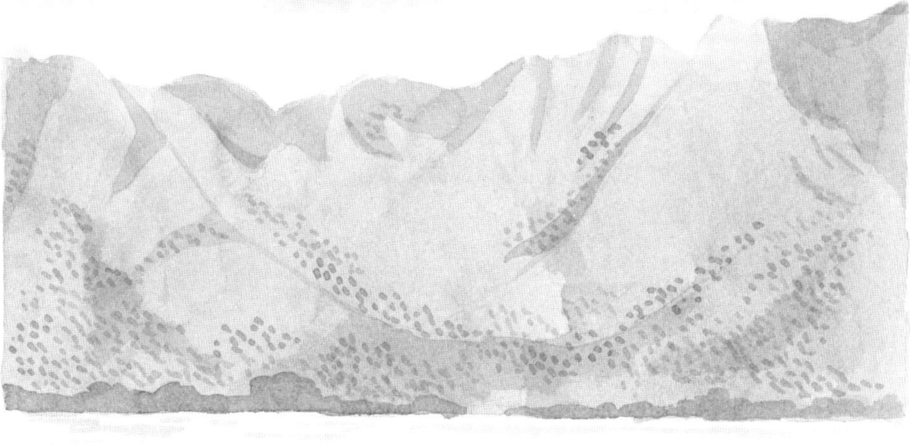

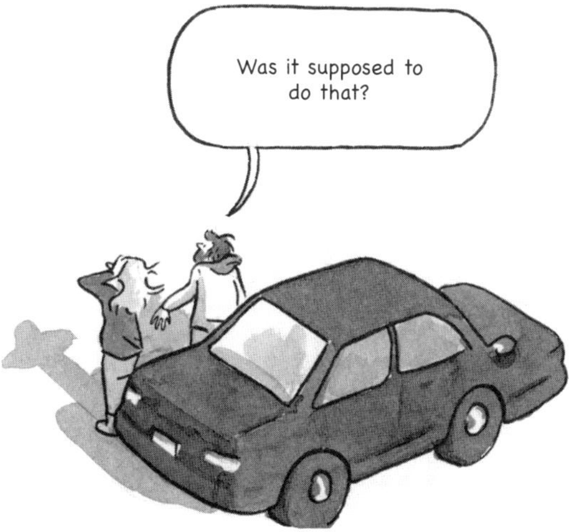
Was it supposed to do that?

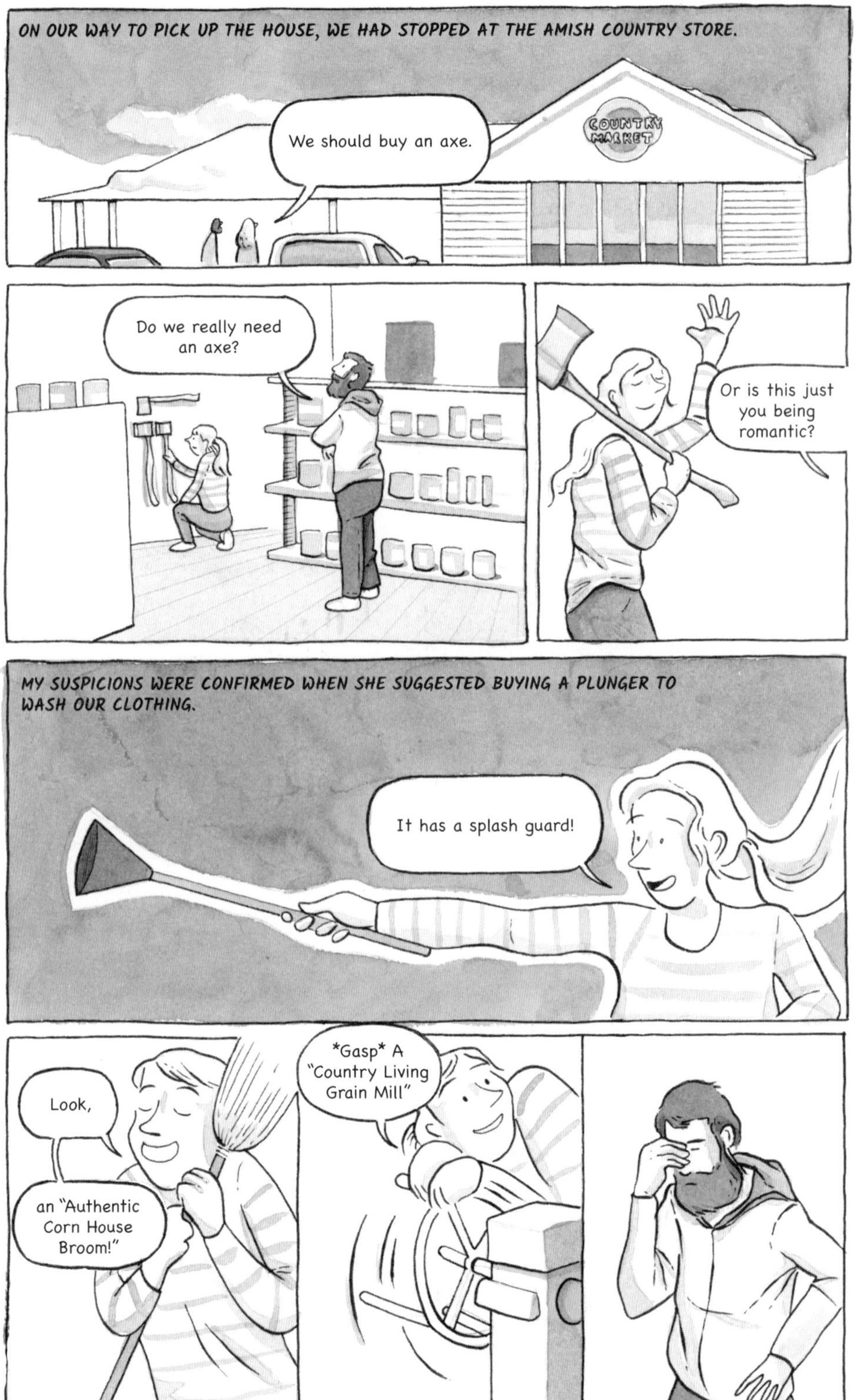

ON OUR WAY TO PICK UP THE HOUSE, WE HAD STOPPED AT THE AMISH COUNTRY STORE.
We should buy an axe.
COUNTRY MARKET
Do we really need an axe?
Or is this just you being romantic?
MY SUSPICIONS WERE CONFIRMED WHEN SHE SUGGESTED BUYING A PLUNGER TO WASH OUR CLOTHING.
It has a splash guard!
Look,
an "Authentic Corn House Broom!"
Gasp A "Country Living Grain Mill"

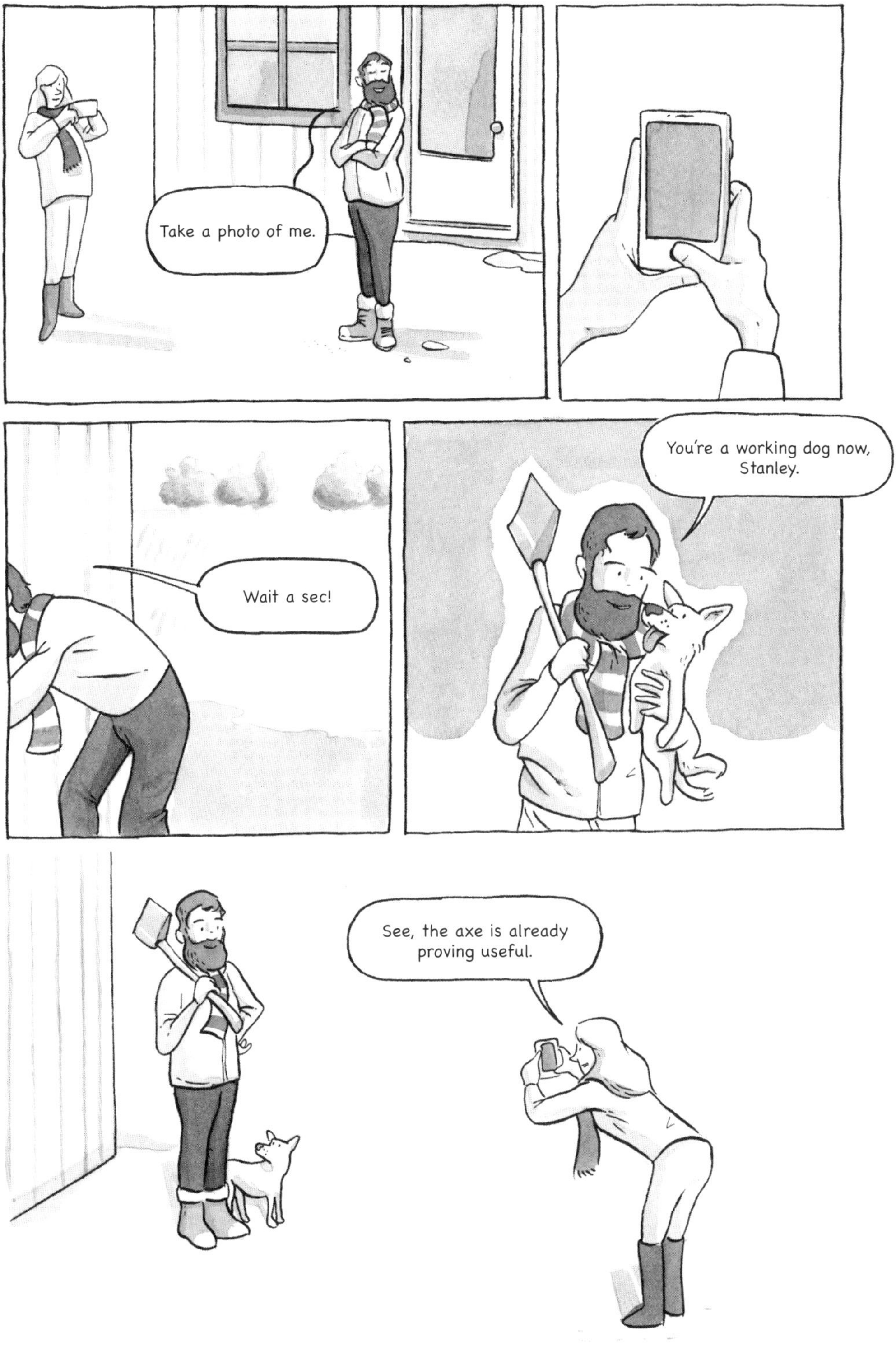
Take a photo of me.
Wait a sec!
You're a working dog now, Stanley.
See, the axe is already proving useful.

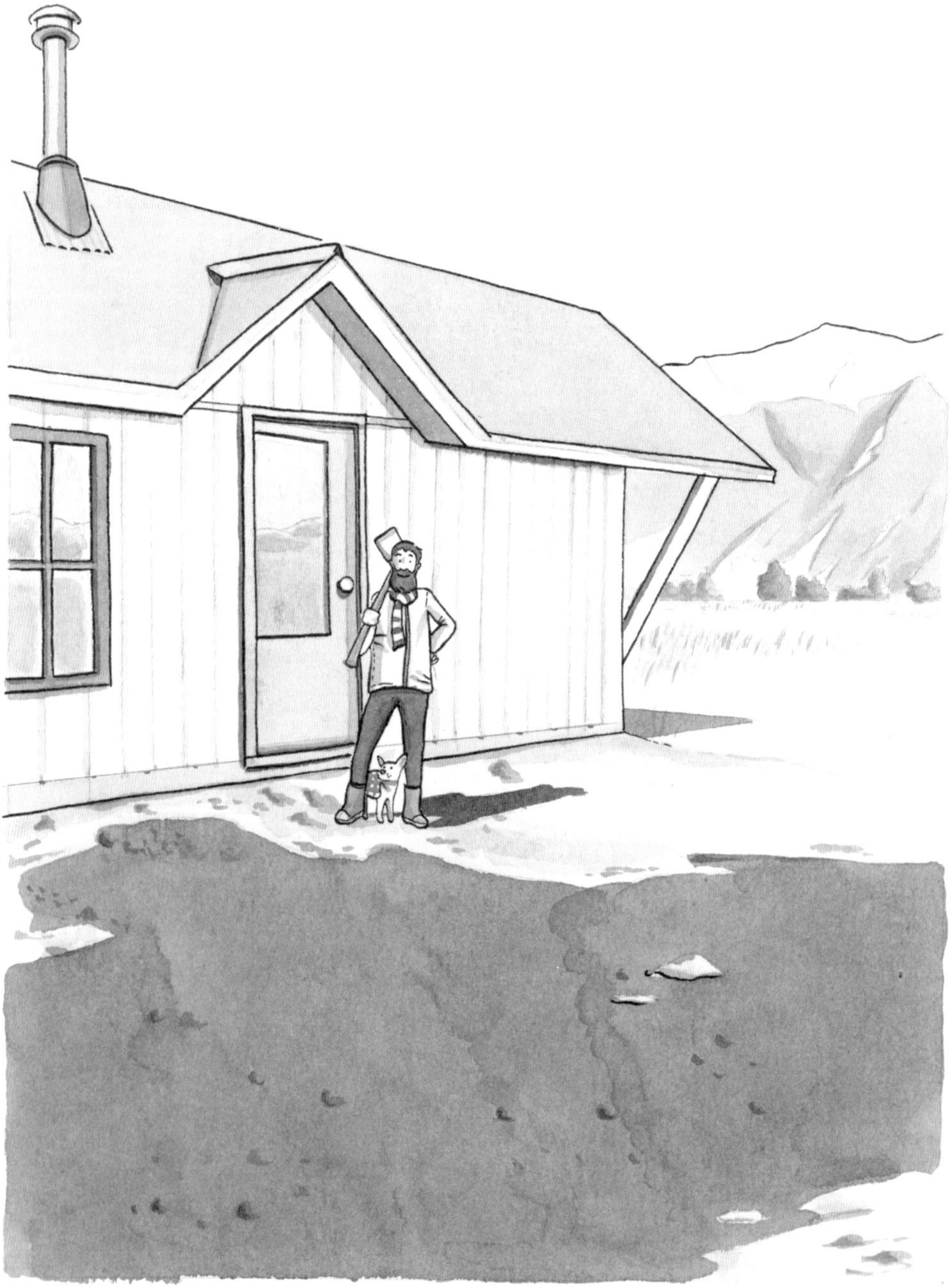

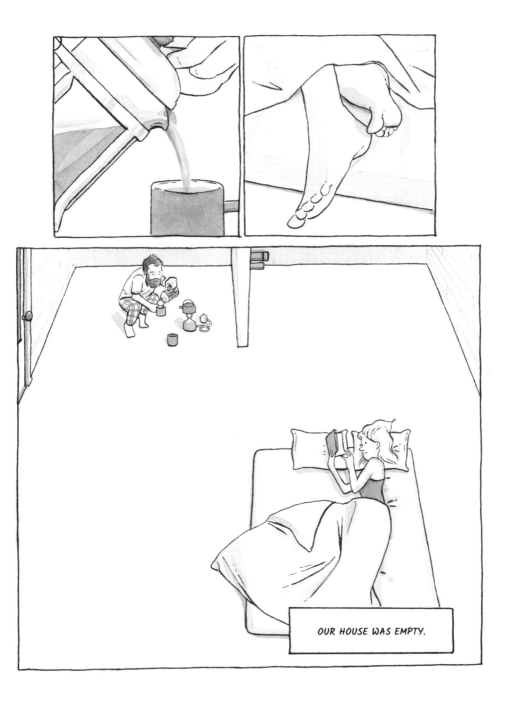

OUR HOUSE WAS EMPTY.

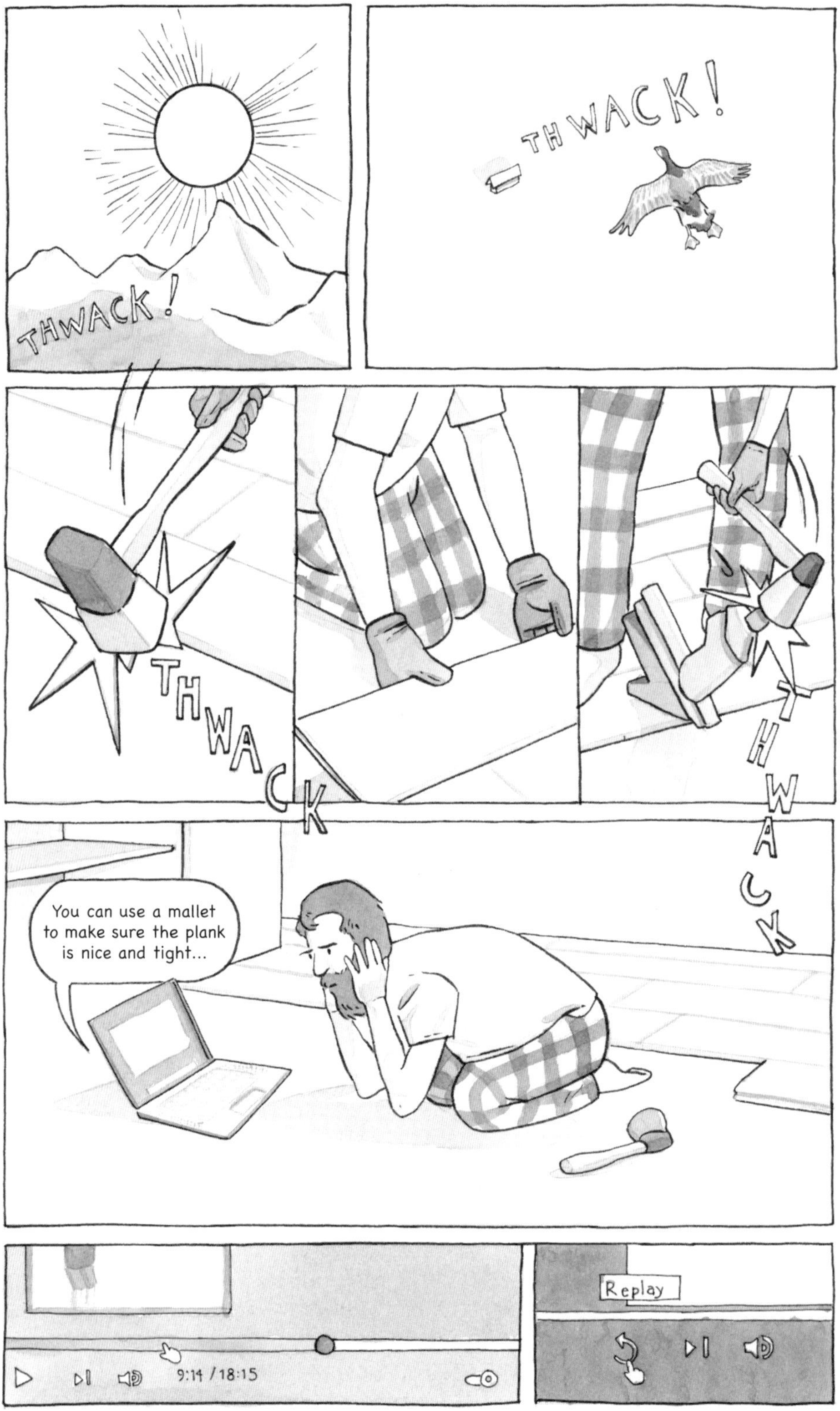
THWACK!
THWACK!
THWACK
THWACK
You can use a mallet to make sure the plank is nice and tight...
9:14 / 18:15
Replay

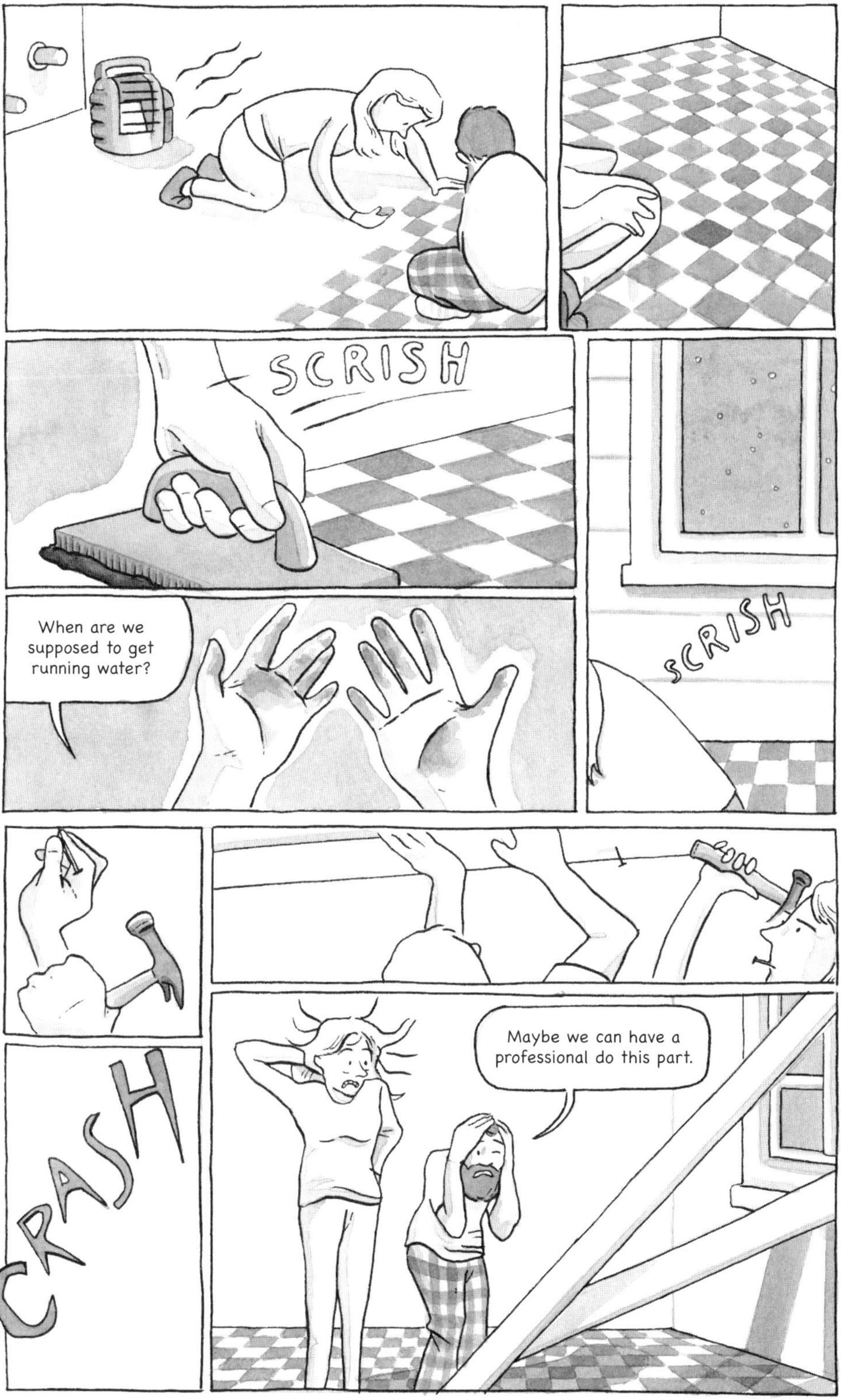
SCRISH
When are we supposed to get running water?
SCRISH
CRASH
Maybe we can have a professional do this part.

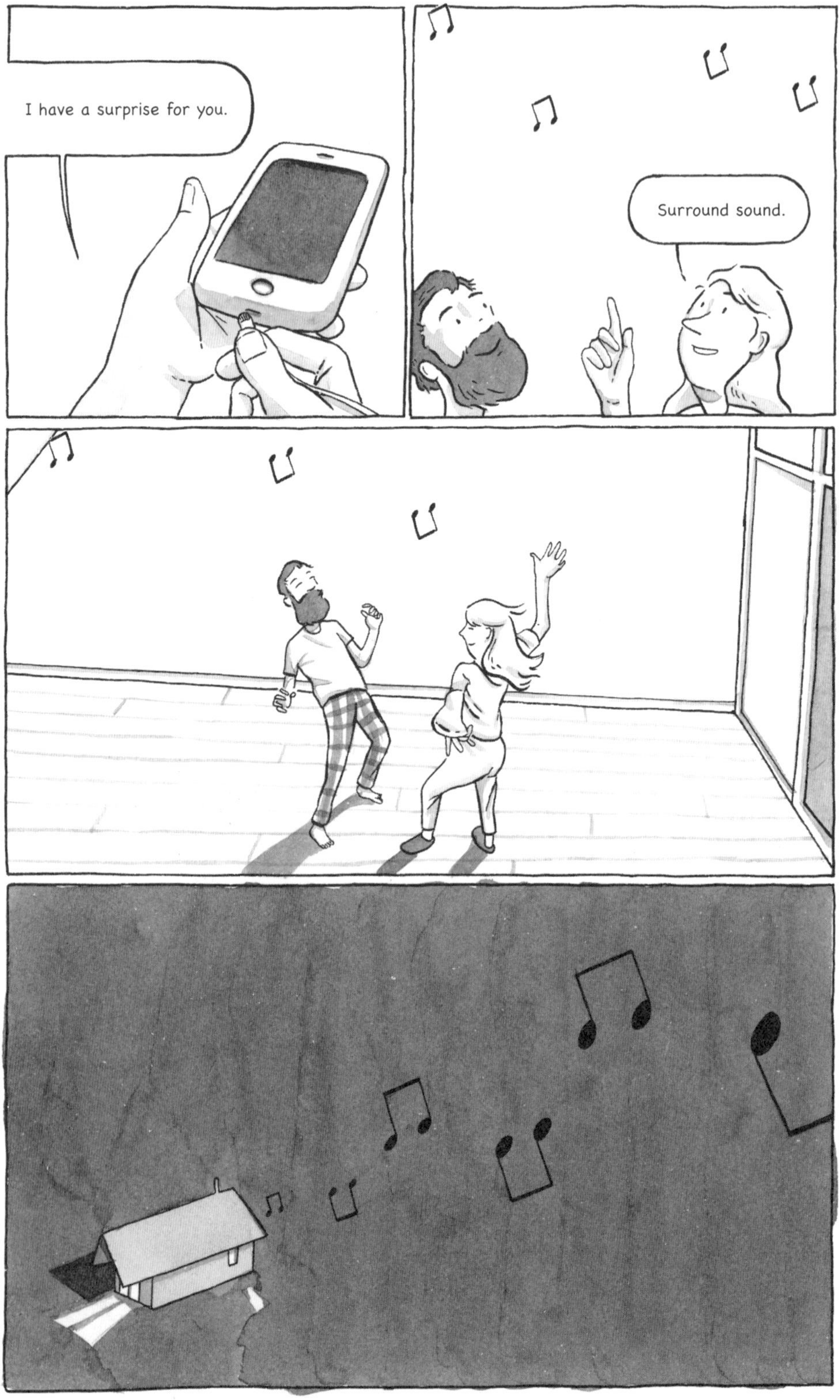
I have a surprise for you.
Surround sound.

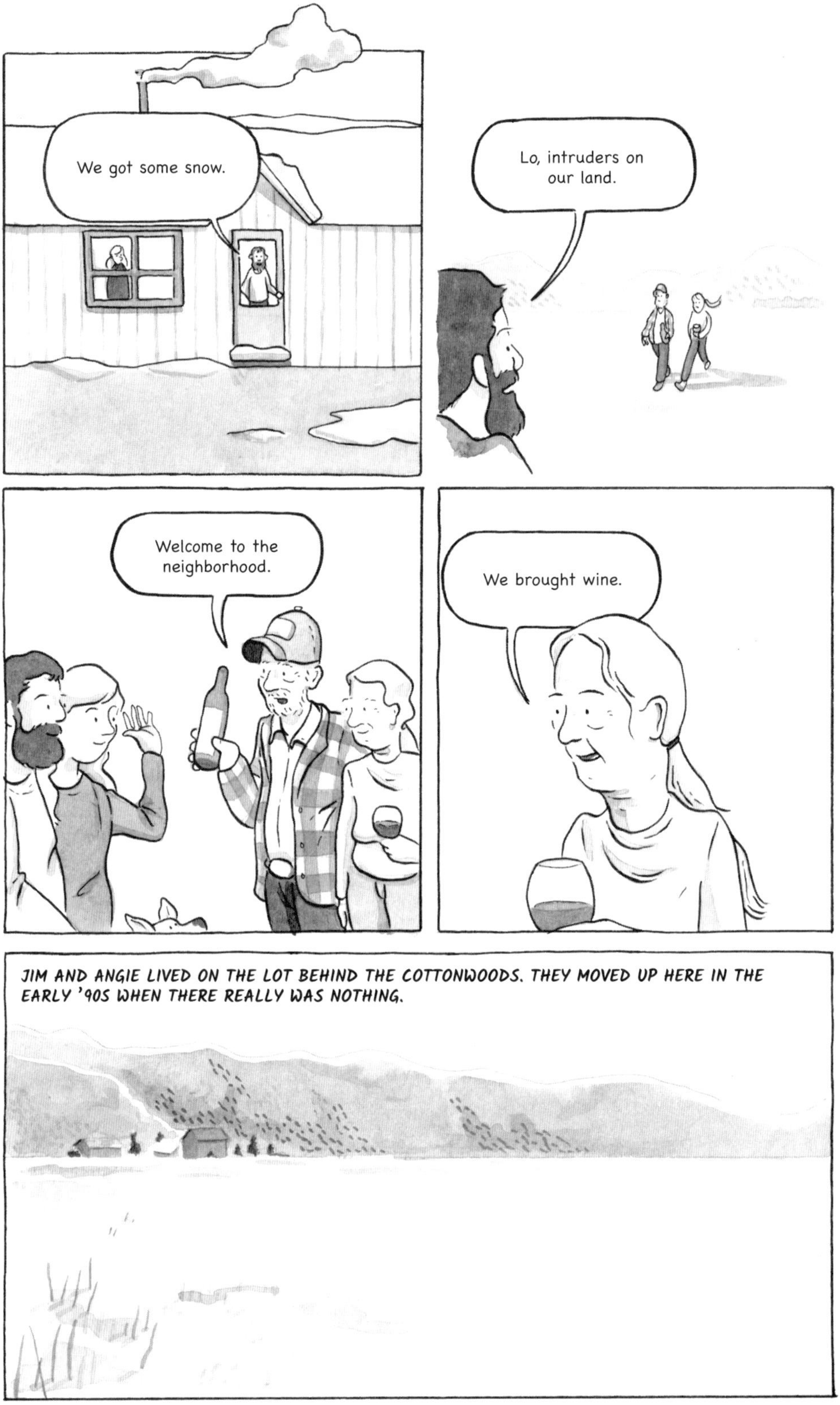
We got some snow.
Lo, intruders on our land.
Welcome to the neighborhood.
We brought wine.
JIM AND ANGIE LIVED ON THE LOT BEHIND THE COTTONWOODS. THEY MOVED UP HERE IN THE EARLY '90S WHEN THERE REALLY WAS NOTHING.

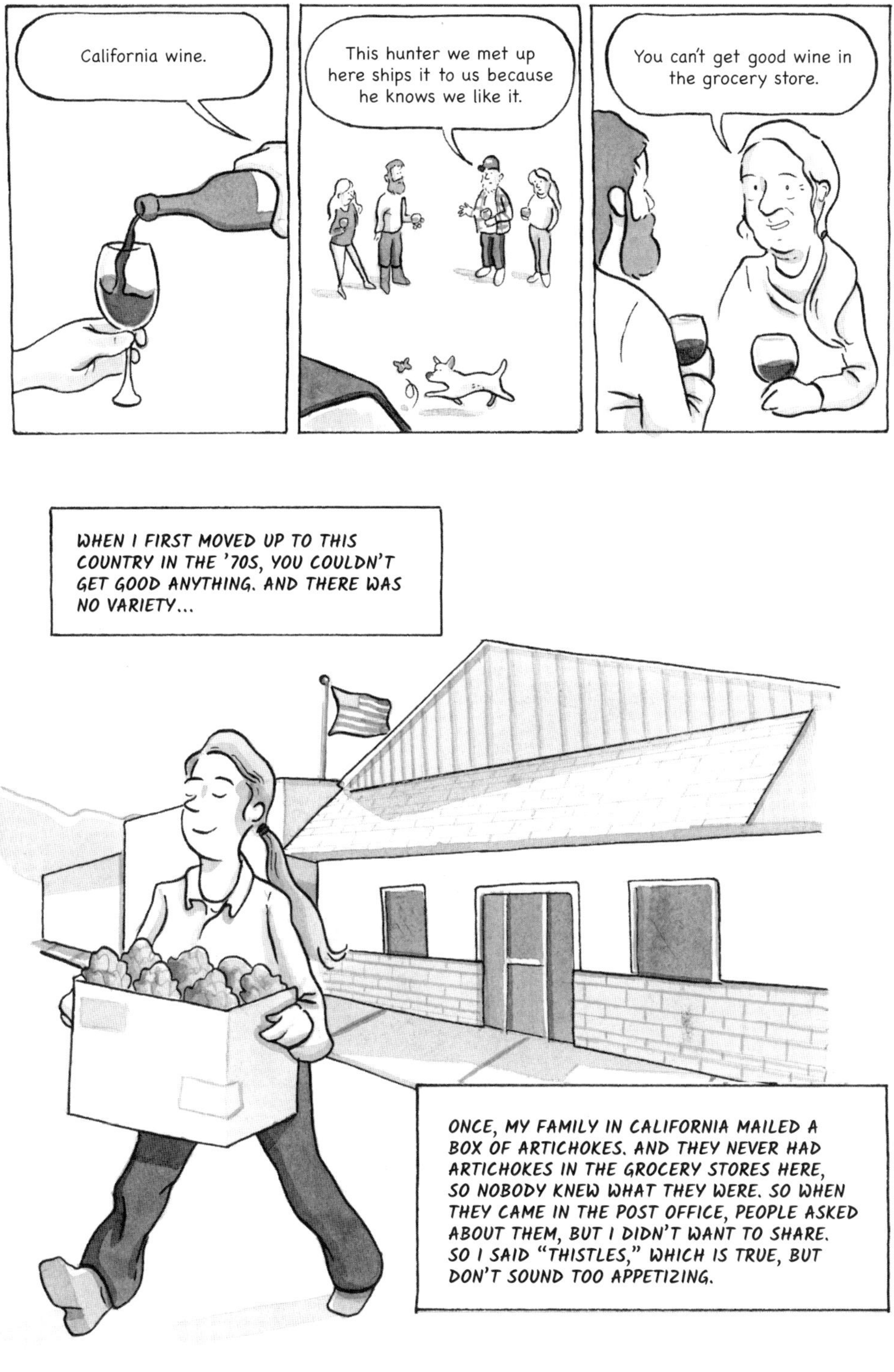
California wine.
This hunter we met up here ships it to us because he knows we like it.
You can't get good wine in the grocery store.
WHEN I FIRST MOVED UP TO THIS COUNTRY IN THE '70S, YOU COULDN'T GET GOOD ANYTHING. AND THERE WAS NO VARIETY...
ONCE, MY FAMILY IN CALIFORNIA MAILED A BOX OF ARTICHOKES. AND THEY NEVER HAD ARTICHOKES IN THE GROCERY STORES HERE, SO NOBODY KNEW WHAT THEY WERE. SO WHEN THEY CAME IN THE POST OFFICE, PEOPLE ASKED ABOUT THEM, BUT I DIDN'T WANT TO SHARE. SO I SAID "THISTLES," WHICH IS TRUE, BUT DON'T SOUND TOO APPETIZING.

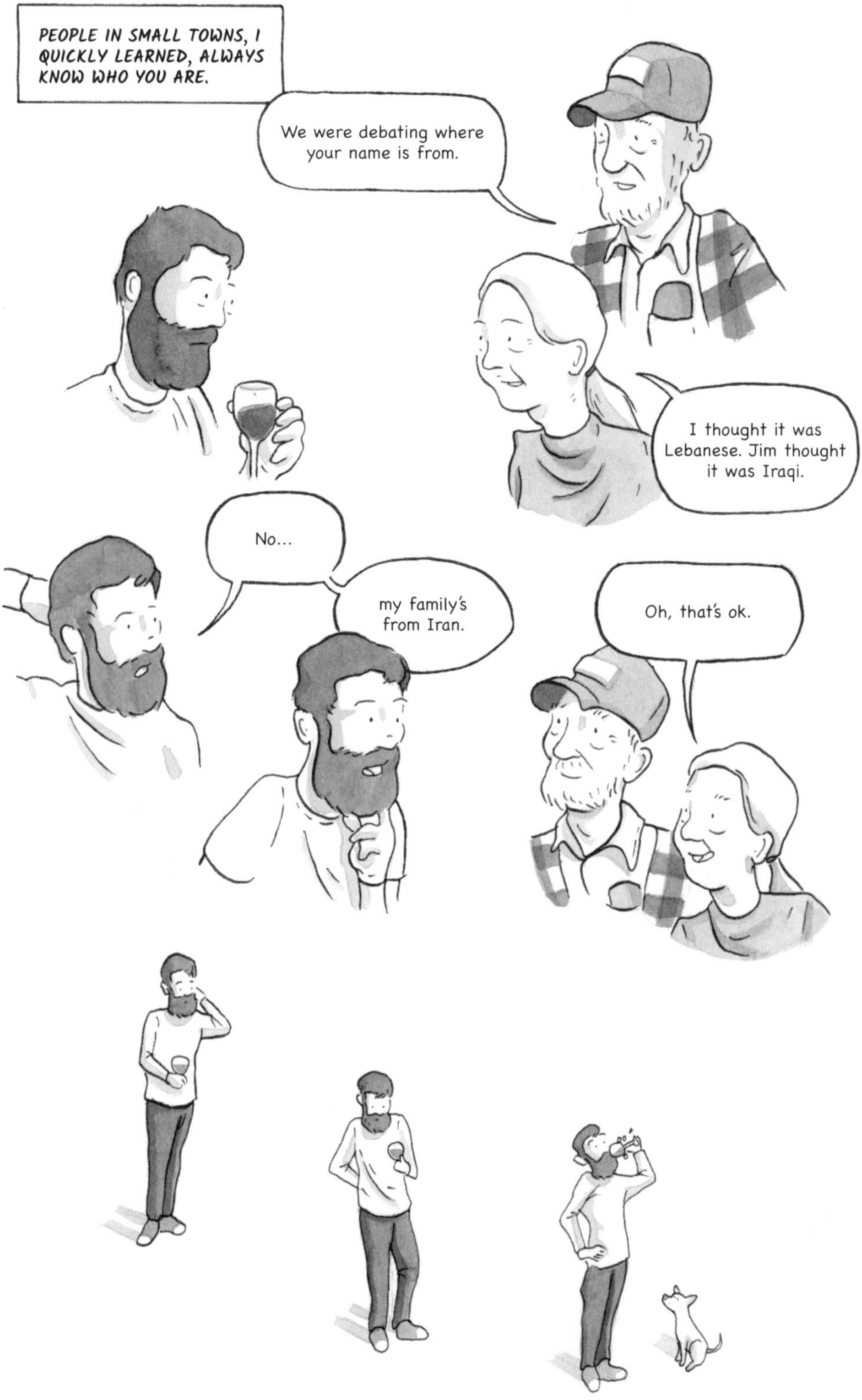
PEOPLE IN SMALL TOWNS, I QUICKLY LEARNED, ALWAYS KNOW WHO YOU ARE.
We were debating where your name is from.
I thought it was Lebanese. Jim thought it was Iraqi.
No...
my family's from Iran.
Oh, that's ok.

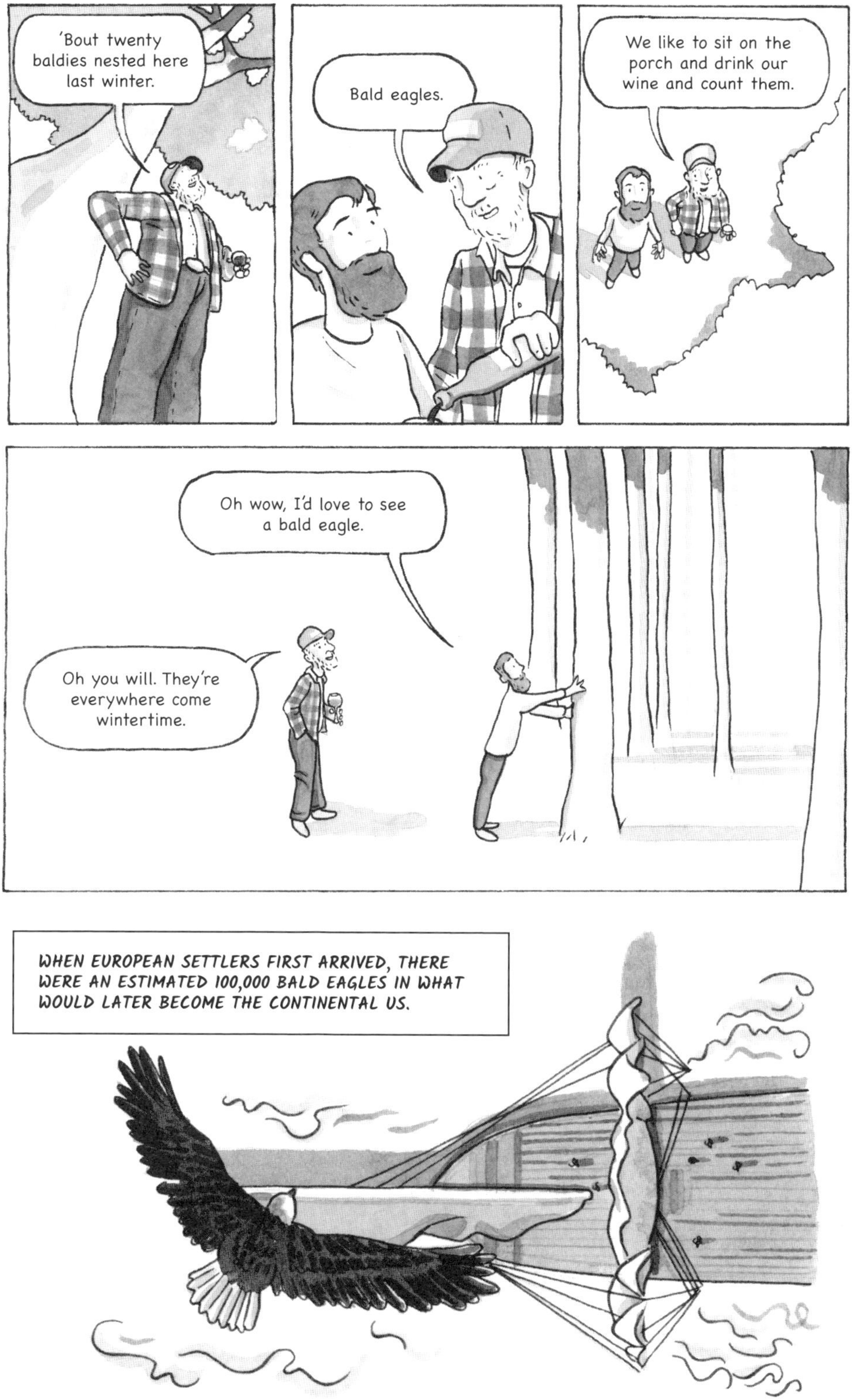
'Bout twenty baldies nested here last winter.
Bald eagles.
We like to sit on the porch and drink our wine and count them.
Oh wow, I'd love to see a bald eagle.
Oh you will. They're everywhere come wintertime.
WHEN EUROPEAN SETTLERS FIRST ARRIVED, THERE WERE AN ESTIMATED 100,000 BALD EAGLES IN WHAT WOULD LATER BECOME THE CONTINENTAL US.

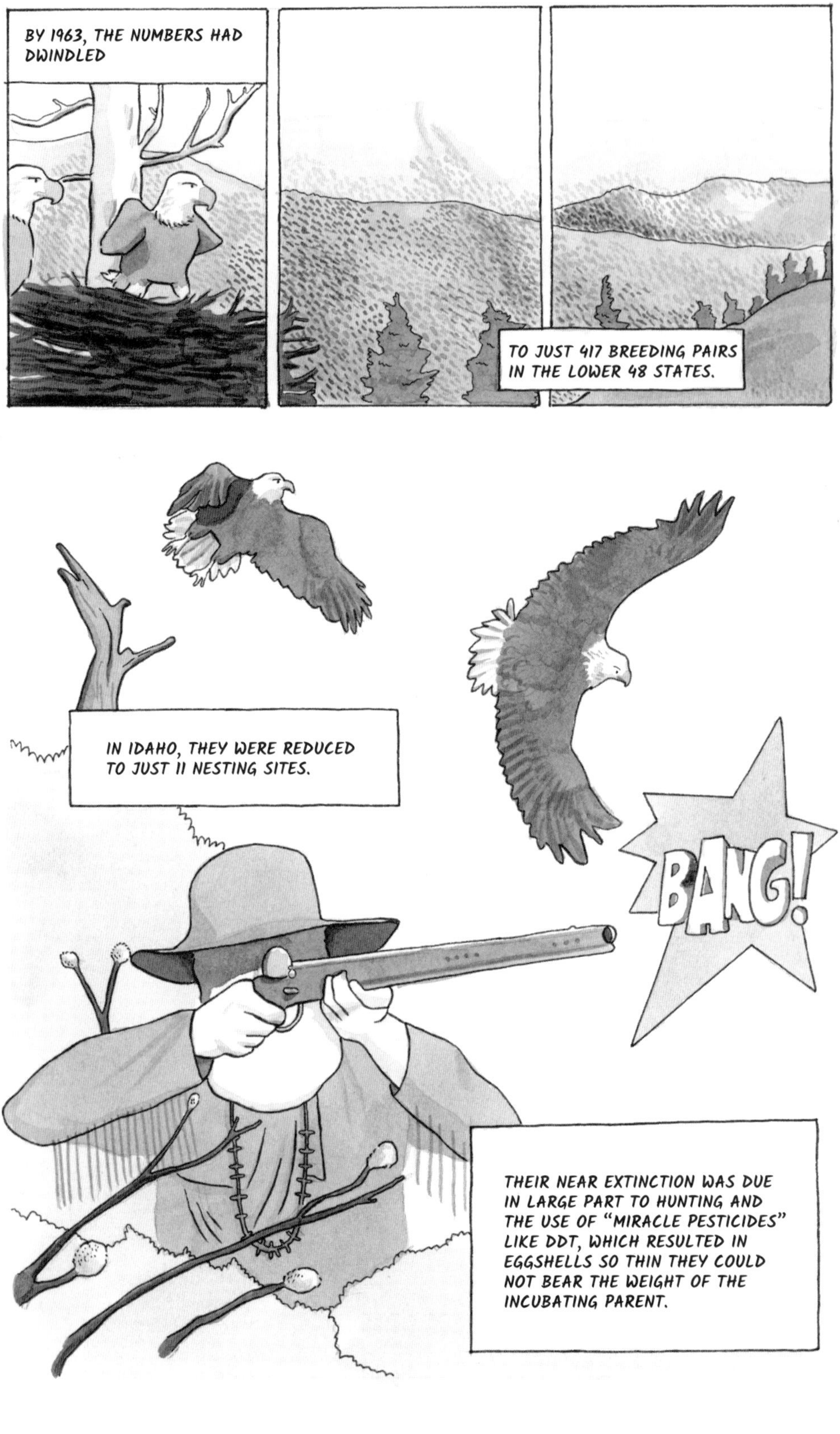
BY 1963, THE NUMBERS HAD DWINDLED
TO JUST 417 BREEDING PAIRS IN THE LOWER 48 STATES.
IN IDAHO, THEY WERE REDUCED TO JUST 11 NESTING SITES.
BANG!
THEIR NEAR EXTINCTION WAS DUE IN LARGE PART TO HUNTING AND THE USE OF "MIRACLE PESTICIDES" LIKE DDT, WHICH RESULTED IN EGGSHELLS SO THIN THEY COULD NOT BEAR THE WEIGHT OF THE INCUBATING PARENT.

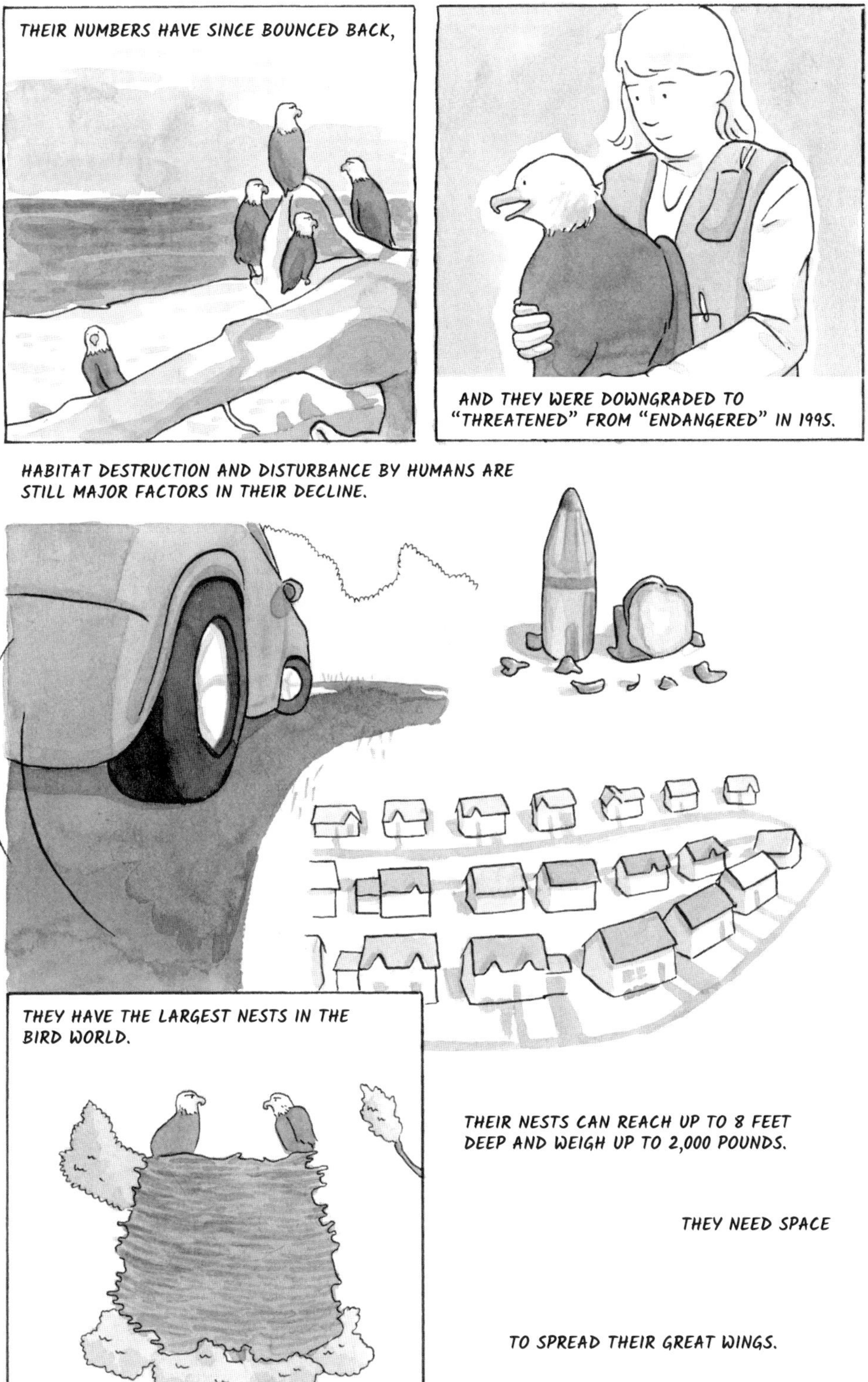
THEIR NUMBERS HAVE SINCE BOUNCED BACK,
AND THEY WERE DOWNGRADED TO "THREATENED" FROM "ENDANGERED" IN 1995.
HABITAT DESTRUCTION AND DISTURBANCE BY HUMANS ARE STILL MAJOR FACTORS IN THEIR DECLINE.
THEY HAVE THE LARGEST NESTS IN THE BIRD WORLD.
THEIR NESTS CAN REACH UP TO 8 FEET DEEP AND WEIGH UP TO 2,000 POUNDS.
THEY NEED SPACE
TO SPREAD THEIR GREAT WINGS.

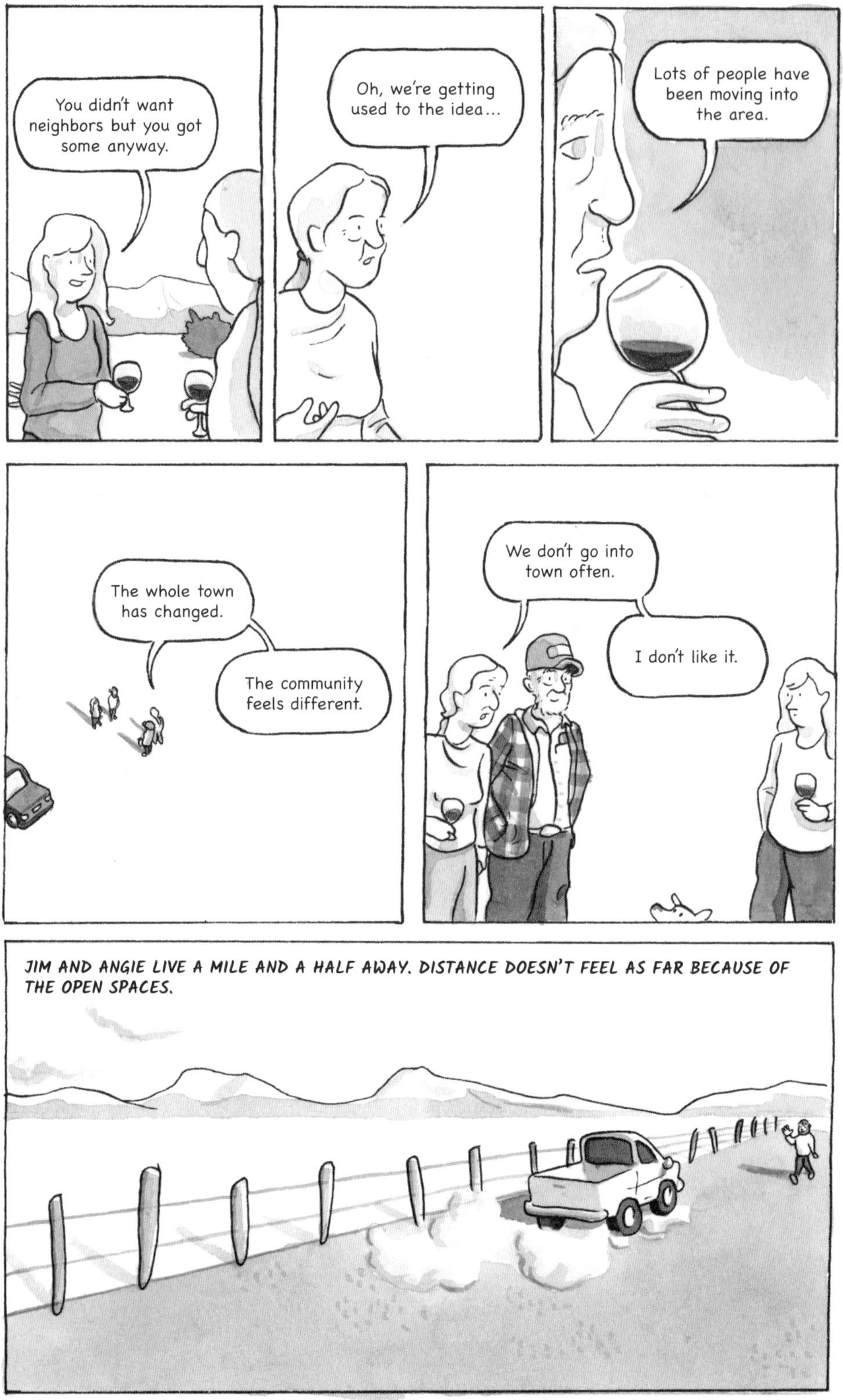
You didn't want neighbors but you got some anyway.
Oh, we're getting used to the idea...
Lots of people have been moving into the area.
The whole town has changed.
The community feels different.
We don't go into town often.
I don't like it.
JIM AND ANGIE LIVE A MILE AND A HALF AWAY. DISTANCE DOESN'T FEEL AS FAR BECAUSE OF THE OPEN SPACES.

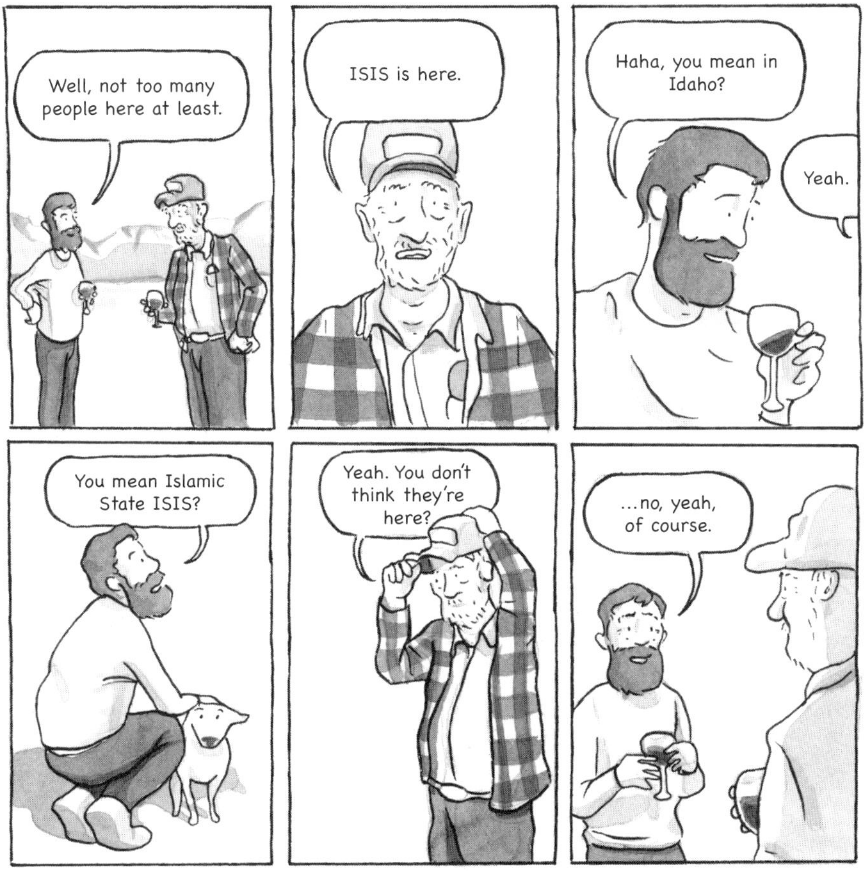
Well, not too many people here at least.
ISIS is here.
Haha, you mean in Idaho?
Yeah.
You mean Islamic State ISIS?
Yeah. You don't think they're here?
...no, yeah, of course.

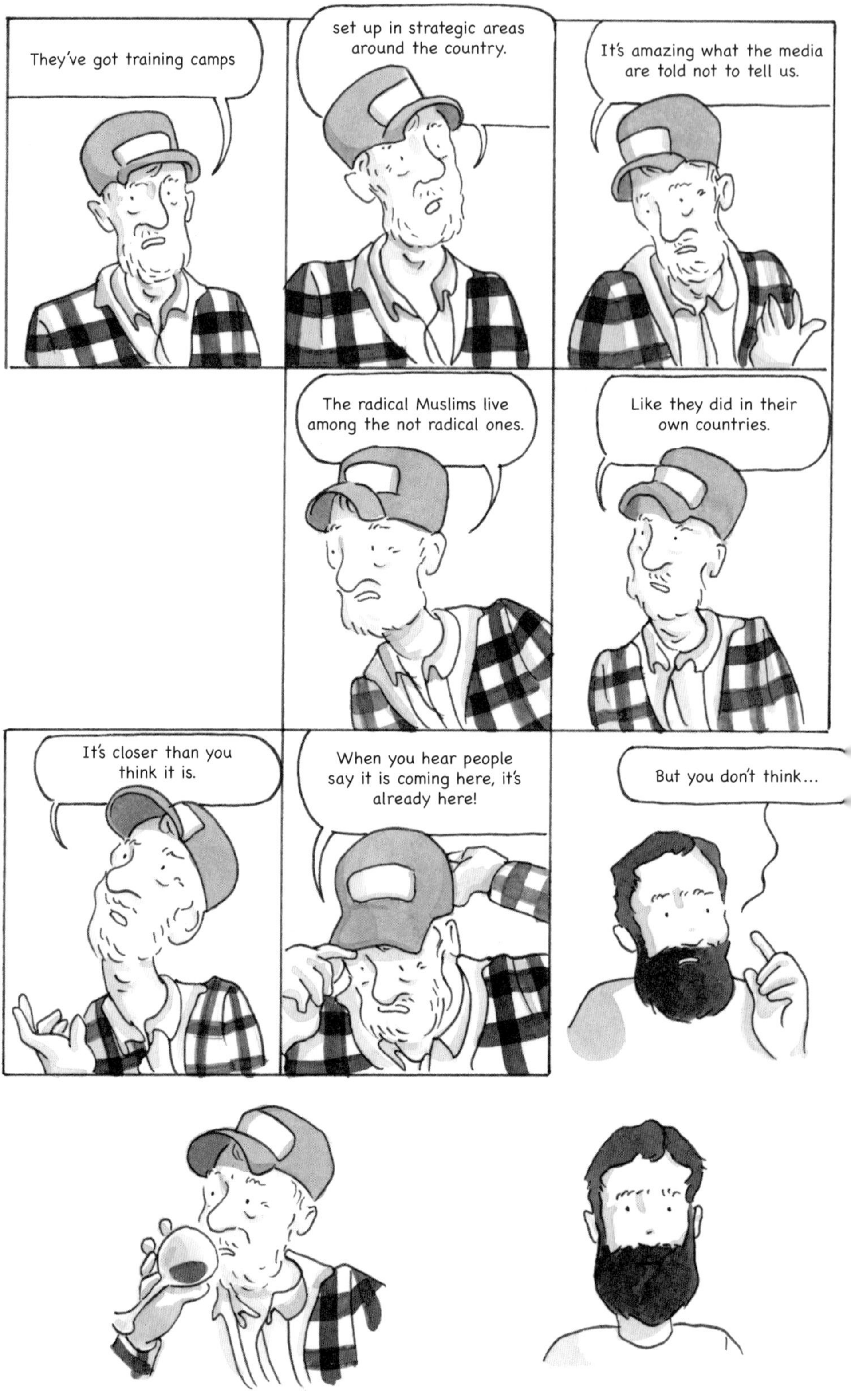
They've got training camps
set up in strategic areas around the country.
It's amazing what the media are told not to tell us.
The radical Muslims live among the not radical ones.
Like they did in their own countries.
It's closer than you think it is.
When you hear people say it is coming here, it's already here!
But you don't think...

I LEARNED THAT JIM IS CONSTANTLY LOOKING FOR WILDLIFE,

BUT AT THE TIME, I THOUGHT HE WAS LOOKING FOR ISIS.

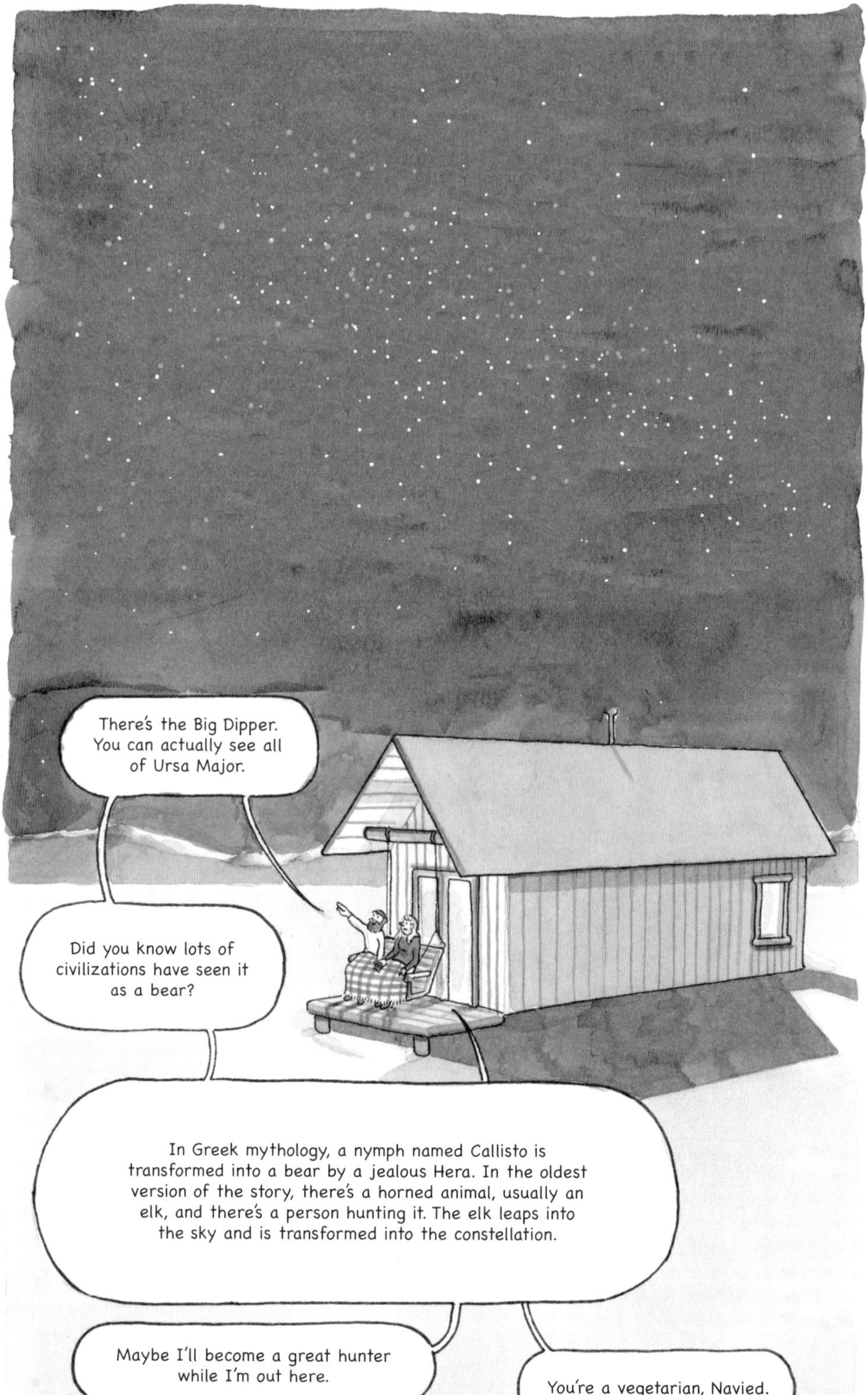
There's the Big Dipper. You can actually see all of Ursa Major.
Did you know lots of civilizations have seen it as a bear?
In Greek mythology, a nymph named Callisto is transformed into a bear by a jealous Hera. In the oldest version of the story, there's a horned animal, usually an elk, and there's a person hunting it. The elk leaps into the sky and is transformed into the constellation.
Maybe I'll become a great hunter while I'm out here.
You're a vegetarian, Navied.

Oh, and that there, that's the white supremacist.

You can see his pointy hat.

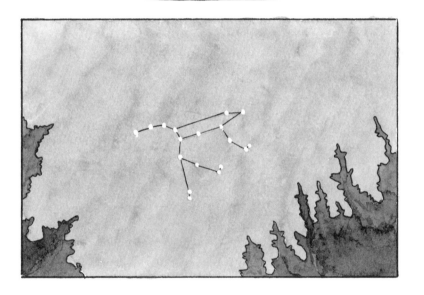

Ooh, and it's Sagittarius.

But instead of a bow, he's holding a gun.

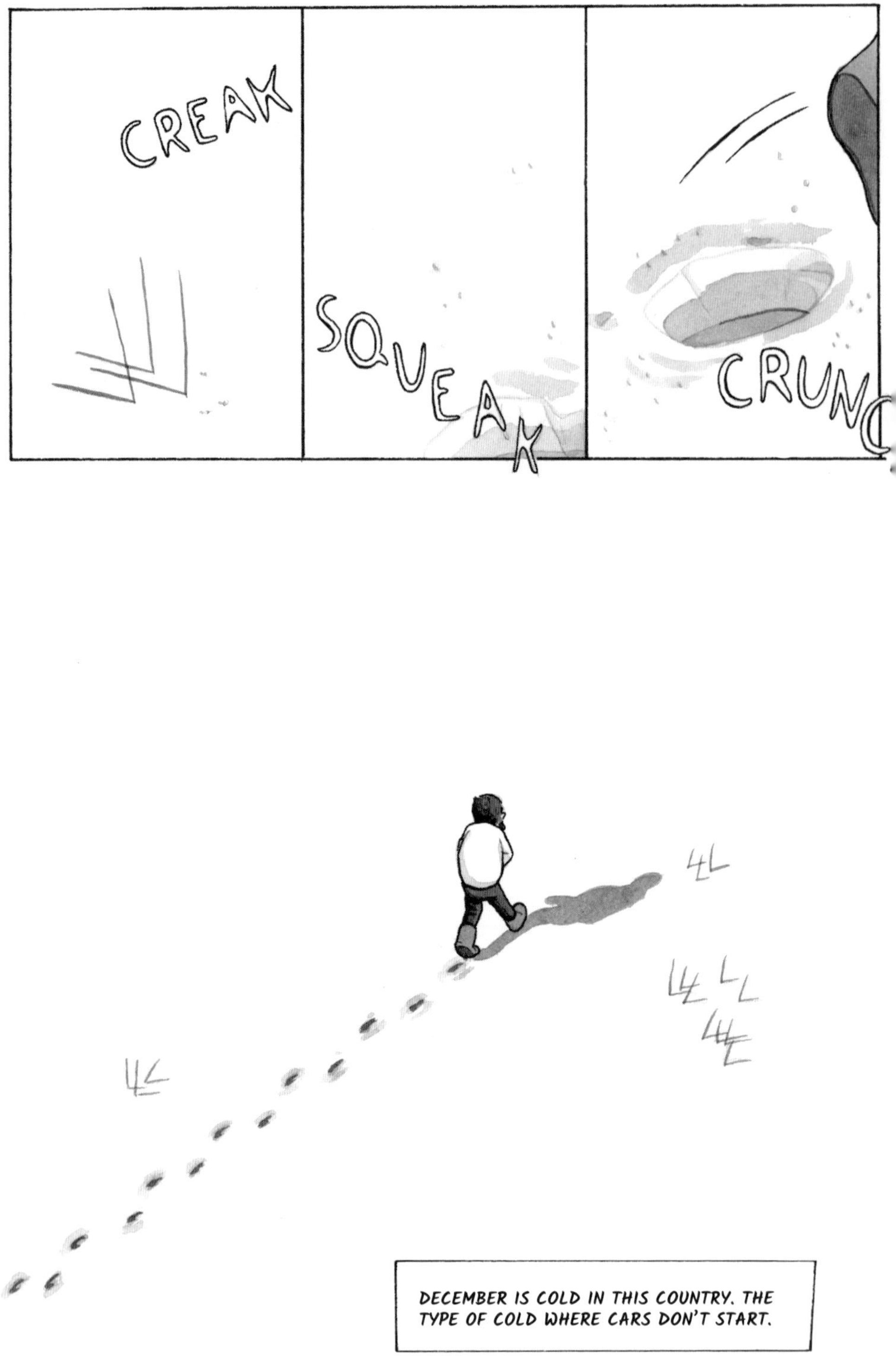
CREAK
SQUEAK
CRUNC
DECEMBER IS COLD IN THIS COUNTRY. THE TYPE OF COLD WHERE CARS DON'T START.

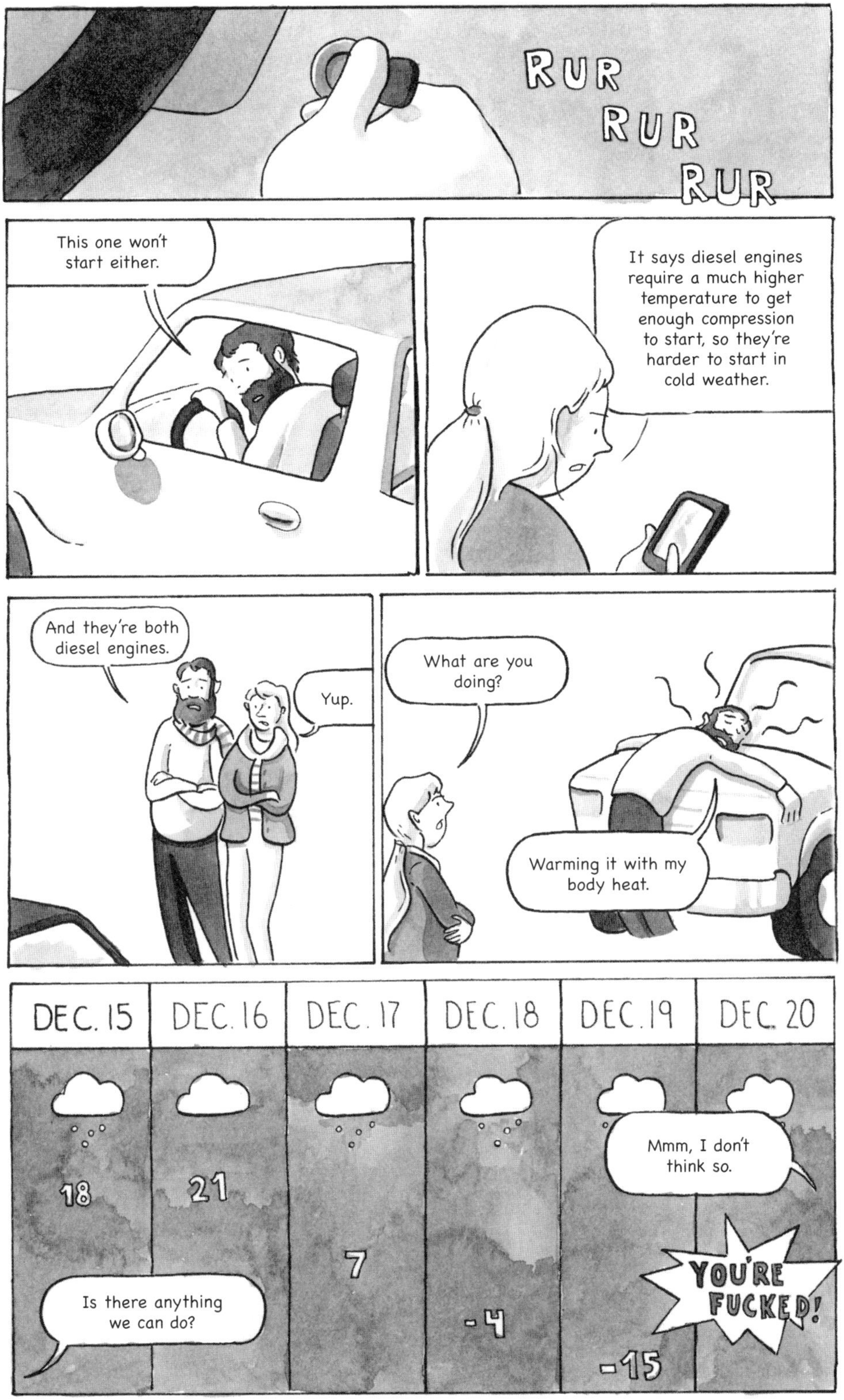
RUR
RUR
RUR
This one won't start either.
It says diesel engines require a much higher temperature to get enough compression to start, so they're harder to start in cold weather.
And they're both diesel engines.
Yup.
What are you doing?
Warming it with my body heat.
DEC. 15
DEC. 16
DEC. 17
DEC. 18
DEC. 19
DEC. 20
18
21
7
-4
-15
Is there anything we can do?
Mmm, I don't think so.
YOU'RE FUCKED!

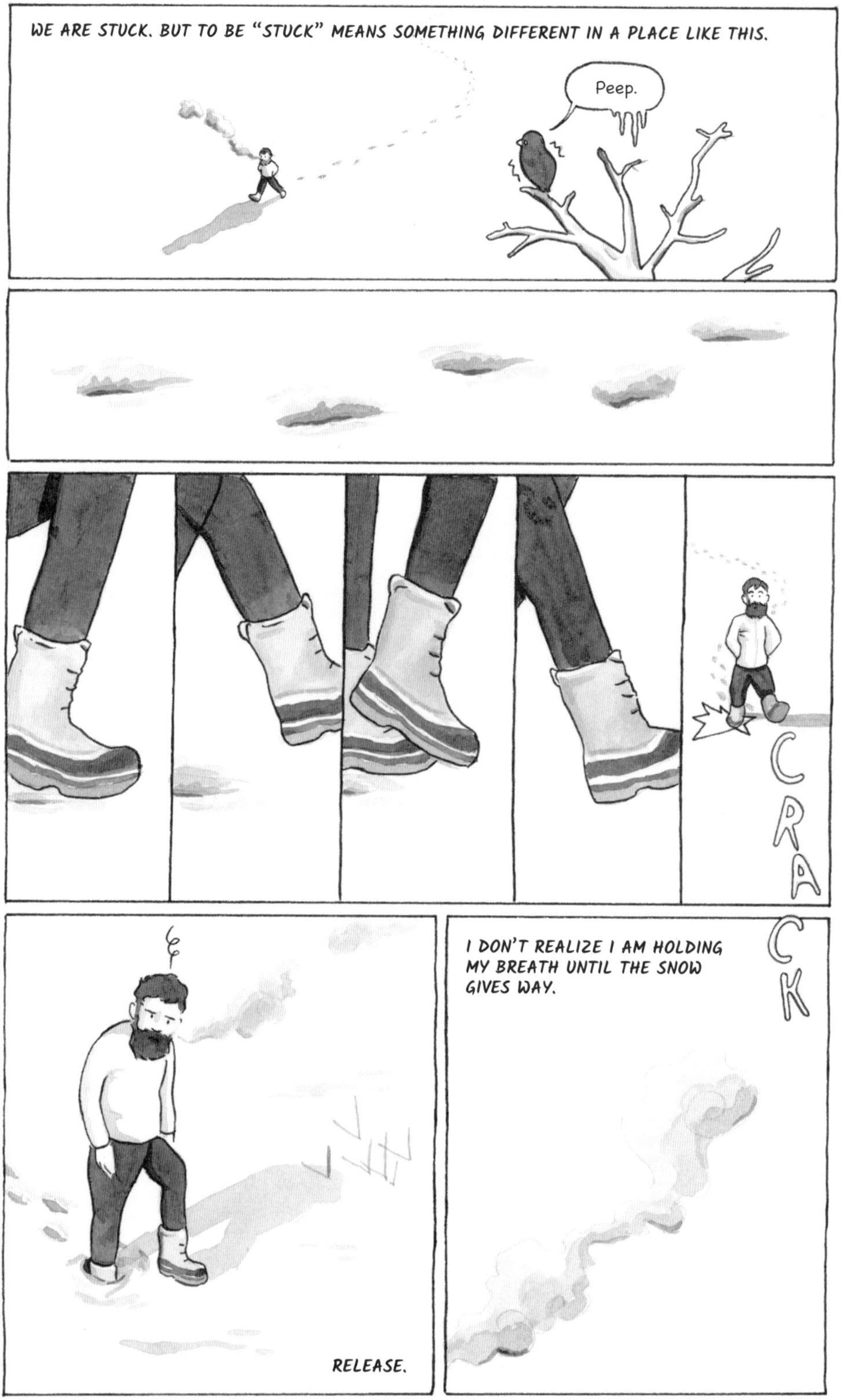

WE ARE STUCK. BUT TO BE "STUCK" MEANS SOMETHING DIFFERENT IN A PLACE LIKE THIS.
Peep.
CRACK
RELEASE.
I DON'T REALIZE I AM HOLDING MY BREATH UNTIL THE SNOW GIVES WAY.

A LAYER OF SNOW IS MADE UP OF TINY GRAINS SURROUNDED BY AIR. MY STEP COMPRESSES THE GRAINS CAUSING THEM TO RUB AGAINST ONE ANOTHER.

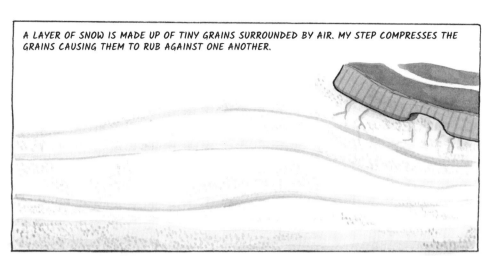

THE LAND OPERATES ON MY BODY.

WHY DID IT GIVE THIS TIME? WHAT WAS UNDER THE SNOW THAT MADE IT UNSTABLE?

ROBERT MACFARLANE WRITES:

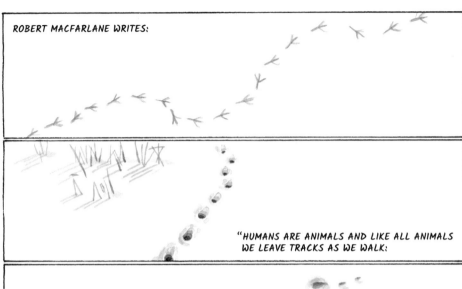

"HUMANS ARE ANIMALS AND LIKE ALL ANIMALS WE LEAVE TRACKS AS WE WALK:

SIGNS OF PASSAGE MADE IN SNOW, SAND, MUD, GRASS, DEW, EARTH OR MOSS...

My, my, Grandma, what big claws you have!

Eep!

Uhhh, Emelie...

WE EASILY FORGET THAT WE ARE TRACK-MAKERS, THOUGH, BECAUSE MOST OF OUR JOURNEYS NOW OCCUR ON ASPHALT AND CONCRETE—AND THESE ARE SUBSTANCES NOT EASILY IMPRESSED."

THIS COUNTRY IS NEW TO US, BUT IT IS HIDDEN NOW, ITS CONTOURS CONSTANTLY SHIFTING.

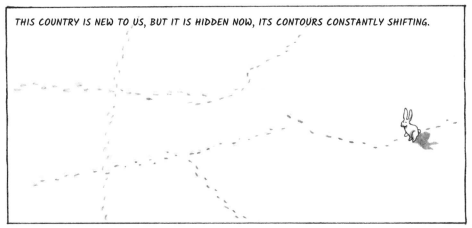

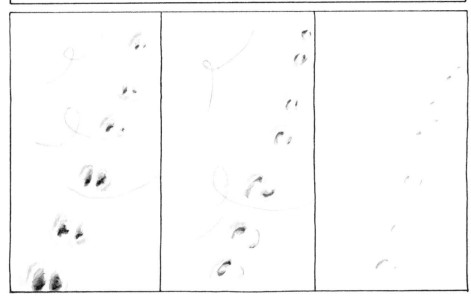

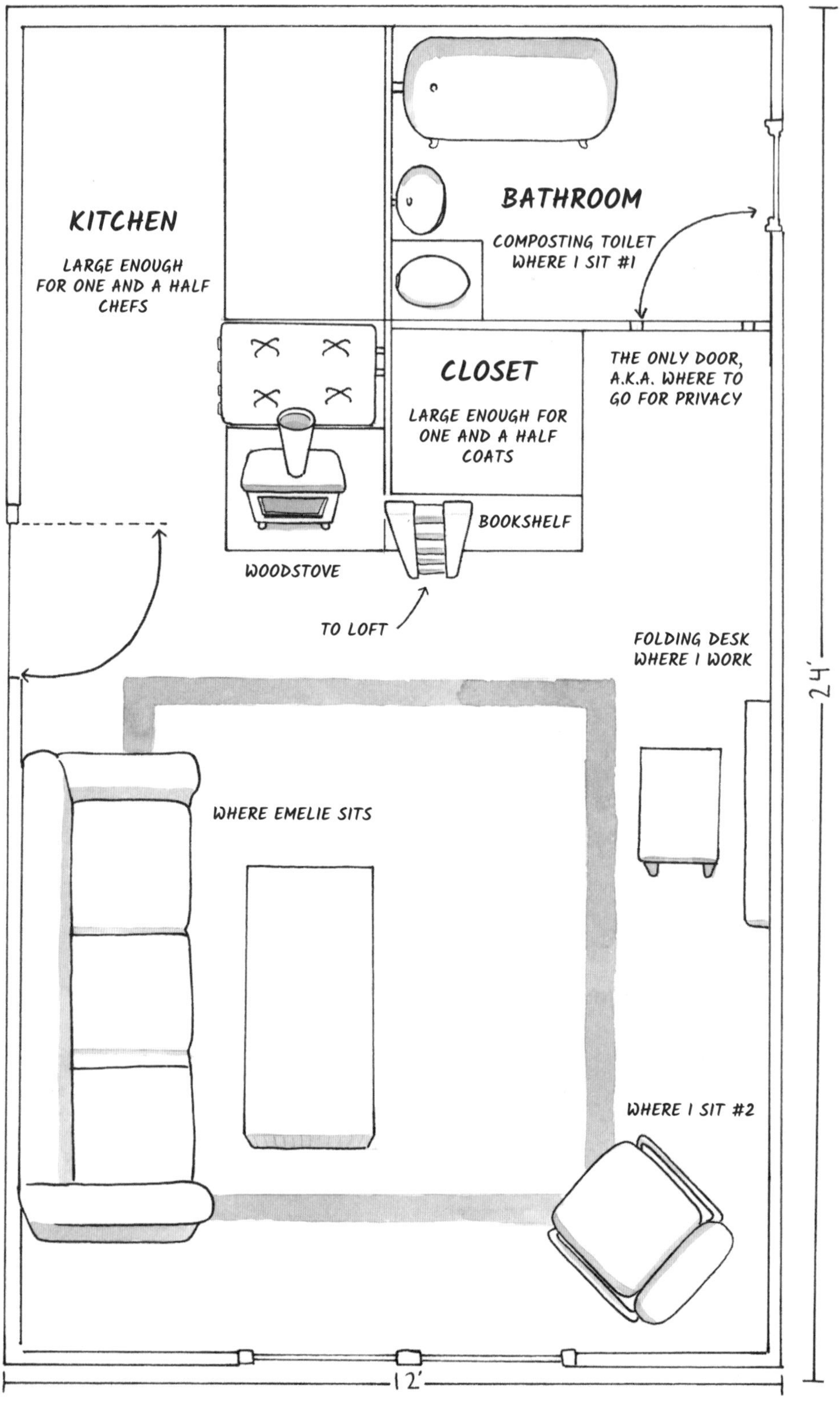
KITCHEN
LARGE ENOUGH FOR ONE AND A HALF CHEFS
BATHROOM
COMPOSTING TOILET WHERE I SIT #1
CLOSET
LARGE ENOUGH FOR ONE AND A HALF COATS
THE ONLY DOOR, A.K.A. WHERE TO GO FOR PRIVACY
BOOKSHELF
WOODSTOVE
TO LOFT
FOLDING DESK WHERE I WORK
WHERE EMELIE SITS
WHERE I SIT #2
24'
12'

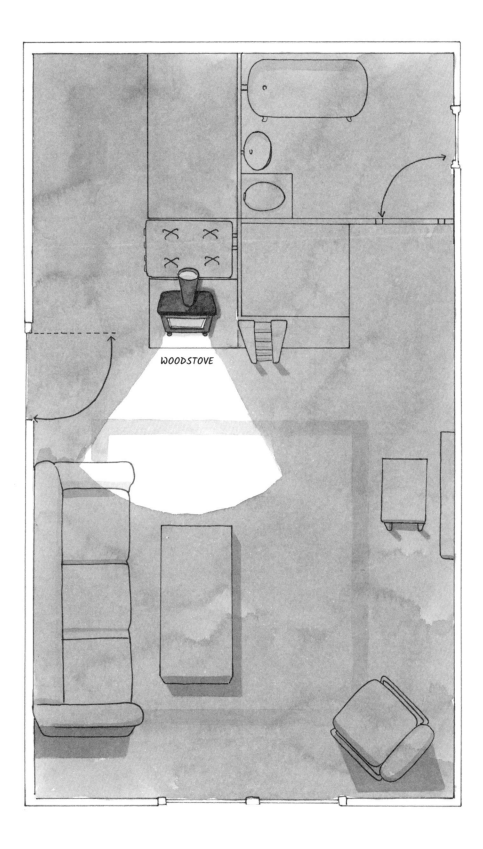

WOODSTOVE

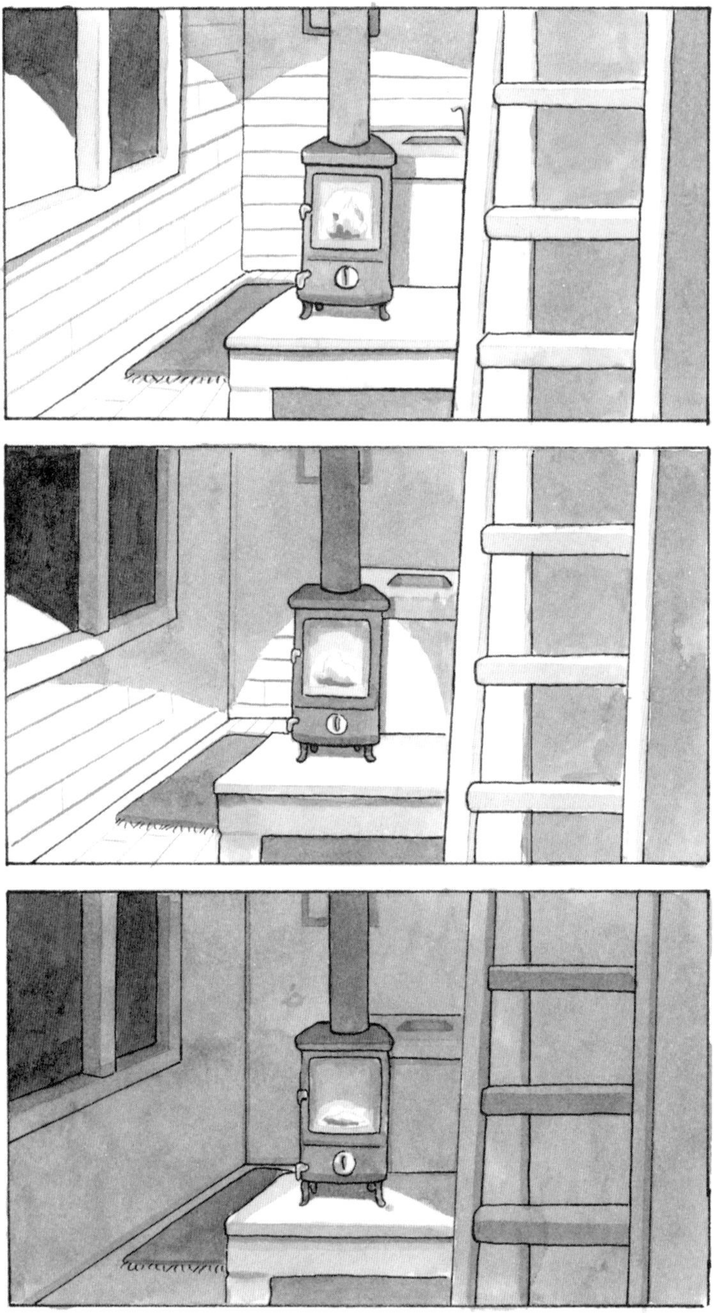

THERE IS A RHYTHM TO WINTER.

I'M LUCKY WHEN I CAN CATCH THE EMBERS OF OUR WOODSTOVE BEFORE THEY'VE GONE OUT.

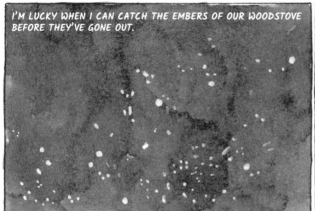

THE HEARTH WAS SO CENTRAL HISTORICALLY THAT IT HAS BEEN GENERALIZED TO MEAN HOME, AS IN "HEARTH AND HOME."

HEARTH DERIVES FROM THE ROOT "KER," MEANING "BURNING, HEAT, FIRE." THIS IS ALSO WHERE WE GET THE WORD "CARBON," THE BUILDING BLOCK OF LIFE.

IN GREEK MYTHOLOGY, HESTIA WAS GODDESS OF THE HEARTH, AND BY EXTENSION OF THE FAMILY, DOMESTICITY, THE HOME, AND EVEN THE STATE.

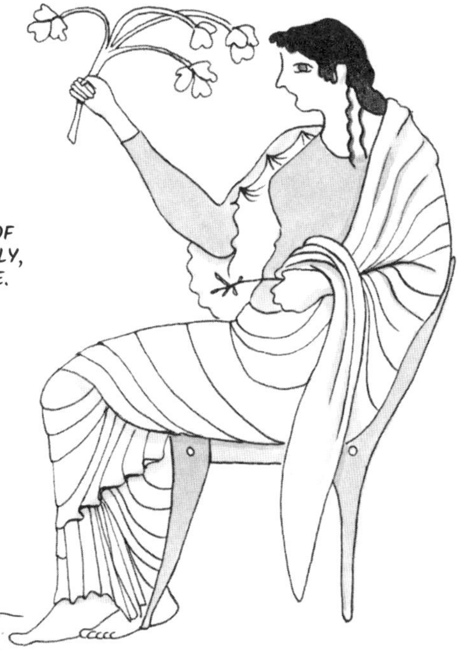

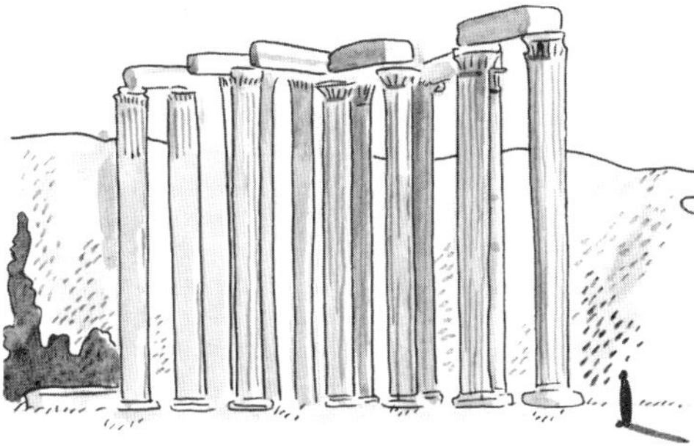

TO EMPHASIZE HER CENTRALITY, HESTIA, FIRSTBORN TO THE TITANS CRONUS AND RHEA, RECEIVED FIRST OFFERING AT EVERY SACRIFICE IN THE HOUSEHOLD.

EVEN CYRUS THE GREAT, FOUNDER OF THE ACHAEMENID EMPIRE, THE FIRST PERSIAN EMPIRE, IS SAID BY THE GREEK HISTORIAN XENOPHON TO HAVE SACRIFICED FIRST TO HESTIA, AND THEN TO ZEUS.

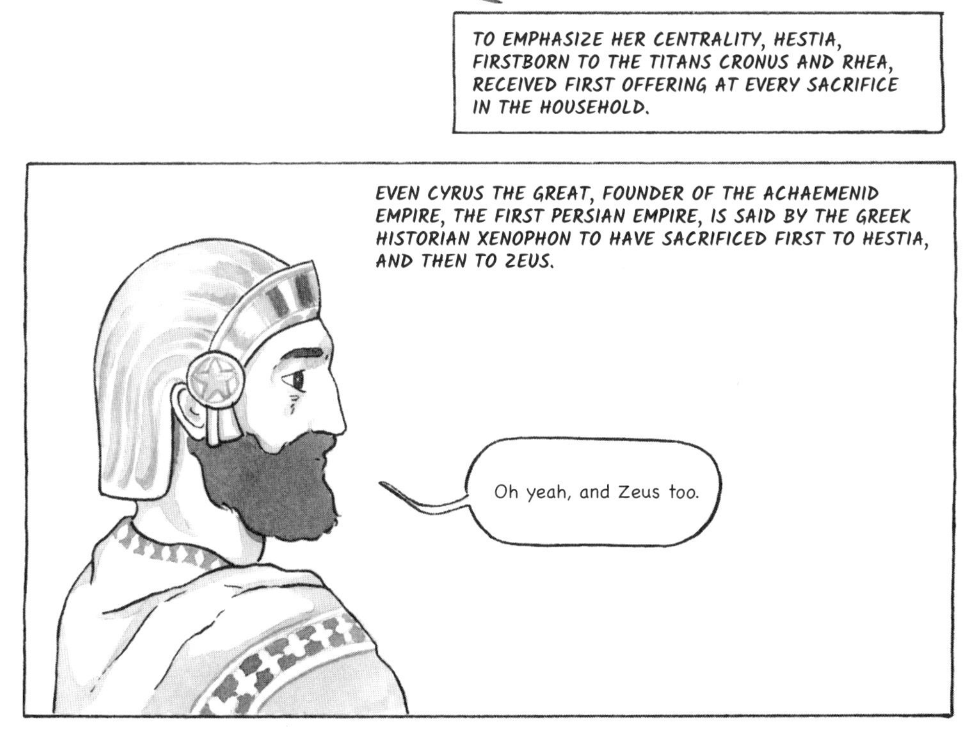
Oh yeah, and Zeus too.

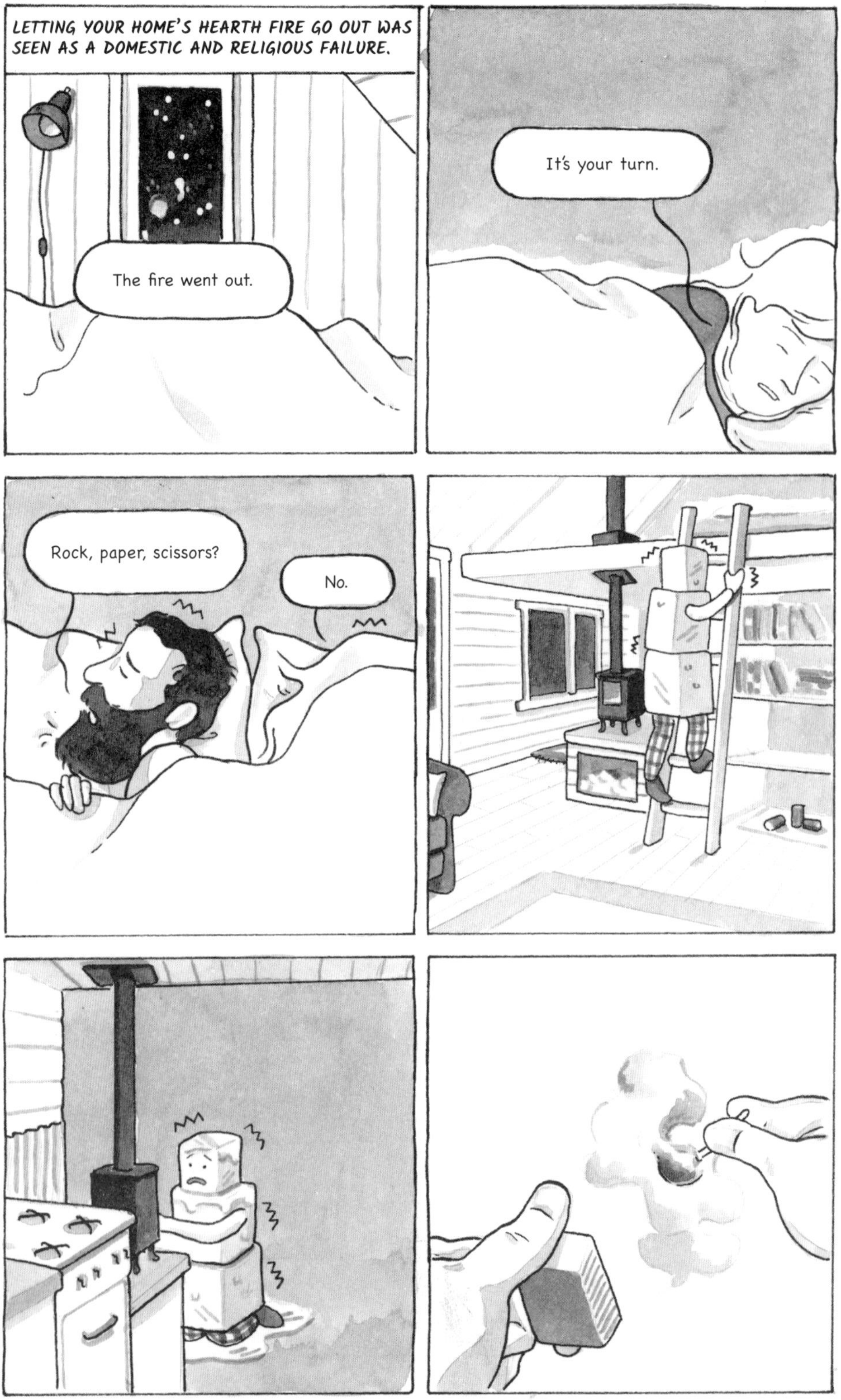
LETTING YOUR HOME'S HEARTH FIRE GO OUT WAS SEEN AS A DOMESTIC AND RELIGIOUS FAILURE.
The fire went out.
It's your turn.
Rock, paper, scissors?
No.

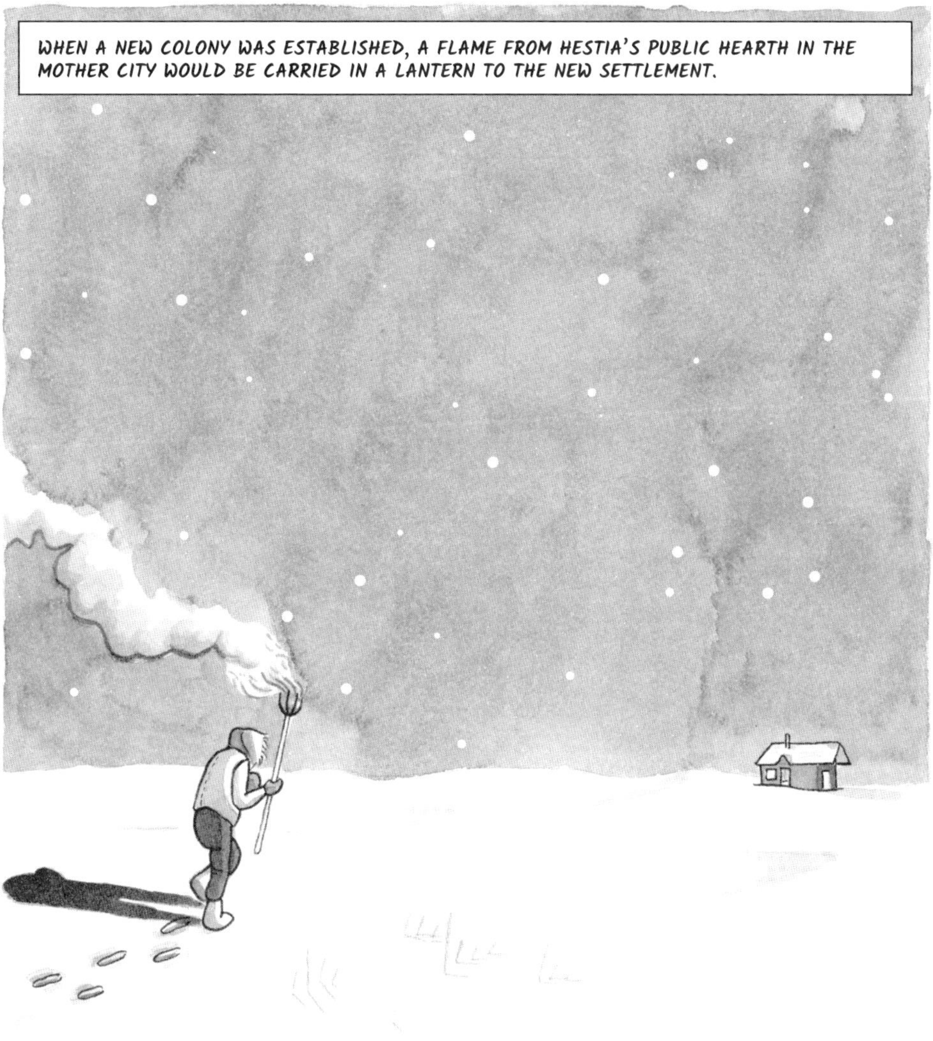
WHEN A NEW COLONY WAS ESTABLISHED, A FLAME FROM HESTIA'S PUBLIC HEARTH IN THE MOTHER CITY WOULD BE CARRIED IN A LANTERN TO THE NEW SETTLEMENT.

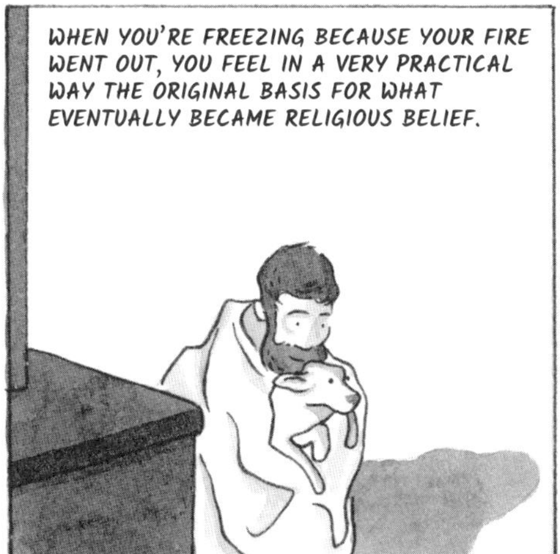
WHEN YOU'RE FREEZING BECAUSE YOUR FIRE WENT OUT, YOU FEEL IN A VERY PRACTICAL WAY THE ORIGINAL BASIS FOR WHAT EVENTUALLY BECAME RELIGIOUS BELIEF.

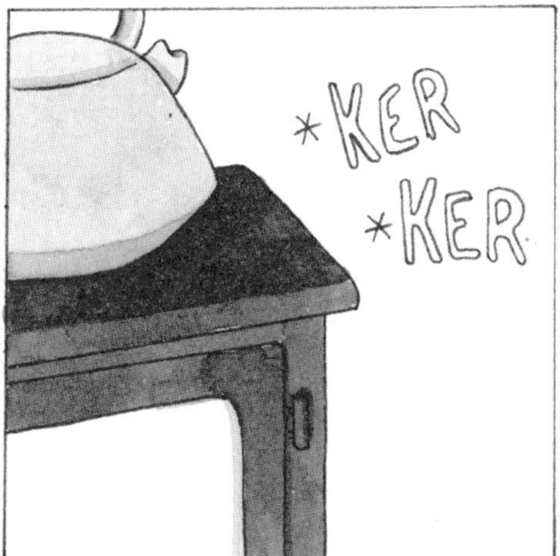
*KER
*KER

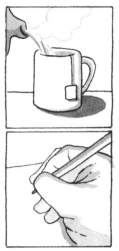

We're out of wood.

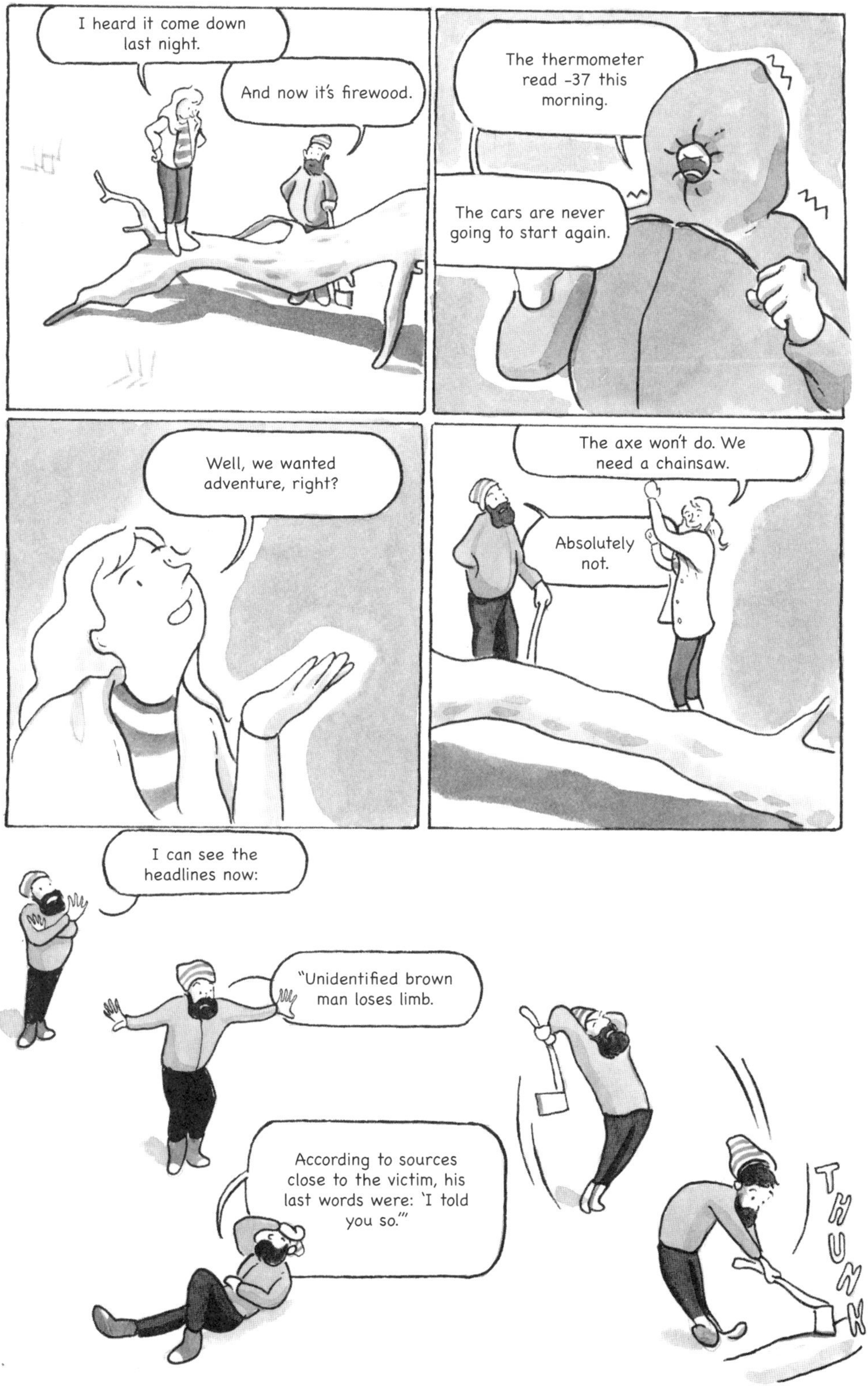
I heard it come down last night.
And now it's firewood.
The thermometer read -37 this morning.
The cars are never going to start again.
Well, we wanted adventure, right?
The axe won't do. We need a chainsaw.
Absolutely not.
I can see the headlines now:
"Unidentified brown man loses limb.
According to sources close to the victim, his last words were: 'I told you so.'"
THUNK

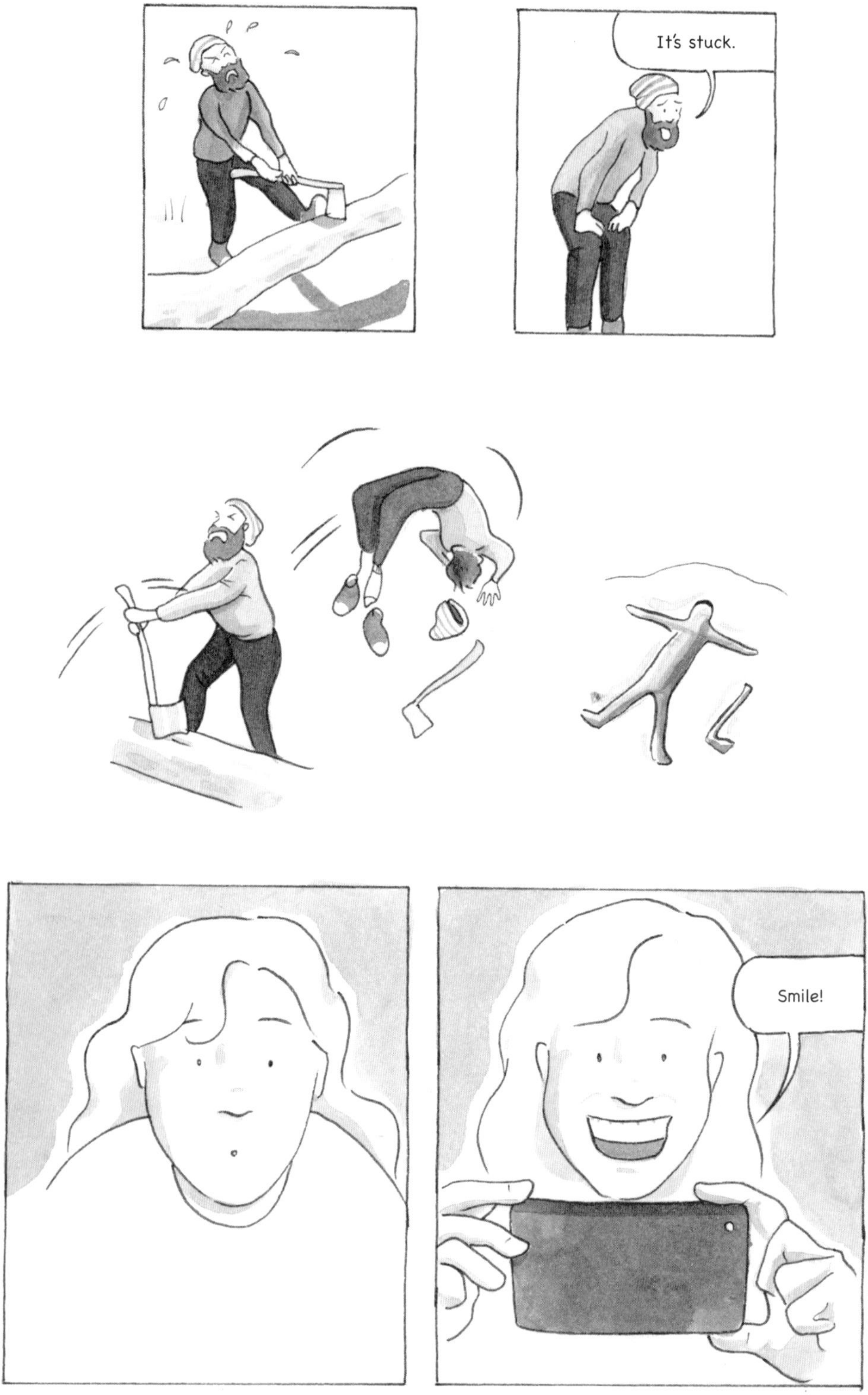
It's stuck.
Smile!

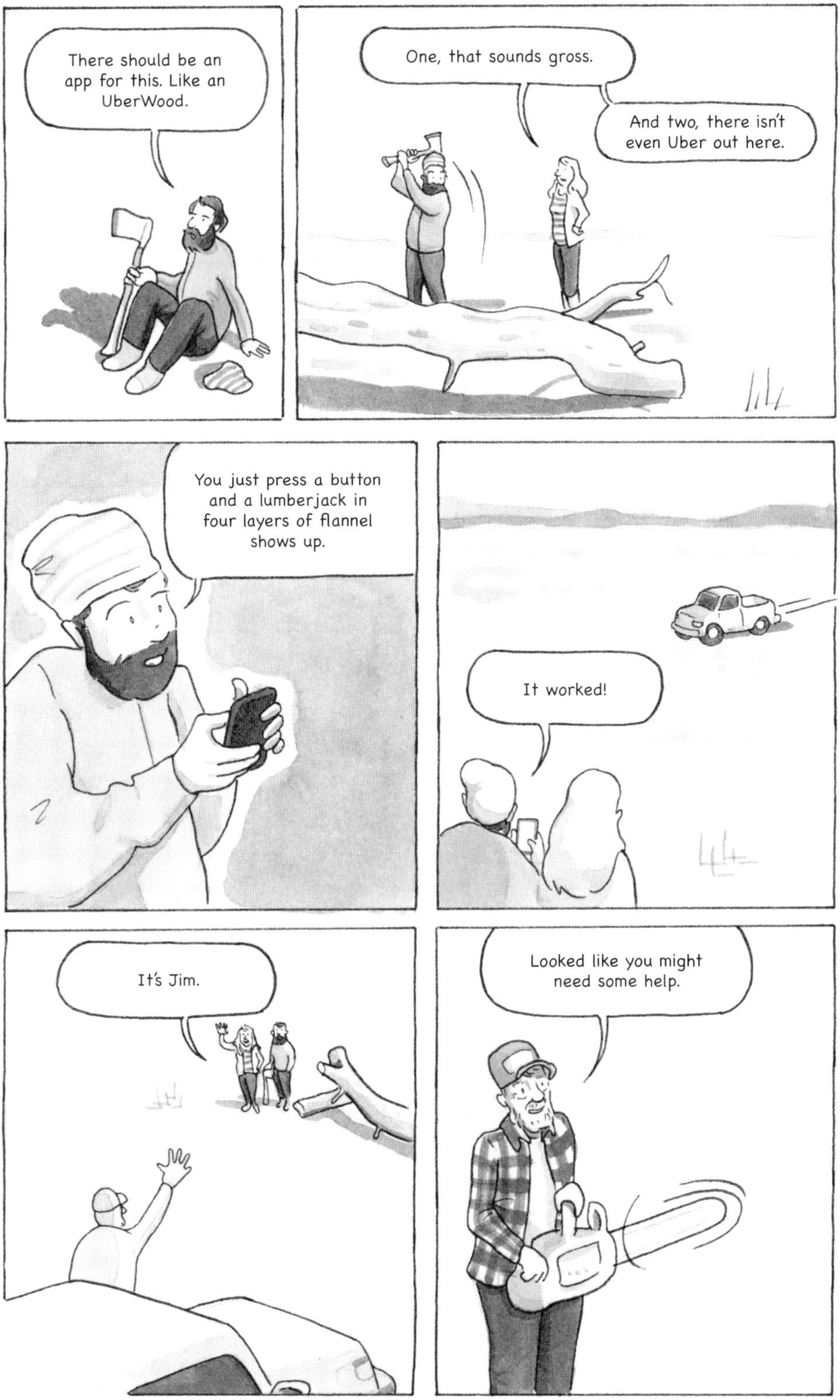
There should be an app for this. Like an UberWood.
One, that sounds gross.
And two, there isn't even Uber out here.
You just press a button and a lumberjack in four layers of flannel shows up.
It worked!
It's Jim.
Looked like you might need some help.

Most people won't even touch cottonwood 'cause it don't burn well and creates a lot of ash.

It grows tall and fast, which means the wood isn't dense. But you use what you've got, right?

Have a look at this. What do you see?

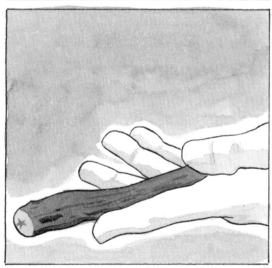

It's a star.

There's an old Indian* legend about cottonwoods and stars. Now, they believed that all things come from the earth. Stars form secretly in the earth, and they drift until they find the roots of the cottonwood tree.

THEY ENTER THE ROOTS AND SLOWLY WORK THEIR WAY UP THROUGH THE TREE AND INTO THE SMALL TWIGS AT THE END OF THE BRANCHES. AND THEY WAIT THERE AND WAIT THERE UNTIL THEY'RE CALLED ON.

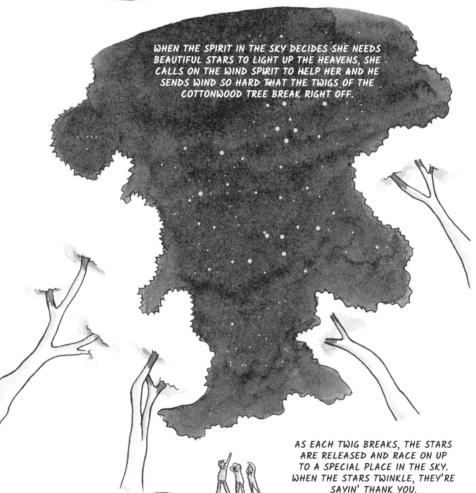

WHEN THE SPIRIT IN THE SKY DECIDES SHE NEEDS BEAUTIFUL STARS TO LIGHT UP THE HEAVENS, SHE CALLS ON THE WIND SPIRIT TO HELP HER AND HE SENDS WIND SO HARD THAT THE TWIGS OF THE COTTONWOOD TREE BREAK RIGHT OFF.

AS EACH TWIG BREAKS, THE STARS ARE RELEASED AND RACE ON UP TO A SPECIAL PLACE IN THE SKY. WHEN THE STARS TWINKLE, THEY'RE SAYIN' THANK YOU.

*HE MEANS THE ARAPAHO AND CHEYENNE.

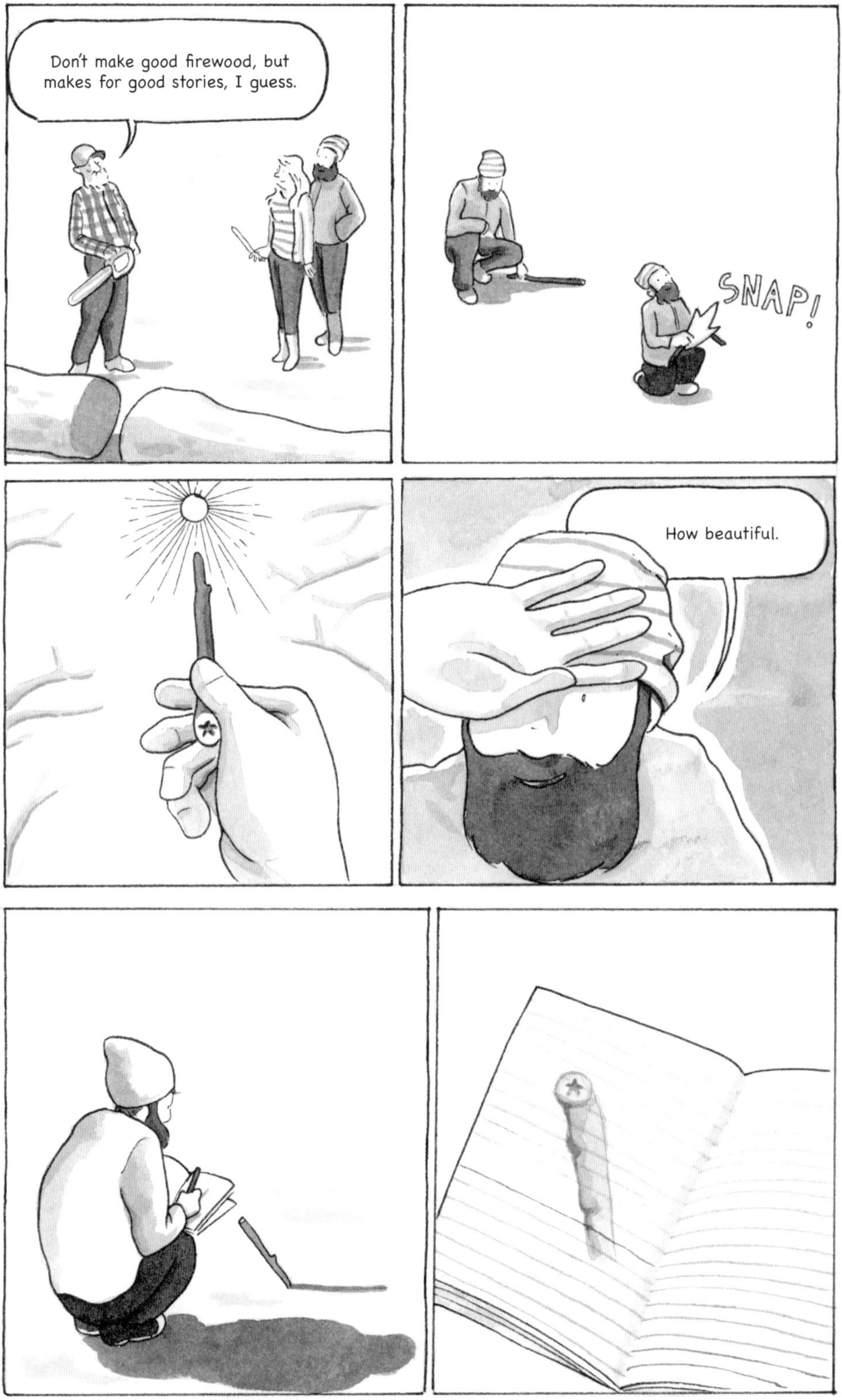
Don't make good firewood, but makes for good stories, I guess.
SNAP!
How beautiful.

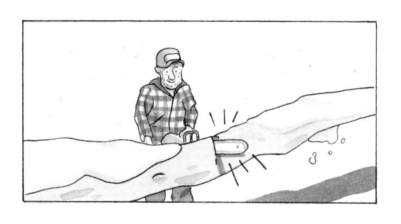

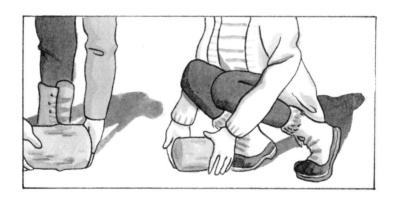

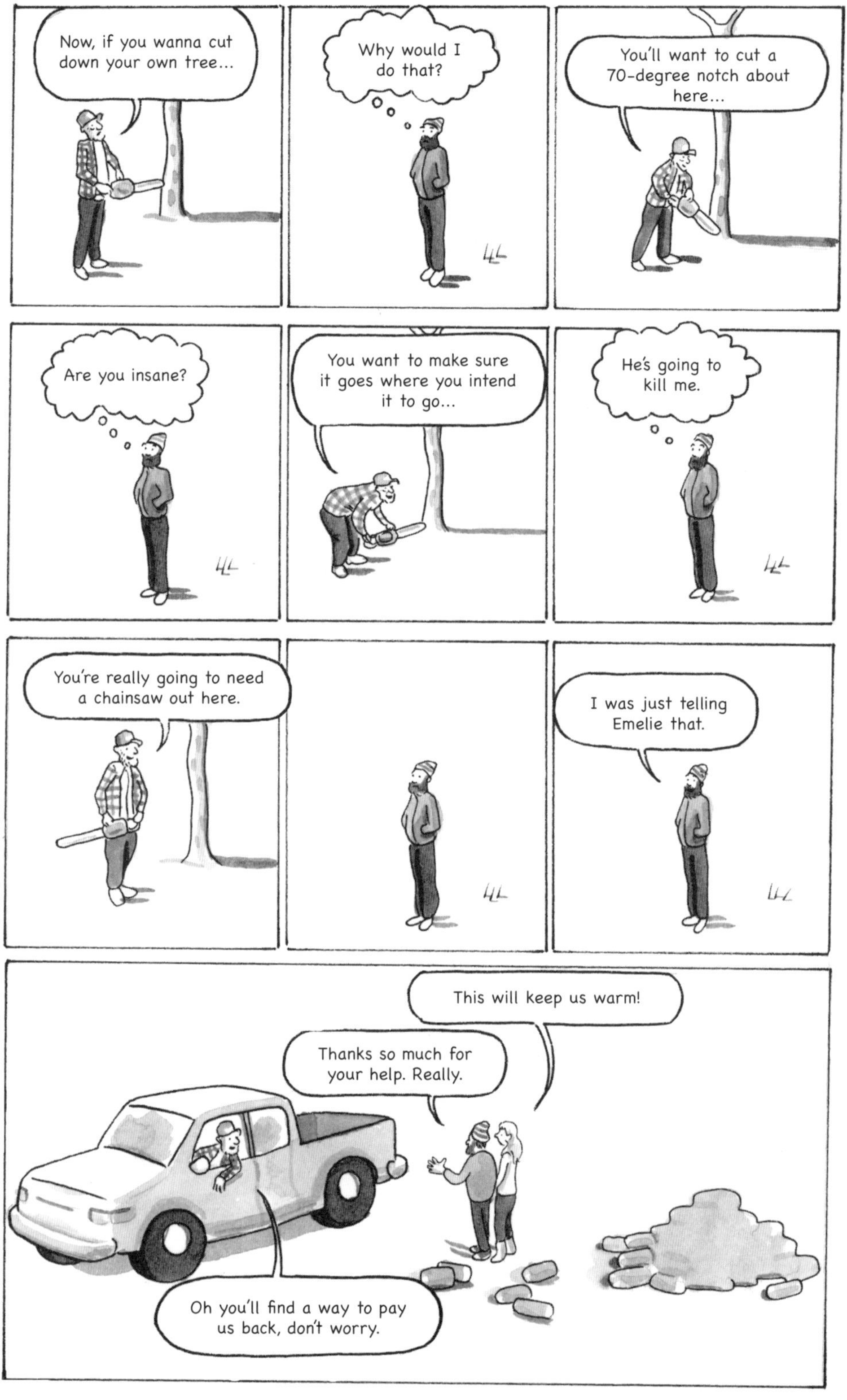
Now, if you wanna cut down your own tree...
Why would I do that?
You'll want to cut a 70-degree notch about here...
Are you insane?
You want to make sure it goes where you intend it to go...
He's going to kill me.
You're really going to need a chainsaw out here.
I was just telling Emelie that.
This will keep us warm!
Thanks so much for your help. Really.
Oh you'll find a way to pay us back, don't worry.

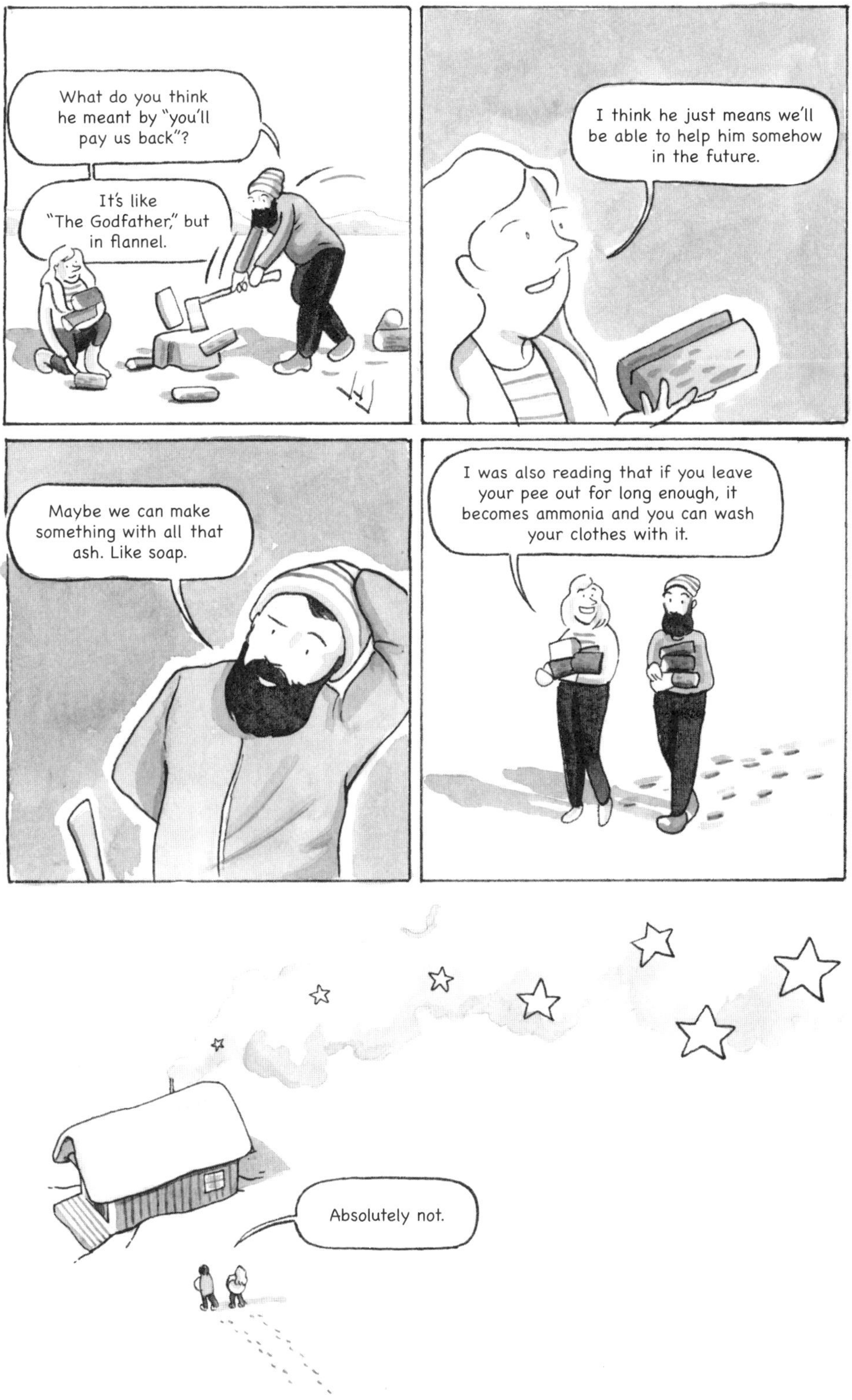
What do you think he meant by "you'll pay us back"?
It's like "The Godfather," but in flannel.
I think he just means we'll be able to help him somehow in the future.
Maybe we can make something with all that ash. Like soap.
I was also reading that if you leave your pee out for long enough, it becomes ammonia and you can wash your clothes with it.
Absolutely not.

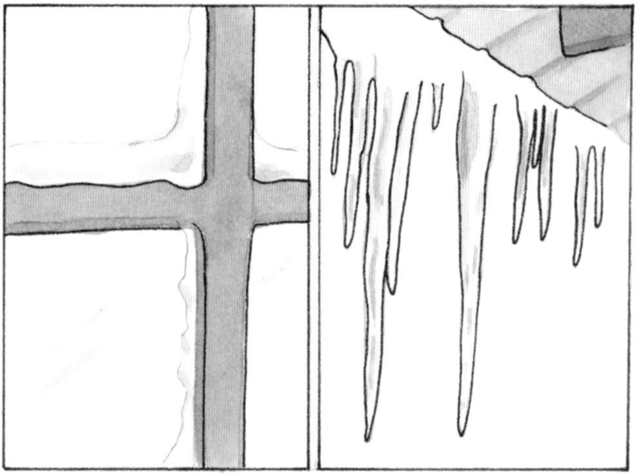

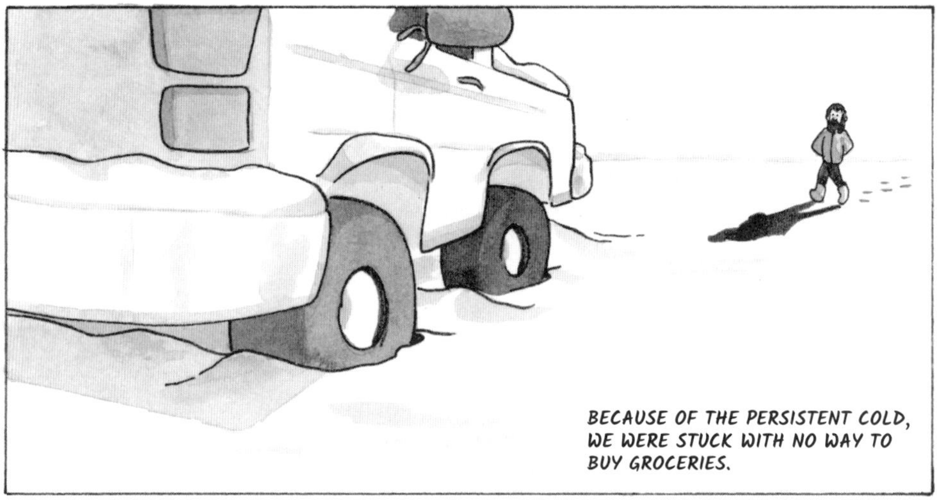
BECAUSE OF THE PERSISTENT COLD, WE WERE STUCK WITH NO WAY TO BUY GROCERIES.

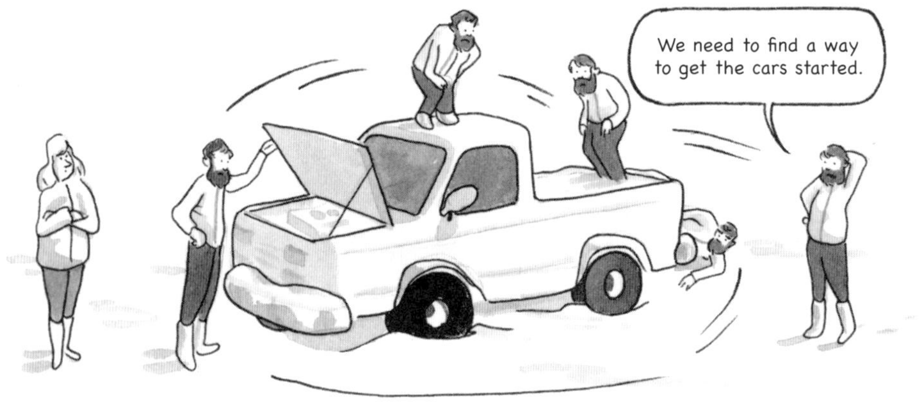
We need to find a way to get the cars started.

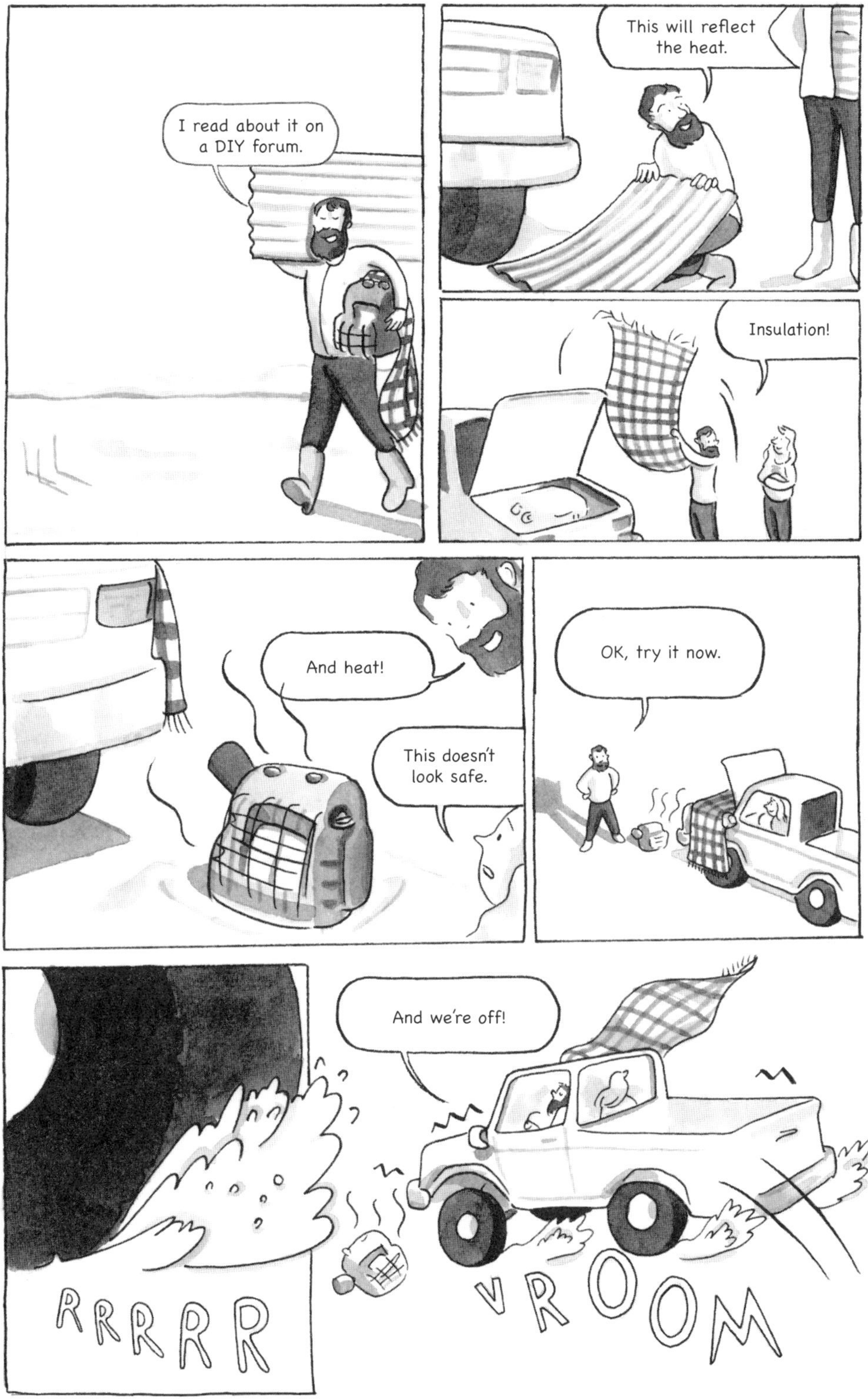
I read about it on a DIY forum.
This will reflect the heat.
Insulation!
And heat!
This doesn't look safe.
OK, try it now.
RRRRR
And we're off!
VROOM

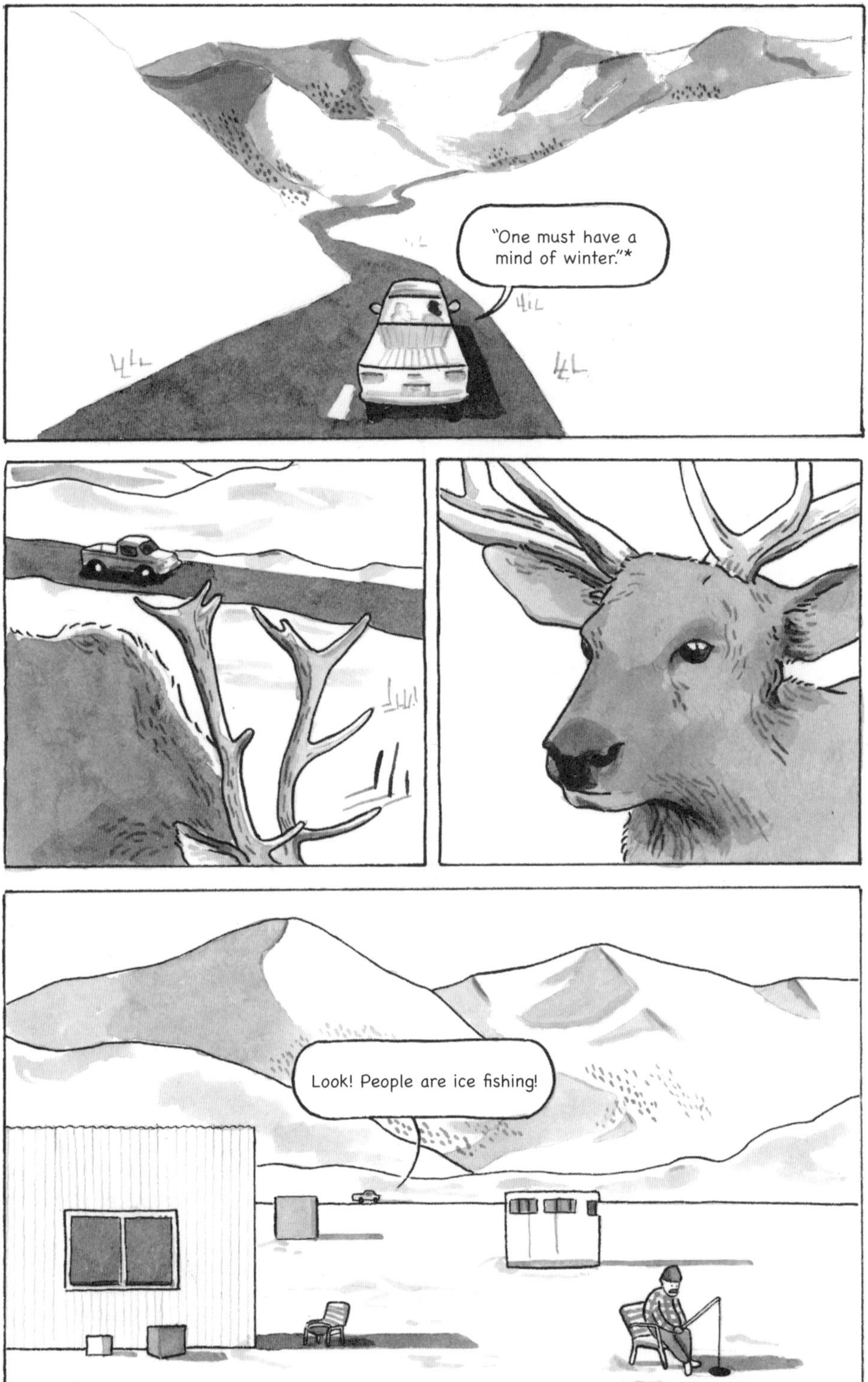
"One must have a mind of winter."*
Look! People are ice fishing!

*WALLACE STEVENS, "THE SNOW MAN"

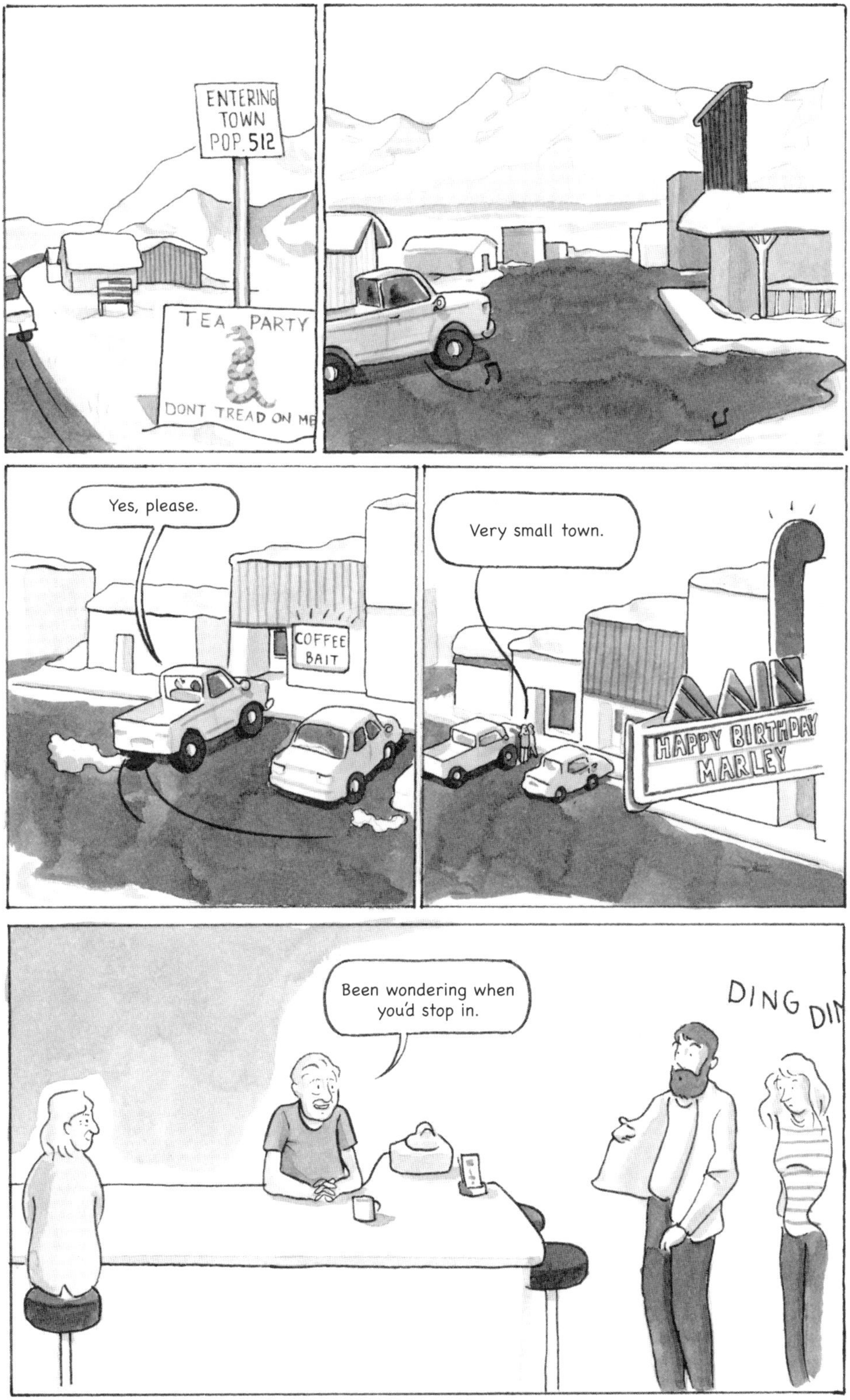
ENTERING TOWN POP. 512
TEA PARTY
DONT TREAD ON ME
Yes, please.
COFFEE BAIT
Very small town.
HAPPY BIRTHDAY MARLEY
Been wondering when you'd stop in.
DING DIN

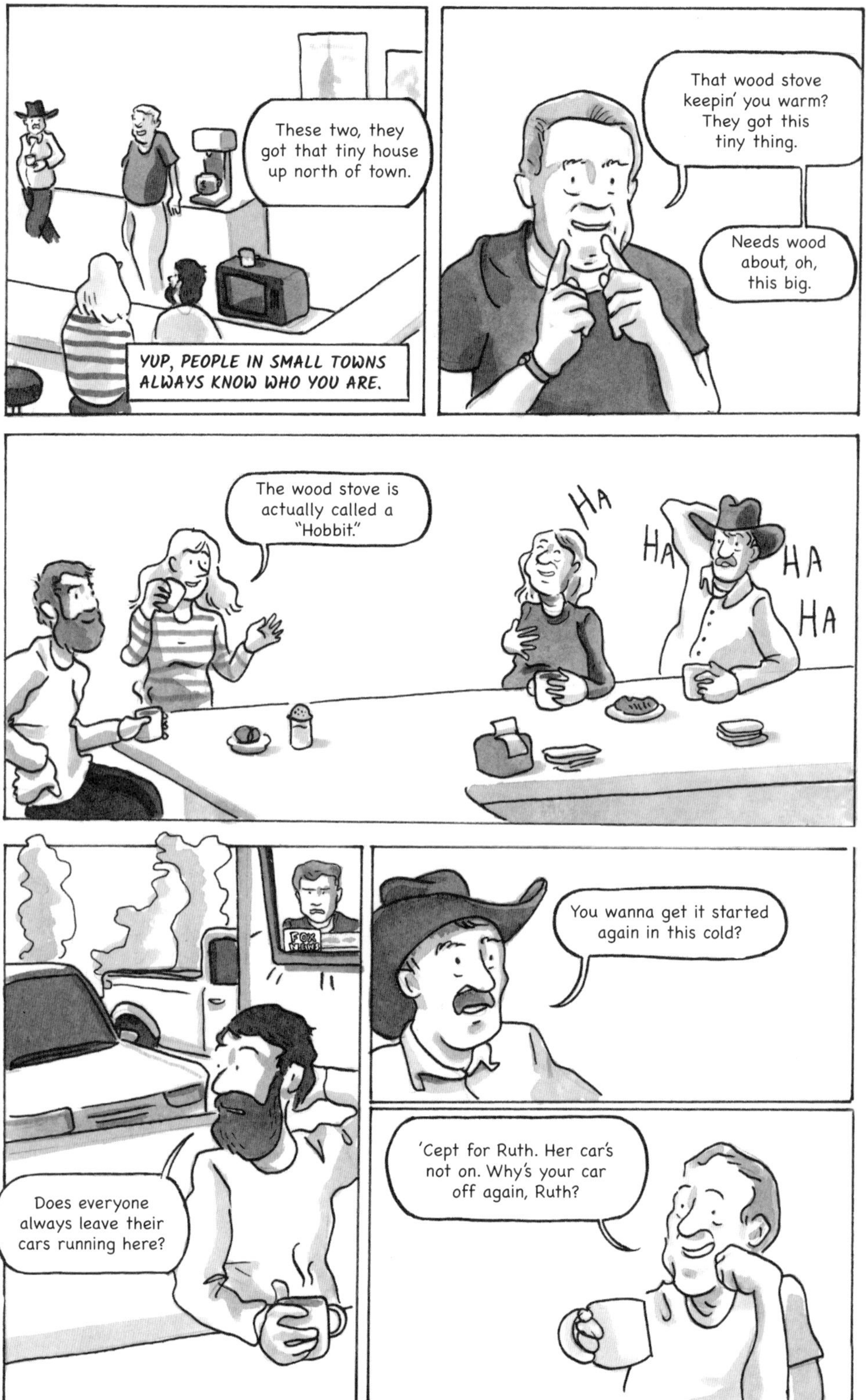
These two, they got that tiny house up north of town.
YUP, PEOPLE IN SMALL TOWNS ALWAYS KNOW WHO YOU ARE.
That wood stove keepin' you warm? They got this tiny thing.
Needs wood about, oh, this big.
The wood stove is actually called a "Hobbit."
HA
HA
HA
HA
FOX NEWS
Does everyone always leave their cars running here?
You wanna get it started again in this cold?
'Cept for Ruth. Her car's not on. Why's your car off again, Ruth?

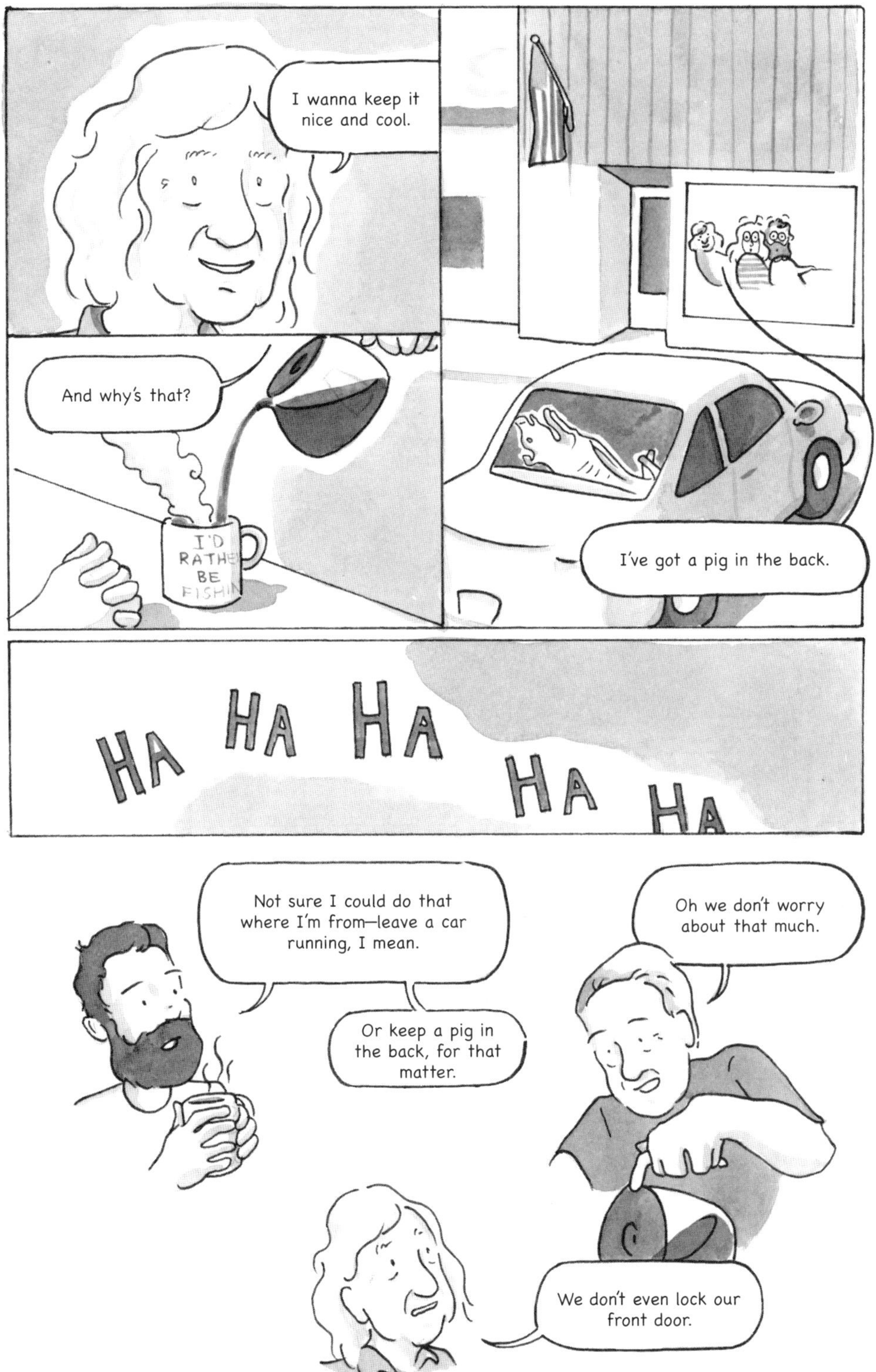
I wanna keep it nice and cool.
And why's that?
I'D RATHER BE FISHIN
I've got a pig in the back.
HA HA HA HA HA
Not sure I could do that where I'm from—leave a car running, I mean.
Or keep a pig in the back, for that matter.
Oh we don't worry about that much.
We don't even lock our front door.

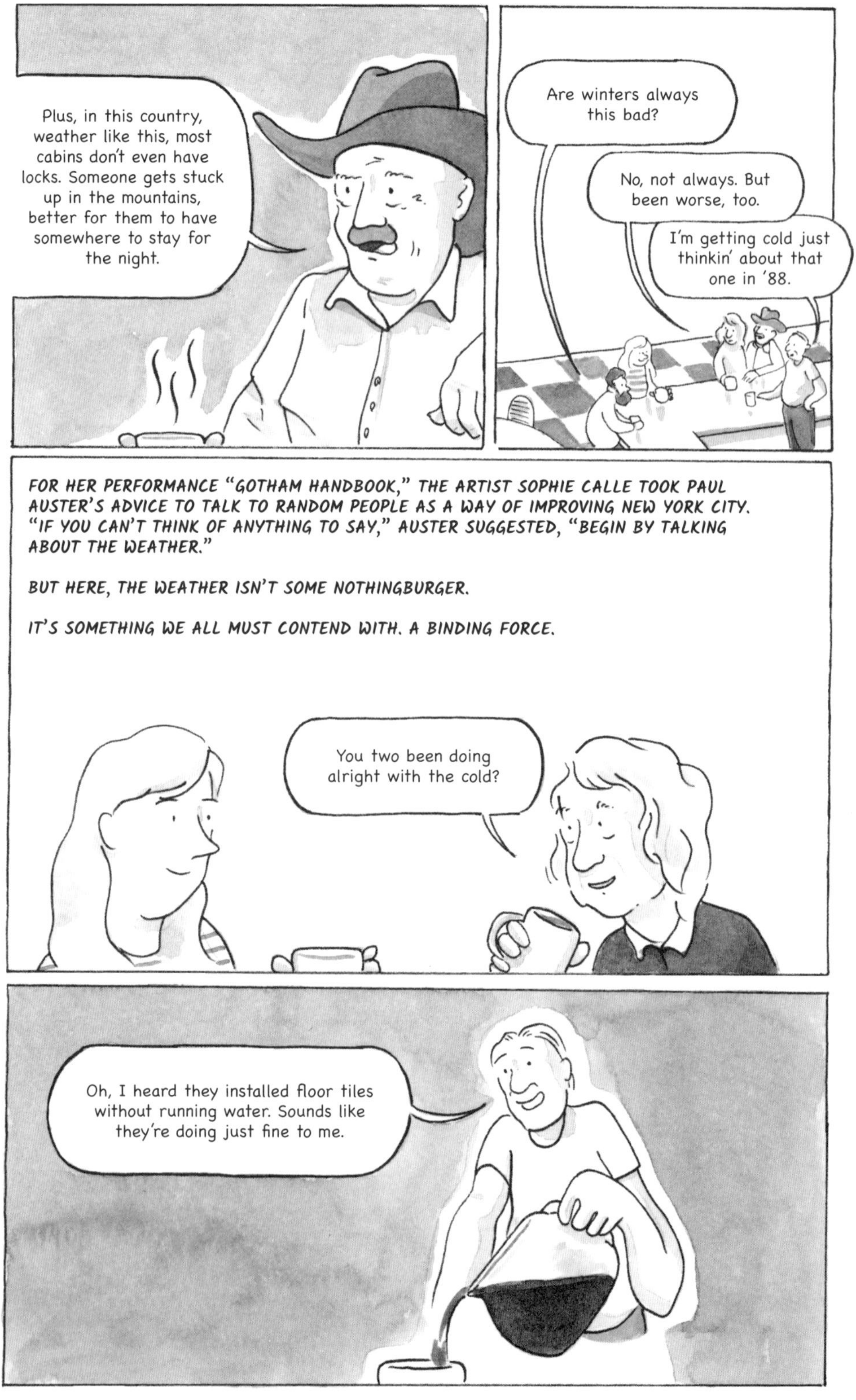
Plus, in this country, weather like this, most cabins don't even have locks. Someone gets stuck up in the mountains, better for them to have somewhere to stay for the night.
Are winters always this bad?
No, not always. But been worse, too.
I'm getting cold just thinkin' about that one in '88.
FOR HER PERFORMANCE "GOTHAM HANDBOOK," THE ARTIST SOPHIE CALLE TOOK PAUL AUSTER'S ADVICE TO TALK TO RANDOM PEOPLE AS A WAY OF IMPROVING NEW YORK CITY. "IF YOU CAN'T THINK OF ANYTHING TO SAY," AUSTER SUGGESTED, "BEGIN BY TALKING ABOUT THE WEATHER."
BUT HERE, THE WEATHER ISN'T SOME NOTHINGBURGER.
IT'S SOMETHING WE ALL MUST CONTEND WITH. A BINDING FORCE.
You two been doing alright with the cold?
Oh, I heard they installed floor tiles without running water. Sounds like they're doing just fine to me.

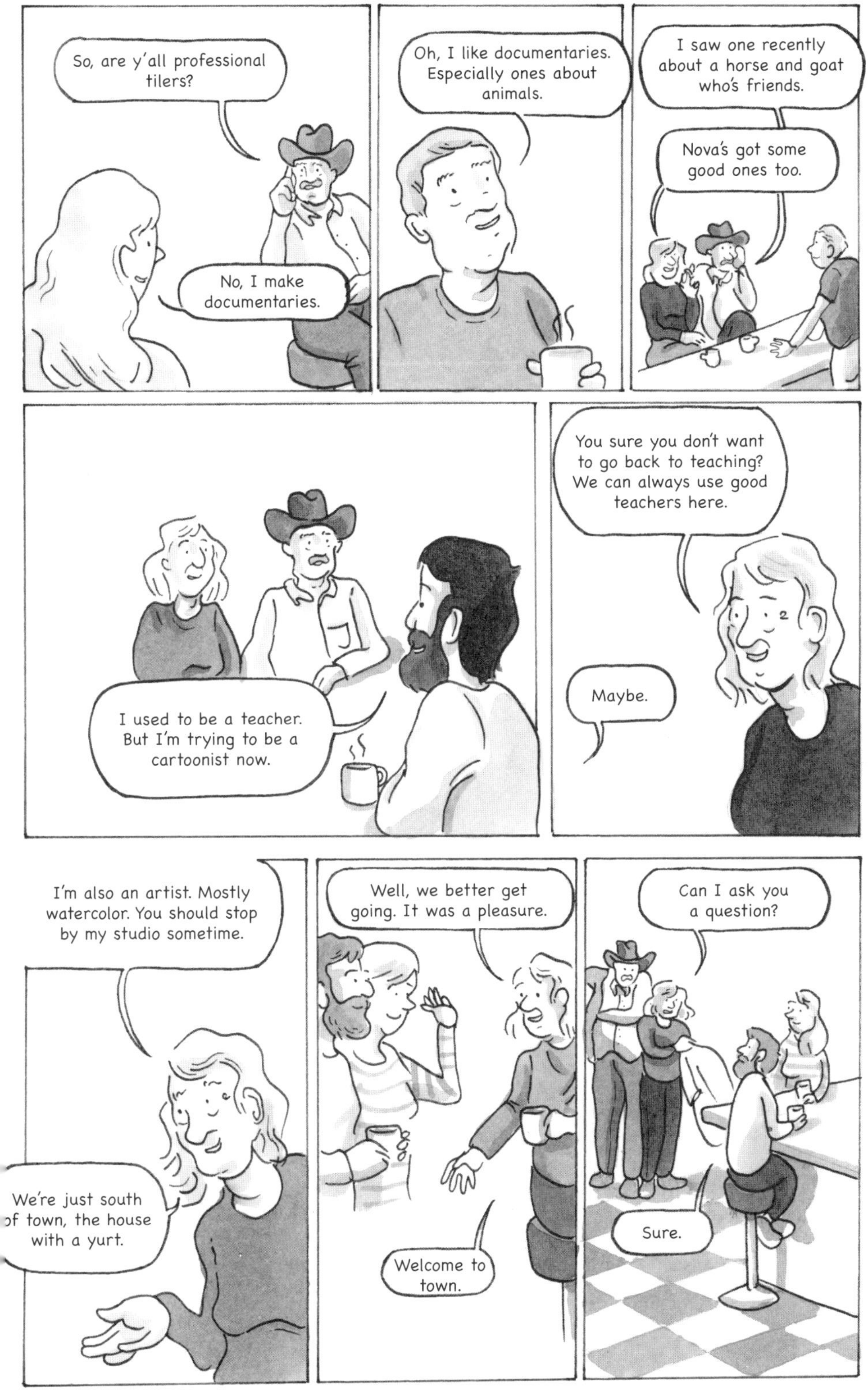
So, are y'all professional tilers?
No, I make documentaries.
Oh, I like documentaries. Especially ones about animals.
I saw one recently about a horse and goat who's friends.
Nova's got some good ones too.
I used to be a teacher. But I'm trying to be a cartoonist now.
You sure you don't want to go back to teaching? We can always use good teachers here.
Maybe.
I'm also an artist. Mostly watercolor. You should stop by my studio sometime.
We're just south of town, the house with a yurt.
Well, we better get going. It was a pleasure.
Welcome to town.
Can I ask you a question?
Sure.

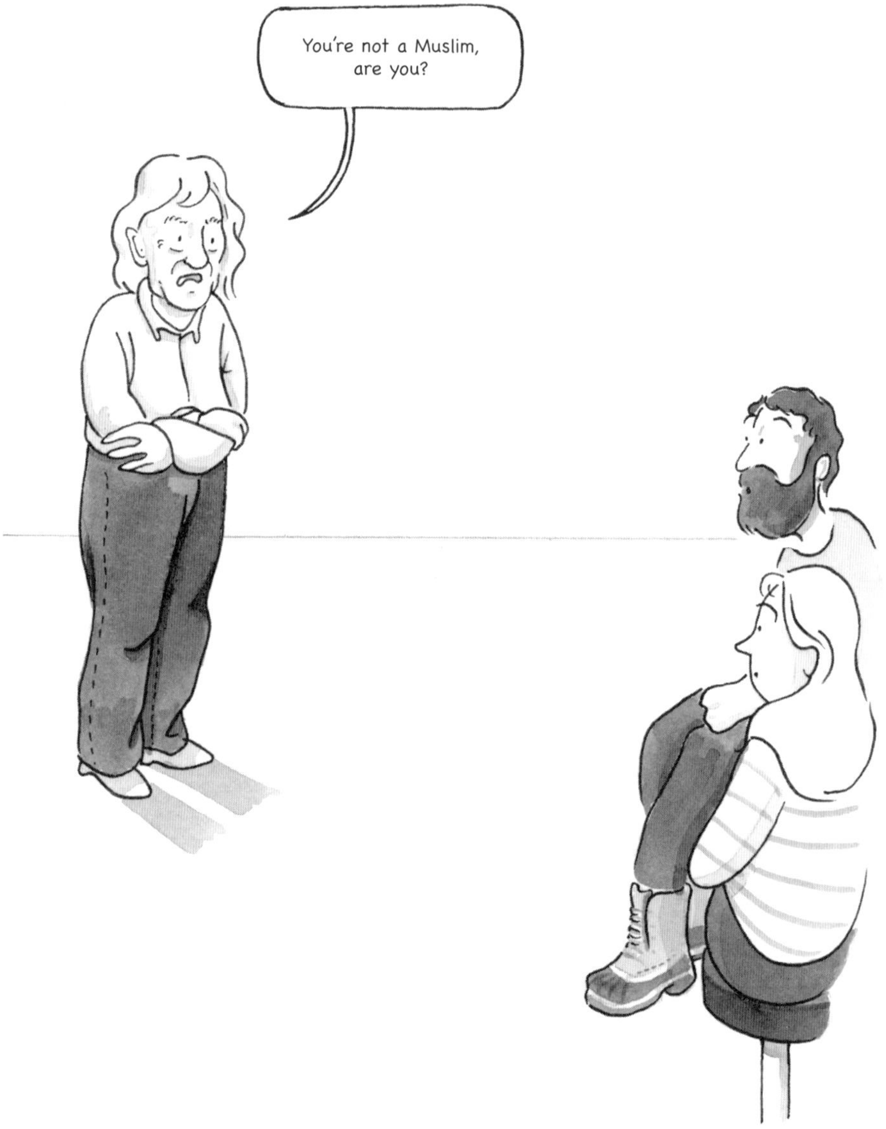
You're not a Muslim, are you?

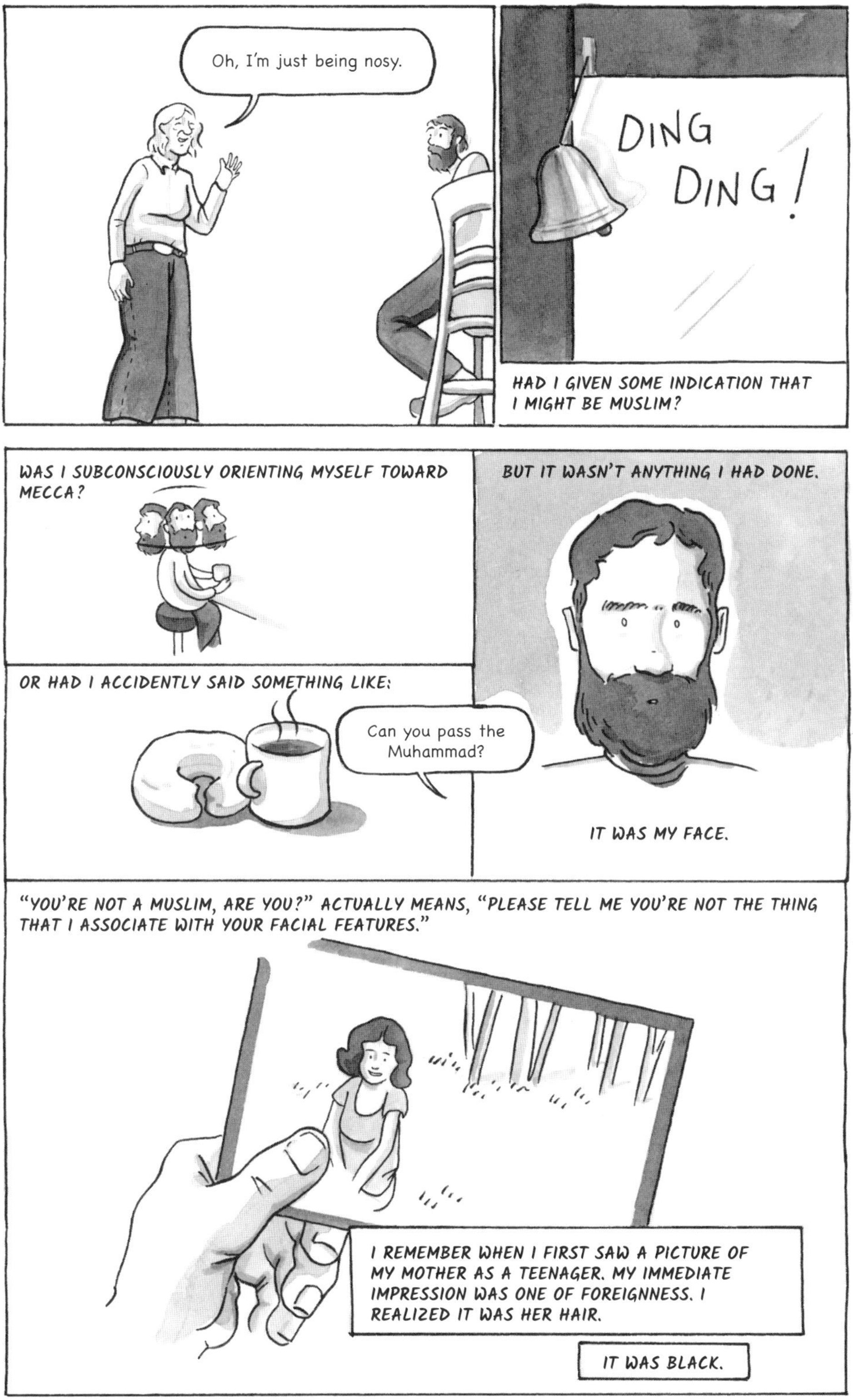
Oh, I'm just being nosy.
DING DING!
HAD I GIVEN SOME INDICATION THAT I MIGHT BE MUSLIM?
WAS I SUBCONSCIOUSLY ORIENTING MYSELF TOWARD MECCA?
OR HAD I ACCIDENTLY SAID SOMETHING LIKE:
Can you pass the Muhammad?
BUT IT WASN'T ANYTHING I HAD DONE.
IT WAS MY FACE.
"YOU'RE NOT A MUSLIM, ARE YOU?" ACTUALLY MEANS, "PLEASE TELL ME YOU'RE NOT THE THING THAT I ASSOCIATE WITH YOUR FACIAL FEATURES."
I REMEMBER WHEN I FIRST SAW A PICTURE OF MY MOTHER AS A TEENAGER. MY IMMEDIATE IMPRESSION WAS ONE OF FOREIGNNESS. I REALIZED IT WAS HER HAIR.
IT WAS BLACK.

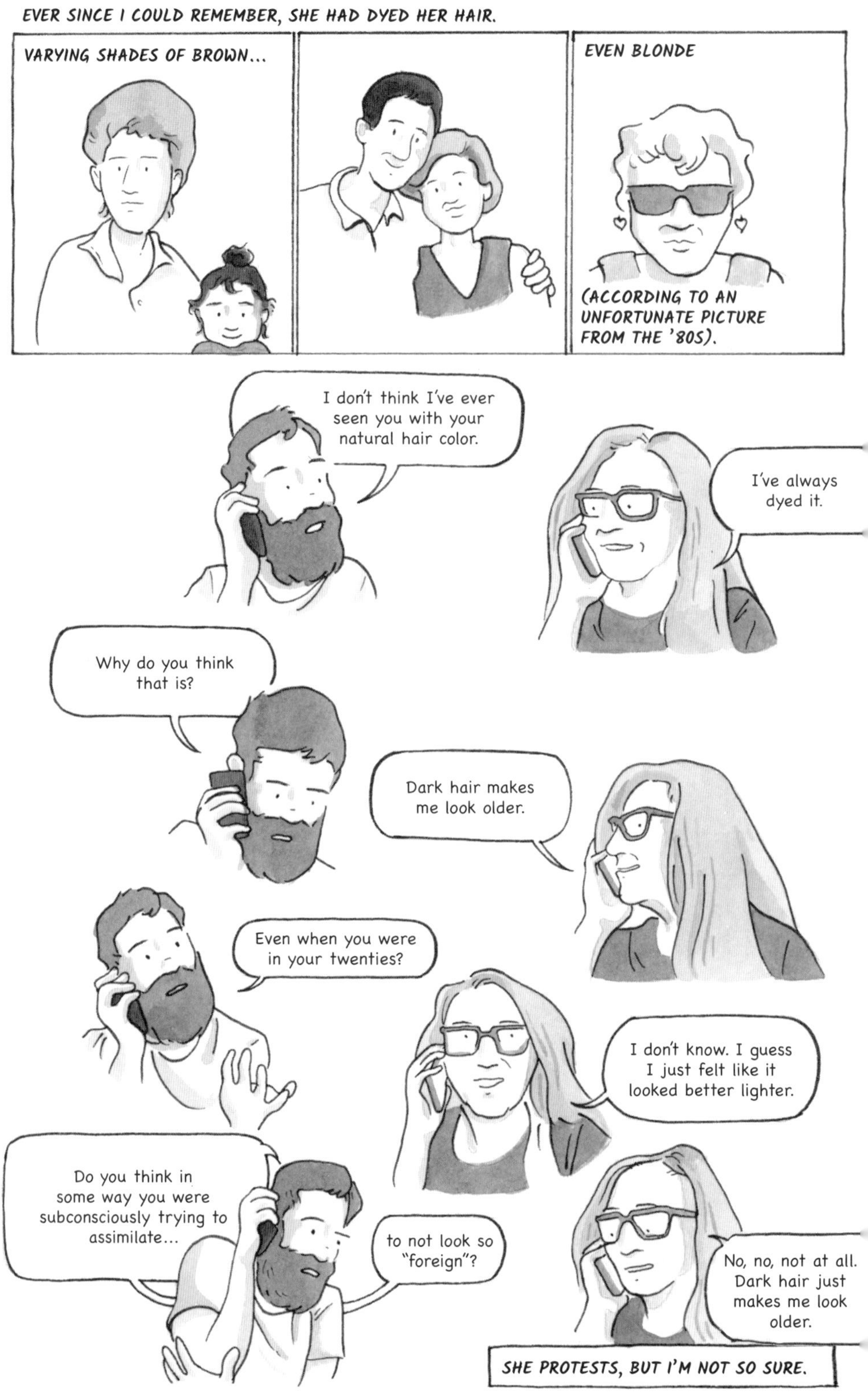

EVER SINCE I COULD REMEMBER, SHE HAD DYED HER HAIR.
VARYING SHADES OF BROWN...
EVEN BLONDE
(ACCORDING TO AN UNFORTUNATE PICTURE FROM THE '80S).
I don't think I've ever seen you with your natural hair color.
I've always dyed it.
Why do you think that is?
Dark hair makes me look older.
Even when you were in your twenties?
I don't know. I guess I just felt like it looked better lighter.
Do you think in some way you were subconsciously trying to assimilate...
to not look so "foreign"?
No, no, not at all. Dark hair just makes me look older.
SHE PROTESTS, BUT I'M NOT SO SURE.

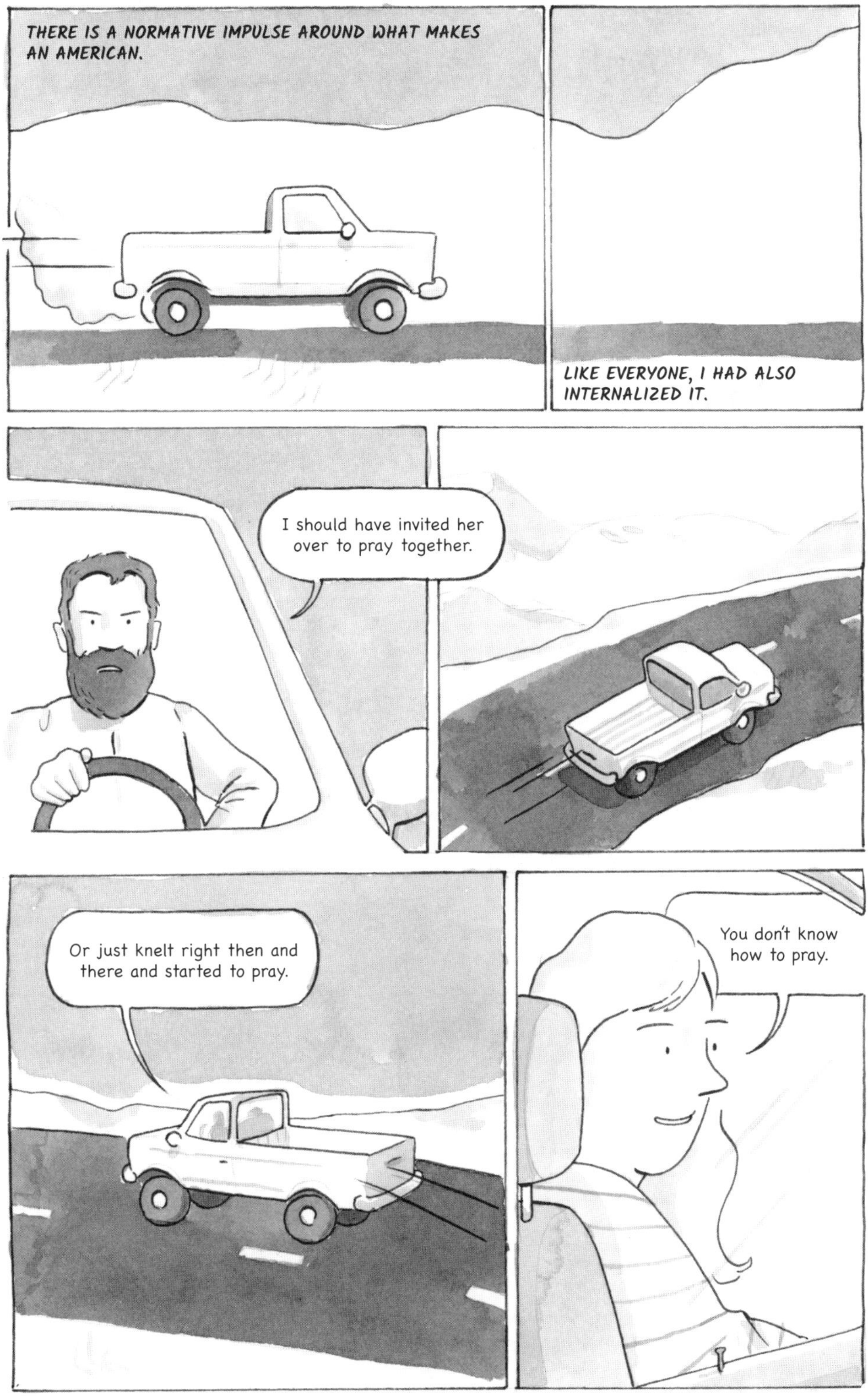
THERE IS A NORMATIVE IMPULSE AROUND WHAT MAKES AN AMERICAN.
LIKE EVERYONE, I HAD ALSO INTERNALIZED IT.
I should have invited her over to pray together.
Or just knelt right then and there and started to pray.
You don't know how to pray.

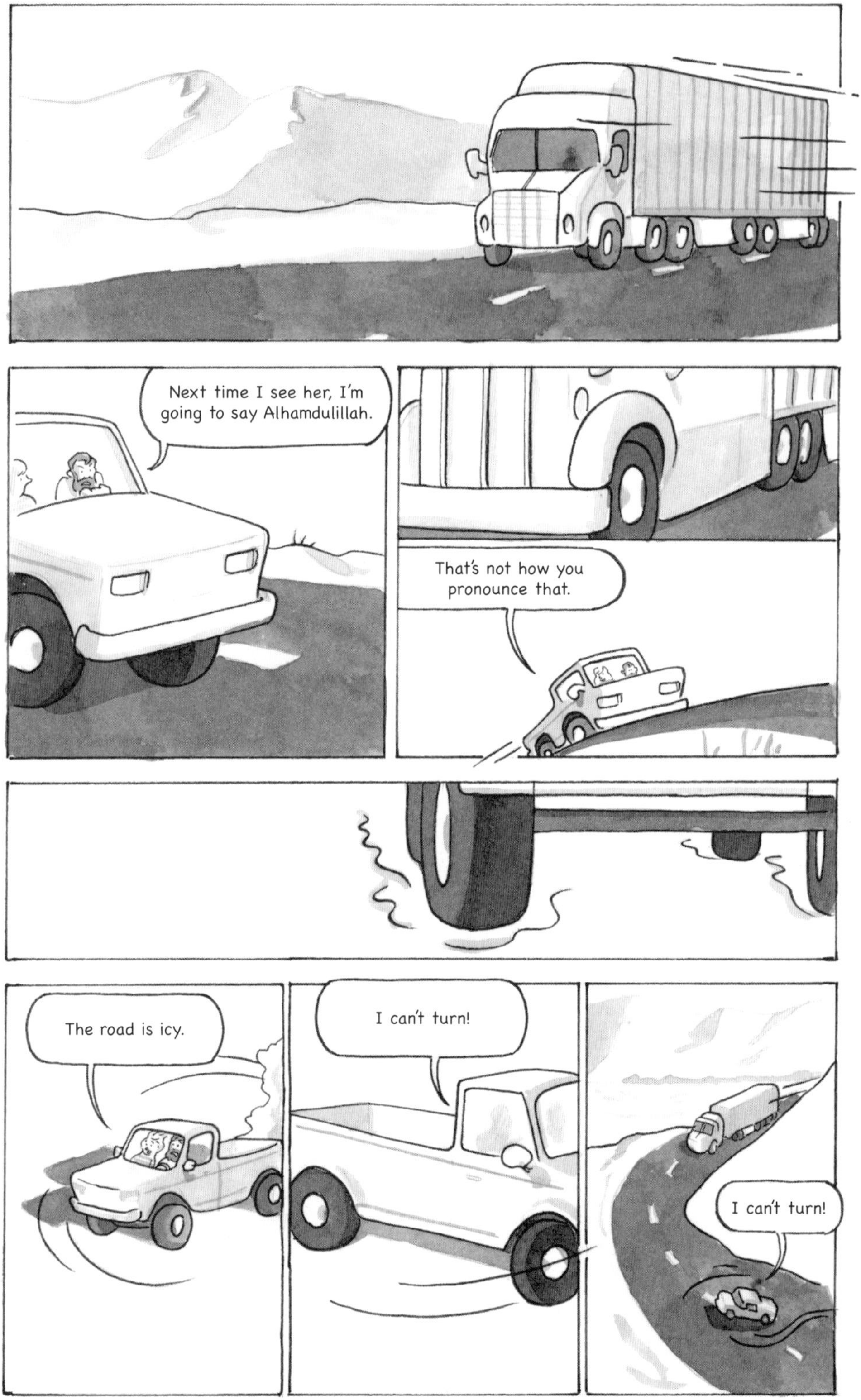
Next time I see her, I'm going to say Alhamdulillah.
That's not how you pronounce that.
The road is icy.
I can't turn!
I can't turn!

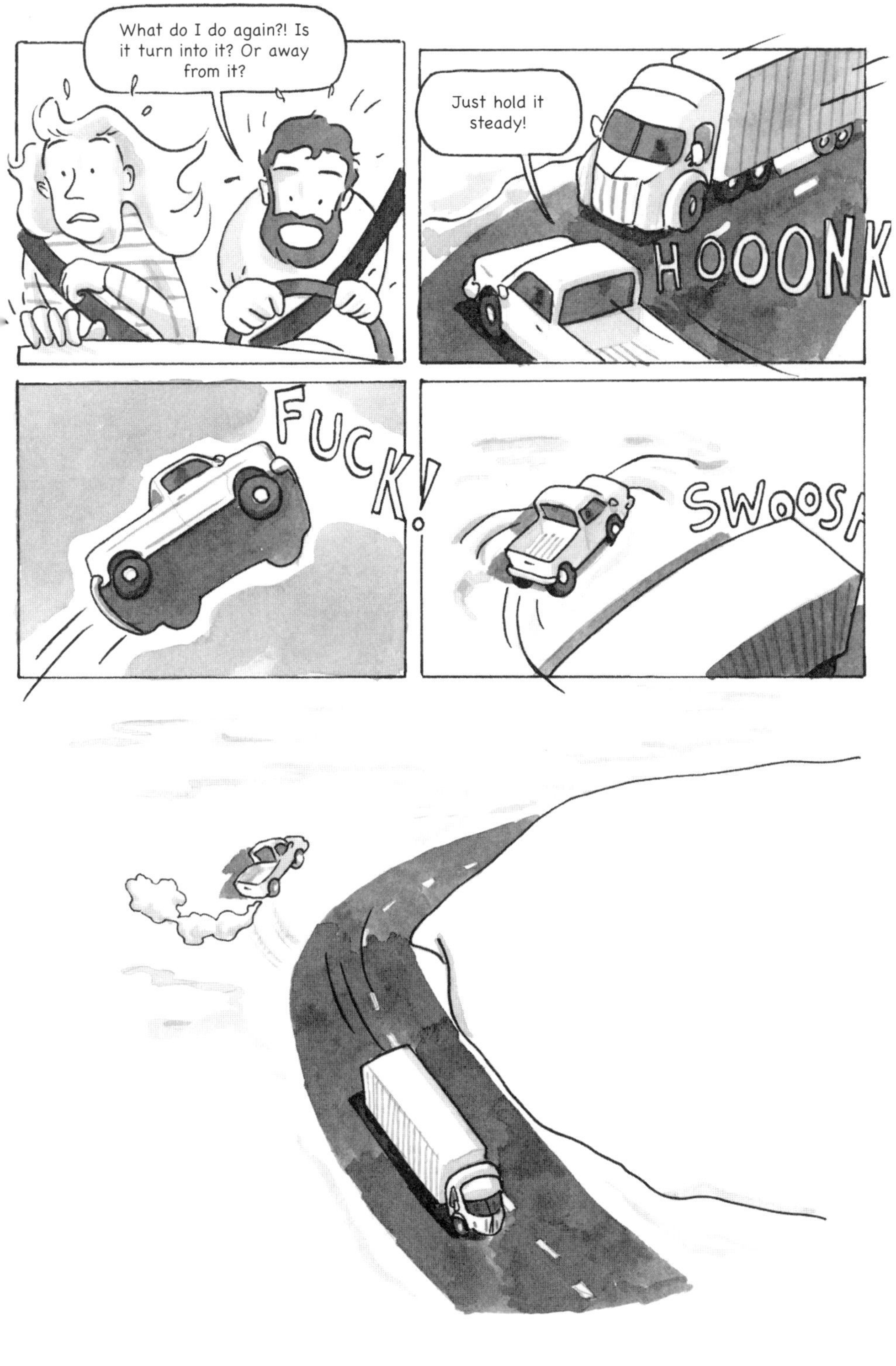
What do I do again?! Is it turn into it? Or away from it?
Just hold it steady!
HOOONK
FUCK!
SWOOSH

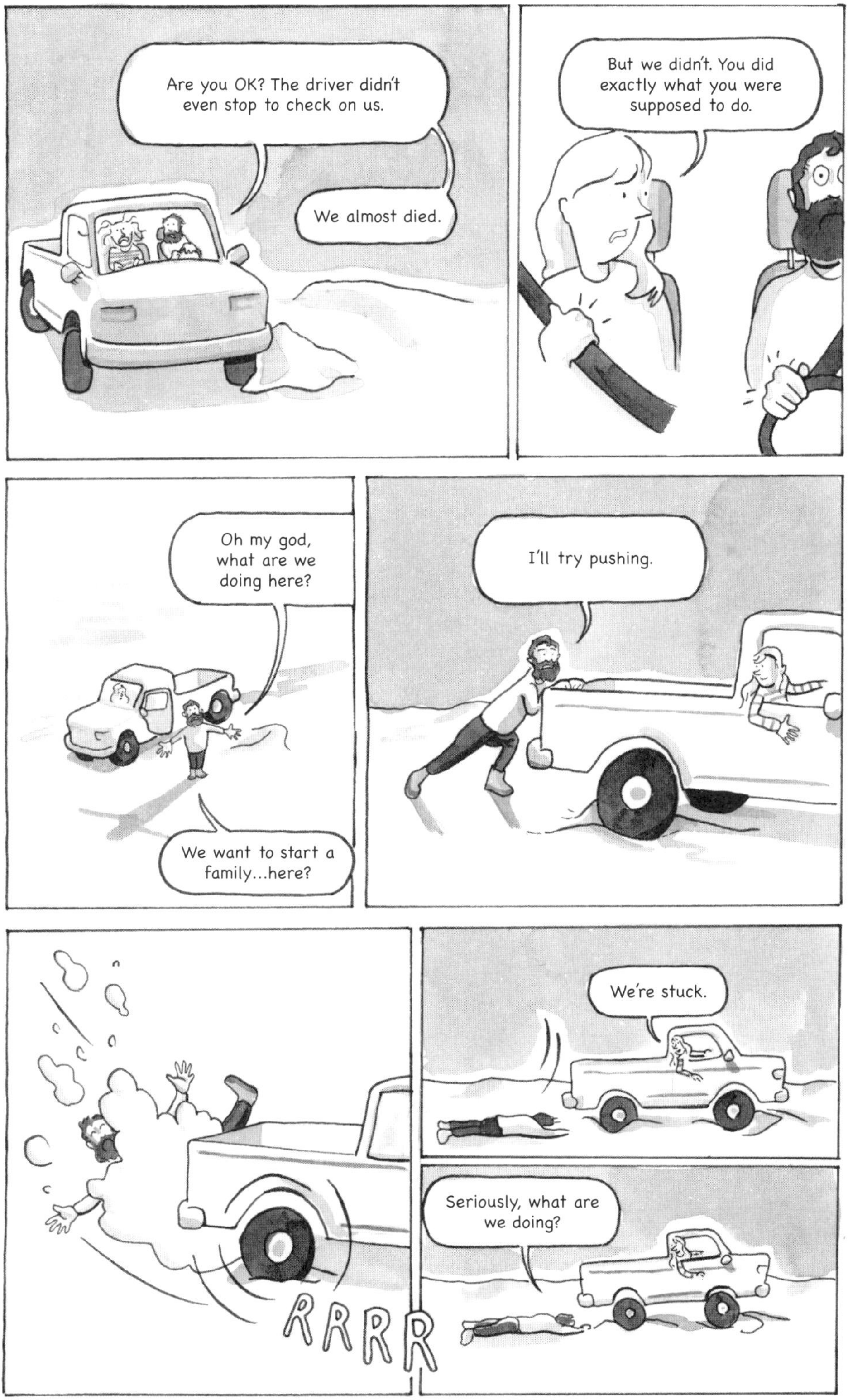
Are you OK? The driver didn't even stop to check on us.
We almost died.
But we didn't. You did exactly what you were supposed to do.
Oh my god, what are we doing here?
We want to start a family...here?
I'll try pushing.
RRRR
We're stuck.
Seriously, what are we doing?

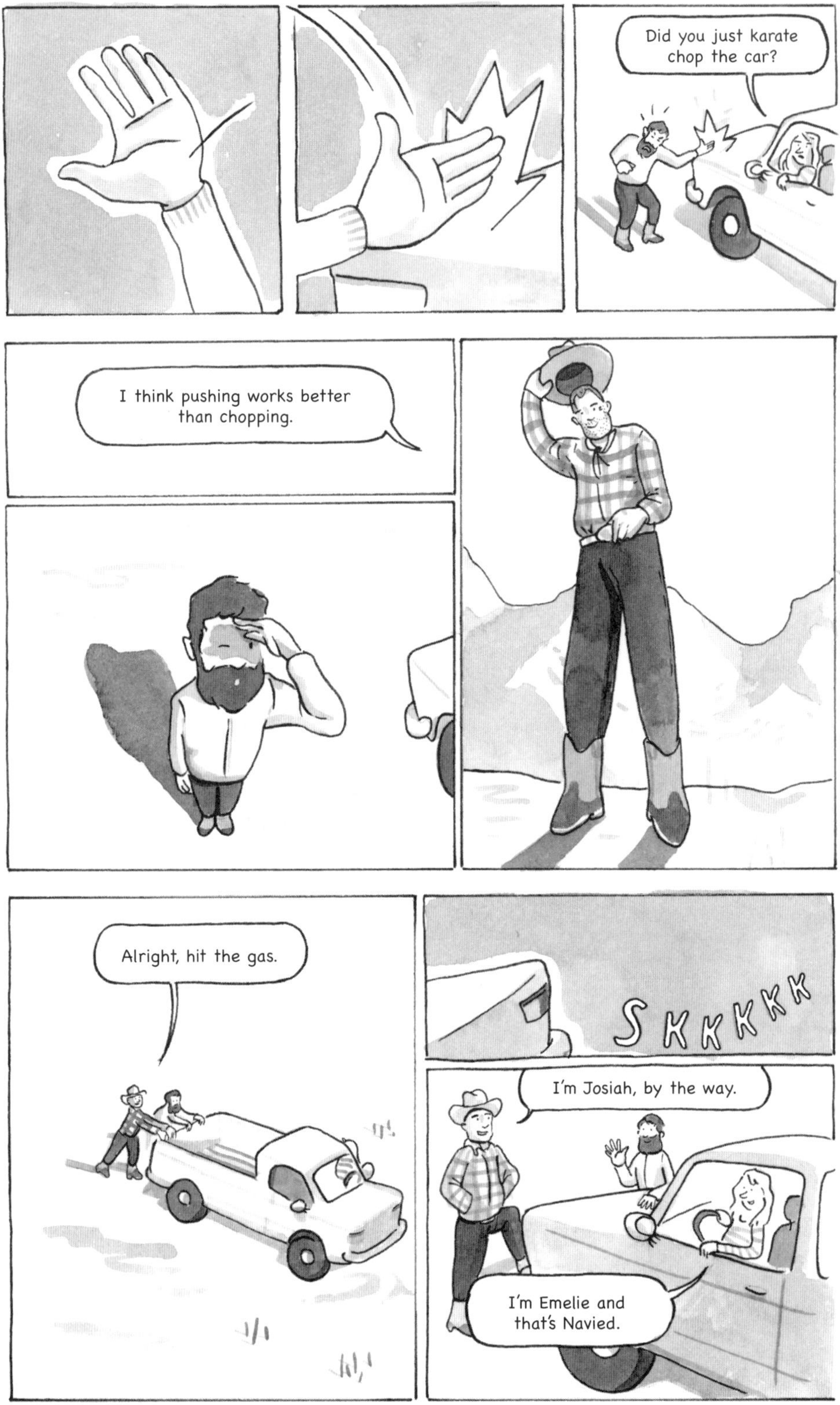
Did you just karate chop the car?
I think pushing works better than chopping.
Alright, hit the gas.
SKKKKK
I'm Josiah, by the way.
I'm Emelie and that's Navied.

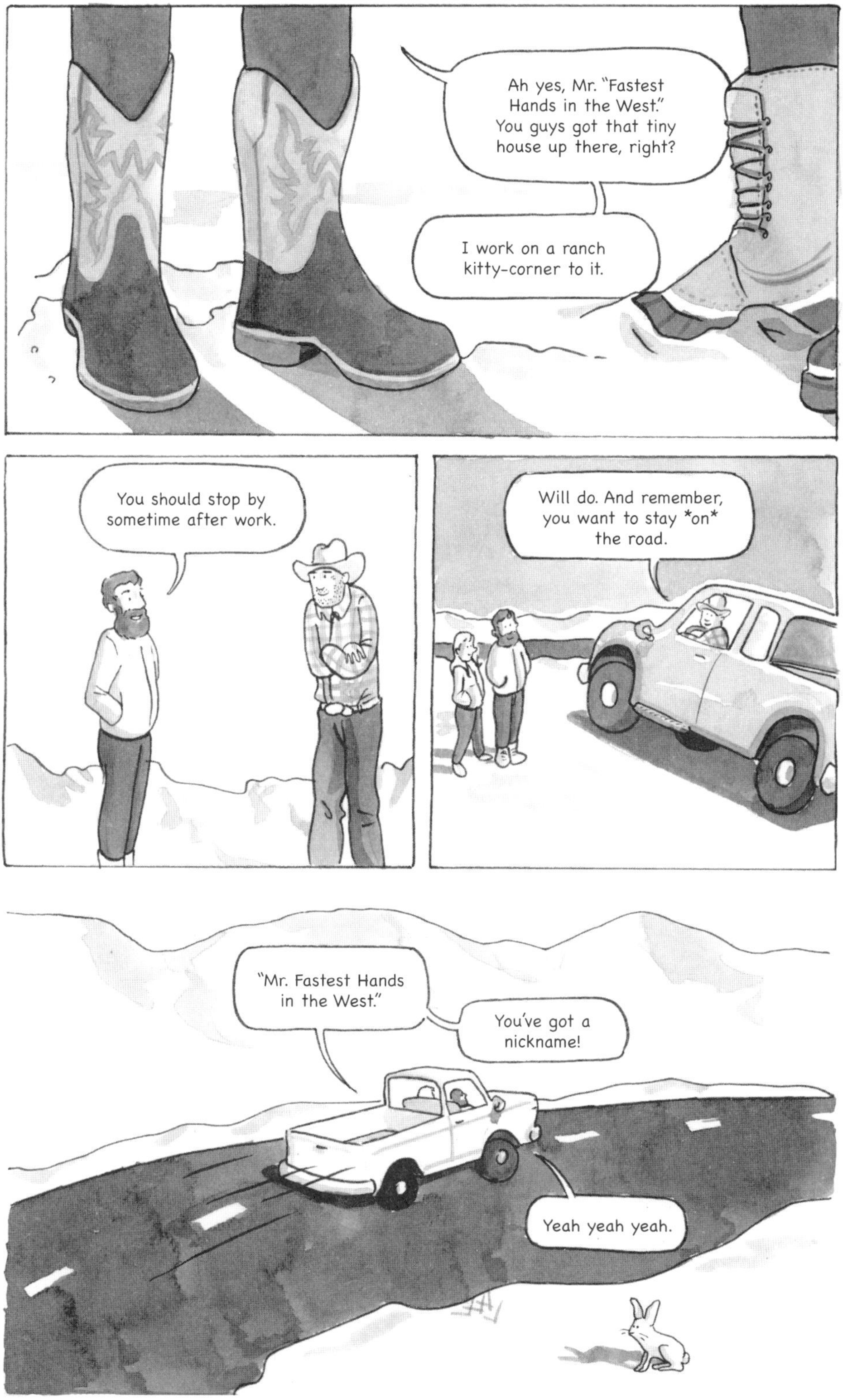
Ah yes, Mr. "Fastest Hands in the West." You guys got that tiny house up there, right?
I work on a ranch kitty-corner to it.
You should stop by sometime after work.
Will do. And remember, you want to stay *on* the road.
"Mr. Fastest Hands in the West."
You've got a nickname!
Yeah yeah yeah.

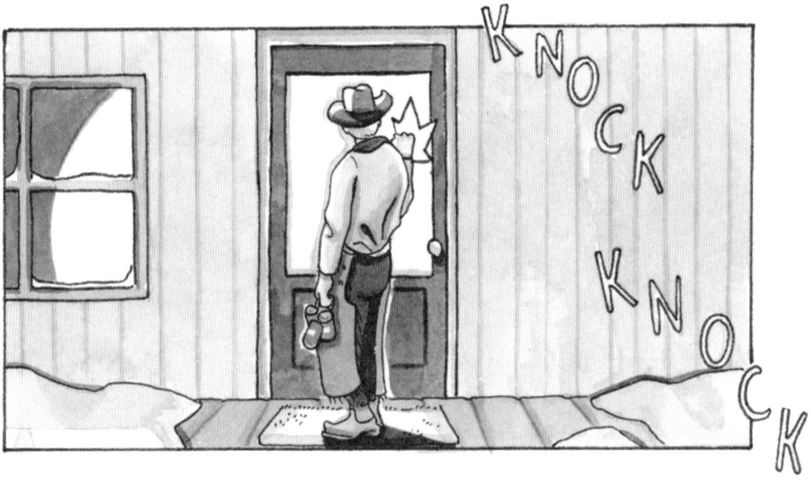
KNOCK
KNOCK

I brought beer.

Well shit. This is cozy.

I don't think I've ever seen someone actually in chaps.

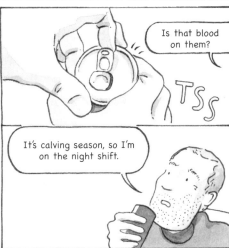

Is that blood on them?

It's calving season, so I'm on the night shift.

This winter's been a bugger. We've lost more calves than normal.

From the cold?

The snow actually.

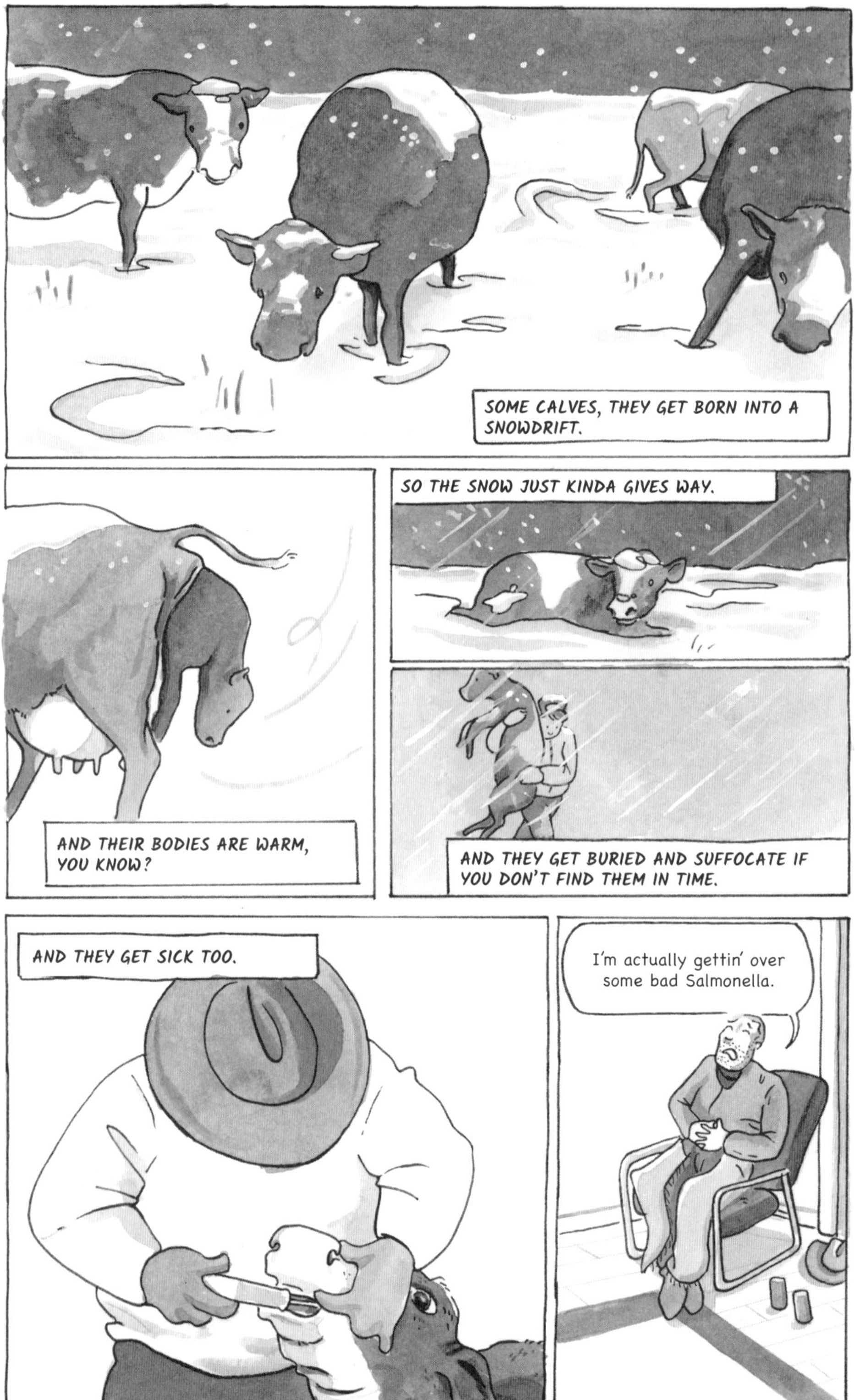
SOME CALVES, THEY GET BORN INTO A SNOWDRIFT.
AND THEIR BODIES ARE WARM, YOU KNOW?
SO THE SNOW JUST KINDA GIVES WAY.
AND THEY GET BURIED AND SUFFOCATE IF YOU DON'T FIND THEM IN TIME.
AND THEY GET SICK TOO.
I'm actually gettin' over some bad Salmonella.

THESE CALVES WERE LIKE A MONTH OLD, SO THEY'RE LIKE 200 POUNDS AND LITERALLY WITHIN 12 HOURS THEY'RE DROPPING DEAD. I MEAN THEY WERE OUT BUCKING AND THEN BOOM.

That's how bad this strain is.

TSSsss

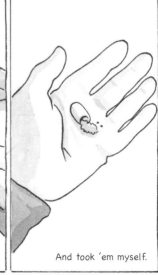

And you can catch it from cows?

Oh yeah. I was given them x and z pills for their Salmonella.

So they're cow pills, but I just cut 'em.

I COULD SEE WHERE THIS WAS GOING.

And took 'em myself.

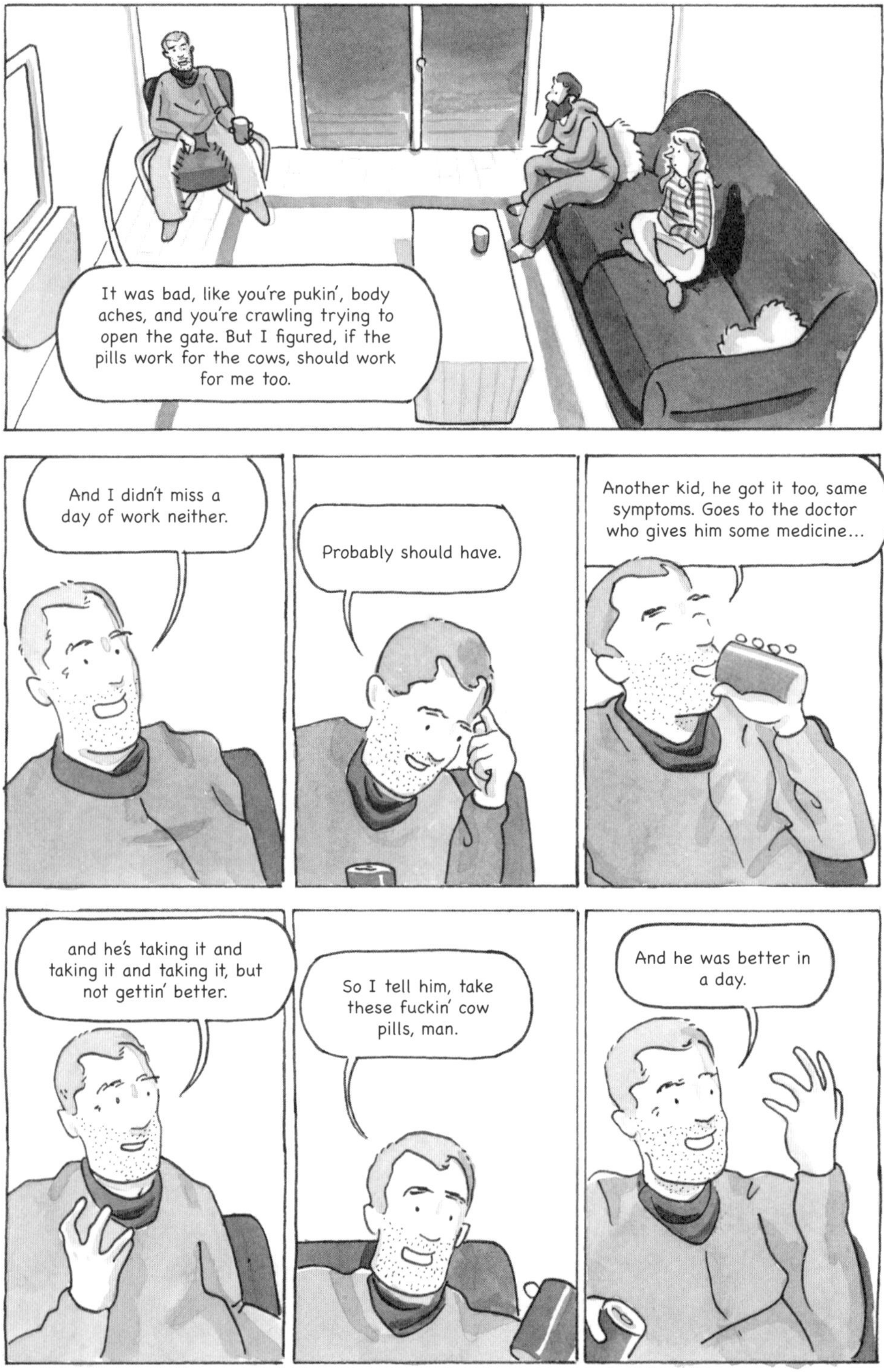

It was bad, like you're pukin', body aches, and you're crawling trying to open the gate. But I figured, if the pills work for the cows, should work for me too.
And I didn't miss a day of work neither.
Probably should have.
Another kid, he got it too, same symptoms. Goes to the doctor who gives him some medicine...
and he's taking it and taking it and taking it, but not gettin' better.
So I tell him, take these fuckin' cow pills, man.
And he was better in a day.

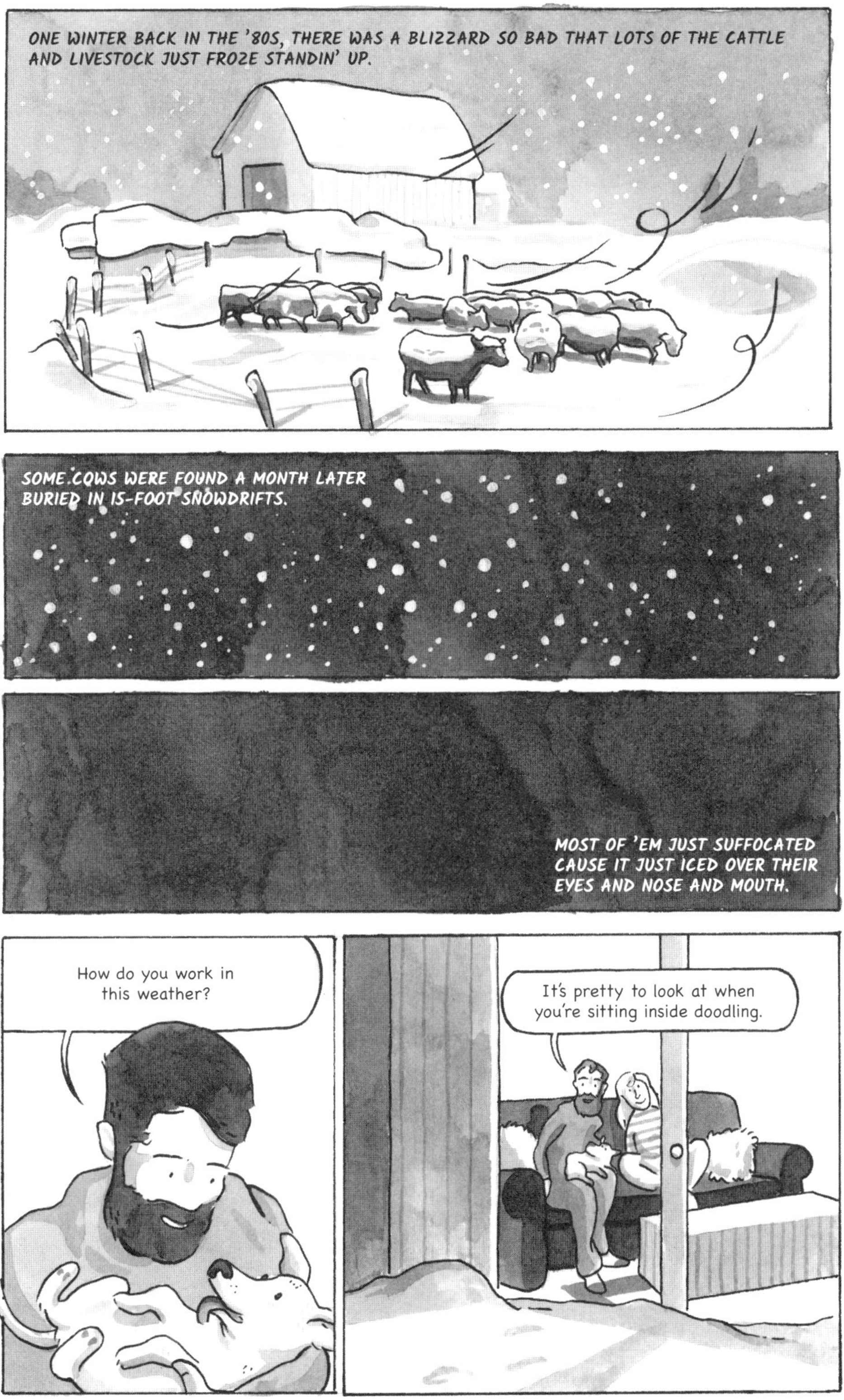
ONE WINTER BACK IN THE '80S, THERE WAS A BLIZZARD SO BAD THAT LOTS OF THE CATTLE AND LIVESTOCK JUST FROZE STANDIN' UP.
SOME COWS WERE FOUND A MONTH LATER BURIED IN 15-FOOT SNOWDRIFTS.
MOST OF 'EM JUST SUFFOCATED CAUSE IT JUST ICED OVER THEIR EYES AND NOSE AND MOUTH.
How do you work in this weather?
It's pretty to look at when you're sitting inside doodling.

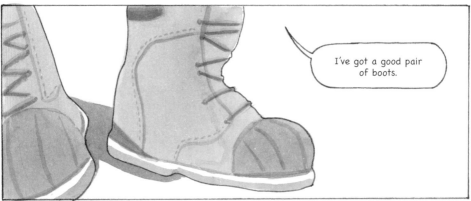

I've got a good pair of boots.

JOSIAH'S BOOTS ARE MASSIVE. JOSIAH IS MASSIVE.

OUR HOME FEELS PARTICULARLY TINY WITH HIM IN IT.

IT DOESN'T HELP THAT I AM IN A ONESIE.

You look like you keep pretty warm yourself in that.

Yeah, you laugh, but do your pants have a flap in the back?

Other years, I literally don't hardly have any problems calving.

Only problems was backwards ones or twins and bad tits. But this winter, they're gettin' run in all the time and pulled.

Pulled as in, pulled?

Pulling the calf out of her. Because of a leg back or head back.

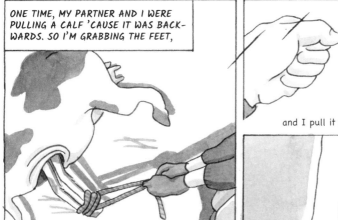

ONE TIME, MY PARTNER AND I WERE PULLING A CALF 'CAUSE IT WAS BACK-WARDS. SO I'M GRABBING THE FEET,

and I pull it out and up, like this.

And my buddy says, "Josiah, are you seeing this?"

And I look down, and this fucker's got two heads.

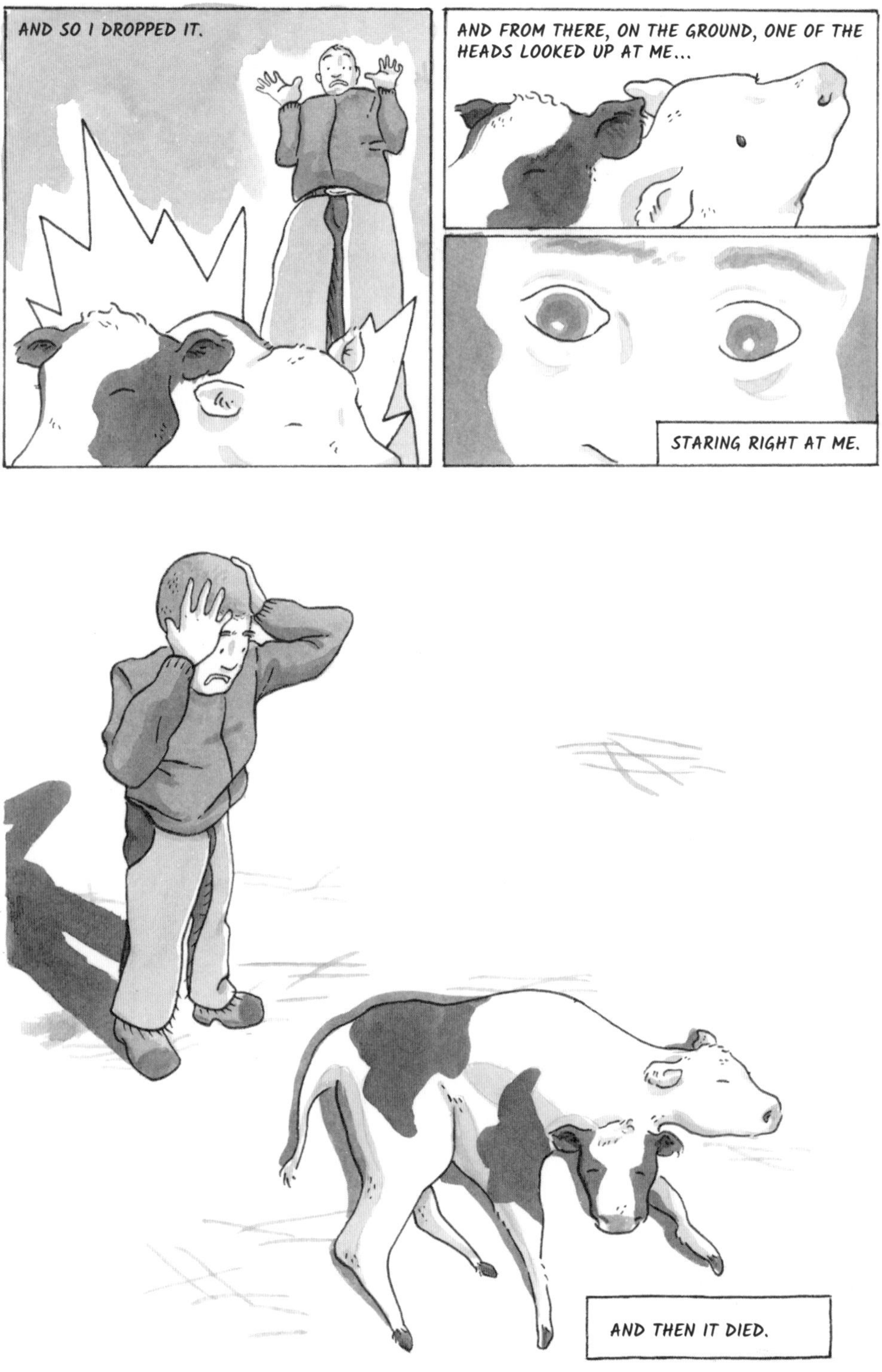
AND SO I DROPPED IT.
AND FROM THERE, ON THE GROUND, ONE OF THE HEADS LOOKED UP AT ME...
STARING RIGHT AT ME.
AND THEN IT DIED.

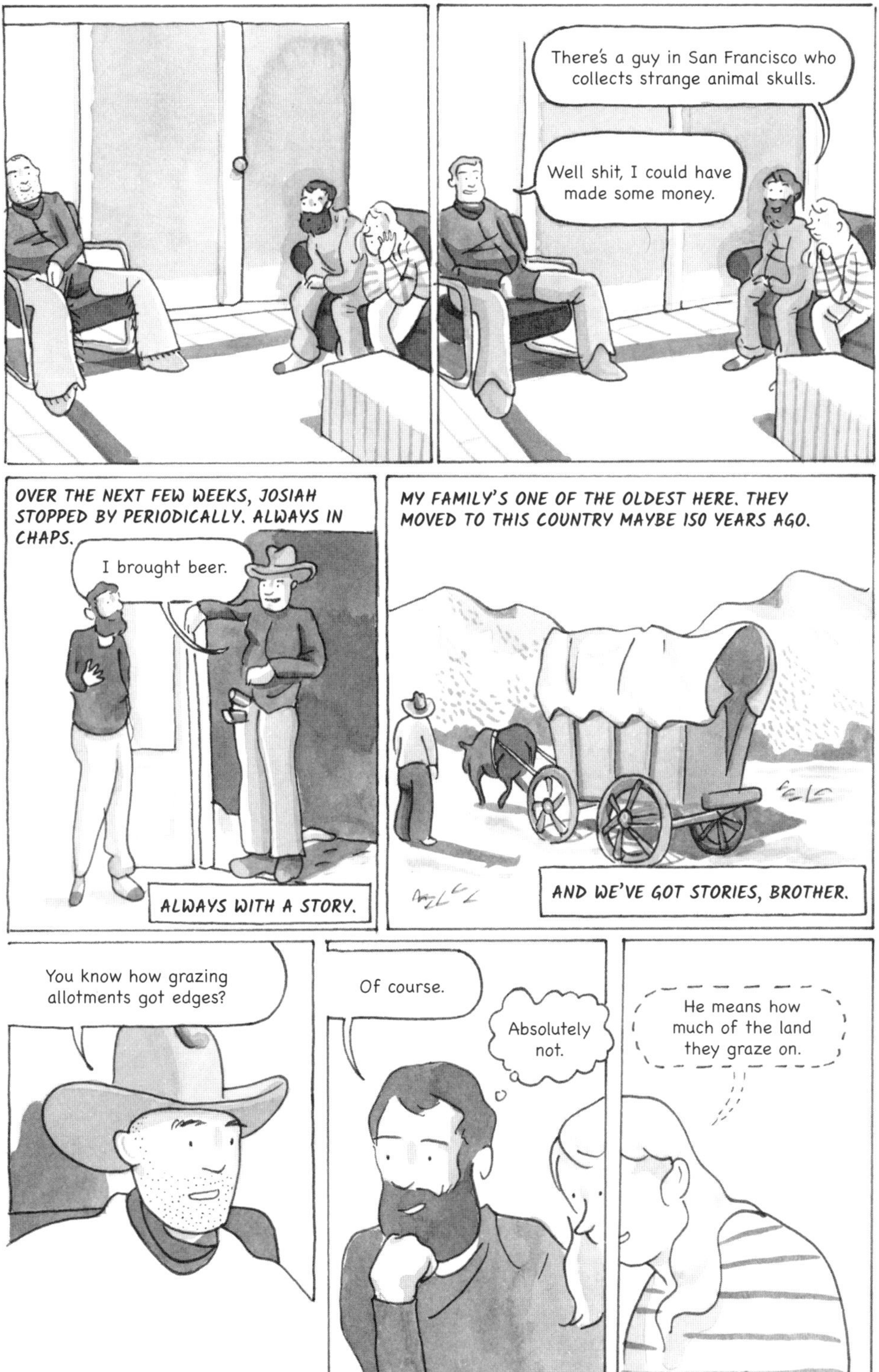
There's a guy in San Francisco who collects strange animal skulls.
Well shit, I could have made some money.
OVER THE NEXT FEW WEEKS, JOSIAH STOPPED BY PERIODICALLY. ALWAYS IN CHAPS.
I brought beer.
ALWAYS WITH A STORY.
MY FAMILY'S ONE OF THE OLDEST HERE. THEY MOVED TO THIS COUNTRY MAYBE 150 YEARS AGO.
AND WE'VE GOT STORIES, BROTHER.
You know how grazing allotments got edges?
Of course.
Absolutely not.
He means how much of the land they graze on.

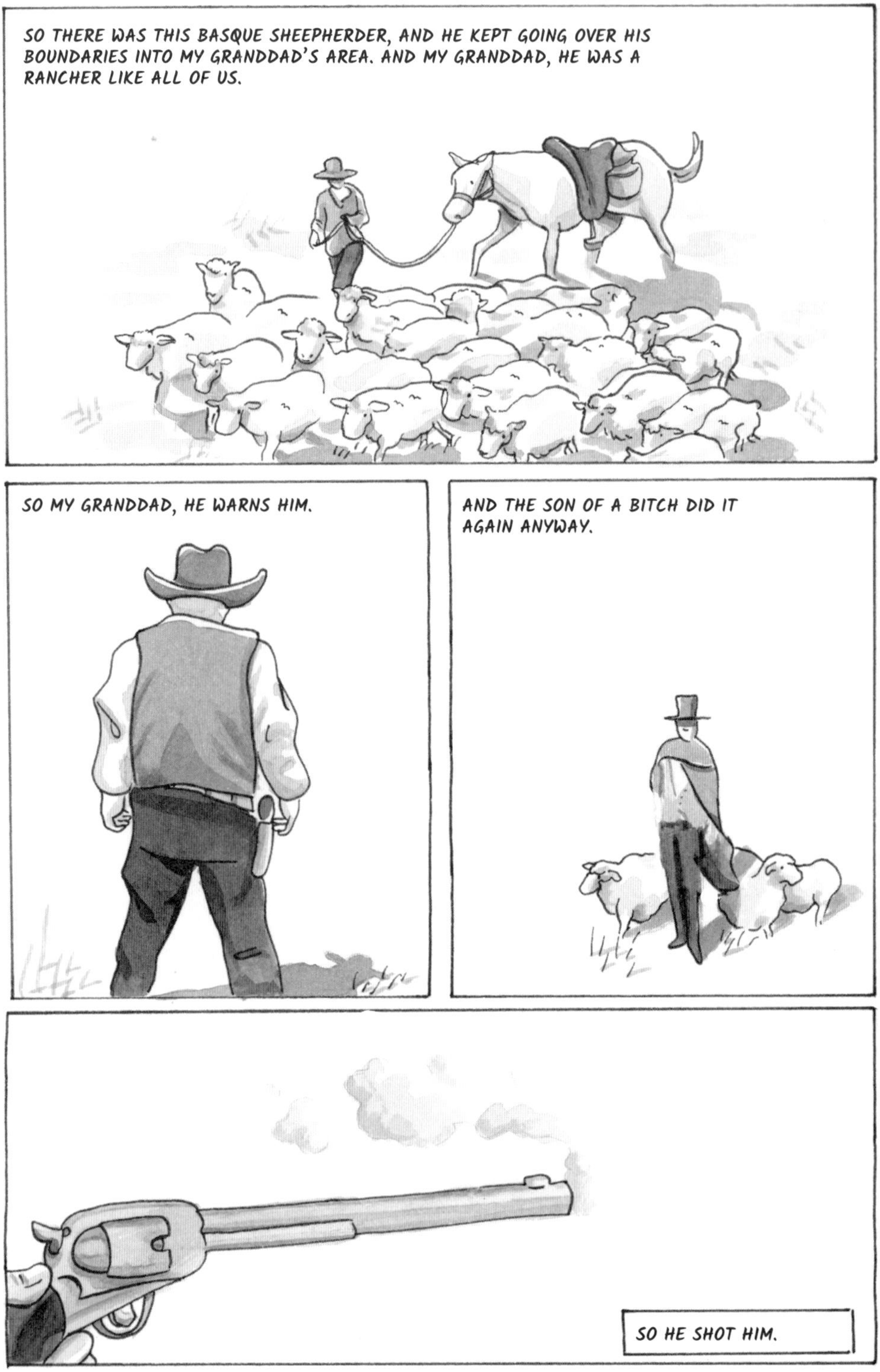
SO THERE WAS THIS BASQUE SHEEPHERDER, AND HE KEPT GOING OVER HIS BOUNDARIES INTO MY GRANDDAD'S AREA. AND MY GRANDDAD, HE WAS A RANCHER LIKE ALL OF US.
SO MY GRANDDAD, HE WARNS HIM.
AND THE SON OF A BITCH DID IT AGAIN ANYWAY.
SO HE SHOT HIM.

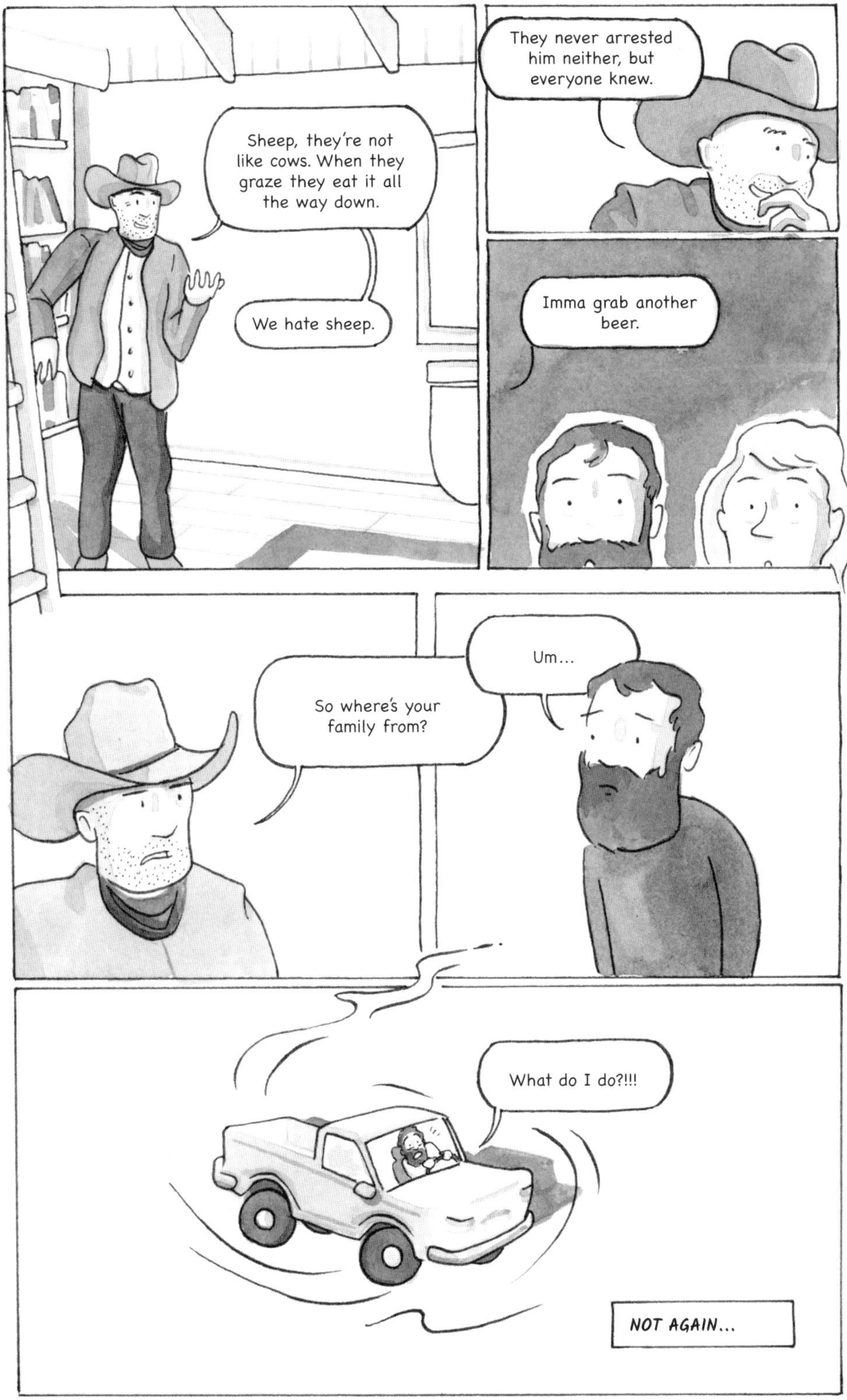

Sheep, they're not like cows. When they graze they eat it all the way down.
We hate sheep.
They never arrested him neither, but everyone knew.
Imma grab another beer.
So where's your family from?
Um...
What do I do?!!!
NOT AGAIN...

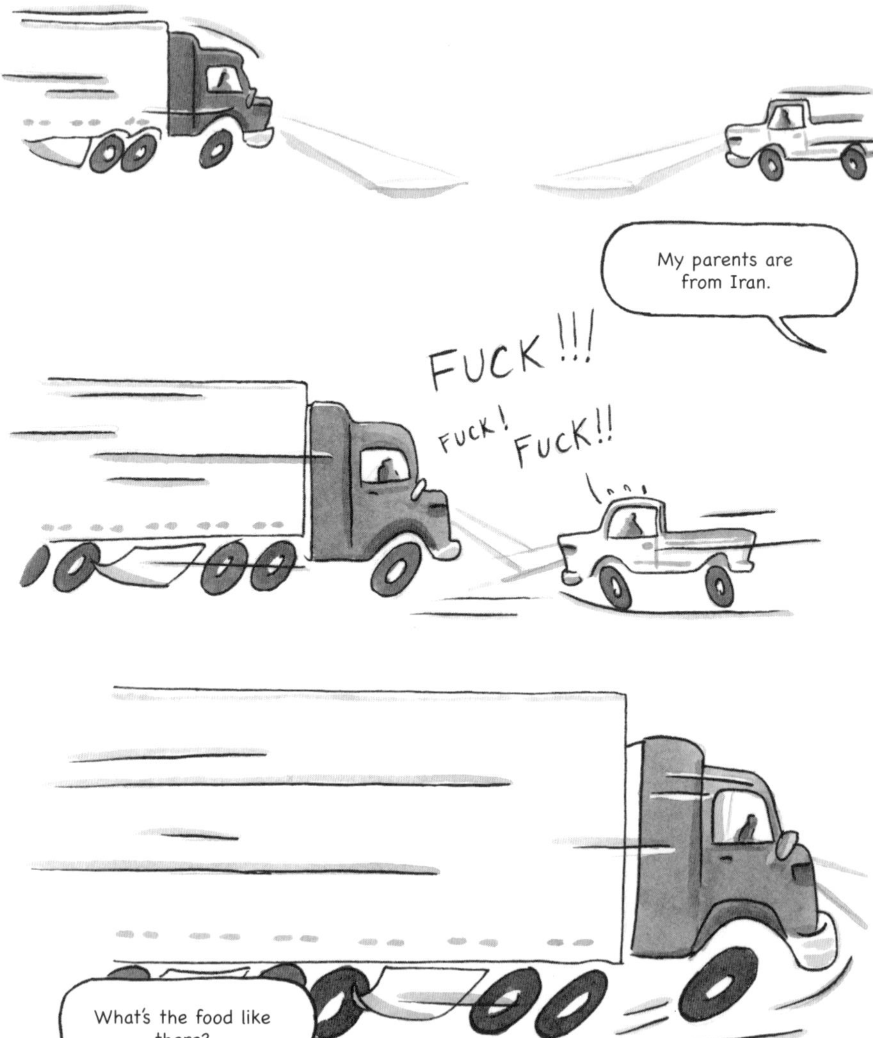
My parents are from Iran.
FUCK!!!
FUCK!
FUCK!!
What's the food like there?

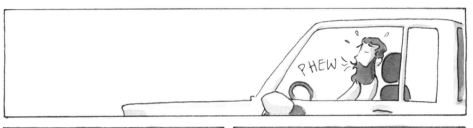

Actually not too different from here. Meat. Lots of meat. Kebabs. I miss my dad's kebabs.

I'll make you some. I bet I can find a recipe online.

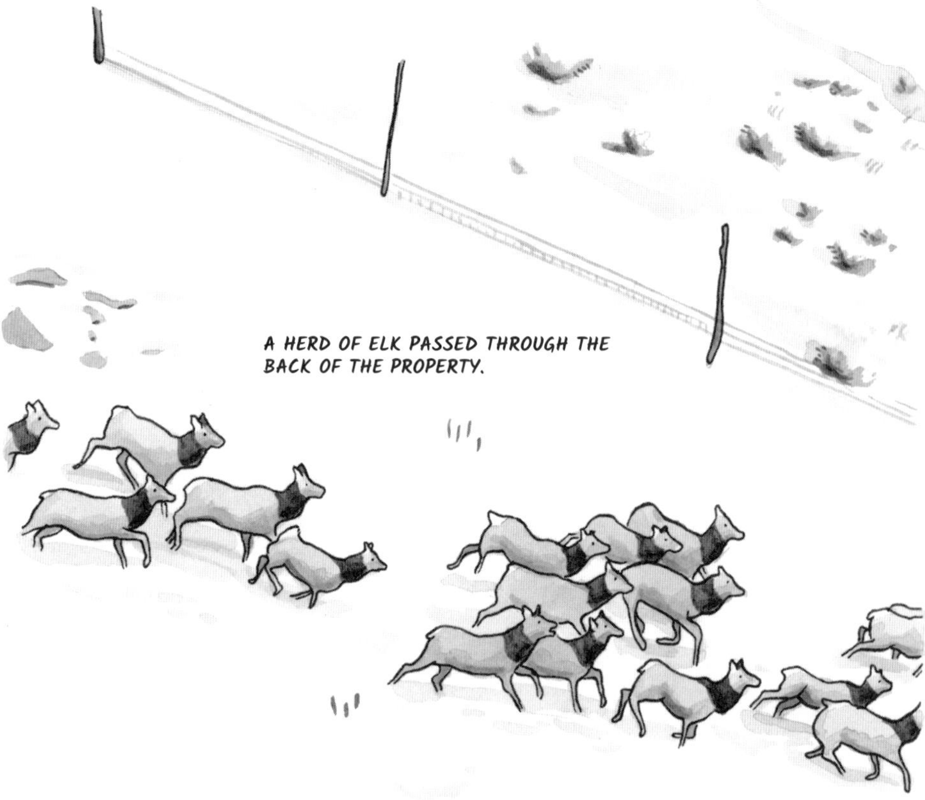
A HERD OF ELK PASSED THROUGH THE
BACK OF THE PROPERTY.

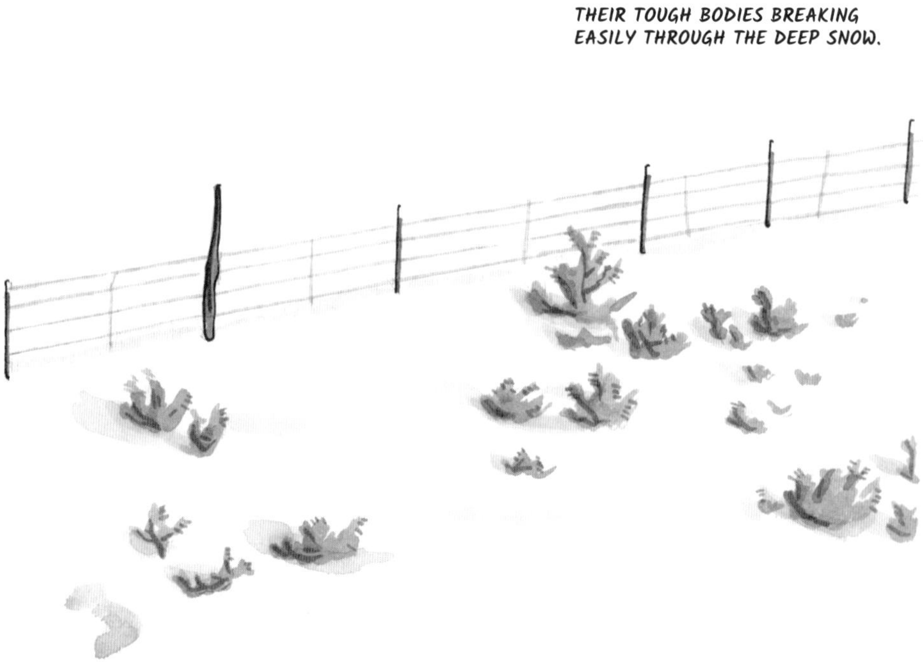
THEIR TOUGH BODIES BREAKING
EASILY THROUGH THE DEEP SNOW.

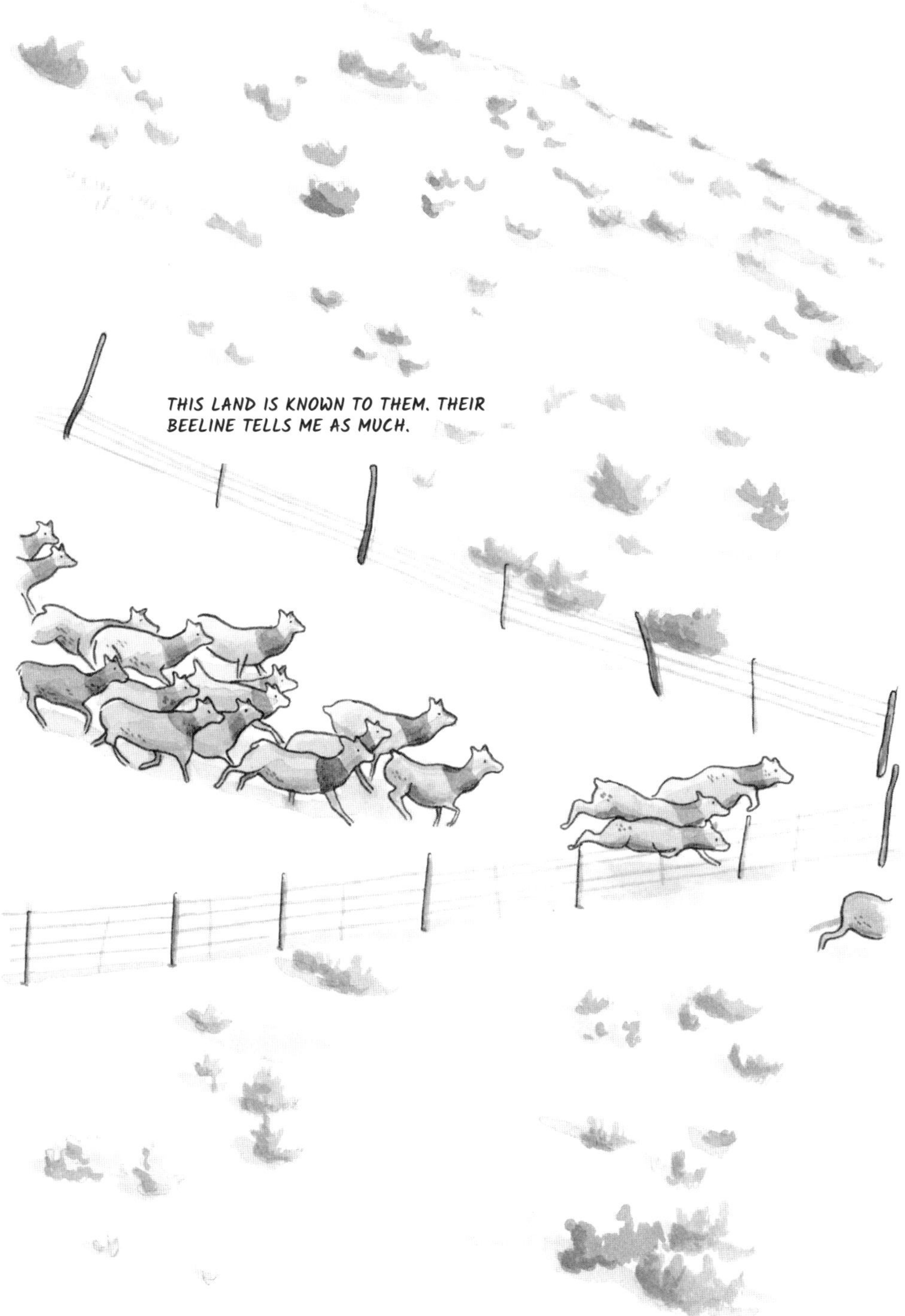
THIS LAND IS KNOWN TO THEM. THEIR BEELINE TELLS ME AS MUCH.
THEY KNOW WHERE THE HELL THEY'RE GOING.

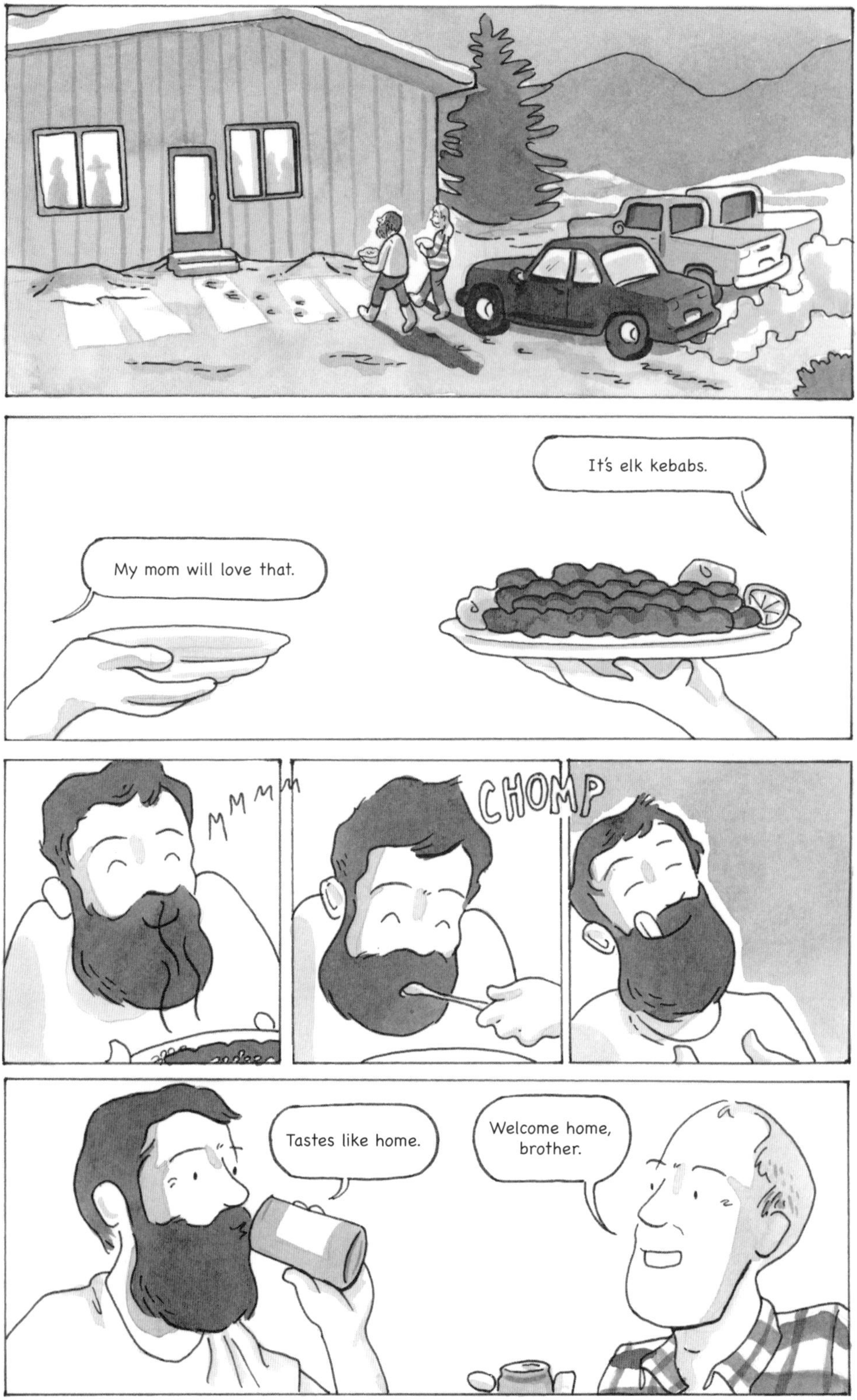
It's elk kebabs.
My mom will love that.
MMMM
CHOMP
Tastes like home.
Welcome home, brother.

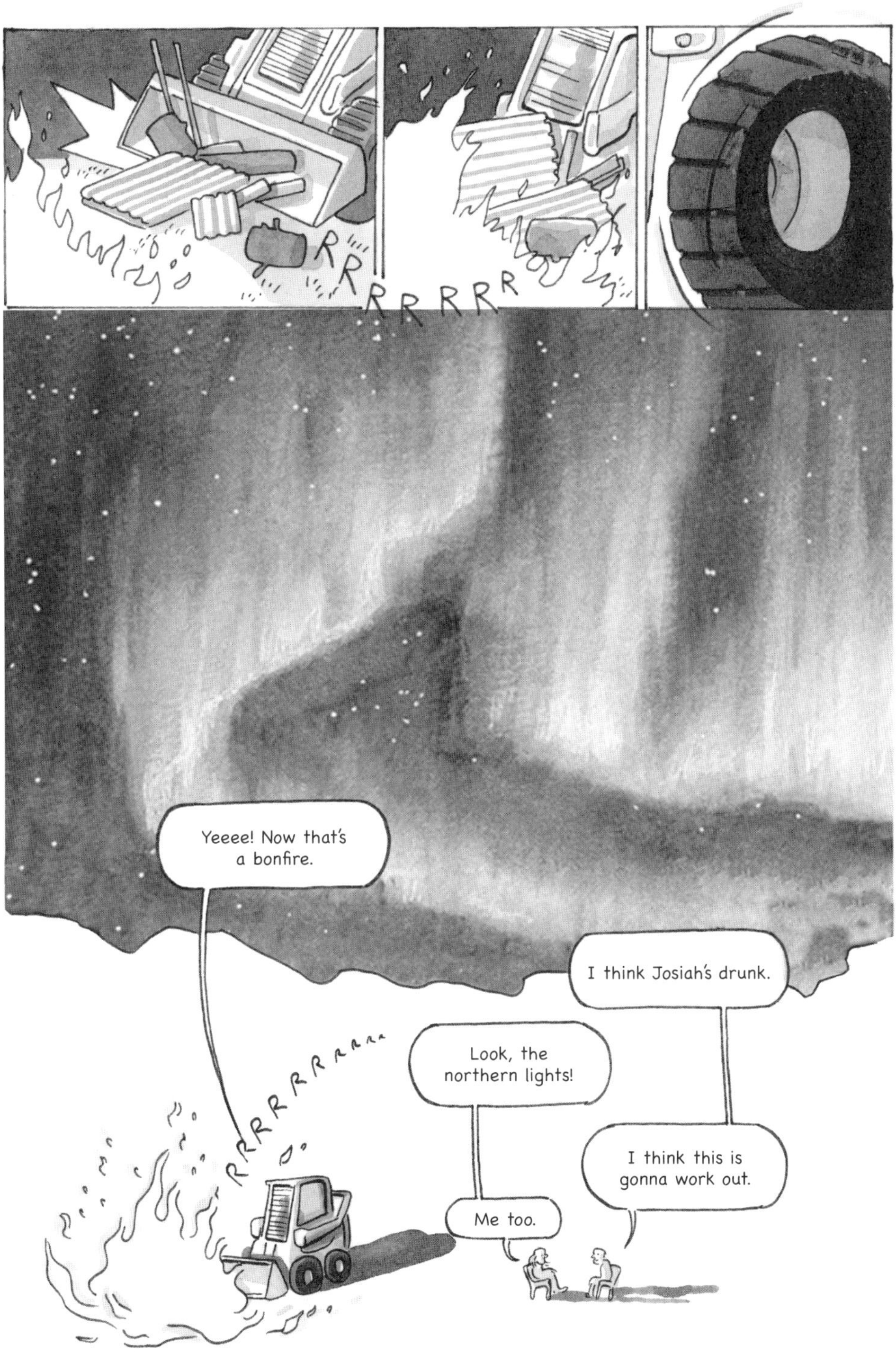
RRRRRRR
Yeeee! Now that's a bonfire.
I think Josiah's drunk.
Look, the northern lights!
RRRRRRRRrrrr
I think this is gonna work out.
Me too.

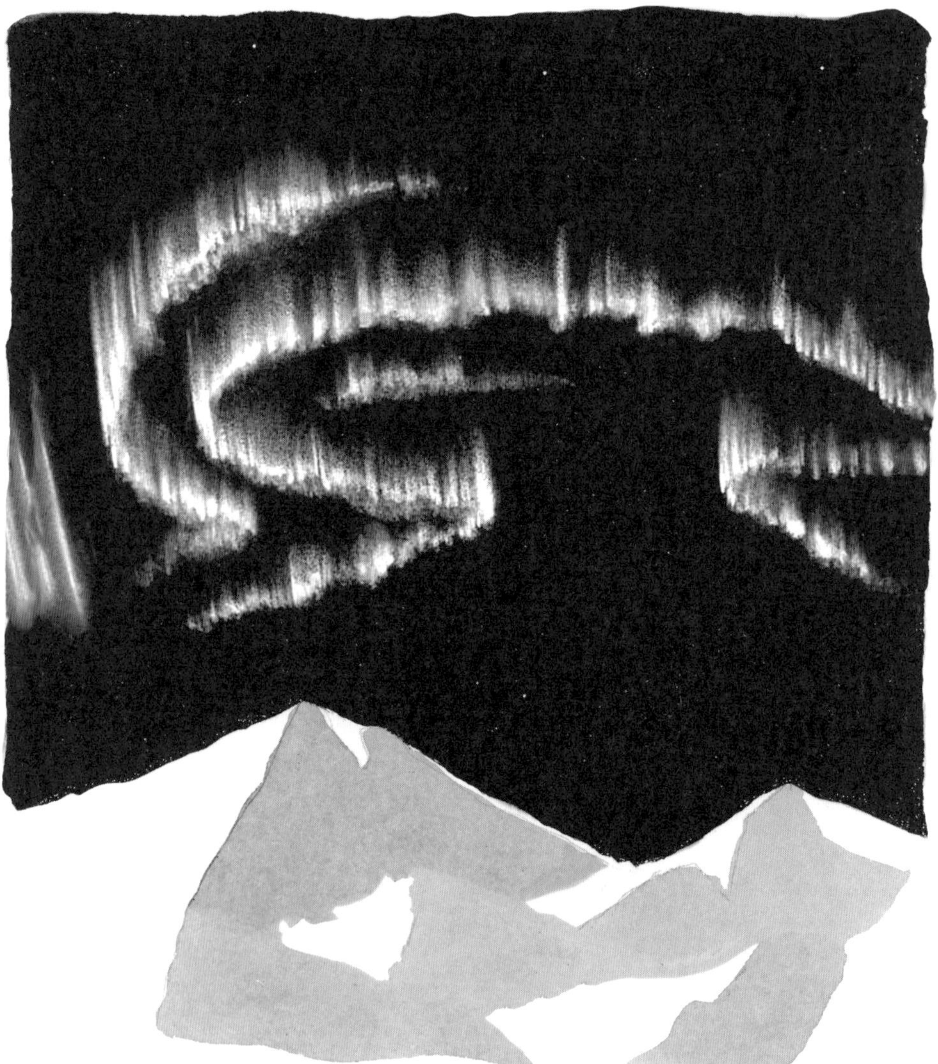

PART II

Spring 2017–Spring 2018

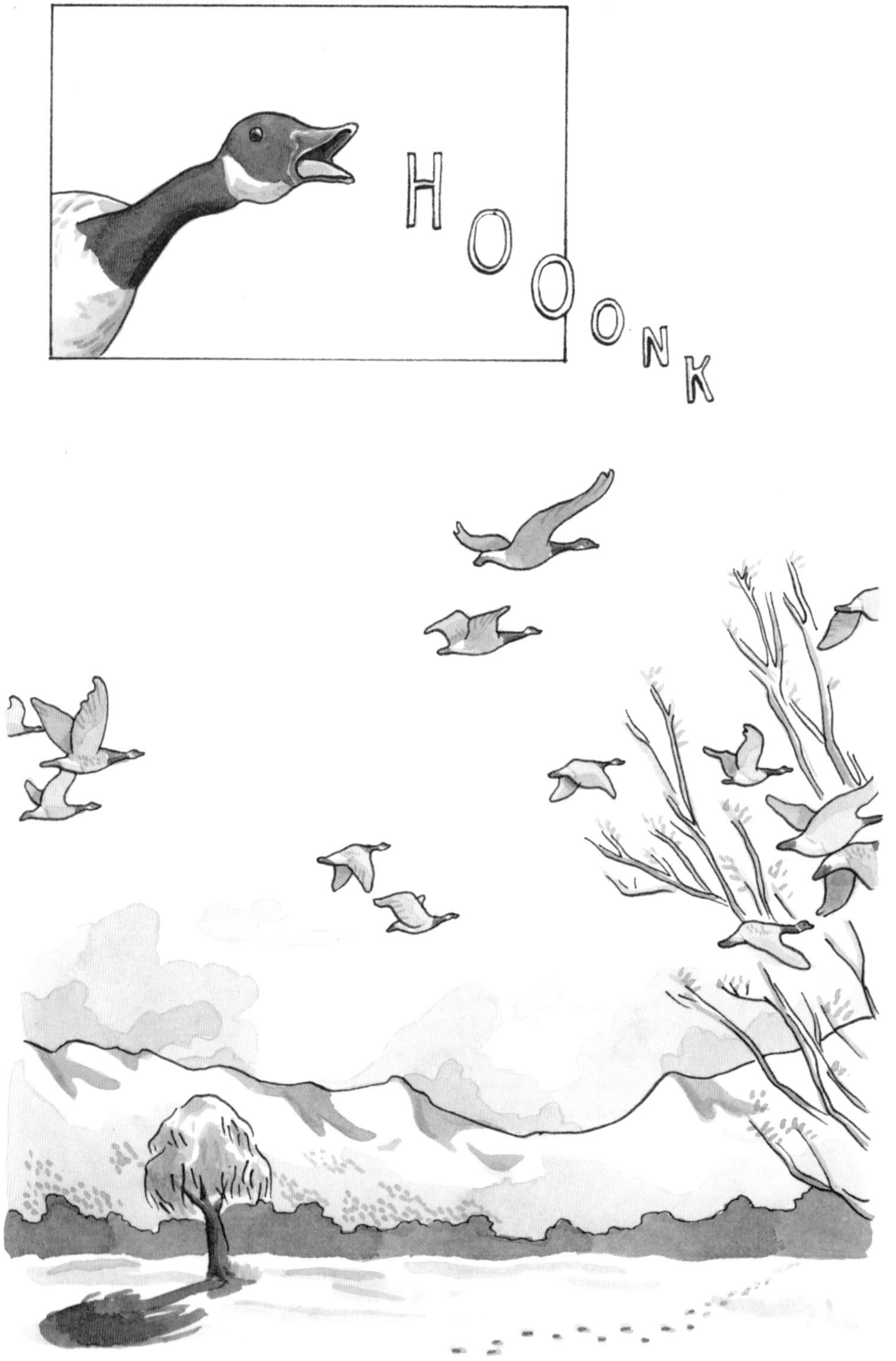
HOOONK

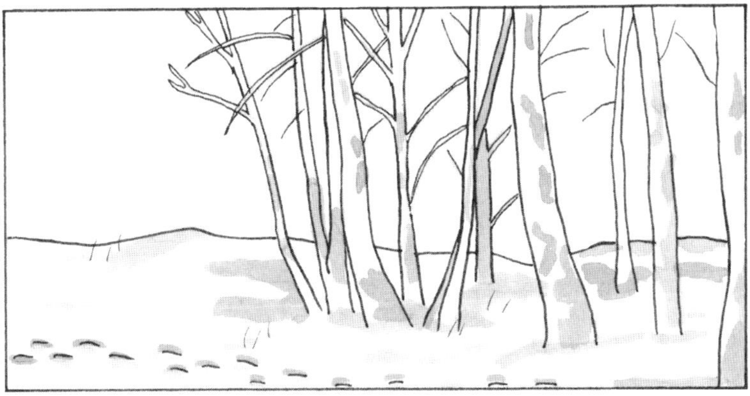

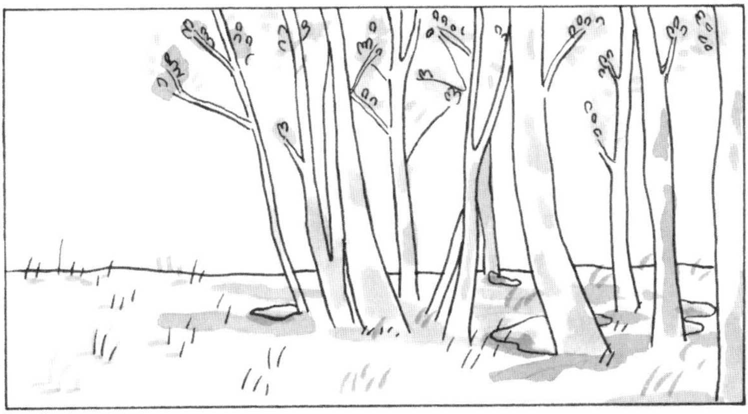

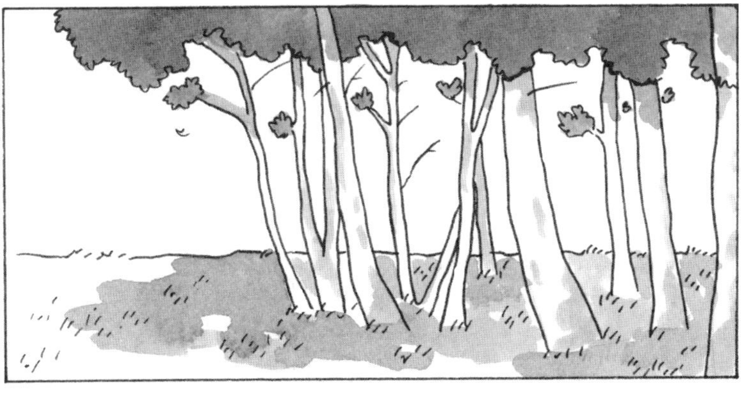

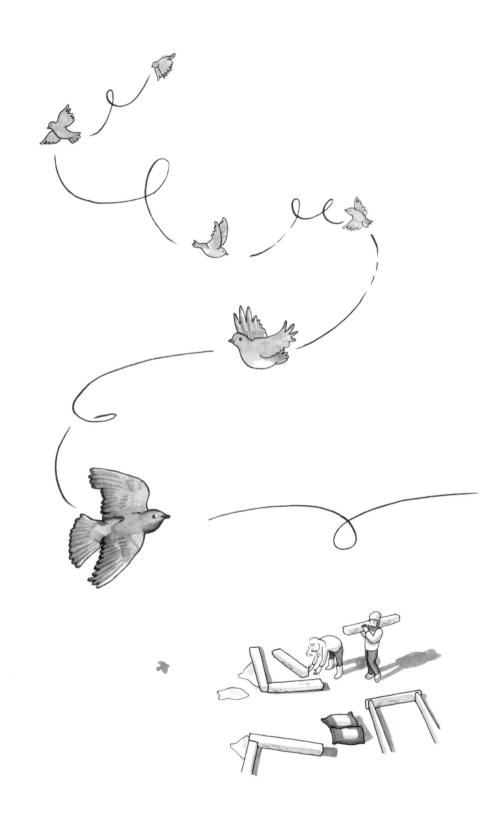

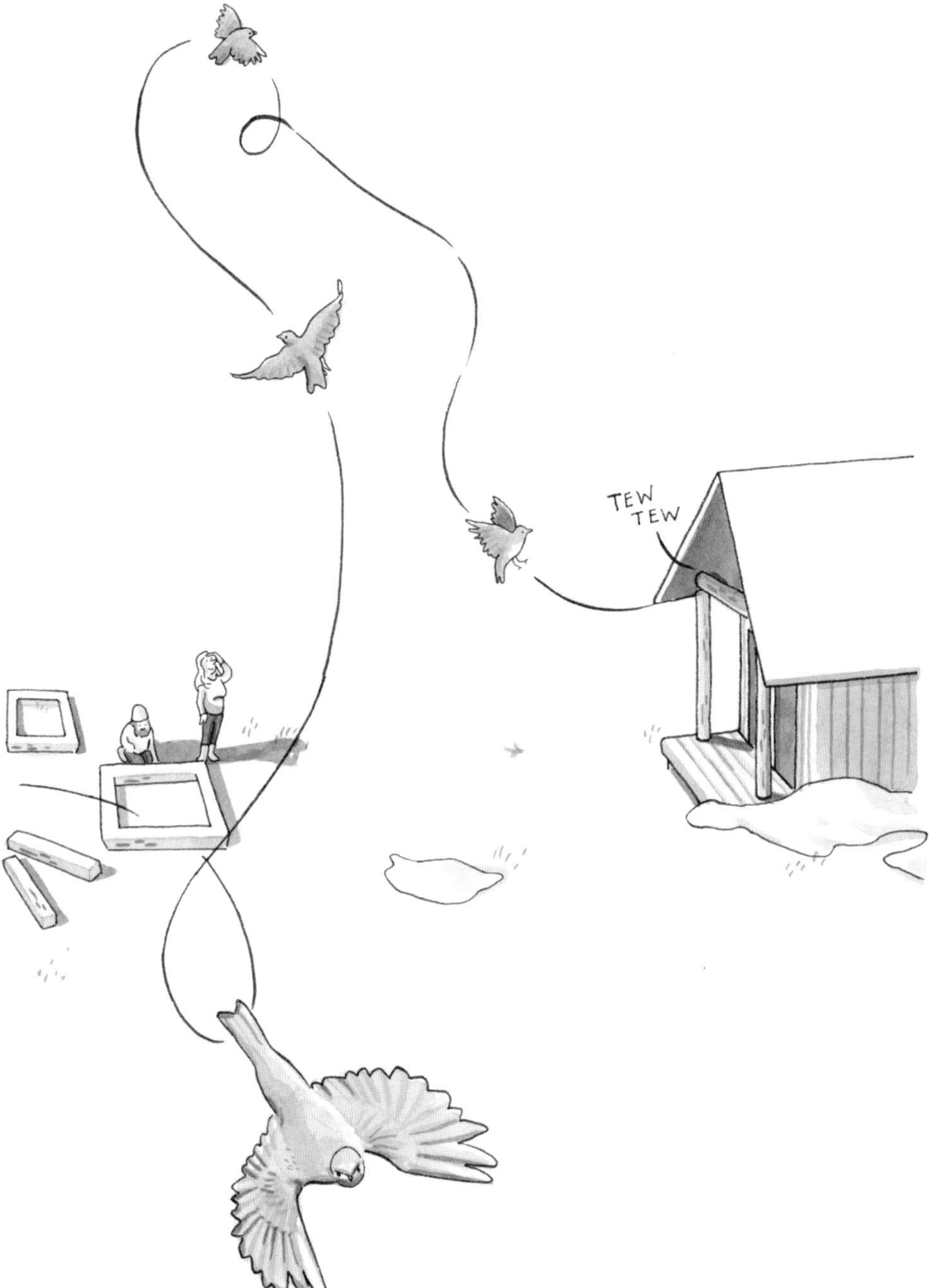
TEW
TEW

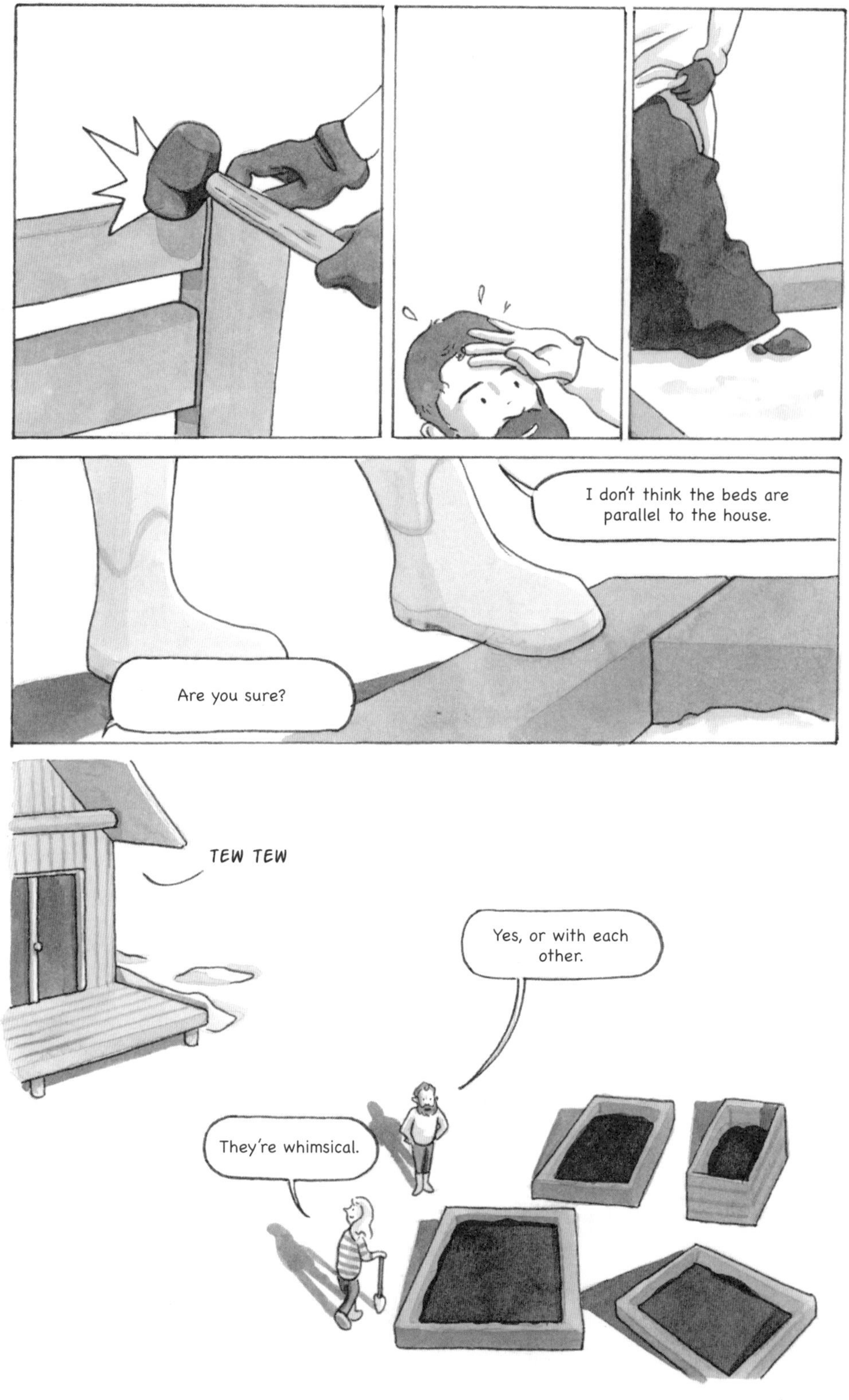
I don't think the beds are parallel to the house.
Are you sure?
TEW TEW
Yes, or with each other.
They're whimsical.

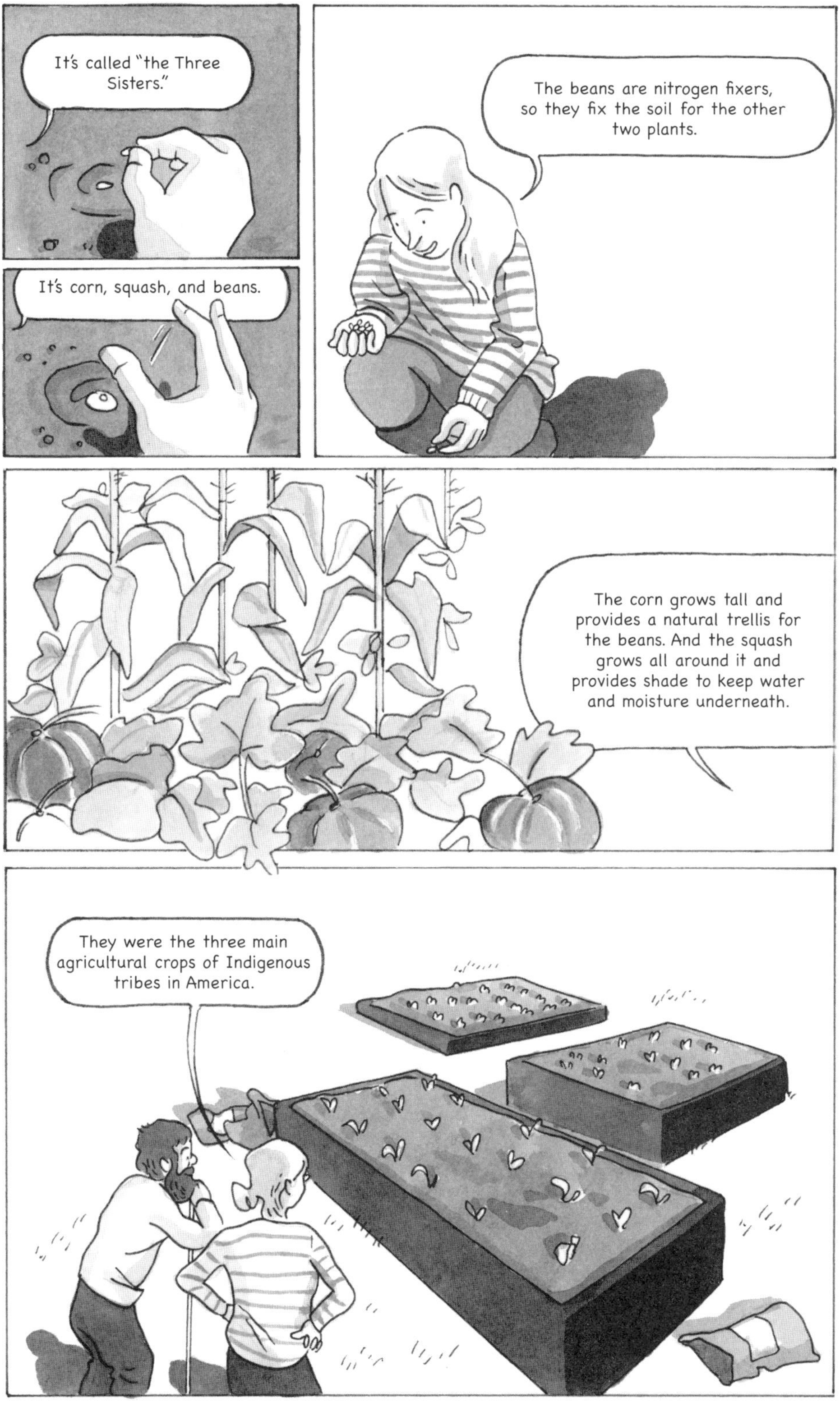
It's called "the Three Sisters."
It's corn, squash, and beans.
The beans are nitrogen fixers, so they fix the soil for the other two plants.
The corn grows tall and provides a natural trellis for the beans. And the squash grows all around it and provides shade to keep water and moisture underneath.
They were the three main agricultural crops of Indigenous tribes in America.

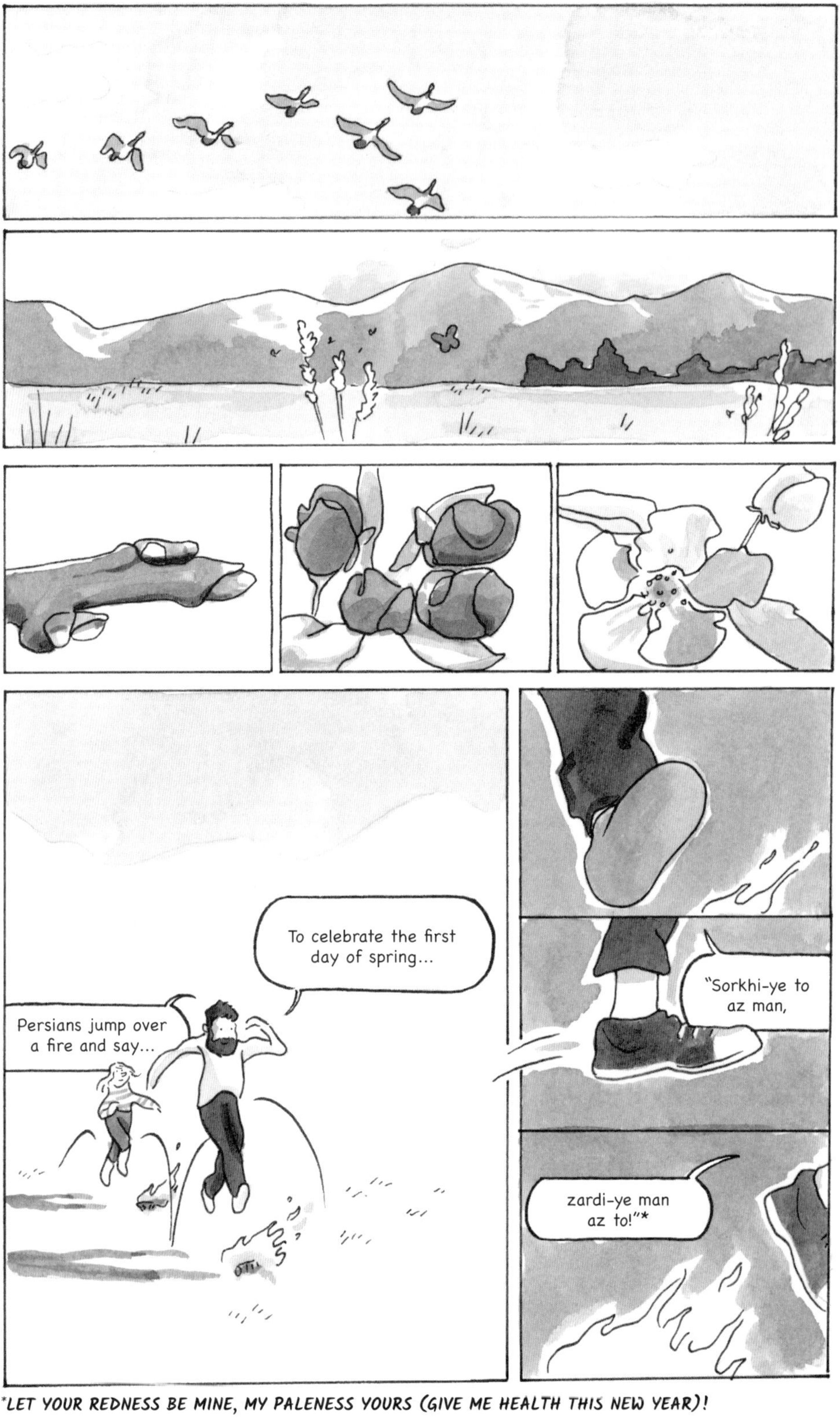
To celebrate the first day of spring...
Persians jump over a fire and say...
"Sorkhi-ye to az man,
zardi-ye man az to!"*

*LET YOUR REDNESS BE MINE, MY PALENESS YOURS (GIVE ME HEALTH THIS NEW YEAR)!

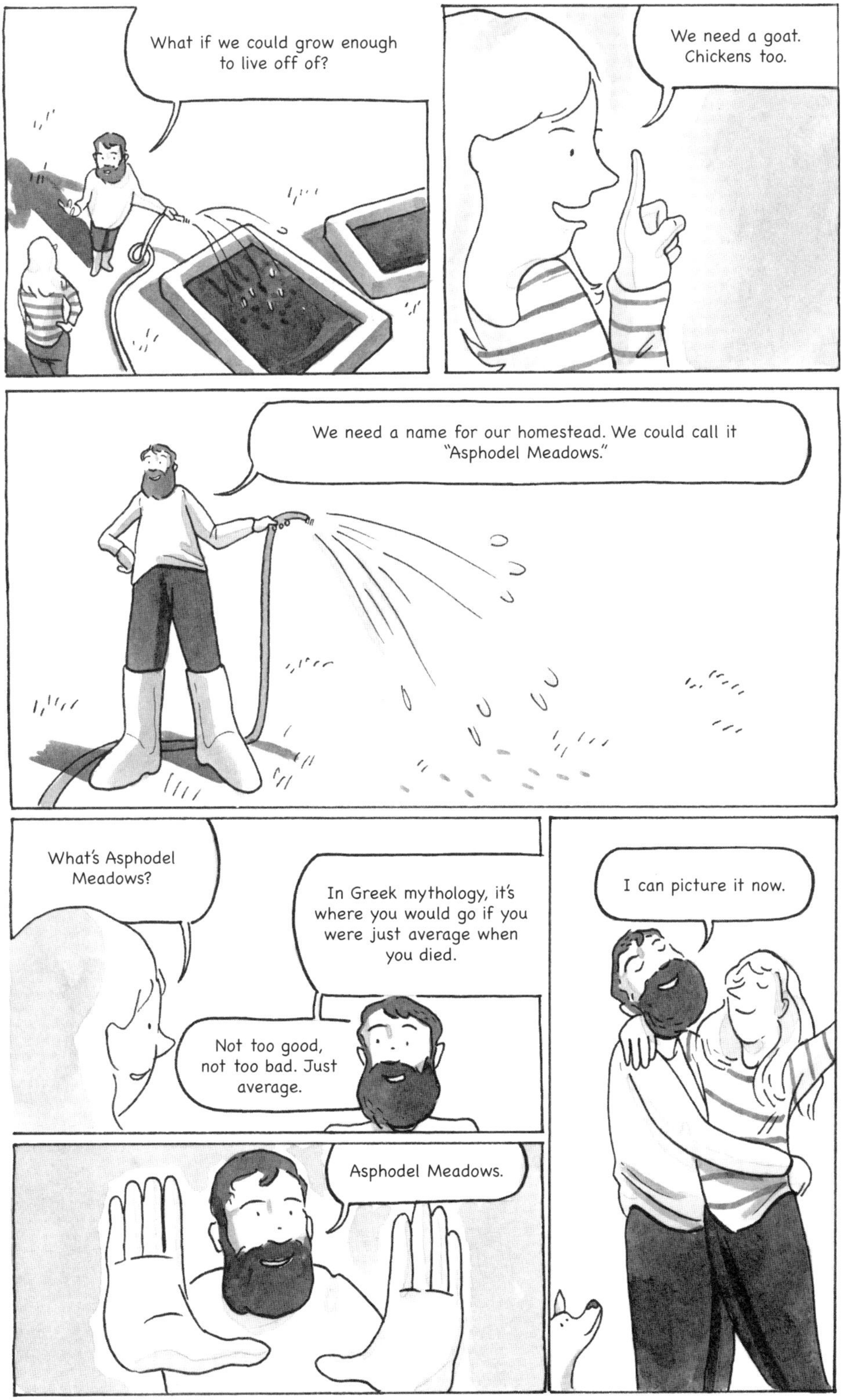
What if we could grow enough to live off of?
We need a goat. Chickens too.
We need a name for our homestead. We could call it "Asphodel Meadows."
What's Asphodel Meadows?
In Greek mythology, it's where you would go if you were just average when you died.
Not too good, not too bad. Just average.
Asphodel Meadows.
I can picture it now.

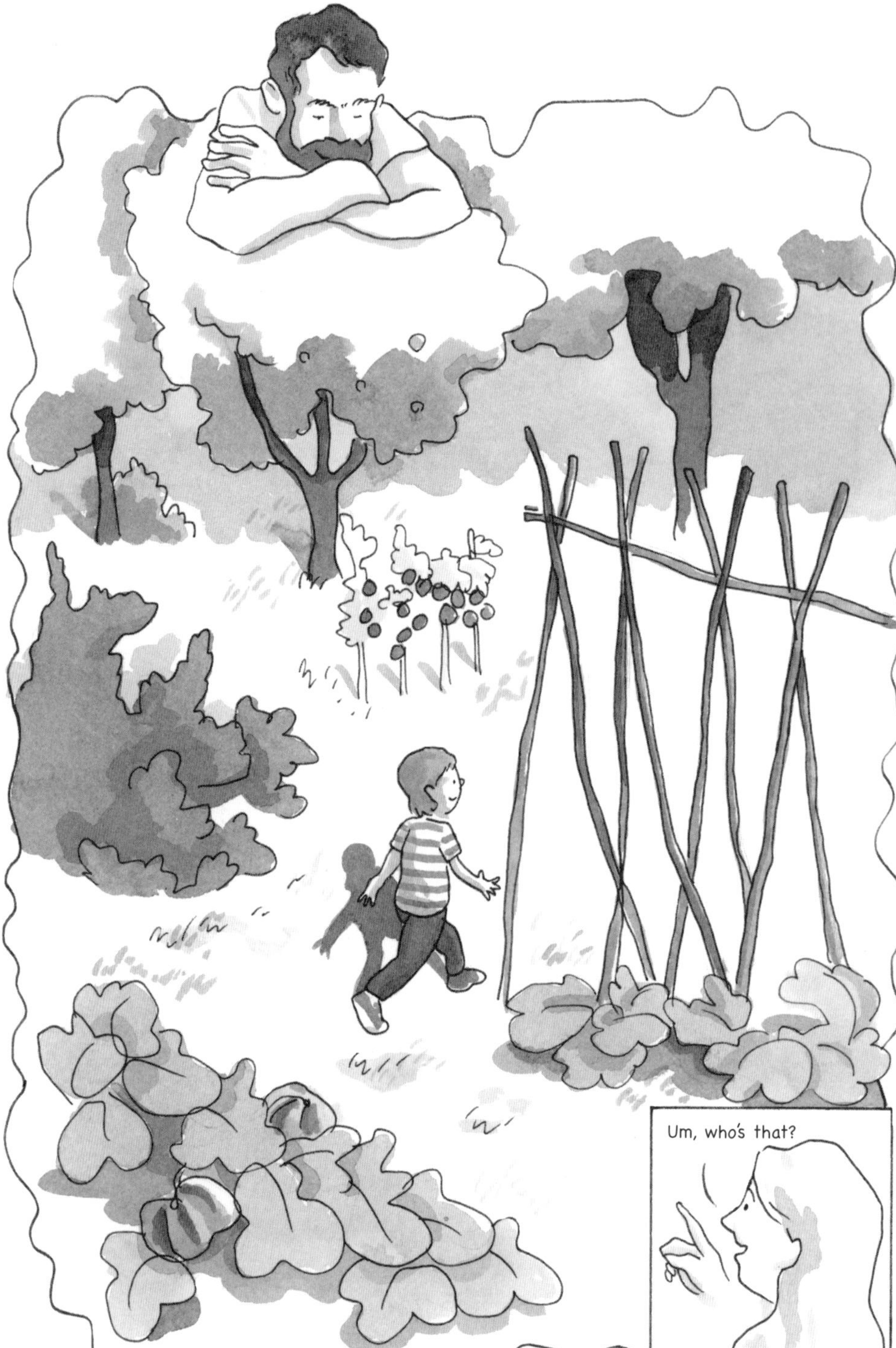
Um, who's that?

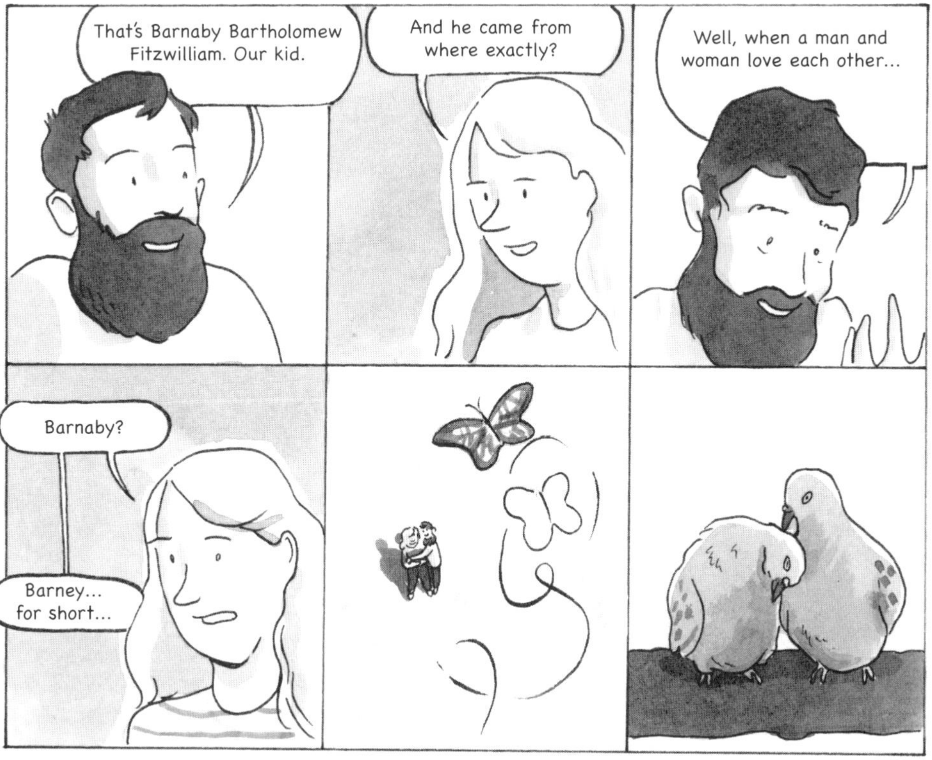
That's Barnaby Bartholomew Fitzwilliam. Our kid.
And he came from where exactly?
Well, when a man and woman love each other...
Barnaby?
Barney... for short...

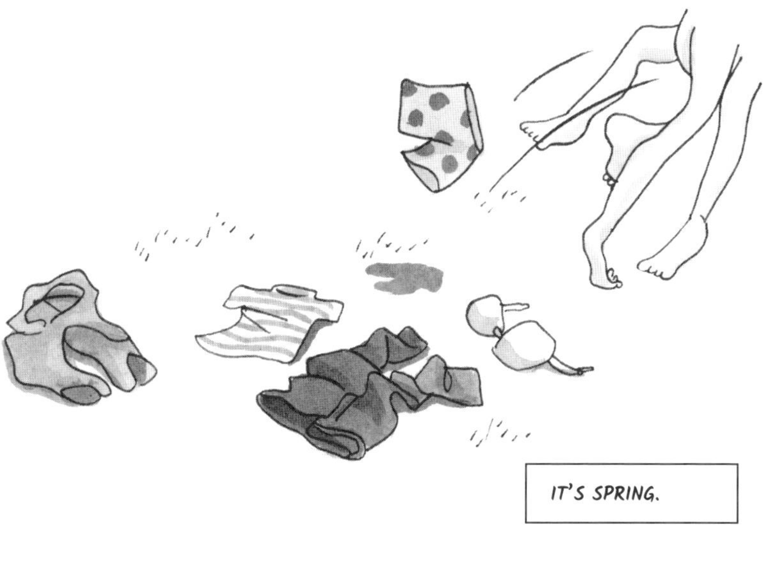
IT'S SPRING.

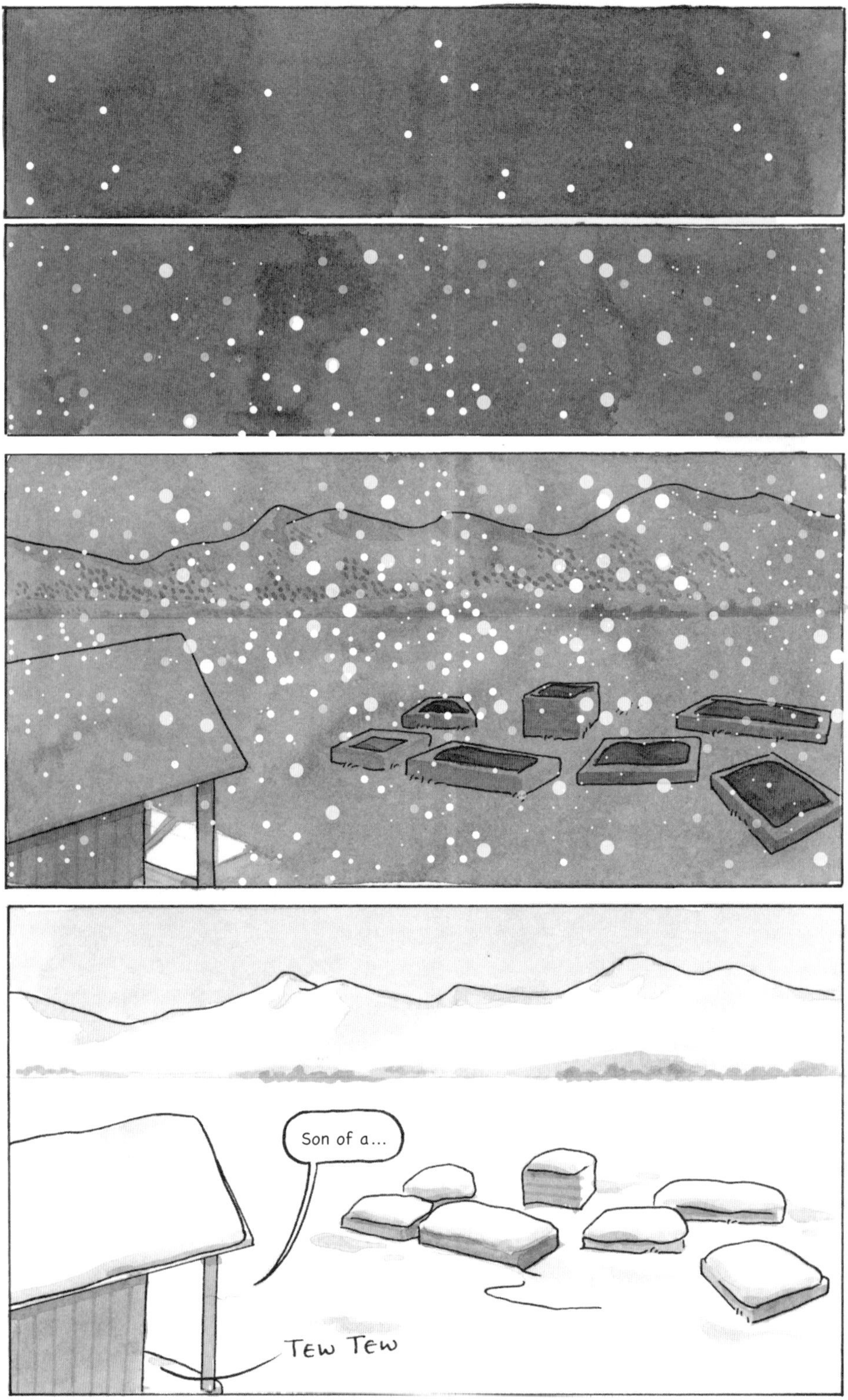
Son of a...
TEW TEW

Where are we going, Nathan?

WE MET NATHAN AND SOFIA AT JOSIAH'S HOUSE.

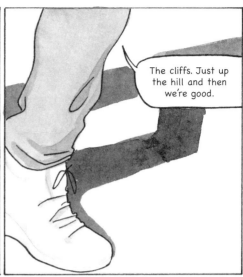

The cliffs. Just up the hill and then we're good.

Sofia, what kind of plant is this?

I think it's just a sagebrush, but it has gauls on it.

It's a growth related to bugs. It does that as a defense mechanism.

Sagebrush is cool.

Sage grouse browse on sagebrush. The sagebrush will put out different tastes to protect itself from getting overbrowsed. So sage grouse roam around and only browse off of new plants regularly.

Now we get a little downhill.

I haven't been up here since I was 12 years old.

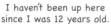

Sofia and I found some new pictographs hiking up by our house this year.

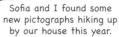

It's not super big like these, just a panel, and it's only hash marks.

If I had to guess, I'd think they represent sheep they ambushed.

The Shoshone are the most diverse and widespread tribe in the west.

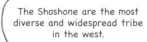

They go from central Idaho all the way down to Mexico. There were little bands.

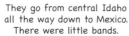

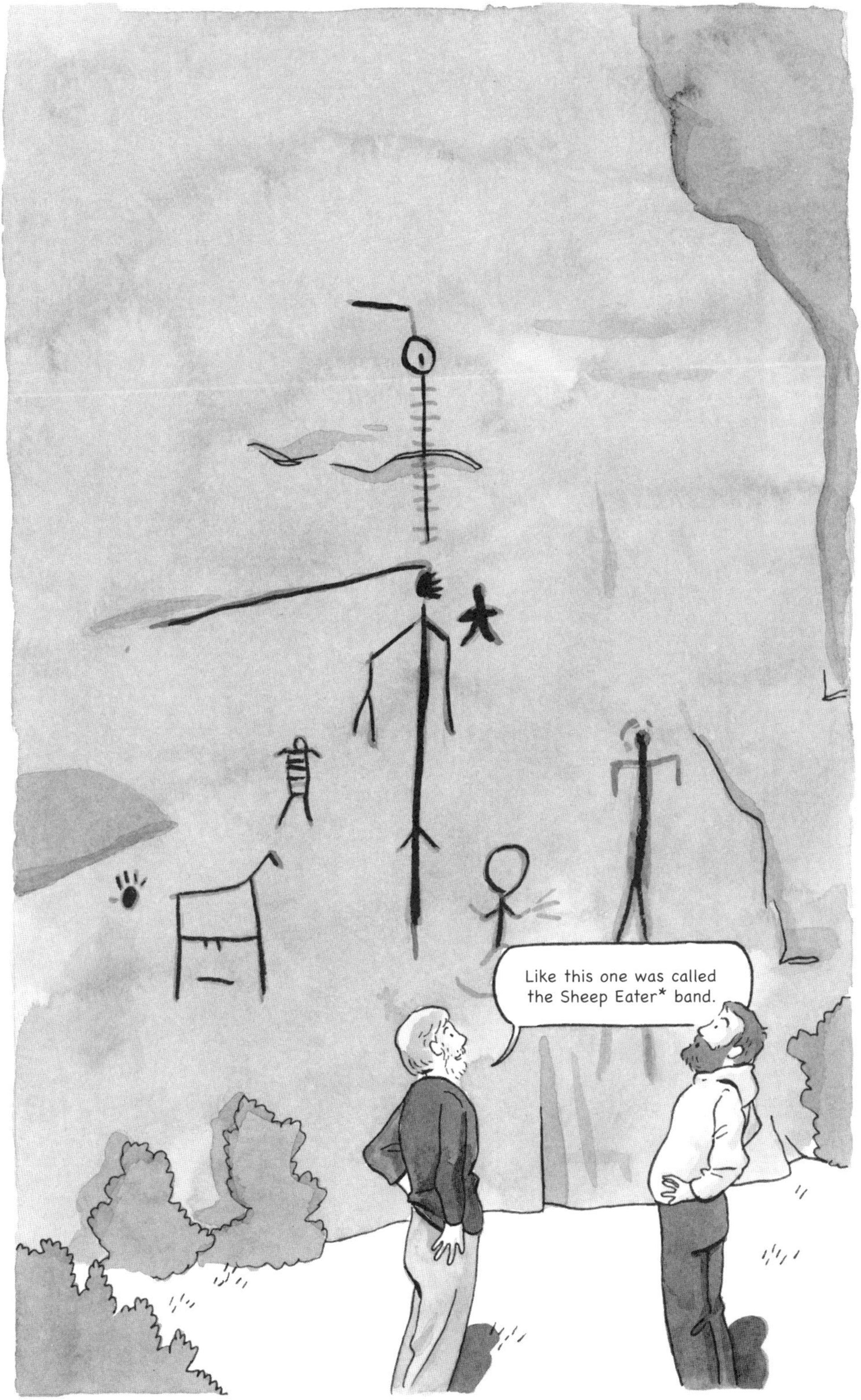
Like this one was called the Sheep Eater* band.

*TUKUDIKA

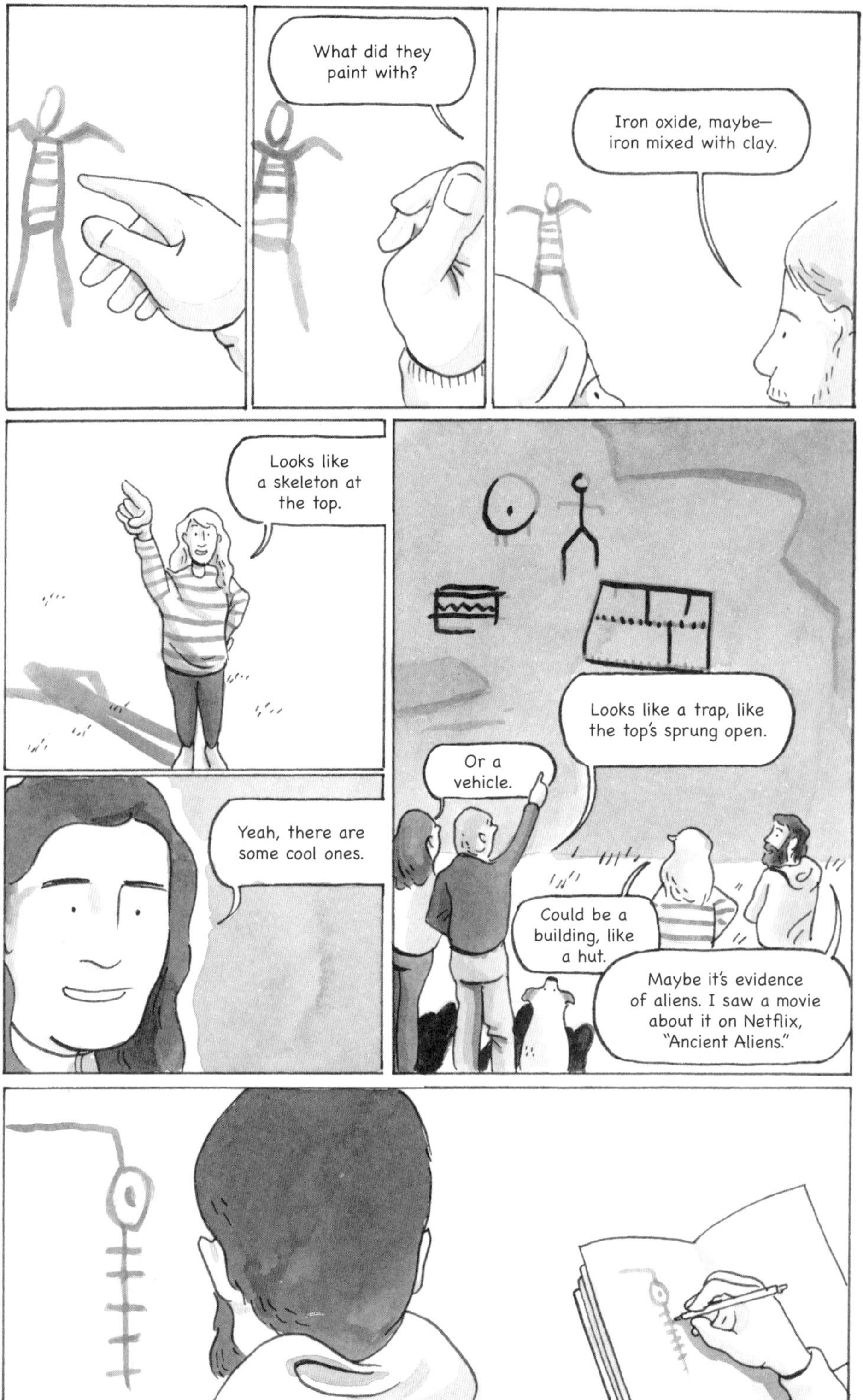
What did they paint with?
Iron oxide, maybe— iron mixed with clay.
Looks like a skeleton at the top.
Yeah, there are some cool ones.
Looks like a trap, like the top's sprung open.
Or a vehicle.
Could be a building, like a hut.
Maybe it's evidence of aliens. I saw a movie about it on Netflix, "Ancient Aliens."

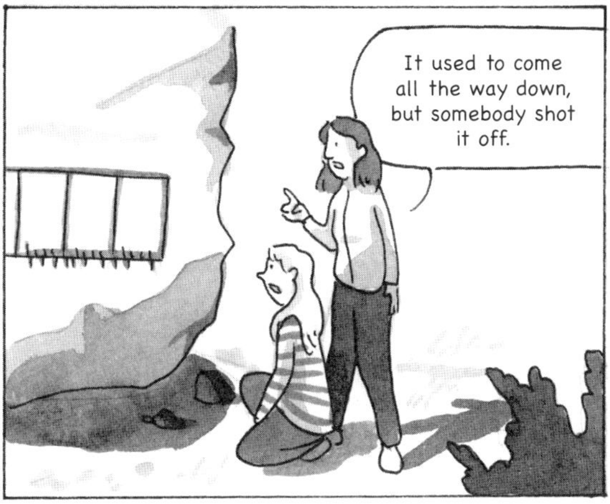
It used to come all the way down, but somebody shot it off.

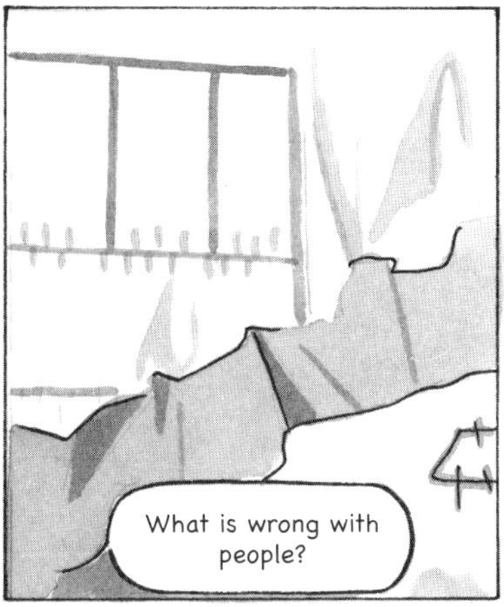
What is wrong with people?

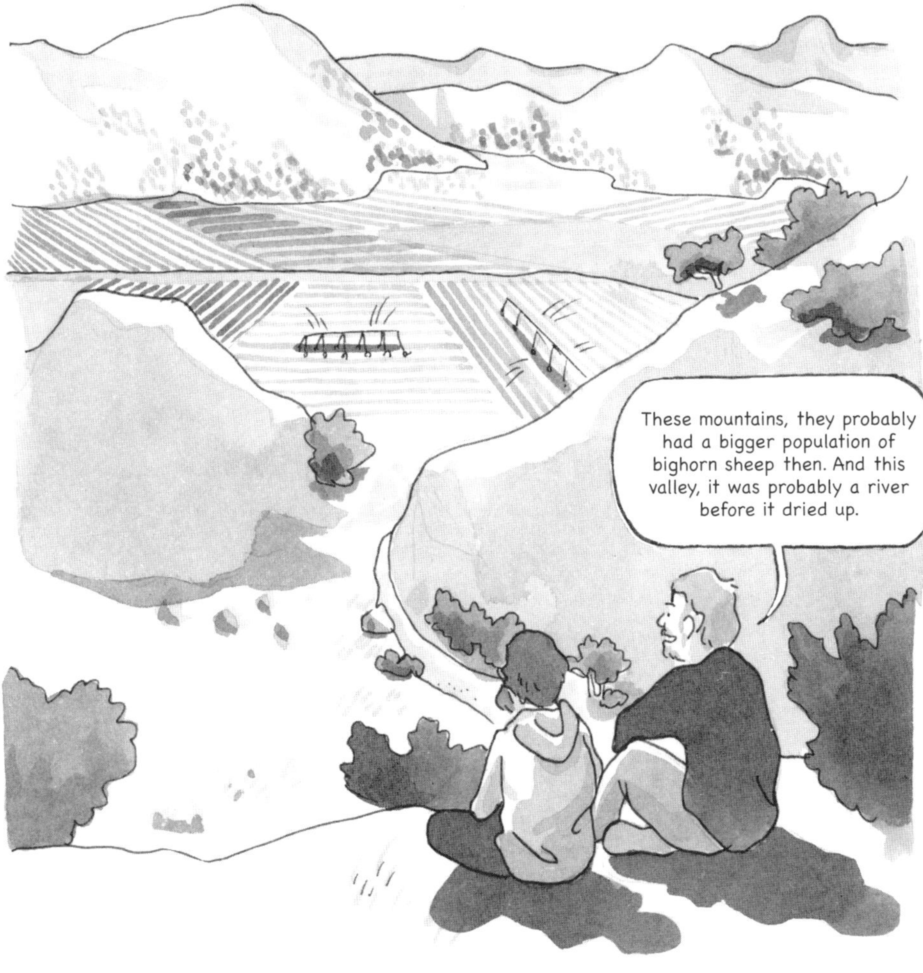
These mountains, they probably had a bigger population of bighorn sheep then. And this valley, it was probably a river before it dried up.

BACK THEN, IT WAS PROBABLY PACKED WITH WILLOWS AND COTTONWOOD TREES. LIKE A JUNGLE, ABOUT A HALF MILE WIDE.

THEY HADN'T DAMMED THE RIVER YET TO IRRIGATE ALL THESE FIELDS.

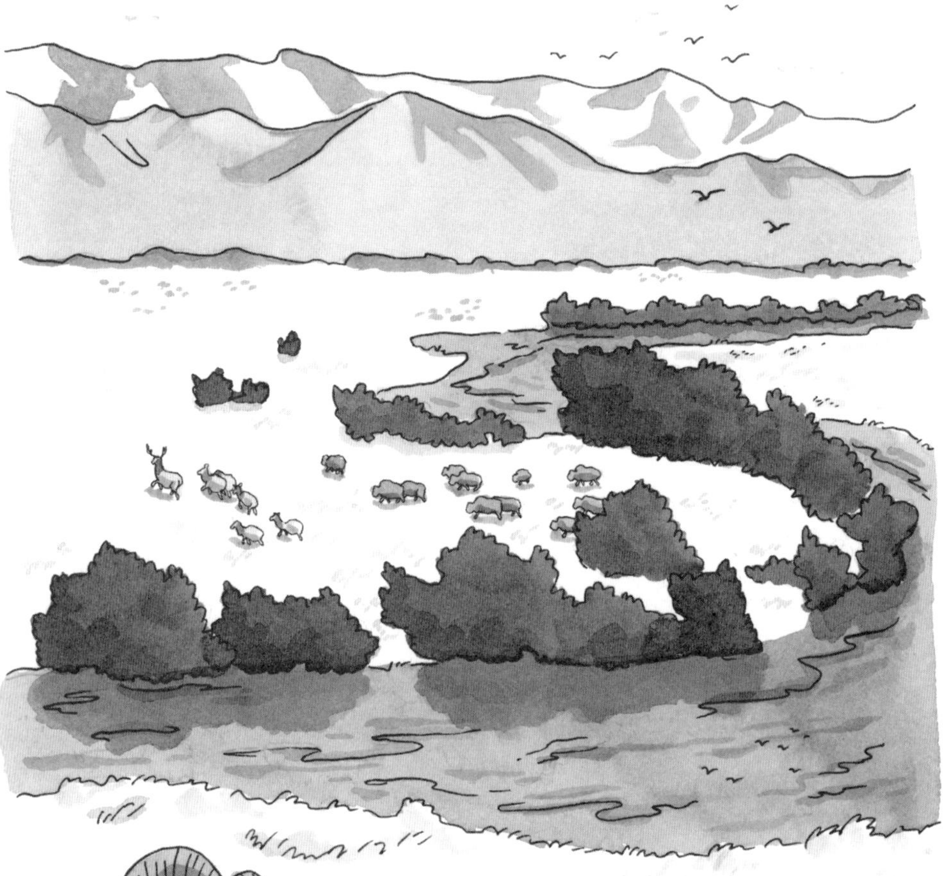

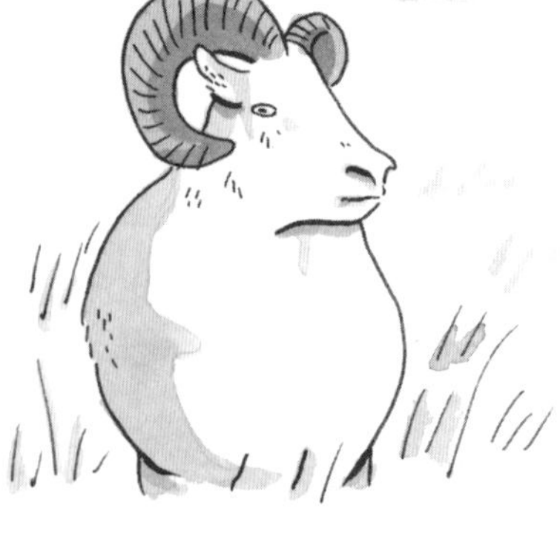

THE SAGEBRUSH STEPPE YOU SEE, IT WAS AROUND THE RIVER. IT WOULD HAVE BEEN FULL OF BISON, PRONGHORN, AND DEER AND MOOSE. AND THE SHEEPEATER SHOSHONE, OF COURSE.

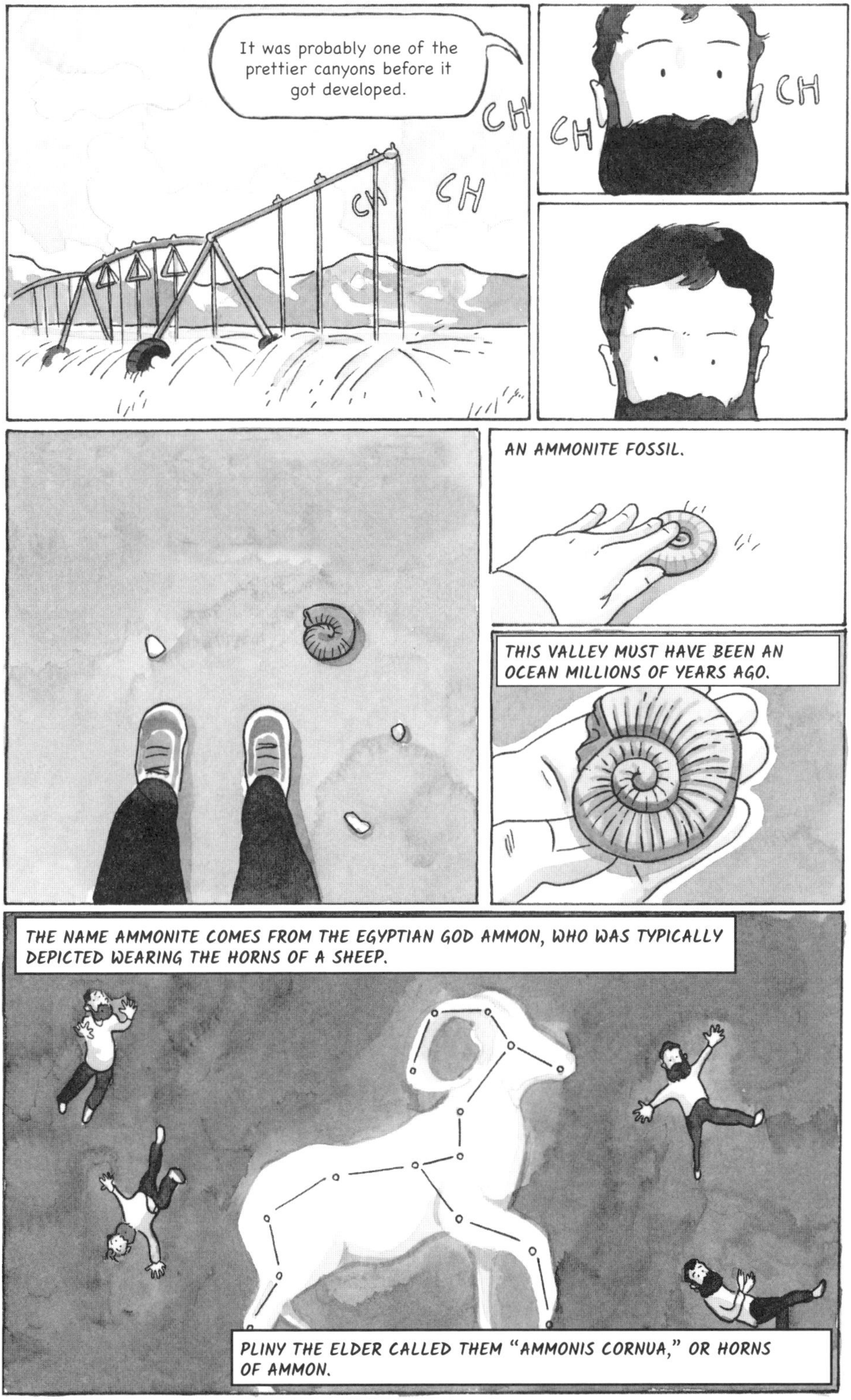
It was probably one of the prettier canyons before it got developed.
CH
CH
CH
CH
CH
AN AMMONITE FOSSIL.
THIS VALLEY MUST HAVE BEEN AN OCEAN MILLIONS OF YEARS AGO.
THE NAME AMMONITE COMES FROM THE EGYPTIAN GOD AMMON, WHO WAS TYPICALLY DEPICTED WEARING THE HORNS OF A SHEEP.
PLINY THE ELDER CALLED THEM "AMMONIS CORNUA," OR HORNS OF AMMON.

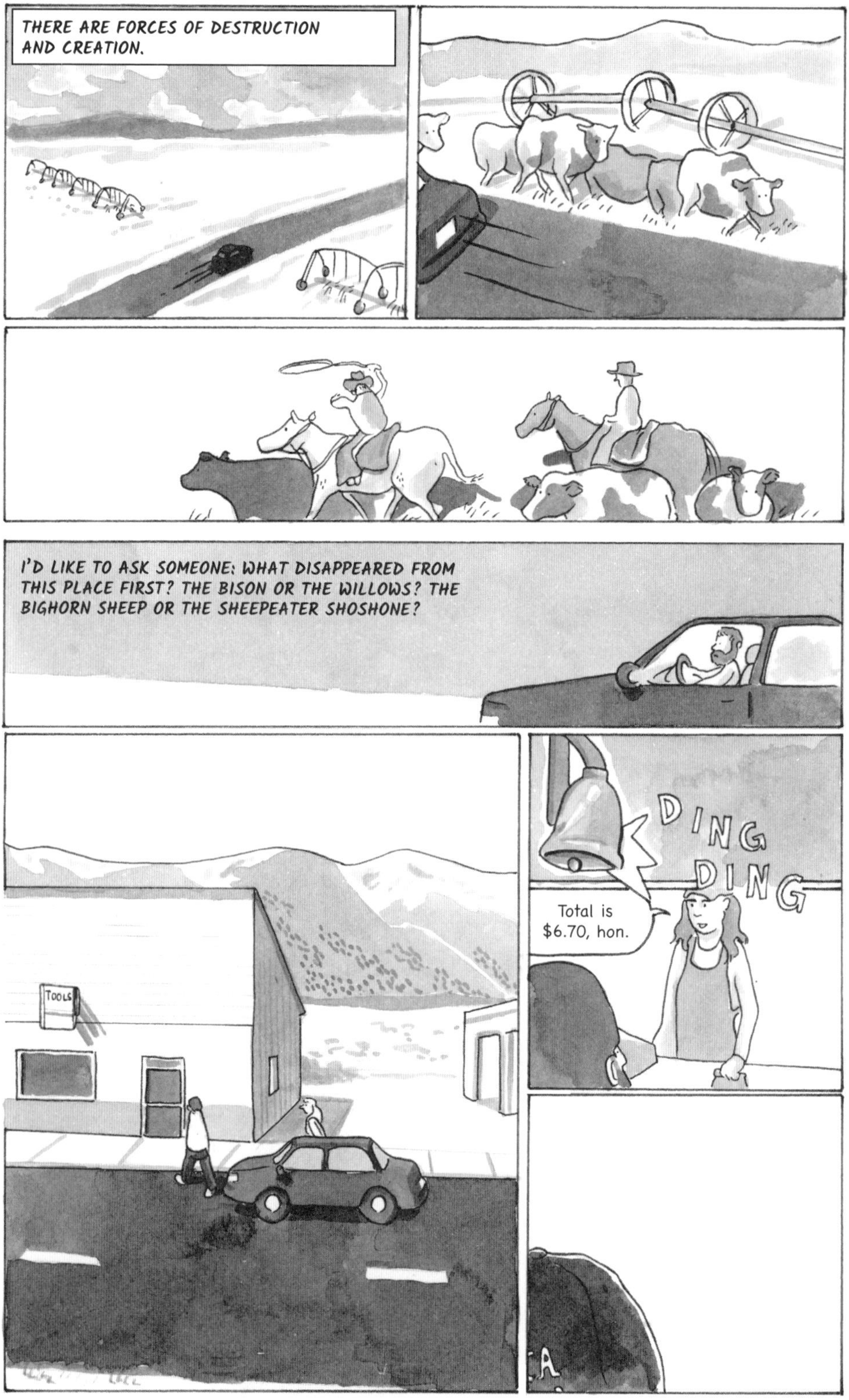
THERE ARE FORCES OF DESTRUCTION AND CREATION.
I'D LIKE TO ASK SOMEONE: WHAT DISAPPEARED FROM THIS PLACE FIRST? THE BISON OR THE WILLOWS? THE BIGHORN SHEEP OR THE SHEEPEATER SHOSHONE?
TOOLS
DING DING
Total is $6.70, hon.

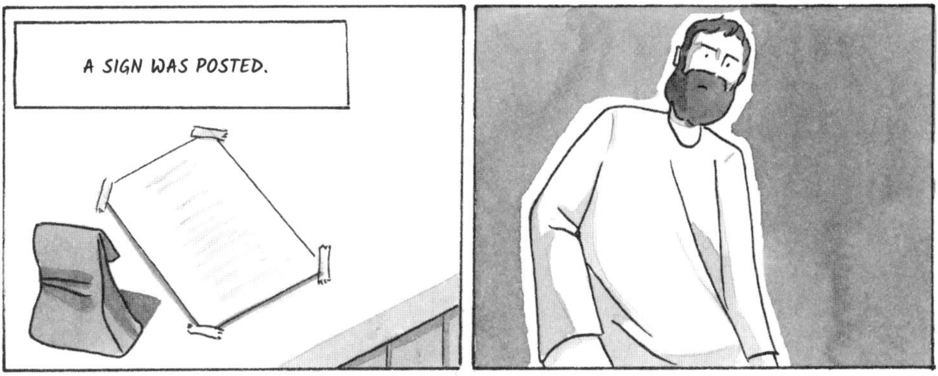
A SIGN WAS POSTED.

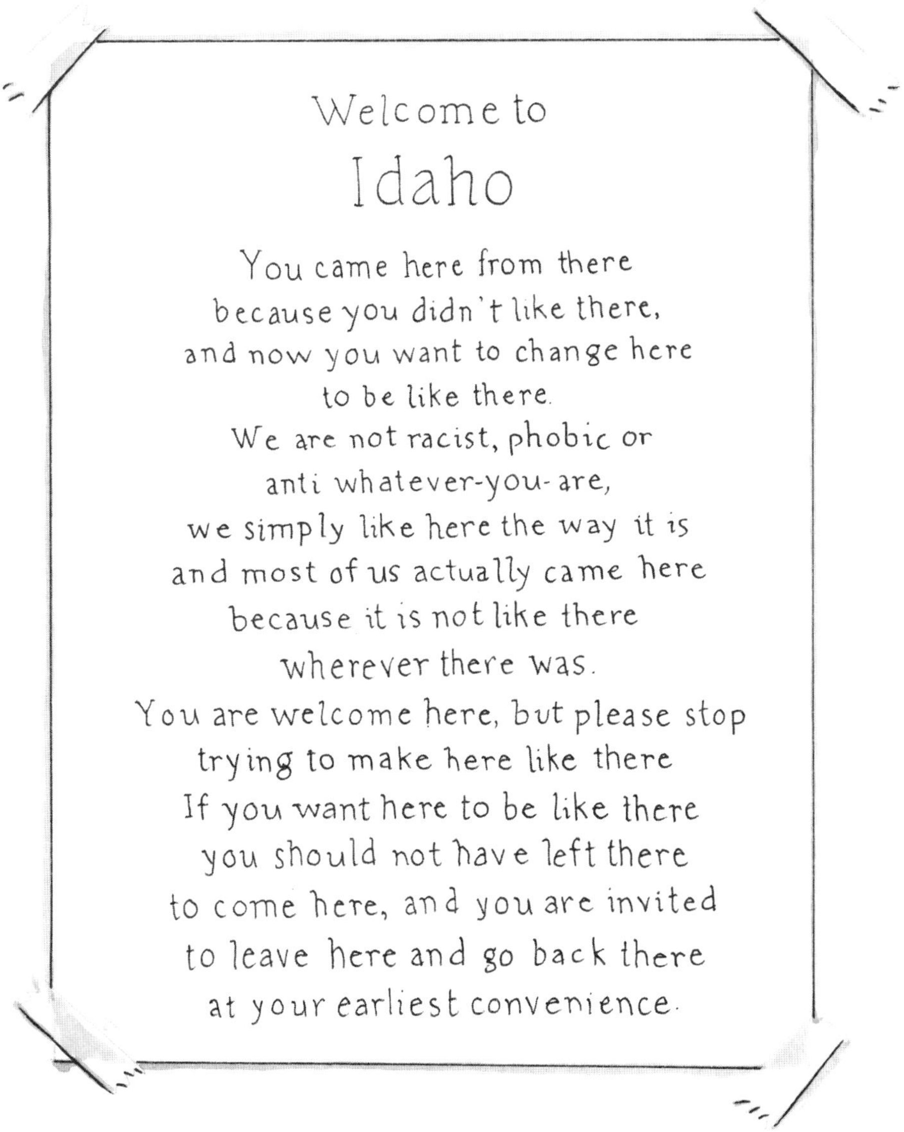
Welcome to
Idaho
You came here from there
because you didn't like there,
and now you want to change here
to be like there.
We are not racist, phobic or
anti whatever-you-are,
we simply like here the way it is
and most of us actually came here
because it is not like there
wherever there was.
You are welcome here, but please stop
trying to make here like there
If you want here to be like there
you should not have left there
to come here, and you are invited
to leave here and go back there
at your earliest convenience.

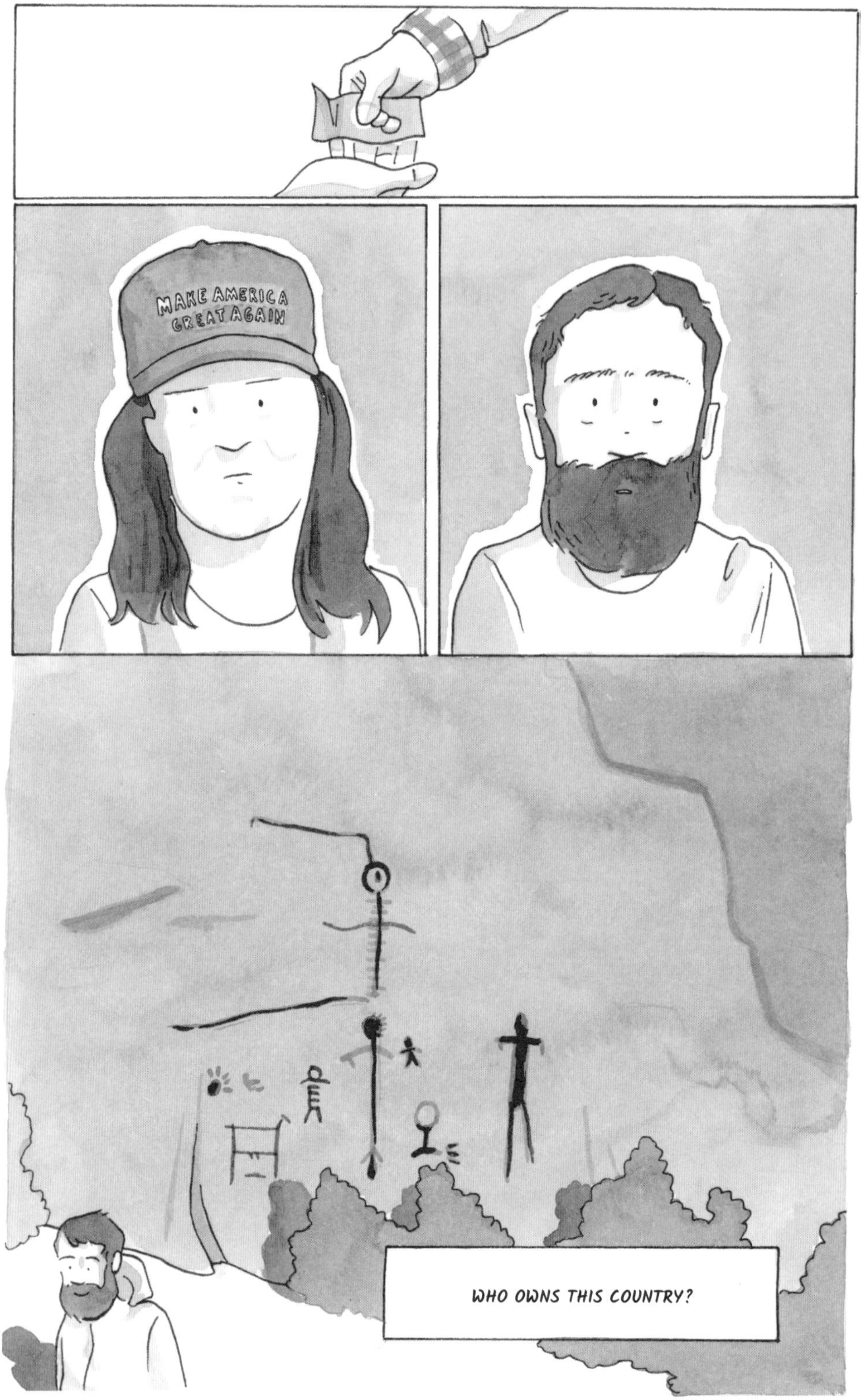
MAKE AMERICA GREAT AGAIN
WHO OWNS THIS COUNTRY?

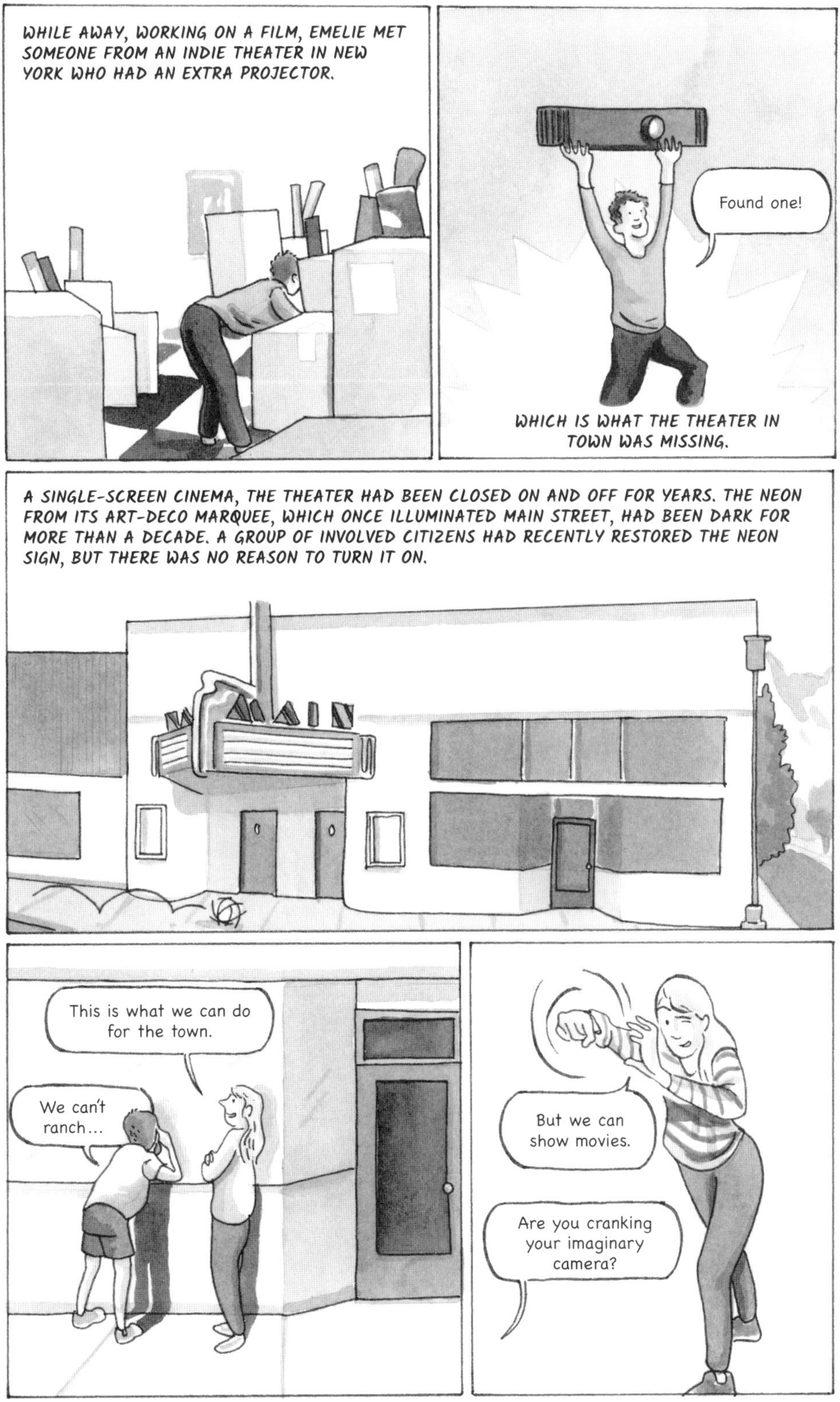
WHILE AWAY, WORKING ON A FILM, EMELIE MET SOMEONE FROM AN INDIE THEATER IN NEW YORK WHO HAD AN EXTRA PROJECTOR.
Found one!
WHICH IS WHAT THE THEATER IN TOWN WAS MISSING.
A SINGLE-SCREEN CINEMA, THE THEATER HAD BEEN CLOSED ON AND OFF FOR YEARS. THE NEON FROM ITS ART-DECO MARQUEE, WHICH ONCE ILLUMINATED MAIN STREET, HAD BEEN DARK FOR MORE THAN A DECADE. A GROUP OF INVOLVED CITIZENS HAD RECENTLY RESTORED THE NEON SIGN, BUT THERE WAS NO REASON TO TURN IT ON.
This is what we can do for the town.
We can't ranch...
But we can show movies.
Are you cranking your imaginary camera?

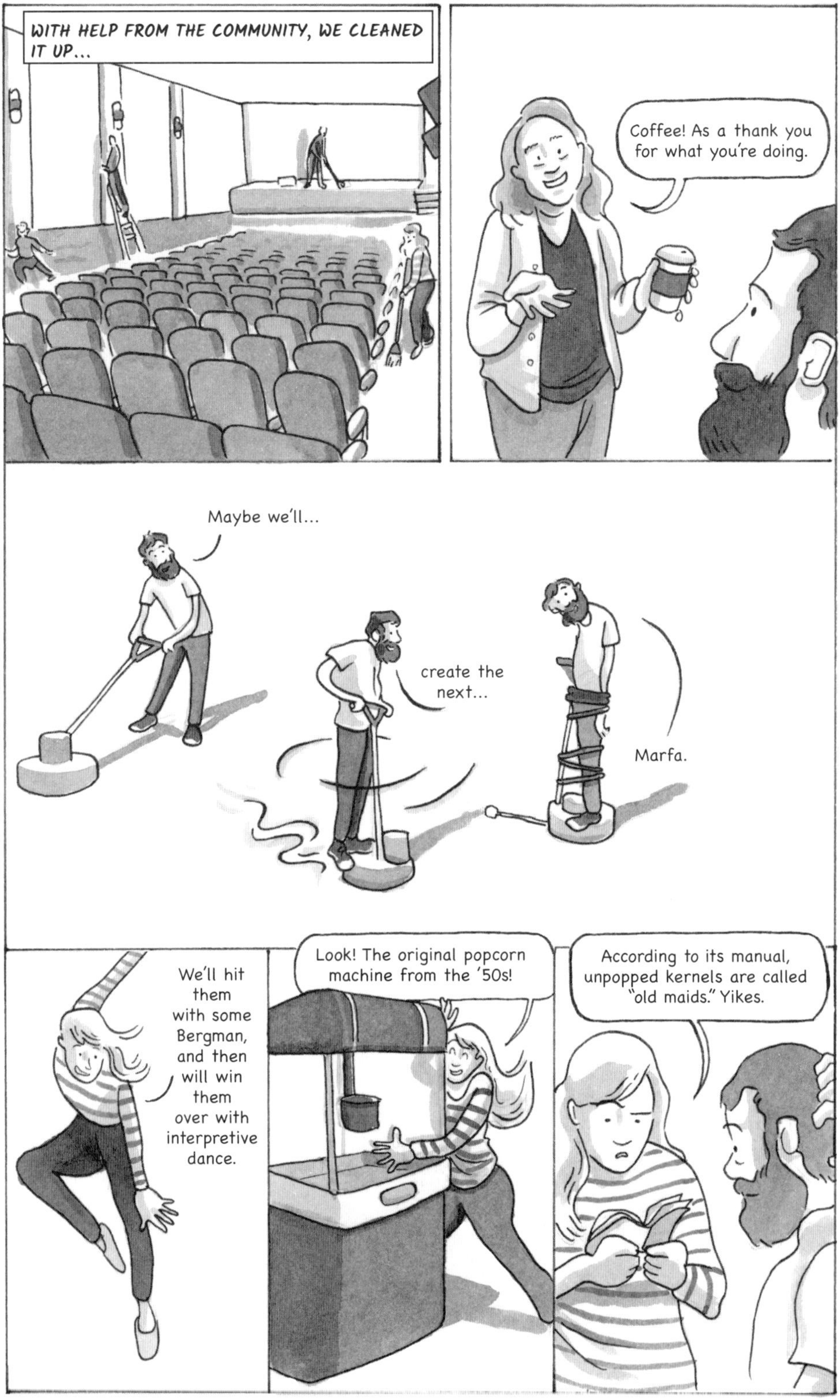
WITH HELP FROM THE COMMUNITY, WE CLEANED IT UP...
Coffee! As a thank you for what you're doing.
Maybe we'll...
create the next...
Marfa.
We'll hit them with some Bergman, and then will win them over with interpretive dance.
Look! The original popcorn machine from the '50s!
According to its manual, unpopped kernels are called "old maids." Yikes.

AND REOPENED IT.

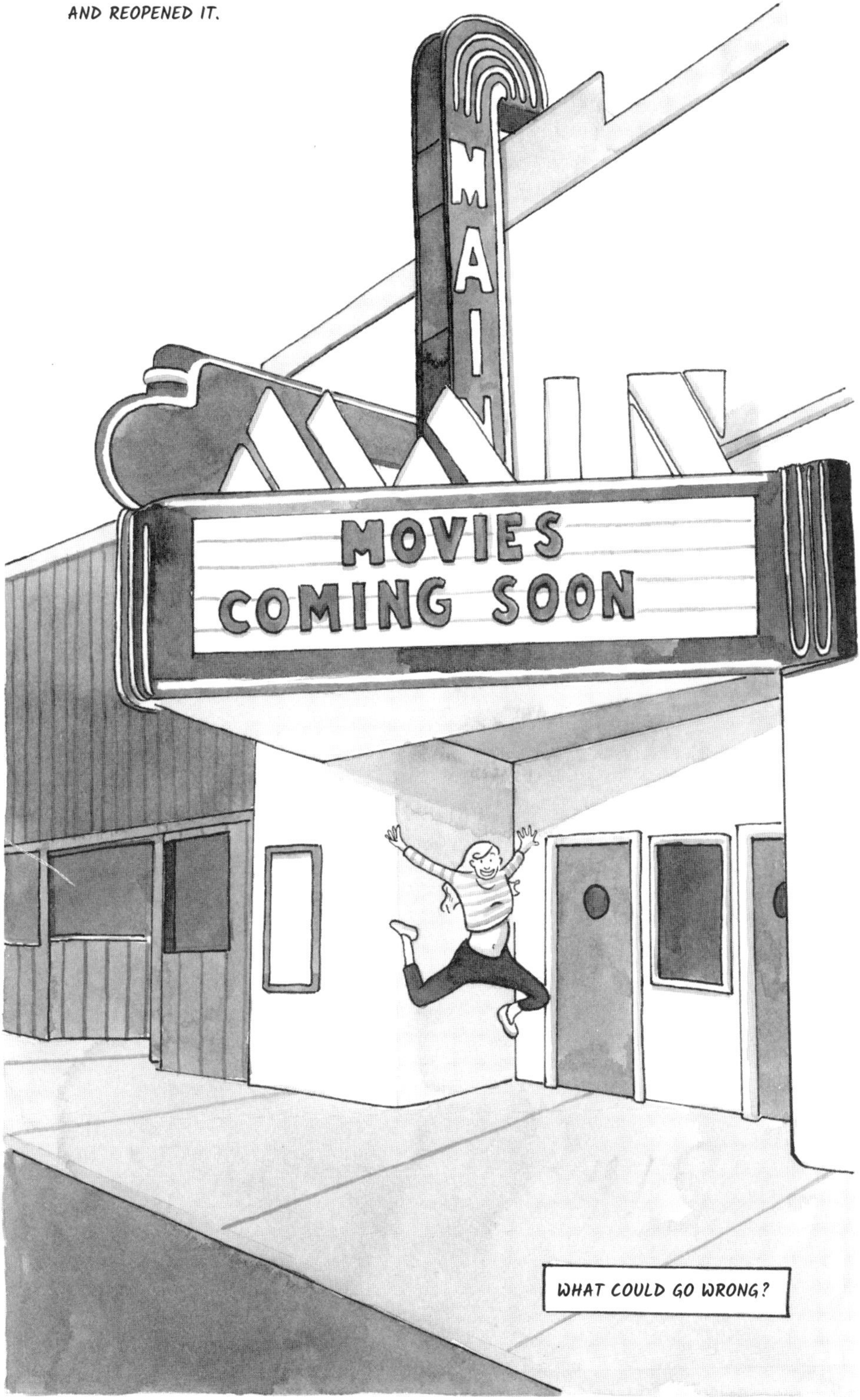
MAIN
MOVIES
COMING SOON
WHAT COULD GO WRONG?

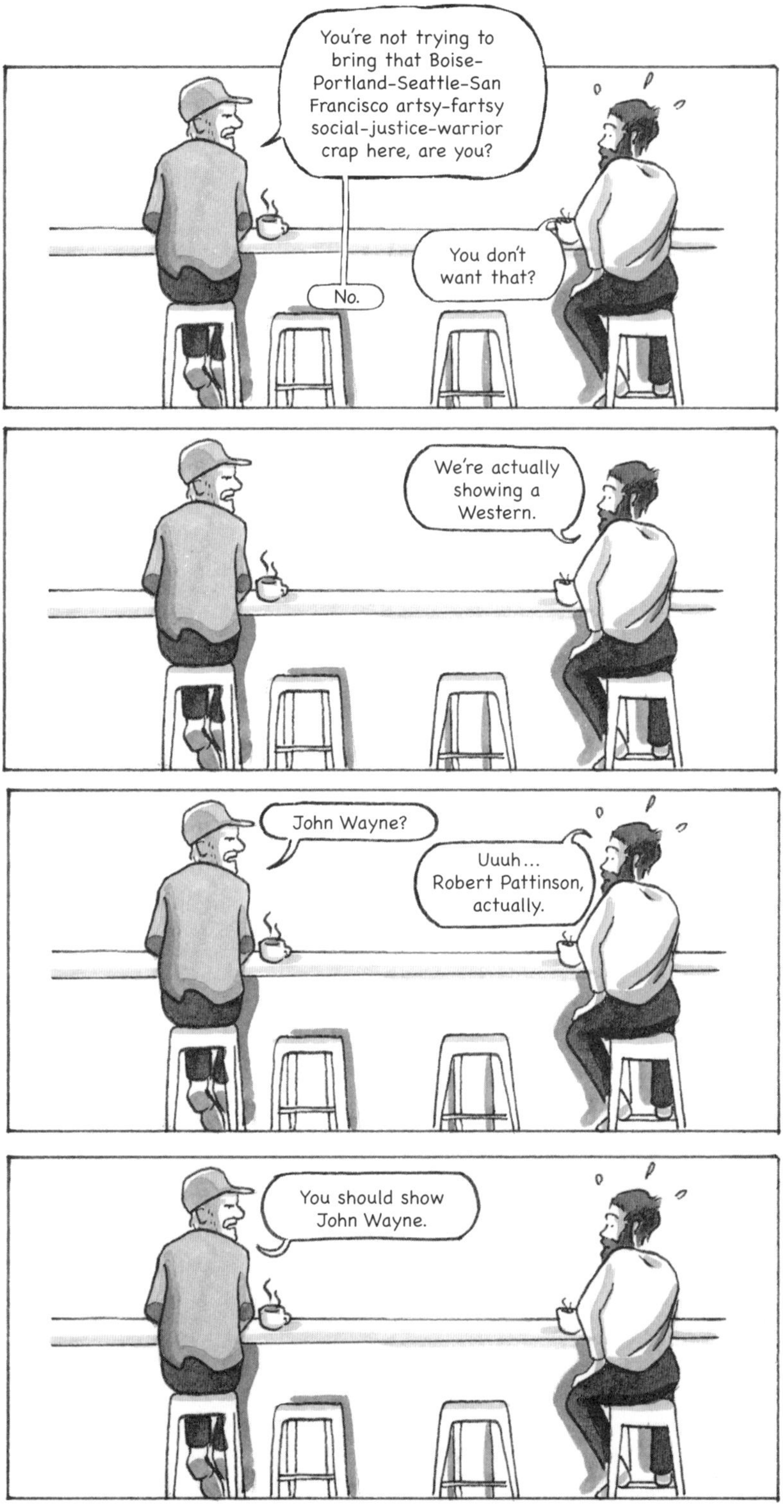
You're not trying to bring that Boise-Portland-Seattle-San Francisco artsy-fartsy social-justice-warrior crap here, are you?
No.
You don't want that?
We're actually showing a Western.
John Wayne?
Uuuh... Robert Pattinson, actually.
You should show John Wayne.

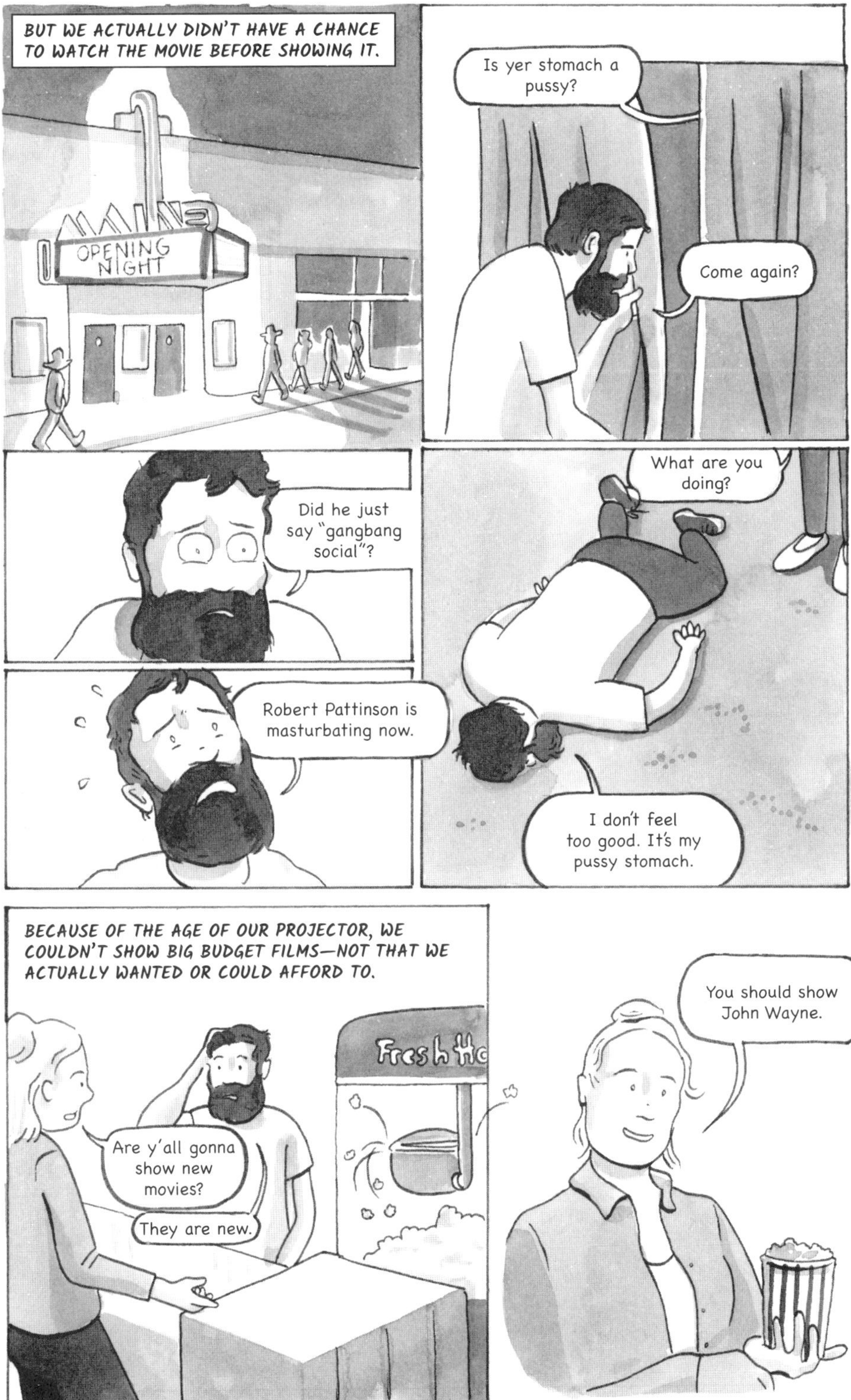
BUT WE ACTUALLY DIDN'T HAVE A CHANCE TO WATCH THE MOVIE BEFORE SHOWING IT.
OPENING NIGHT
Is yer stomach a pussy?
Come again?
Did he just say "gangbang social"?
What are you doing?
Robert Pattinson is masturbating now.
I don't feel too good. It's my pussy stomach.
BECAUSE OF THE AGE OF OUR PROJECTOR, WE COULDN'T SHOW BIG BUDGET FILMS—NOT THAT WE ACTUALLY WANTED OR COULD AFFORD TO.
Are y'all gonna show new movies?
They are new.
You should show John Wayne.

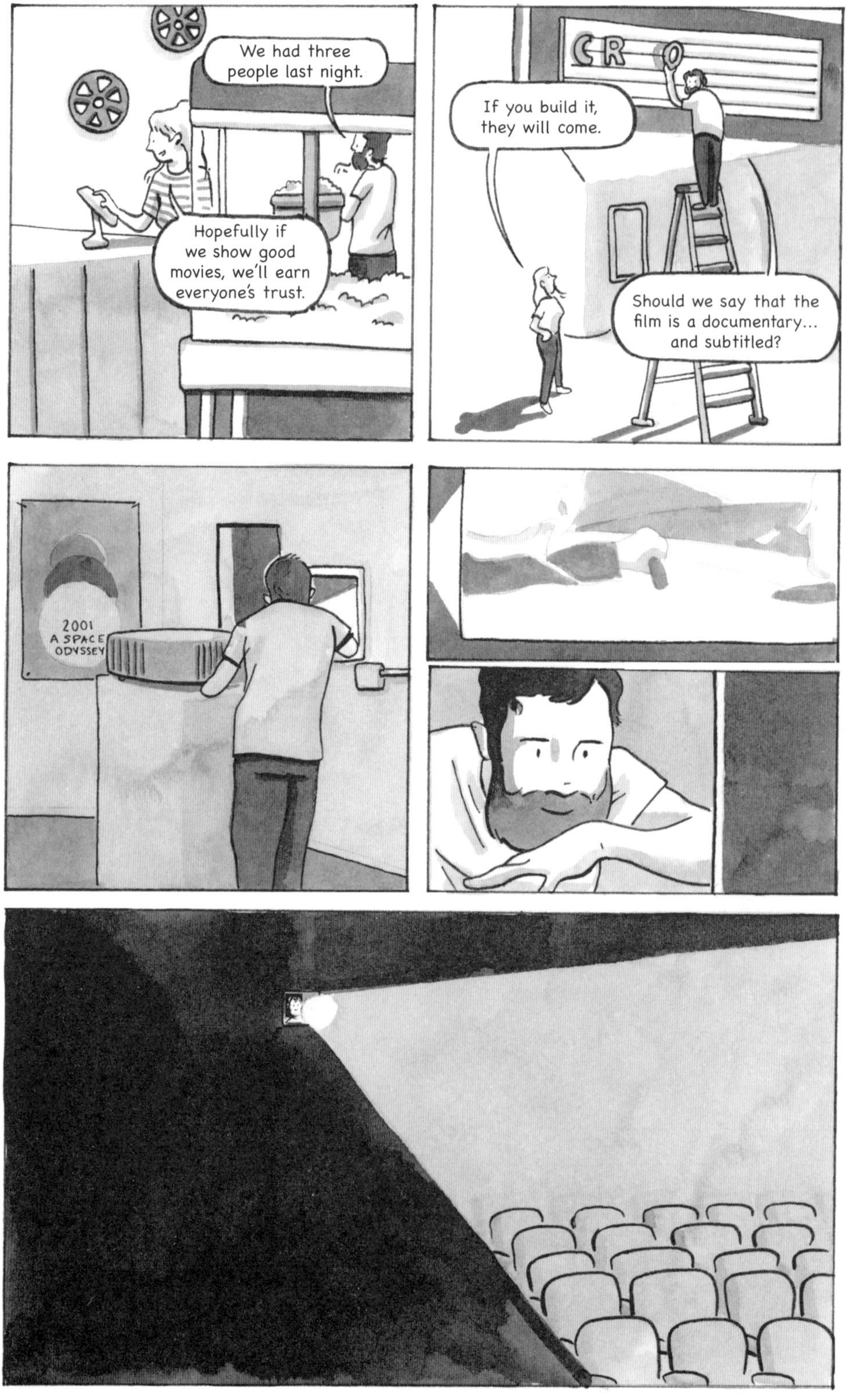
We had three people last night.
Hopefully if we show good movies, we'll earn everyone's trust.
CR O
If you build it, they will come.
Should we say that the film is a documentary... and subtitled?
2001 A SPACE ODYSSEY

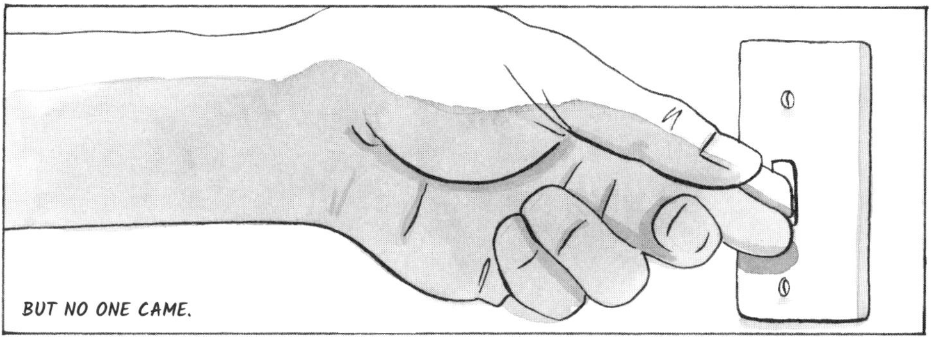
BUT NO ONE CAME.

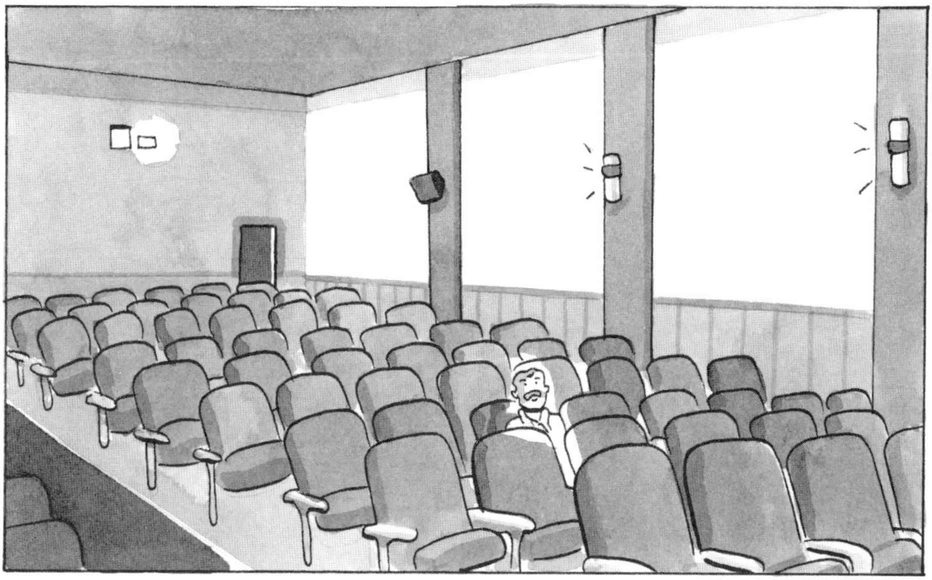

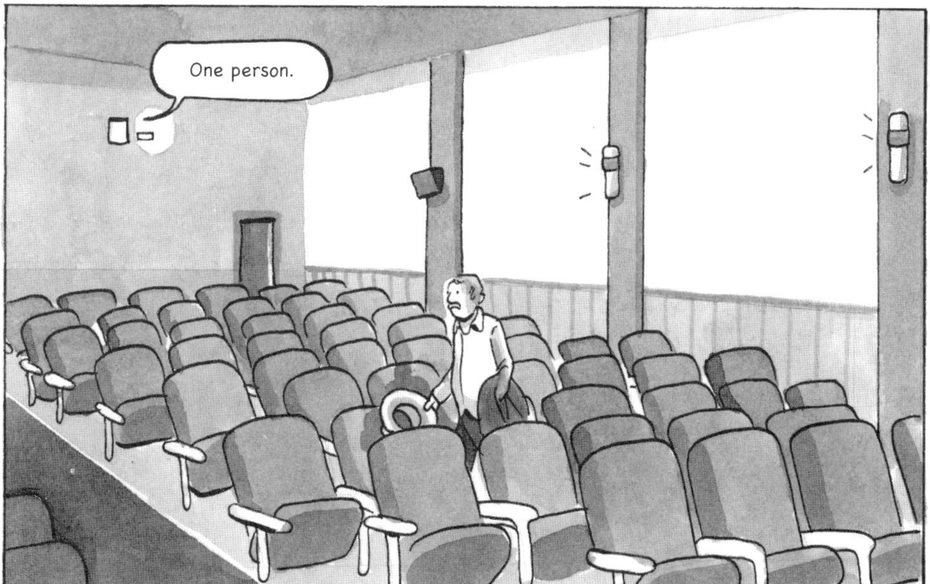
One person.

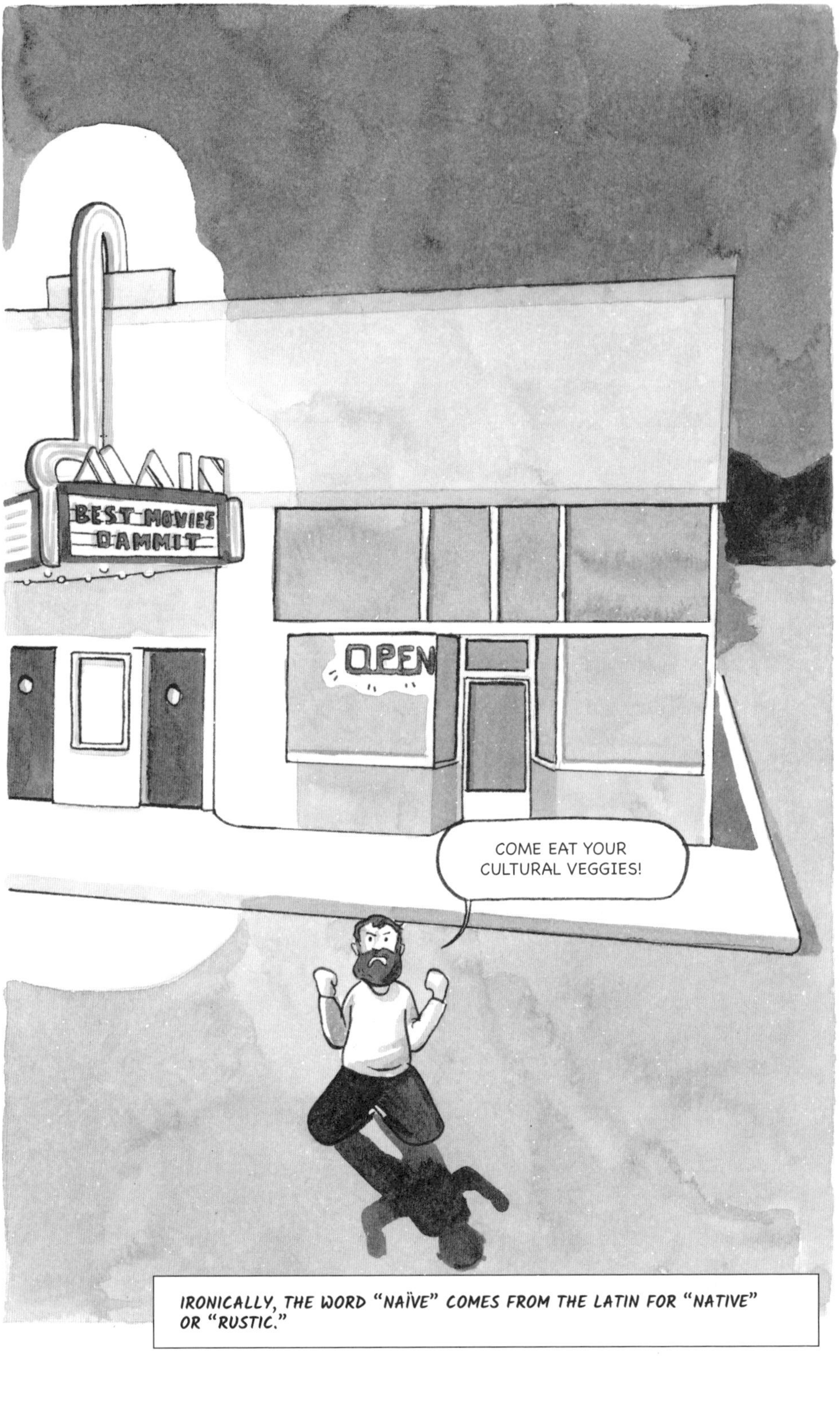
BEST MOVIES
DAMMIT
OPEN
COME EAT YOUR CULTURAL VEGGIES!
IRONICALLY, THE WORD "NAÏVE" COMES FROM THE LATIN FOR "NATIVE" OR "RUSTIC."

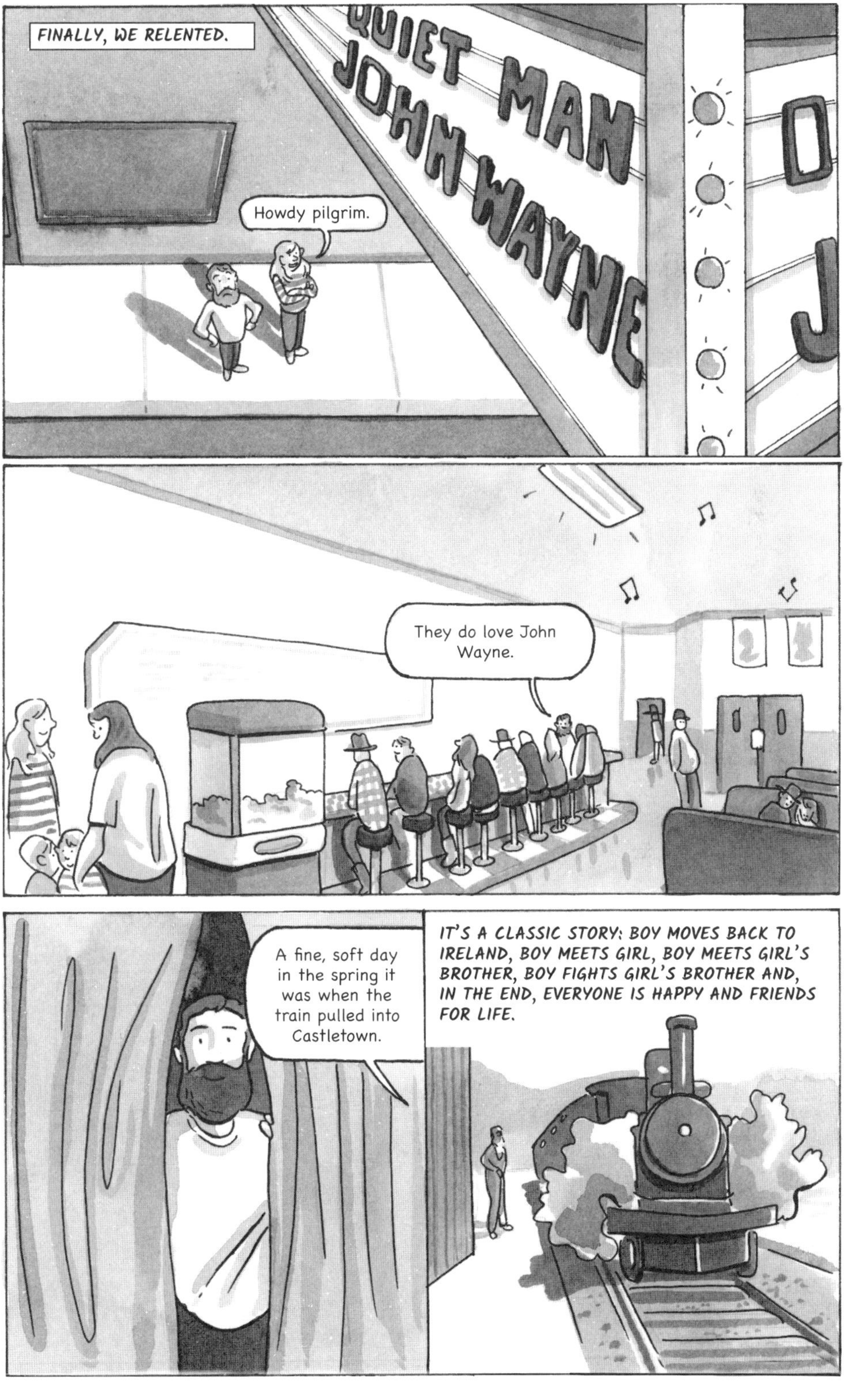
FINALLY, WE RELENTED.
QUIET MAN
JOHN WAYNE
Howdy pilgrim.
They do love John Wayne.
A fine, soft day in the spring it was when the train pulled into Castletown.
IT'S A CLASSIC STORY: BOY MOVES BACK TO IRELAND, BOY MEETS GIRL, BOY MEETS GIRL'S BROTHER, BOY FIGHTS GIRL'S BROTHER AND, IN THE END, EVERYONE IS HAPPY AND FRIENDS FOR LIFE.

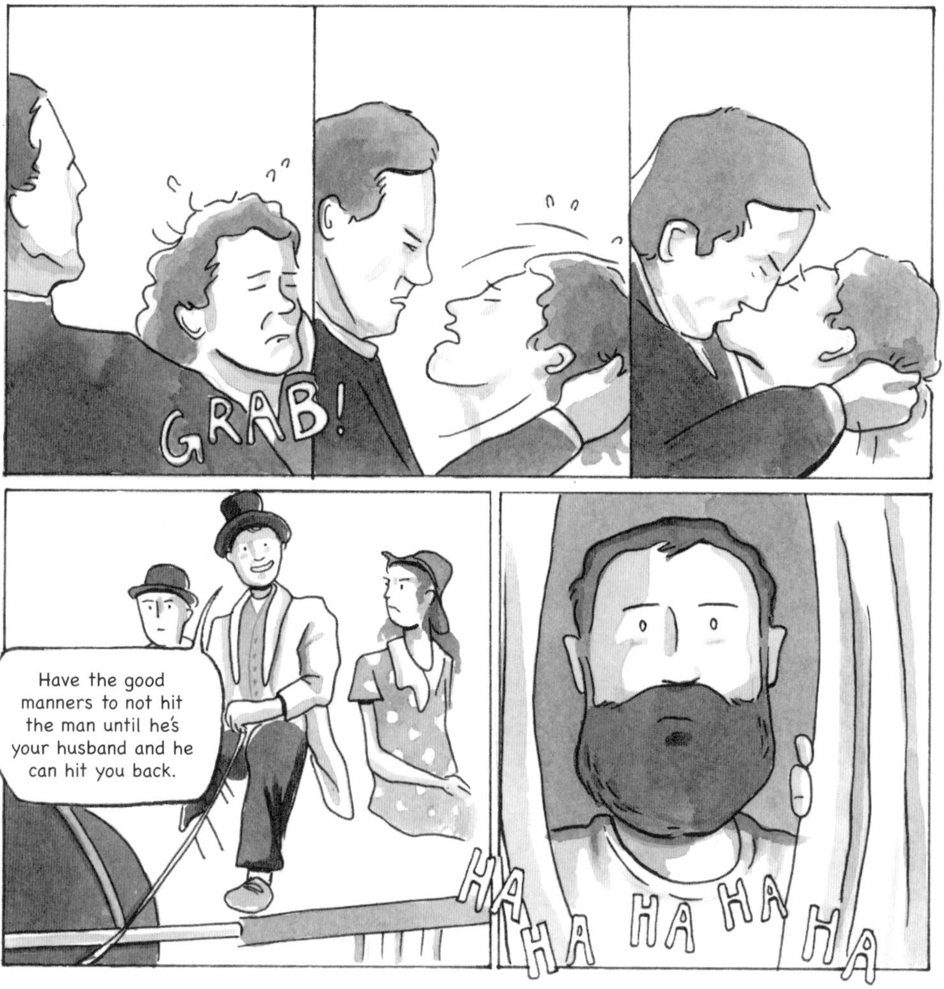
GRAB!
Have the good manners to not hit the man until he's your husband and he can hit you back.
HA HA HA HA HA HA

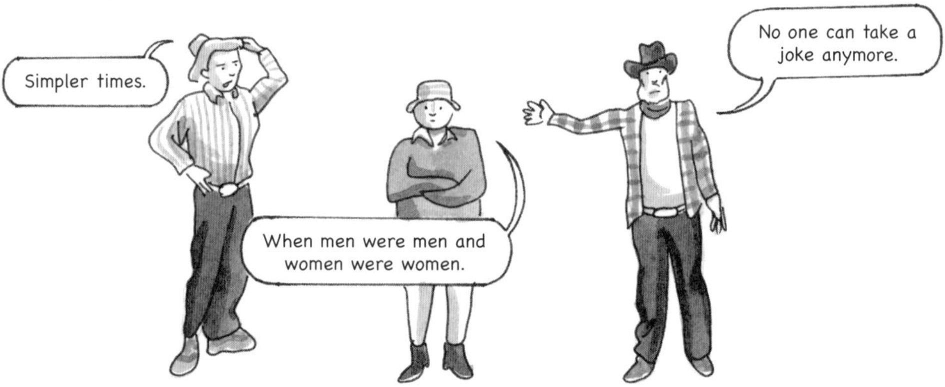
Simpler times.
When men were men and women were women.
No one can take a joke anymore.

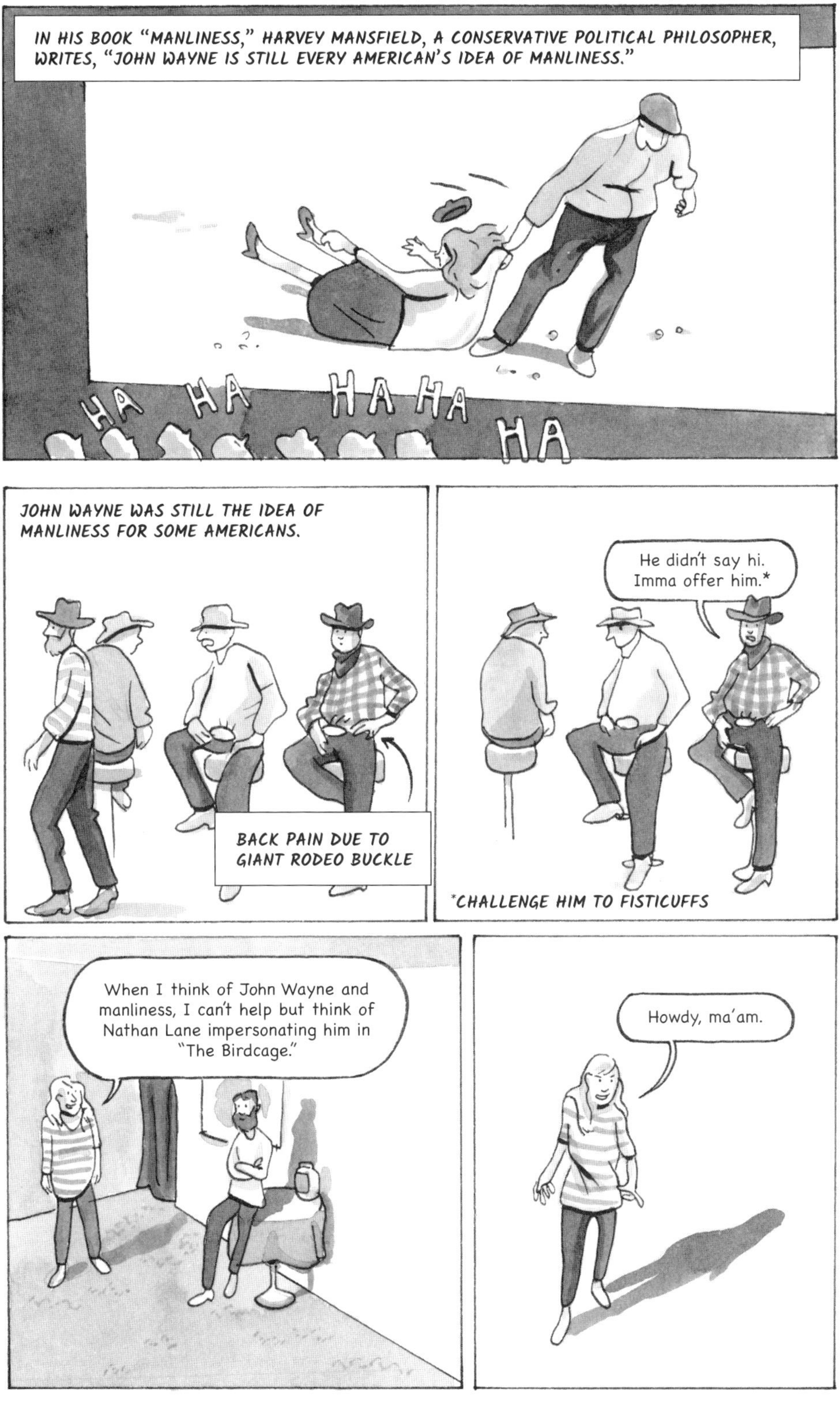
IN HIS BOOK "MANLINESS," HARVEY MANSFIELD, A CONSERVATIVE POLITICAL PHILOSOPHER, WRITES, "JOHN WAYNE IS STILL EVERY AMERICAN'S IDEA OF MANLINESS."
HA HA HA HA HA
JOHN WAYNE WAS STILL THE IDEA OF MANLINESS FOR SOME AMERICANS.
BACK PAIN DUE TO GIANT RODEO BUCKLE
He didn't say hi. Imma offer him.*
*CHALLENGE HIM TO FISTICUFFS
When I think of John Wayne and manliness, I can't help but think of Nathan Lane impersonating him in "The Birdcage."
Howdy, ma'am.

DON'T GET ME WRONG. I AM A FAN OF JOHN FORD. THE MOUNTAINS HERE ARE REMINISCENT OF HIS FILM VISTAS. AND I REMEMBER THE FIRST TIME I SAW A YOUNG JOHN WAYNE IN FORD'S "STAGECOACH," I WAS MESMERIZED.

I'm the Ringo Kid.

No, I'm the Ringo Kid.

AND IT IS JUST A MOVIE. BUT ONE WHOSE IDEALIZED VISION OF THE PAST—WHICH MASKS MISOGYNY AND DEEPLY CONSERVATIVE VALUES—FELT ALL TOO SIMILAR TO THE TOWN ITSELF.

AND THEY SHOWED UP.

AND THEY LAUGHED.

AND SAW THEMSELVES REFLECTED BACK.

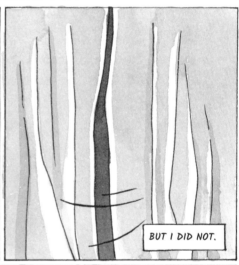

BUT I DID NOT.

FALL CAME, AND EVEN WITH THE ADDITION OF OLD REPERTORY FILMS, THINGS DID NOT IMPROVE. THE COLDER TEMPERATURES DIDN'T HELP EITHER.

STAR WARS

OPE

It'll cost a fortune to heat this place.

Maybe we can buy our one customer a coat.

We can't keep volunteering our time for something nobody wants.

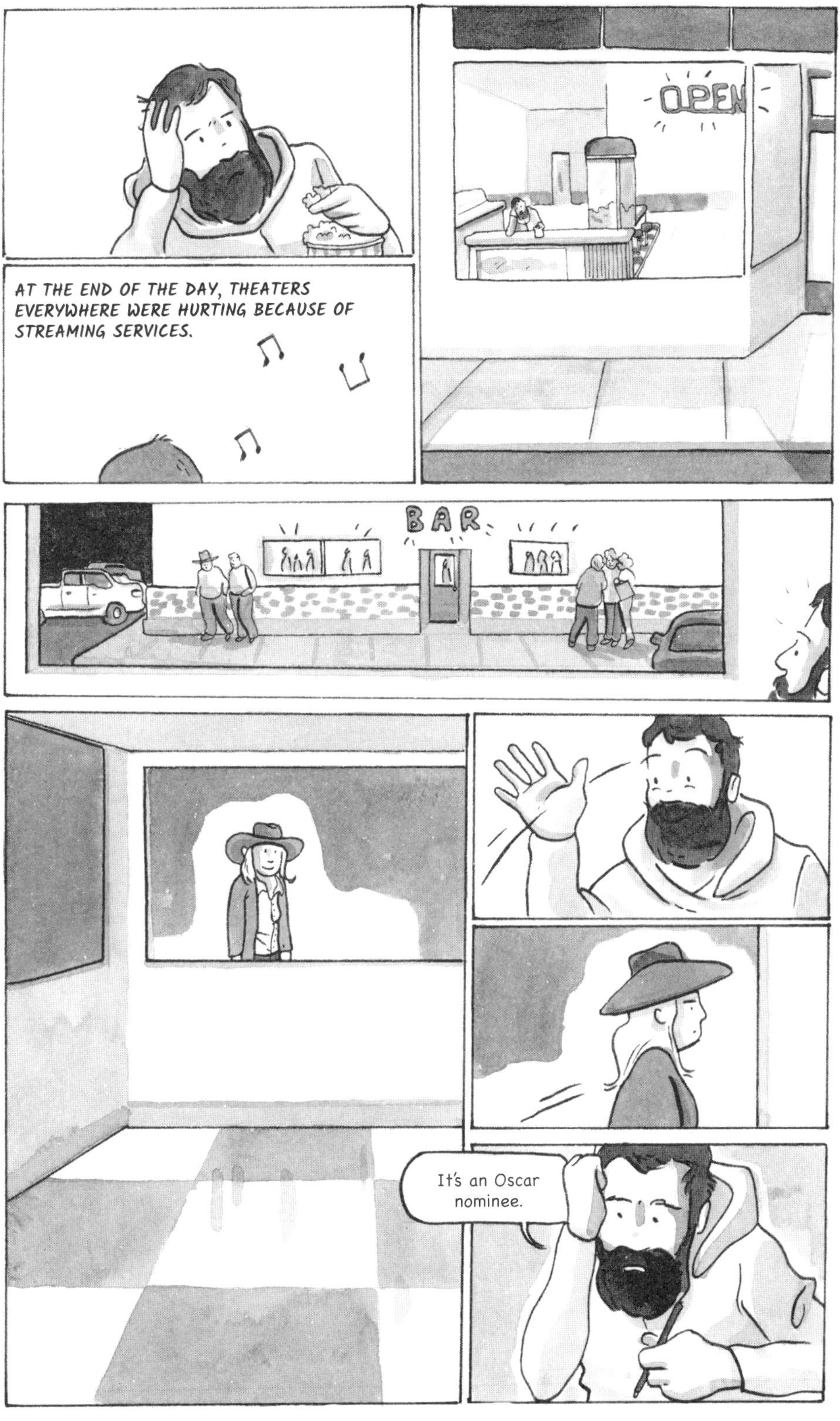
OPEN
AT THE END OF THE DAY, THEATERS EVERYWHERE WERE HURTING BECAUSE OF STREAMING SERVICES.
BAR
It's an Oscar nominee.

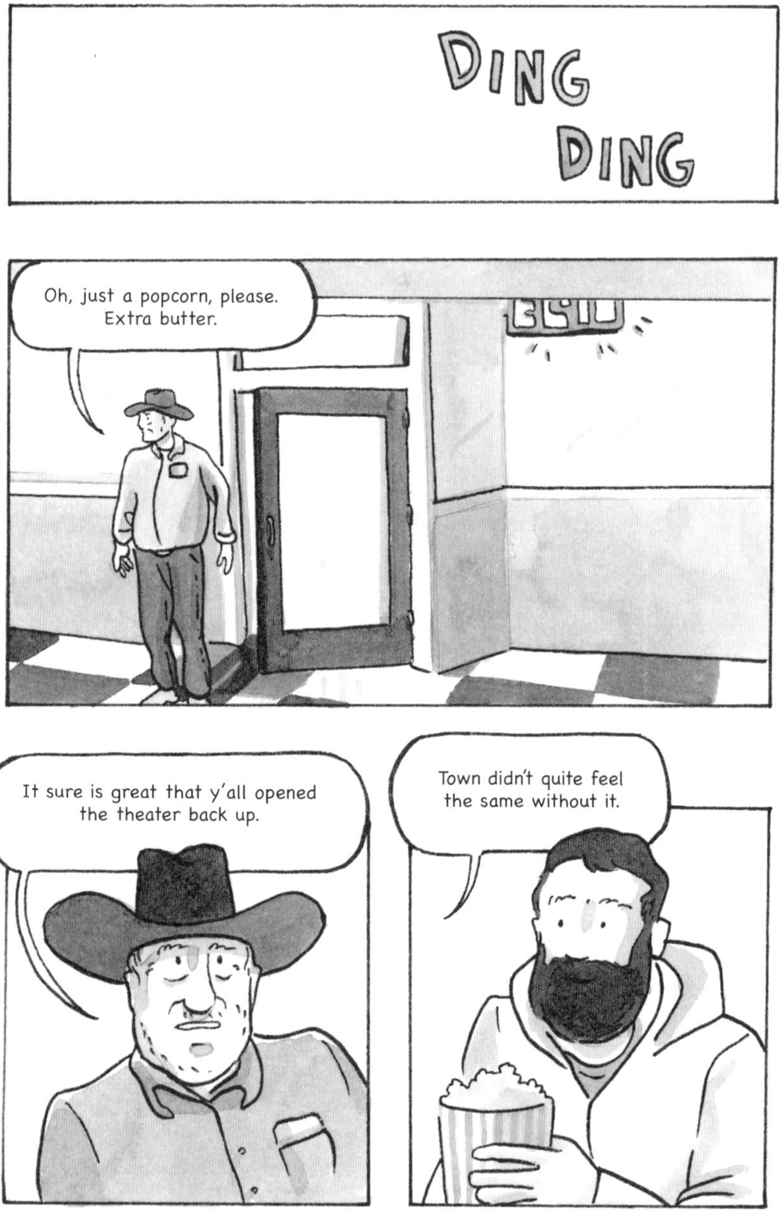
DING
DING
Oh, just a popcorn, please. Extra butter.
It sure is great that y'all opened the theater back up.
Town didn't quite feel the same without it.

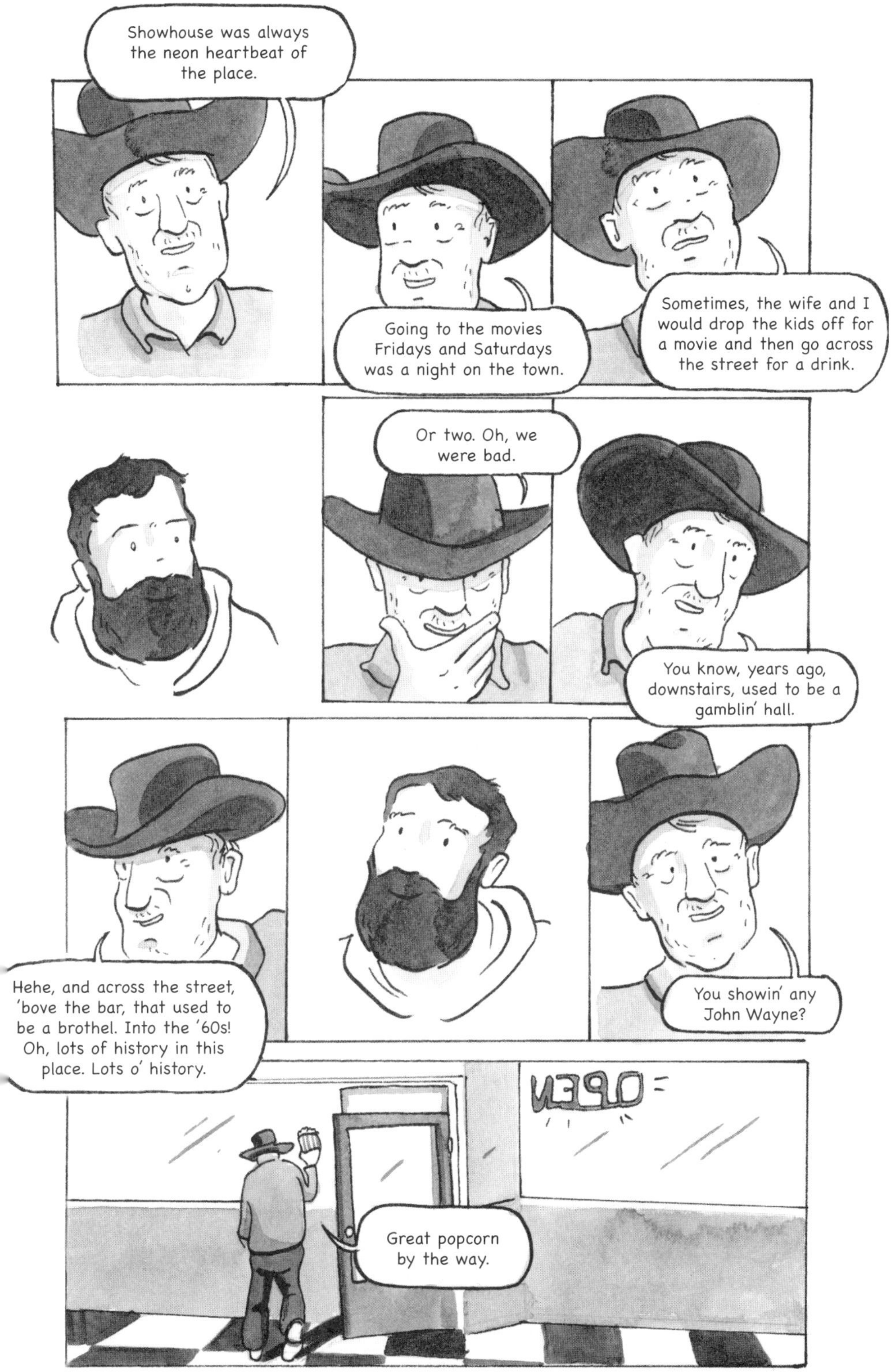
Showhouse was always the neon heartbeat of the place.
Going to the movies Fridays and Saturdays was a night on the town.
Sometimes, the wife and I would drop the kids off for a movie and then go across the street for a drink.
Or two. Oh, we were bad.
You know, years ago, downstairs, used to be a gamblin' hall.
Hehe, and across the street, 'bove the bar, that used to be a brothel. Into the '60s! Oh, lots of history in this place. Lots o' history.
You showin' any John Wayne?
OPEN
Great popcorn by the way.

AFTER WE CLOSED THE THEATER, WE LEARNED THAT BACK IN THE DAY,
WHEN FILM WAS STILL SHOWN ON PRINT, REELS WOULD BE SMUGGLED FROM
A WEALTHY TOWN OVER THE MOUNTAIN. THIS ALLOWED THE TOWN TO SEE
NEW MOVIES WITHOUT HAVING TO LICENSE THEM.

THE THEATER HAD NEVER BEEN VIABLE.

WHICH WAS FITTING.

AND ROMANTIC.

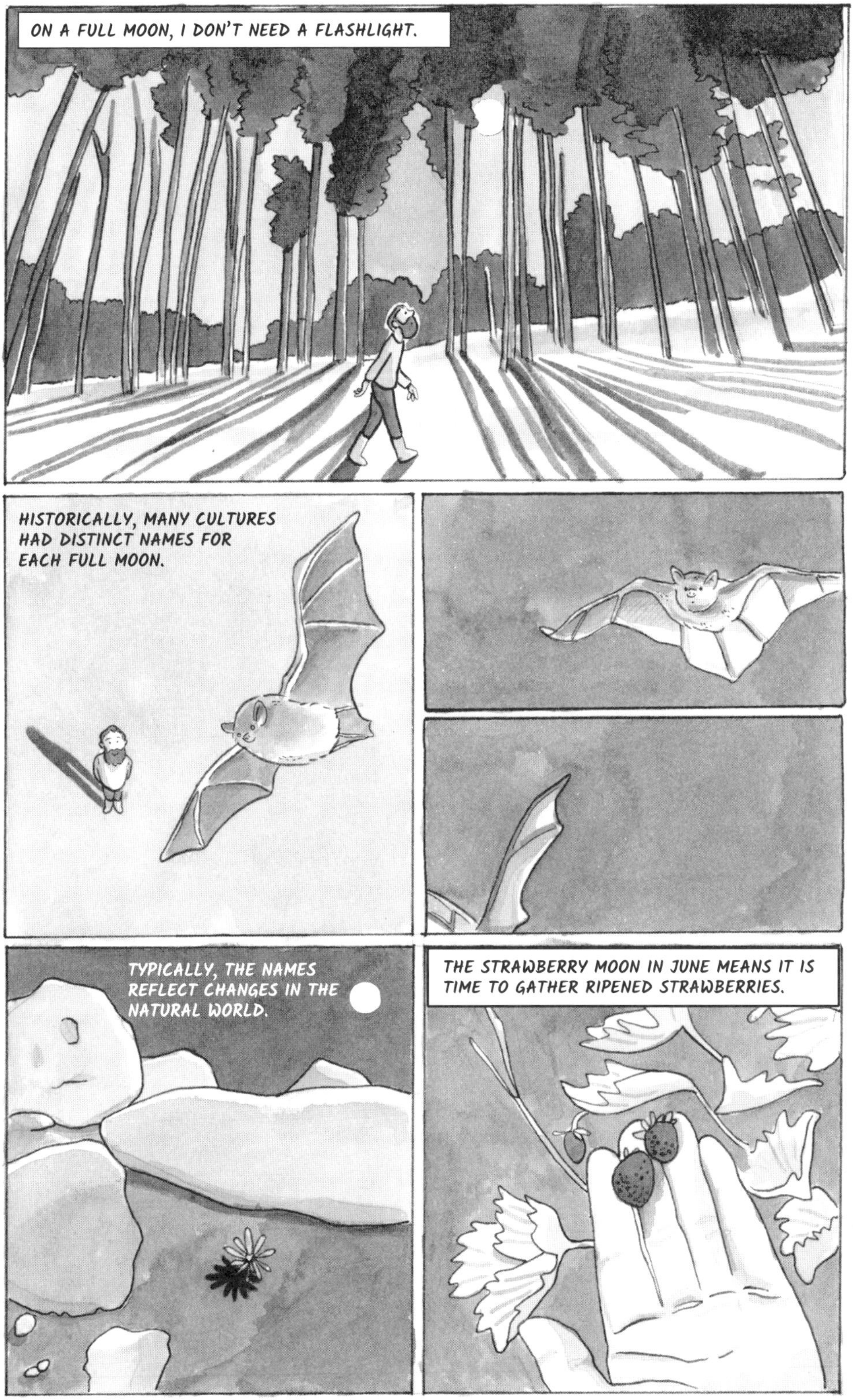
ON A FULL MOON, I DON'T NEED A FLASHLIGHT.
HISTORICALLY, MANY CULTURES HAD DISTINCT NAMES FOR EACH FULL MOON.
TYPICALLY, THE NAMES REFLECT CHANGES IN THE NATURAL WORLD.
THE STRAWBERRY MOON IN JUNE MEANS IT IS TIME TO GATHER RIPENED STRAWBERRIES.

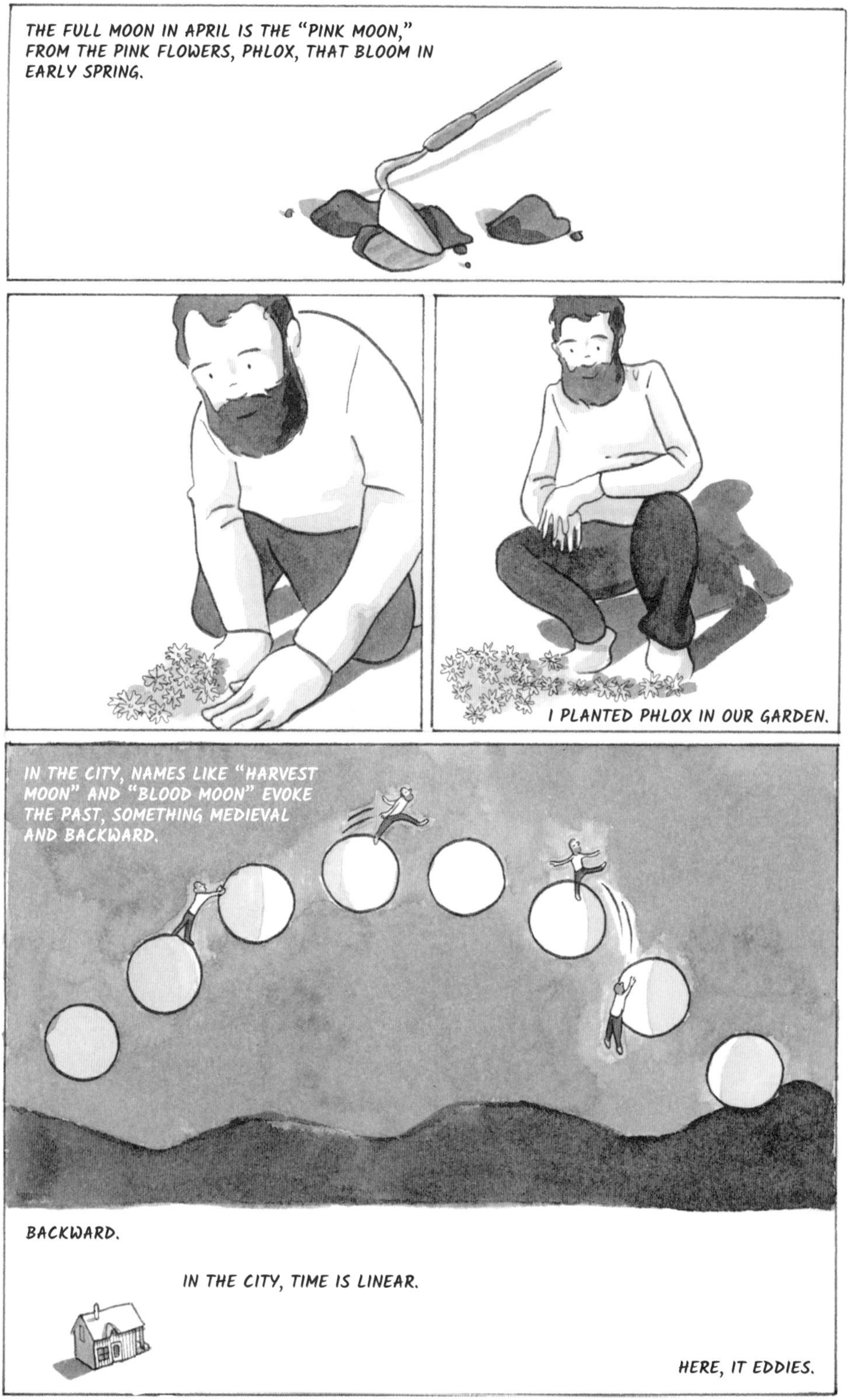
THE FULL MOON IN APRIL IS THE "PINK MOON," FROM THE PINK FLOWERS, PHLOX, THAT BLOOM IN EARLY SPRING.
I PLANTED PHLOX IN OUR GARDEN.
IN THE CITY, NAMES LIKE "HARVEST MOON" AND "BLOOD MOON" EVOKE THE PAST, SOMETHING MEDIEVAL AND BACKWARD.
BACKWARD.
IN THE CITY, TIME IS LINEAR.
HERE, IT EDDIES.

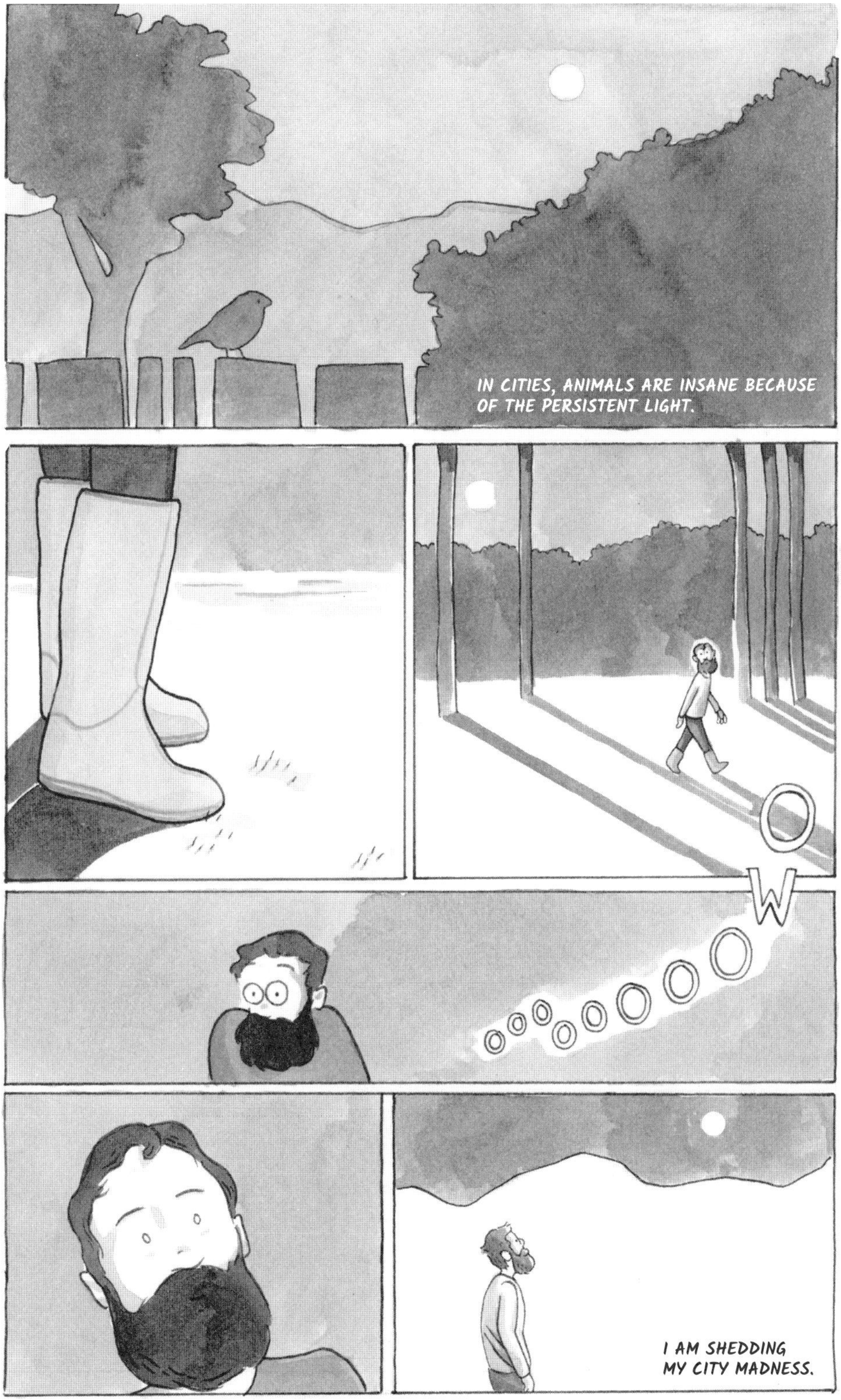
IN CITIES, ANIMALS ARE INSANE BECAUSE OF THE PERSISTENT LIGHT.
OOOOOOOOOOOW
I AM SHEDDING MY CITY MADNESS.

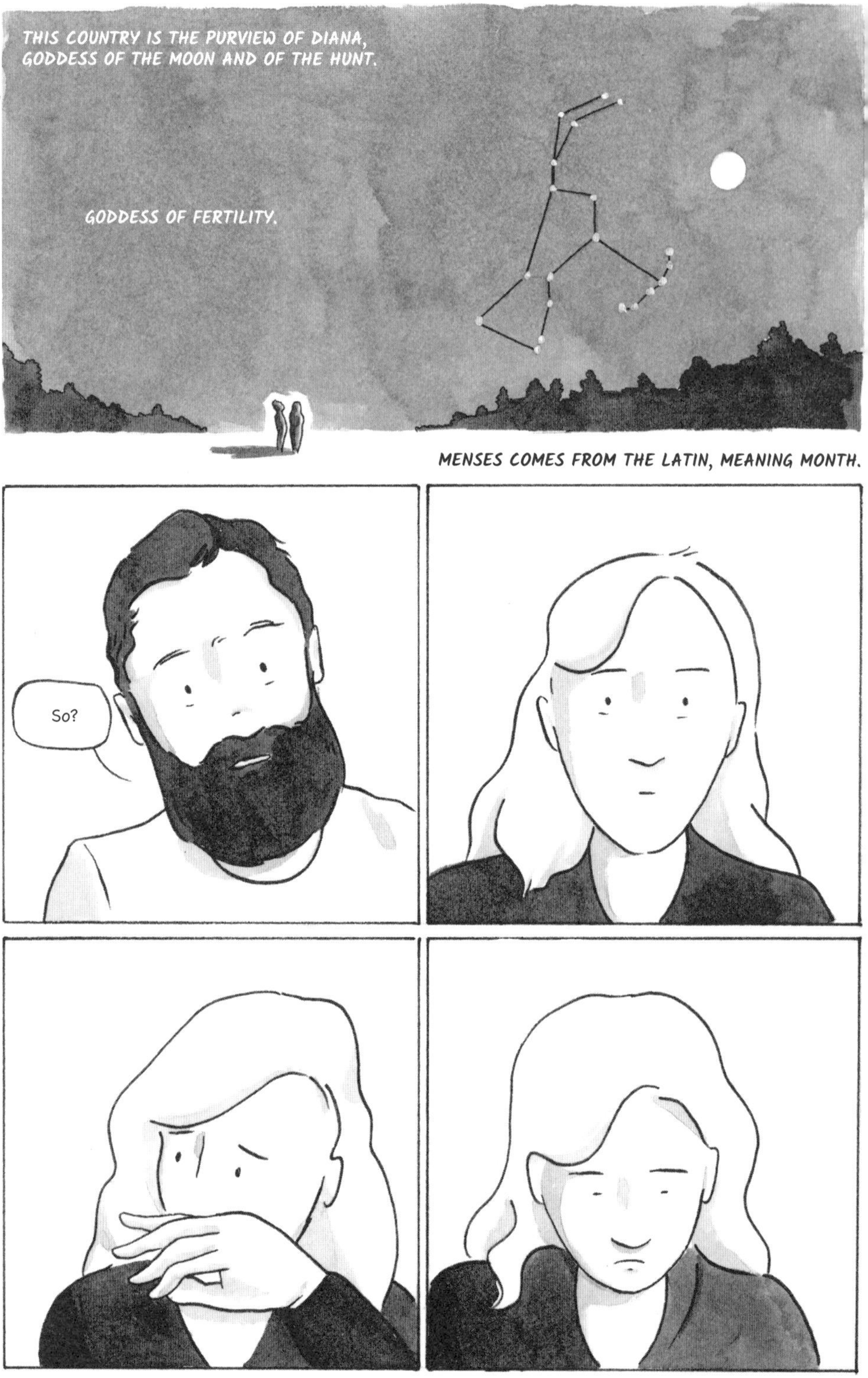
THIS COUNTRY IS THE PURVIEW OF DIANA, GODDESS OF THE MOON AND OF THE HUNT.
GODDESS OF FERTILITY.
MENSES COMES FROM THE LATIN, MEANING MONTH.
So?

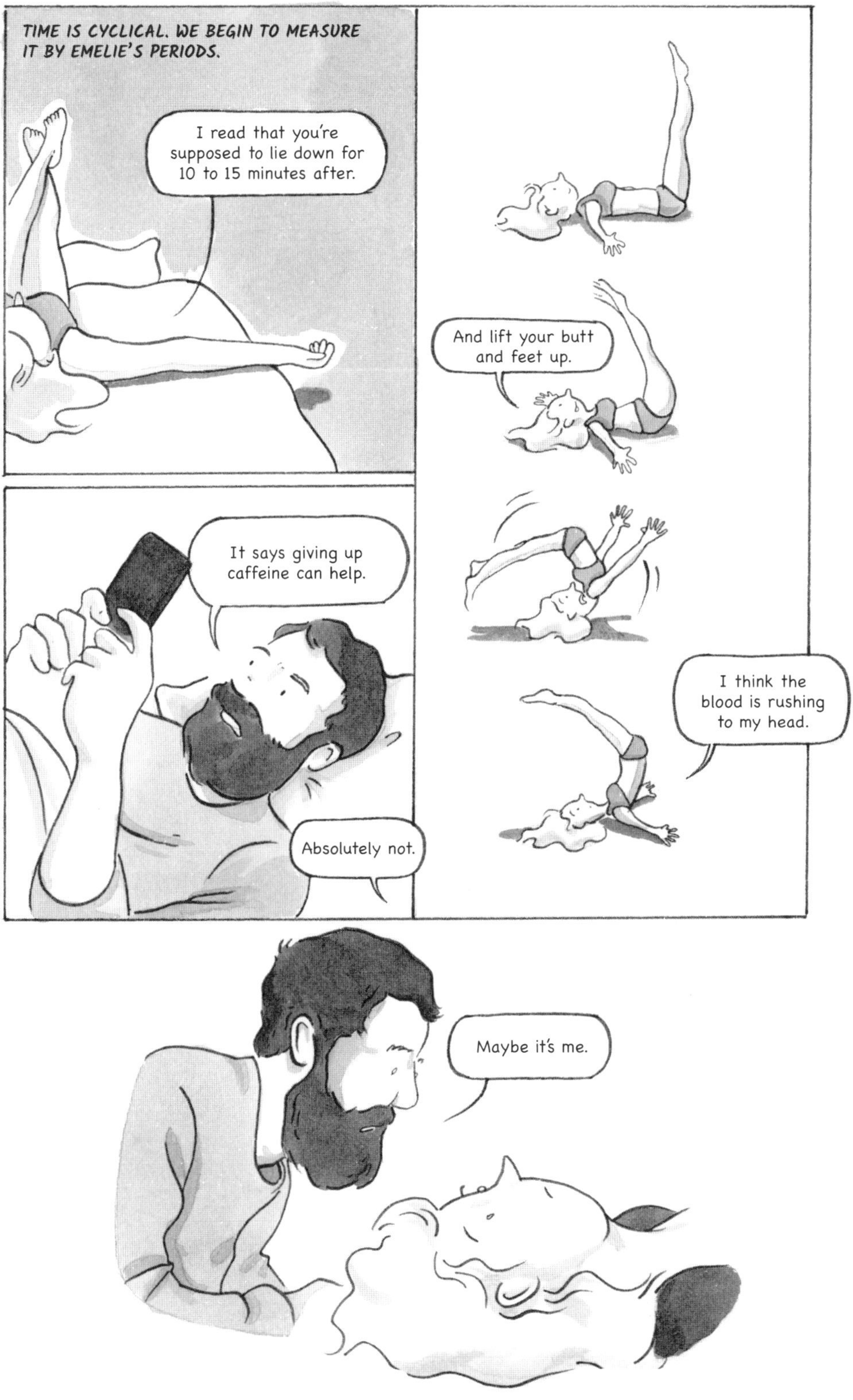
TIME IS CYCLICAL. WE BEGIN TO MEASURE IT BY EMELIE'S PERIODS.
I read that you're supposed to lie down for 10 to 15 minutes after.
And lift your butt and feet up.
It says giving up caffeine can help.
Absolutely not.
I think the blood is rushing to my head.
Maybe it's me.

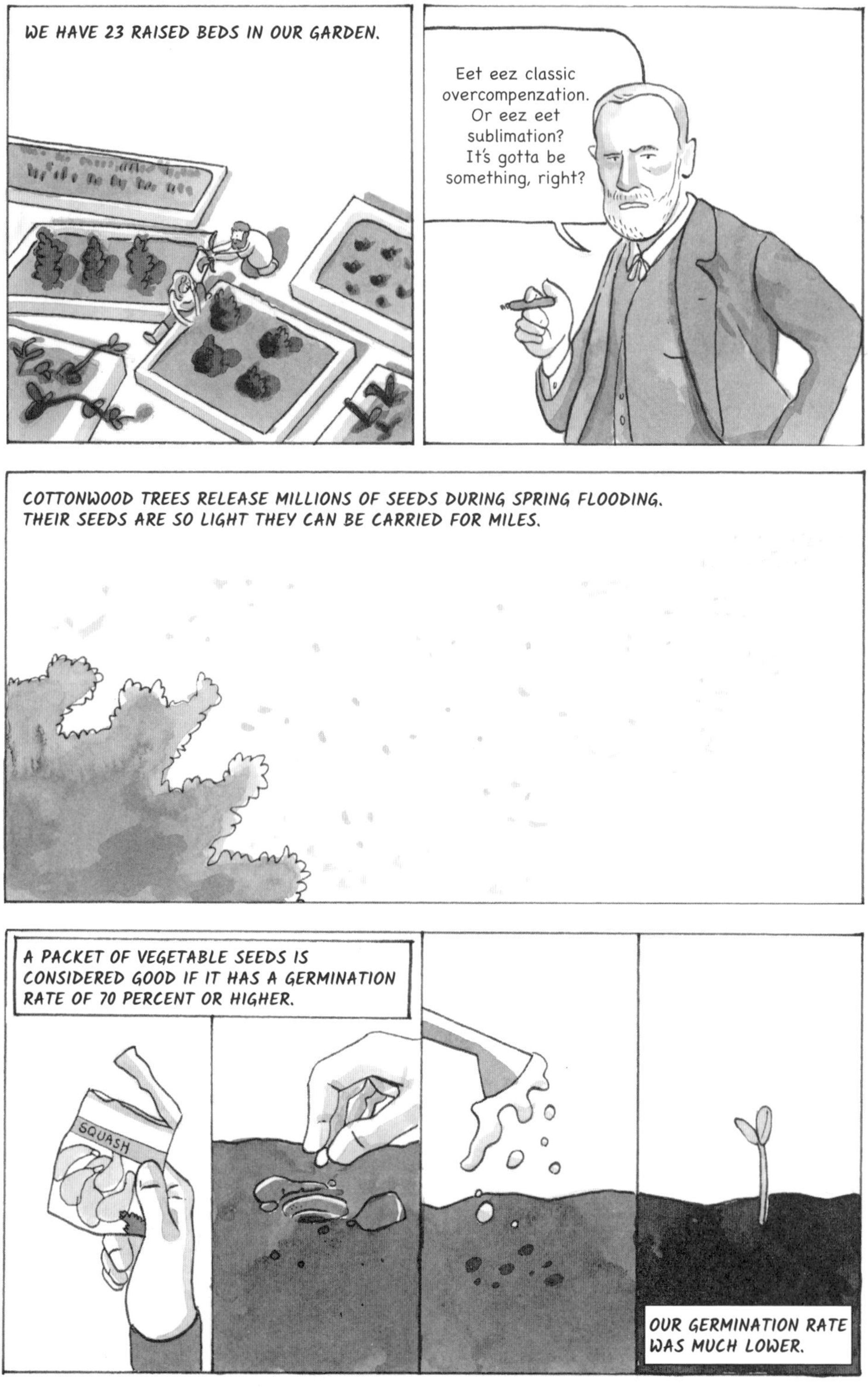
WE HAVE 23 RAISED BEDS IN OUR GARDEN.
Eet eez classic overcompenzation. Or eez eet sublimation? It's gotta be something, right?
COTTONWOOD TREES RELEASE MILLIONS OF SEEDS DURING SPRING FLOODING. THEIR SEEDS ARE SO LIGHT THEY CAN BE CARRIED FOR MILES.
A PACKET OF VEGETABLE SEEDS IS CONSIDERED GOOD IF IT HAS A GERMINATION RATE OF 70 PERCENT OR HIGHER.
SQUASH
OUR GERMINATION RATE WAS MUCH LOWER.

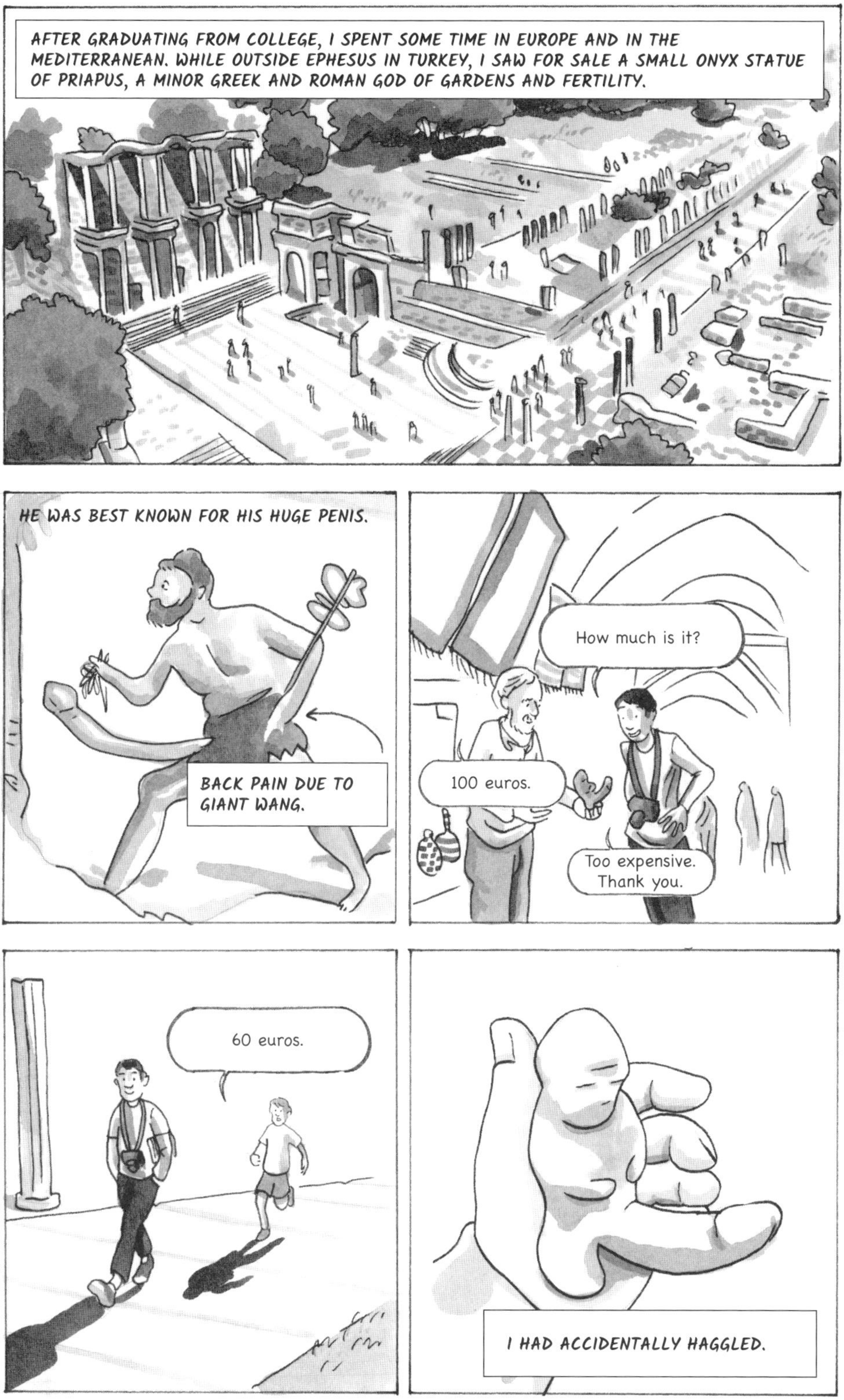
AFTER GRADUATING FROM COLLEGE, I SPENT SOME TIME IN EUROPE AND IN THE MEDITERRANEAN. WHILE OUTSIDE EPHESUS IN TURKEY, I SAW FOR SALE A SMALL ONYX STATUE OF PRIAPUS, A MINOR GREEK AND ROMAN GOD OF GARDENS AND FERTILITY.
HE WAS BEST KNOWN FOR HIS HUGE PENIS.
BACK PAIN DUE TO GIANT WANG.
How much is it?
100 euros.
Too expensive. Thank you.
60 euros.
I HAD ACCIDENTALLY HAGGLED.

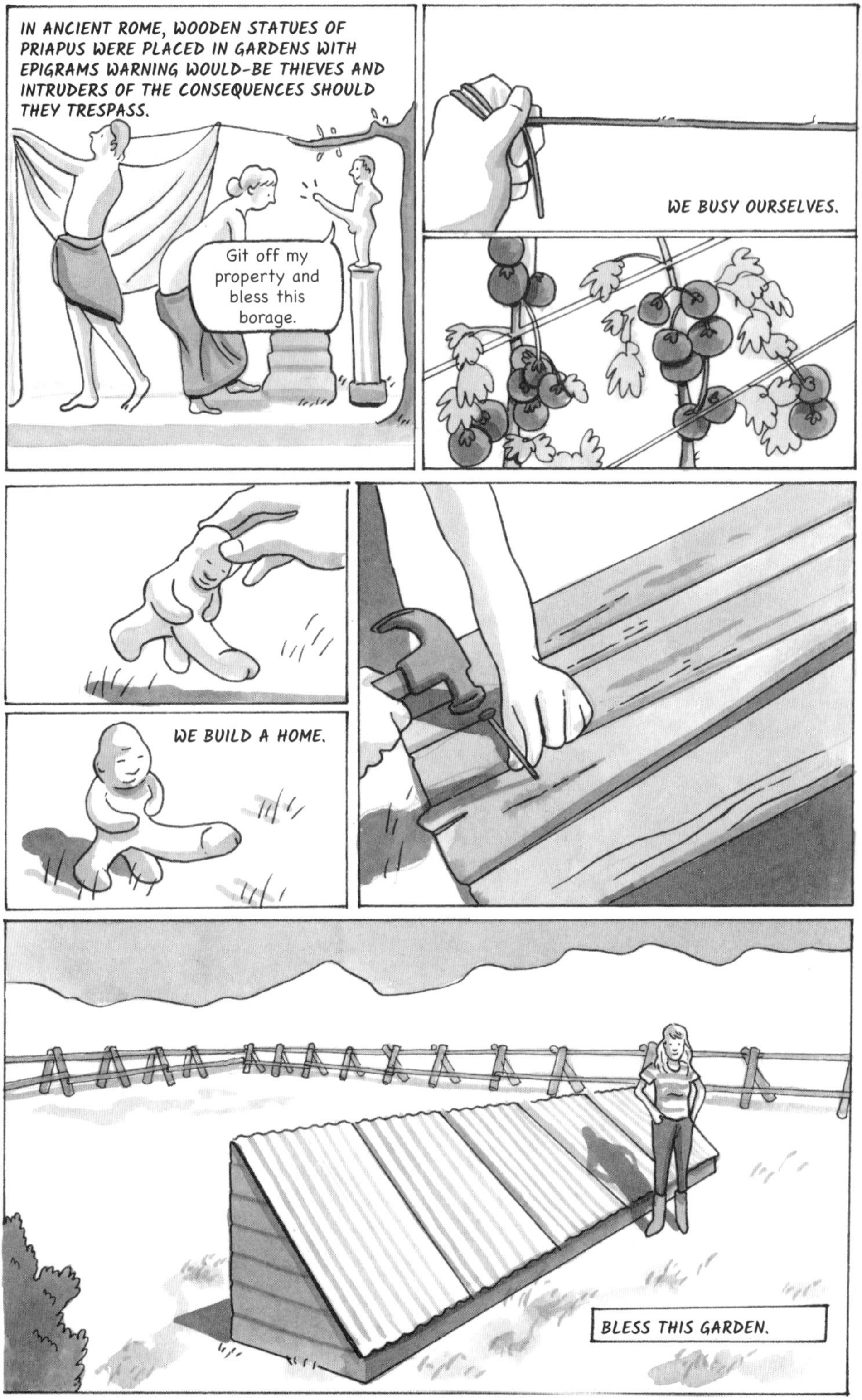
IN ANCIENT ROME, WOODEN STATUES OF PRIAPUS WERE PLACED IN GARDENS WITH EPIGRAMS WARNING WOULD-BE THIEVES AND INTRUDERS OF THE CONSEQUENCES SHOULD THEY TRESPASS.
Git off my property and bless this borage.
WE BUSY OURSELVES.
WE BUILD A HOME.
BLESS THIS GARDEN.

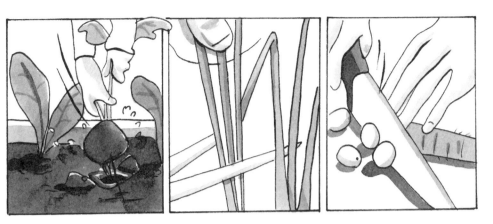

APRIL IS ALSO KNOWN AS THE "EGG MOON," LIKELY
BECAUSE BIRDS BEGIN TO LAY THEIR EGGS AFTER A LONG
AND BARREN WINTER.

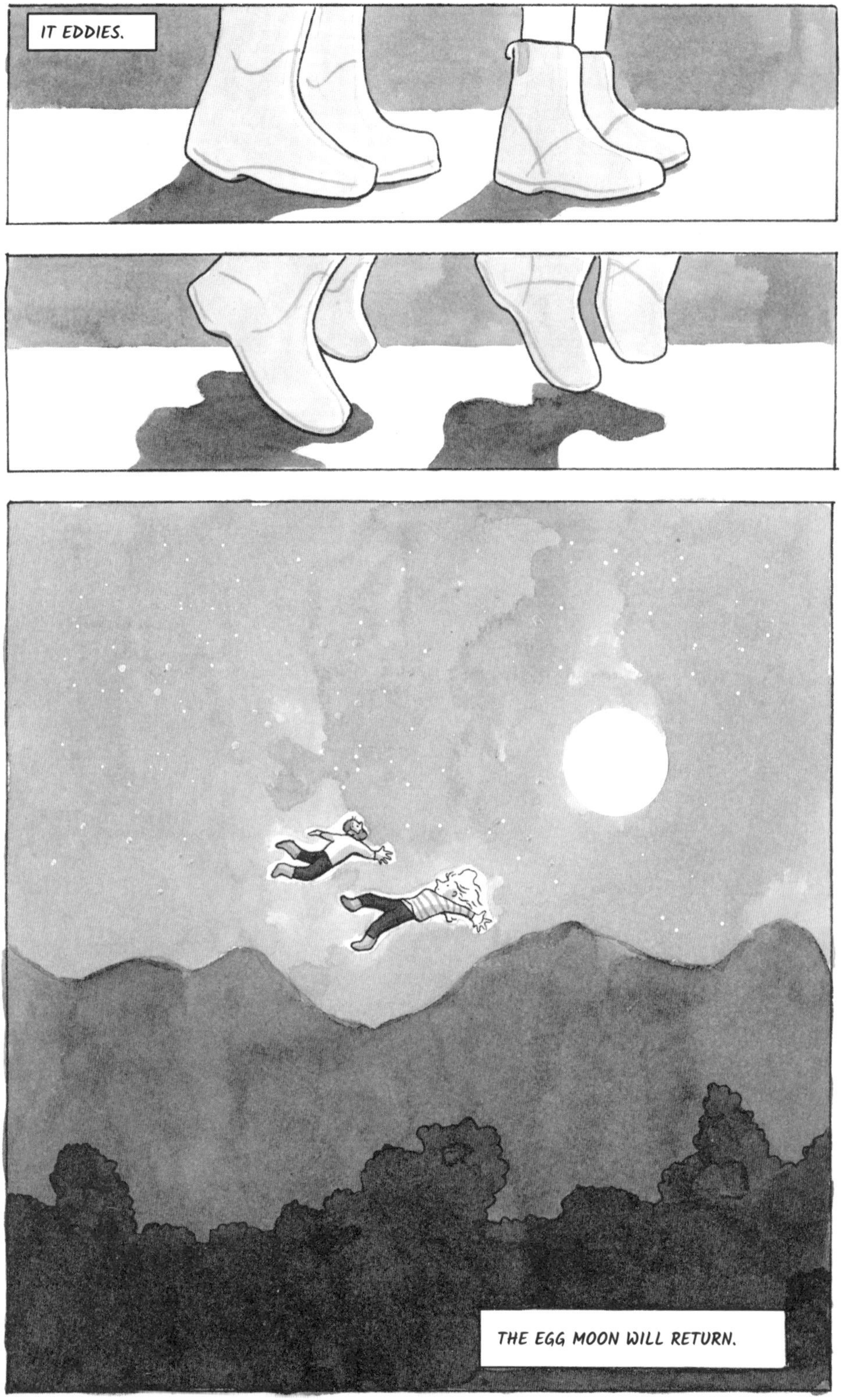
IT EDDIES.
THE EGG MOON WILL RETURN.

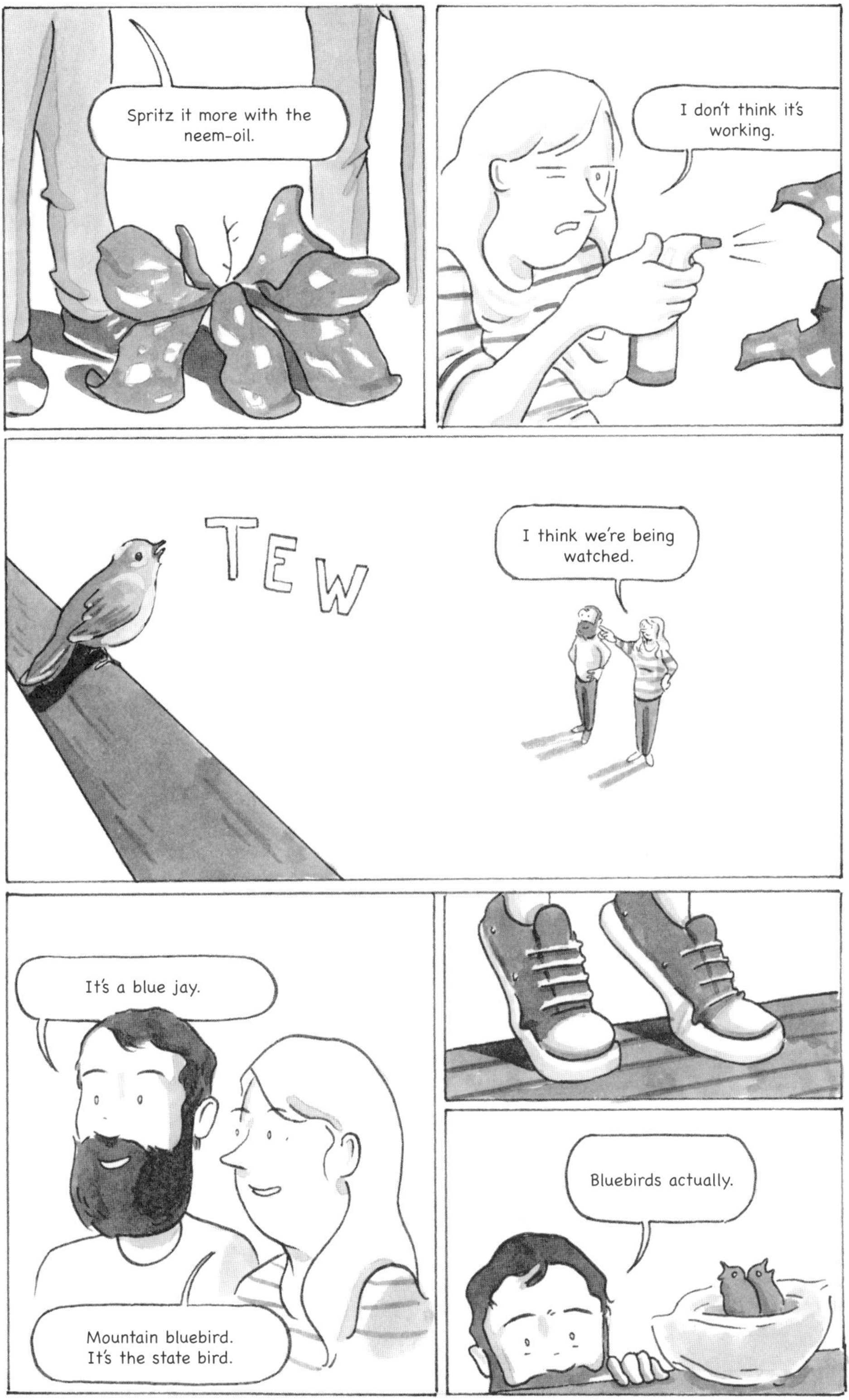
Spritz it more with the neem-oil.
I don't think it's working.
TEW
I think we're being watched.
It's a blue jay.
Mountain bluebird. It's the state bird.
Bluebirds actually.

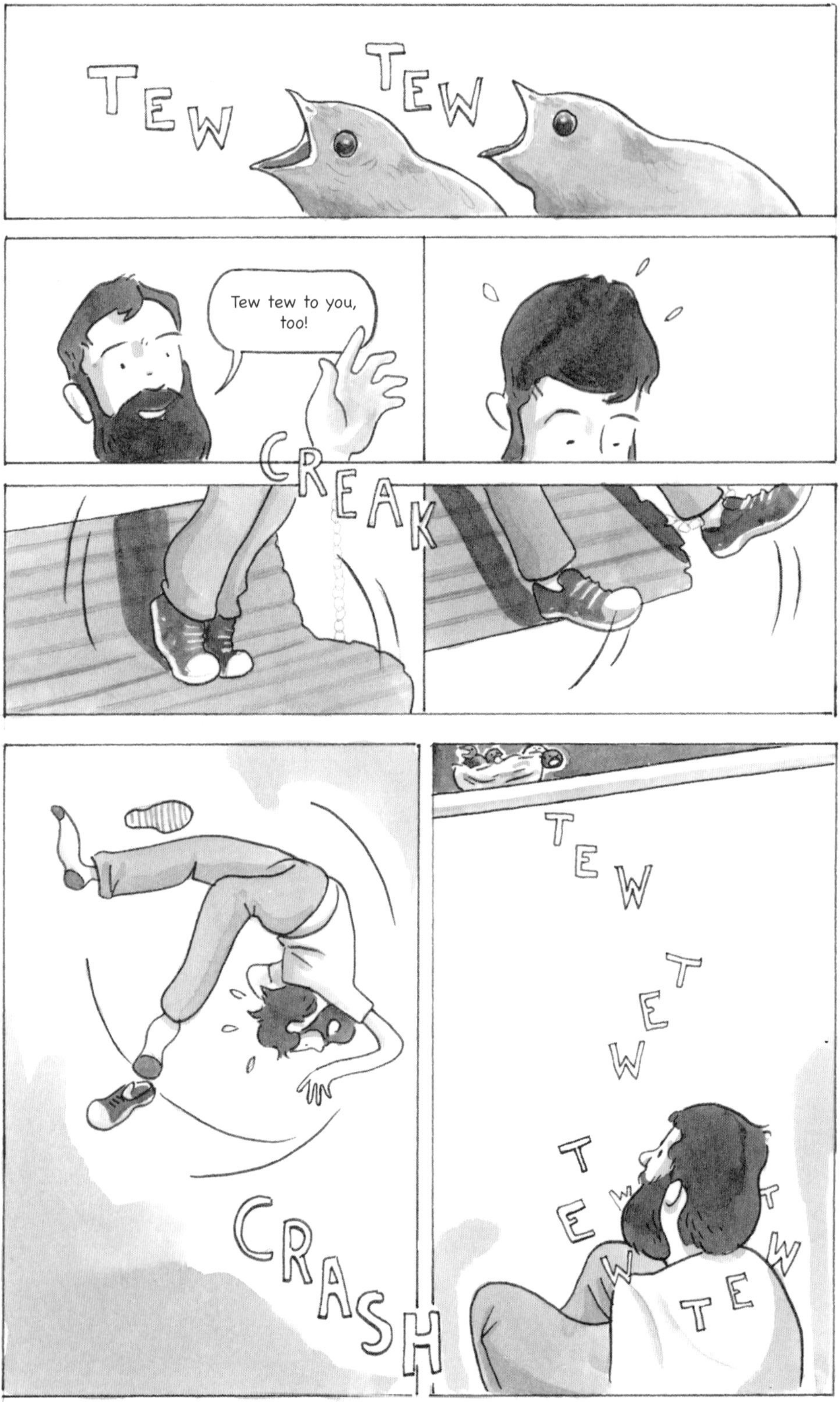

TEW TEW
Tew tew to you, too!
CREAK
CRASH
TEW
TWET
TEW
TEW
TEW

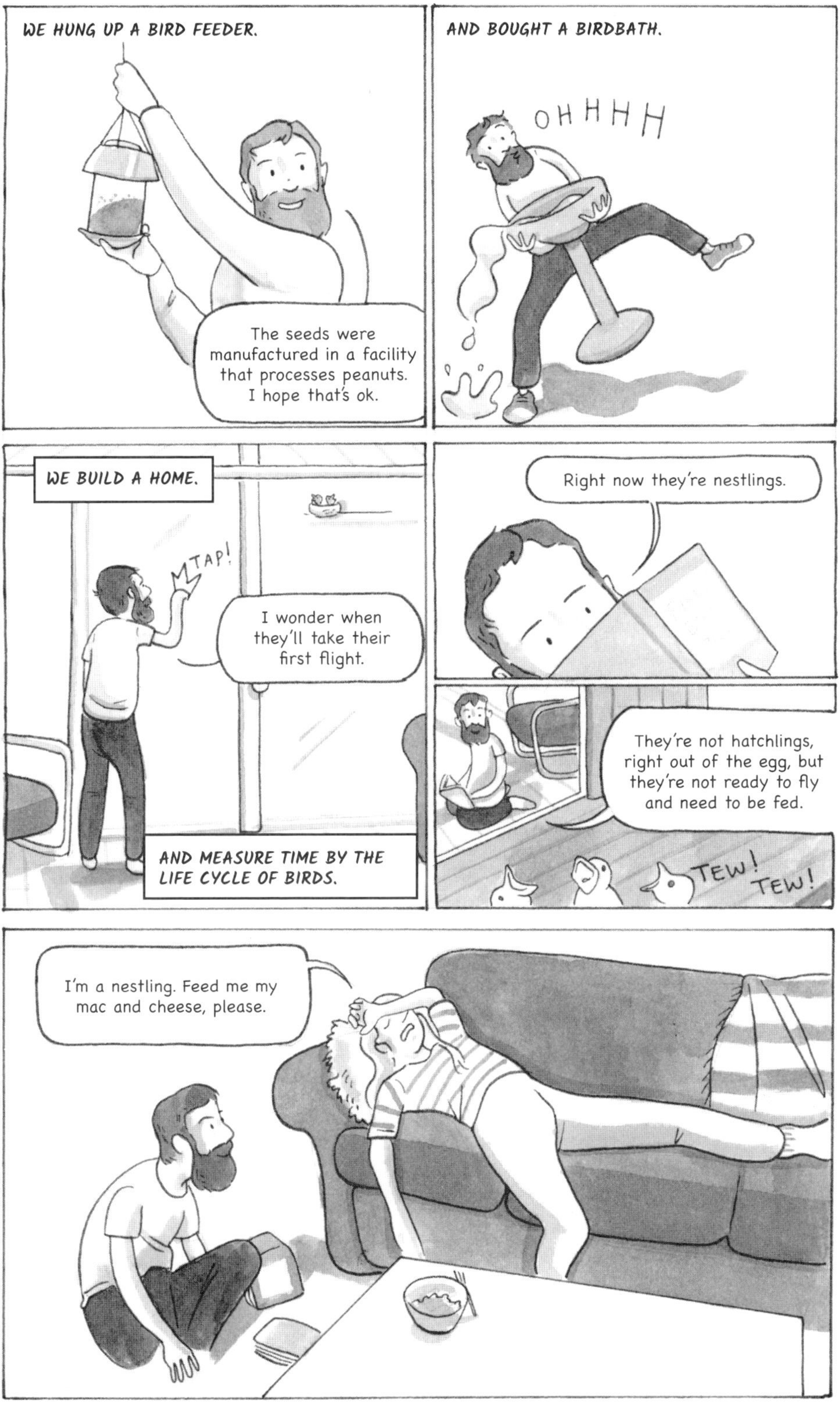

WE HUNG UP A BIRD FEEDER.
The seeds were manufactured in a facility that processes peanuts. I hope that's ok.
AND BOUGHT A BIRDBATH.
OHHHH
WE BUILD A HOME.
TAP!
I wonder when they'll take their first flight.
AND MEASURE TIME BY THE LIFE CYCLE OF BIRDS.
Right now they're nestlings.
They're not hatchlings, right out of the egg, but they're not ready to fly and need to be fed.
TEW! TEW!
I'm a nestling. Feed me my mac and cheese, please.

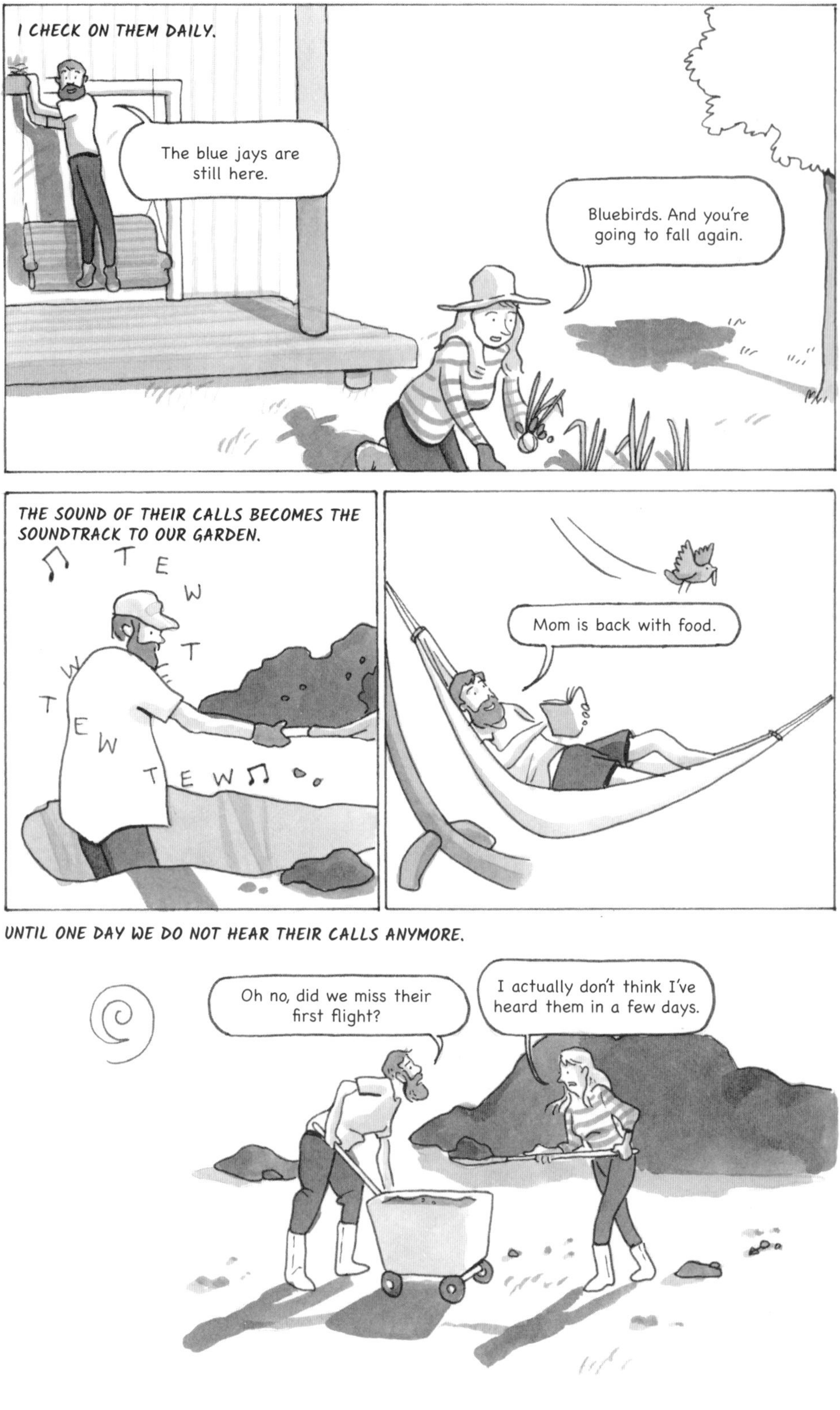
I CHECK ON THEM DAILY.
The blue jays are still here.
Bluebirds. And you're going to fall again.
THE SOUND OF THEIR CALLS BECOMES THE SOUNDTRACK TO OUR GARDEN.
TEW
TEW
TEW
TEW
Mom is back with food.
UNTIL ONE DAY WE DO NOT HEAR THEIR CALLS ANYMORE.
Oh no, did we miss their first flight?
I actually don't think I've heard them in a few days.

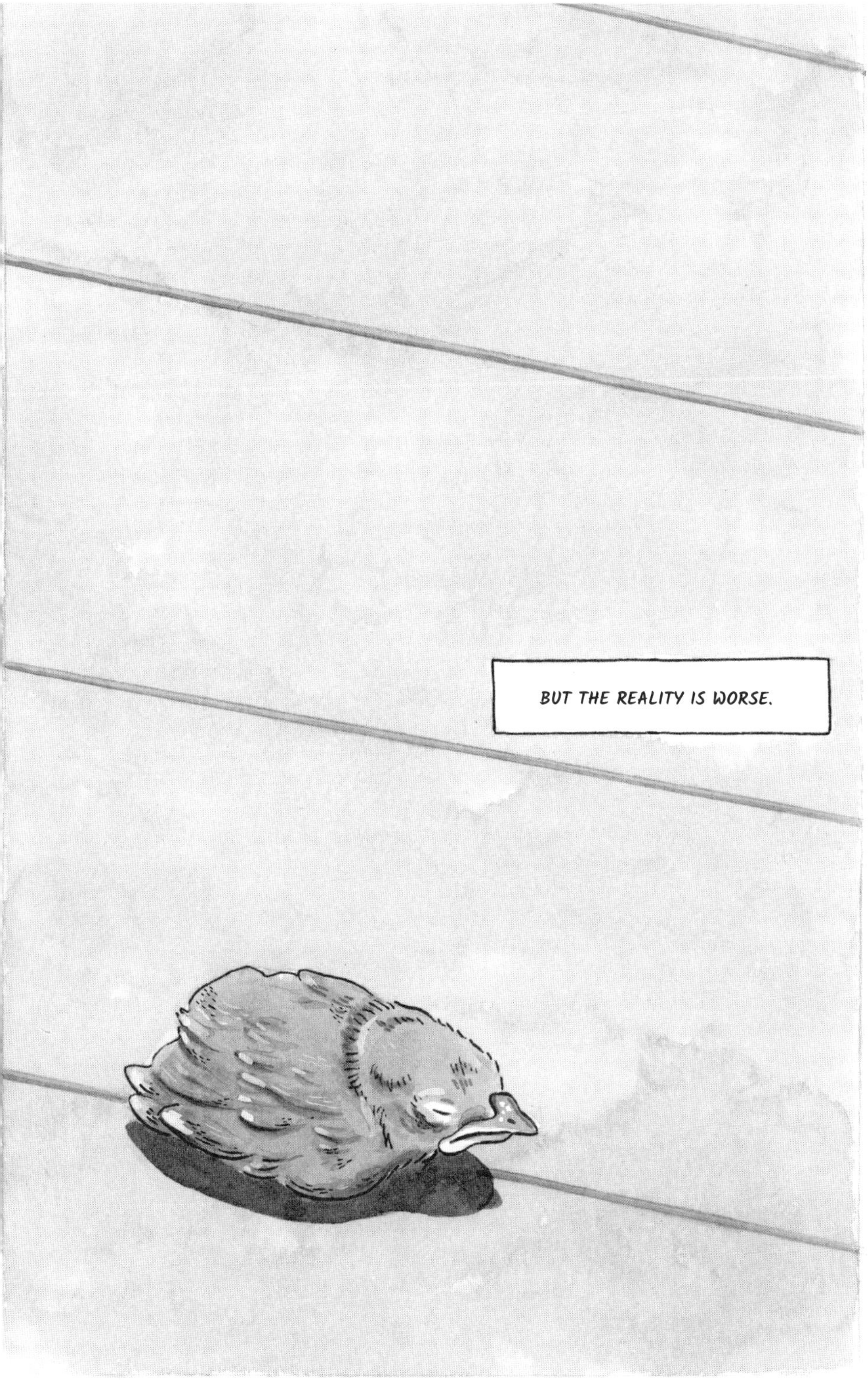
BUT THE REALITY IS WORSE.

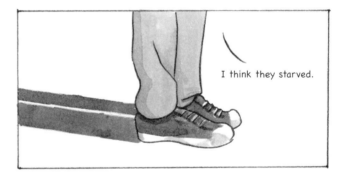

I think they starved.

IF ONE BIRD PARENT DIES OR DISAPPEARS, PARTICULARLY DURING THE NESTLING STAGE, THE REMAINING PARENT MAY ABANDON THE NEST TO SEARCH FOR A NEW MATE AND START OVER.

SINCE TWO PARENTS NEED TO WORK TOGETHER TO FEED THEIR NESTLINGS AND THEMSELVES, THE LOSS OF ONE PARENT MAY DOOM THE NESTLINGS.

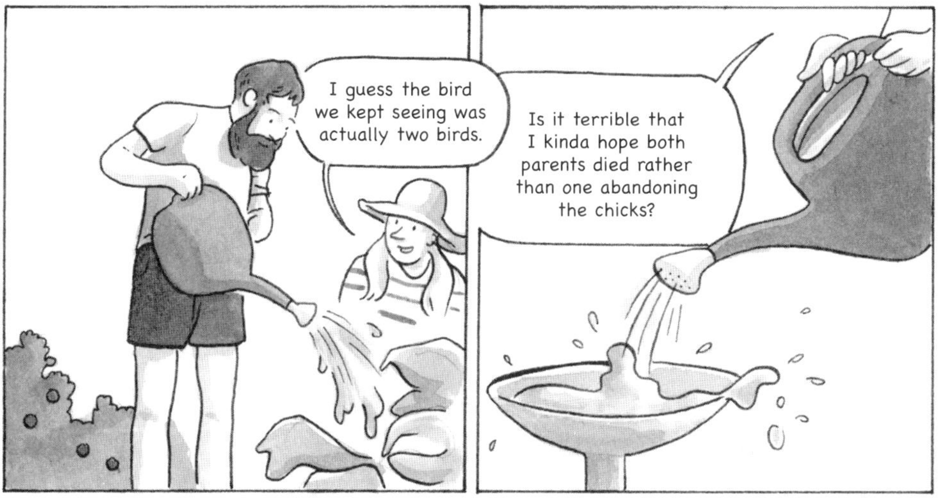
I guess the bird we kept seeing was actually two birds.
Is it terrible that I kinda hope both parents died rather than one abandoning the chicks?

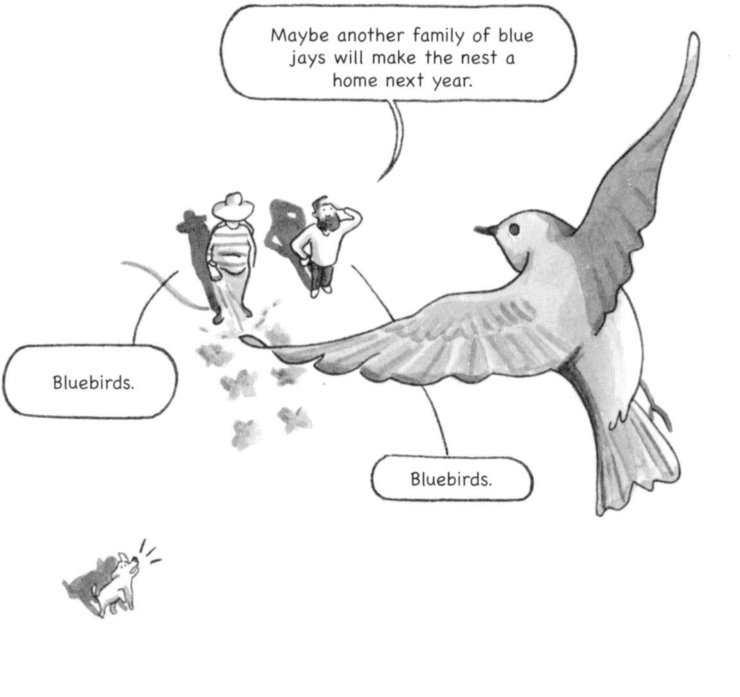
Maybe another family of blue jays will make the nest a home next year.
Bluebirds.
Bluebirds.

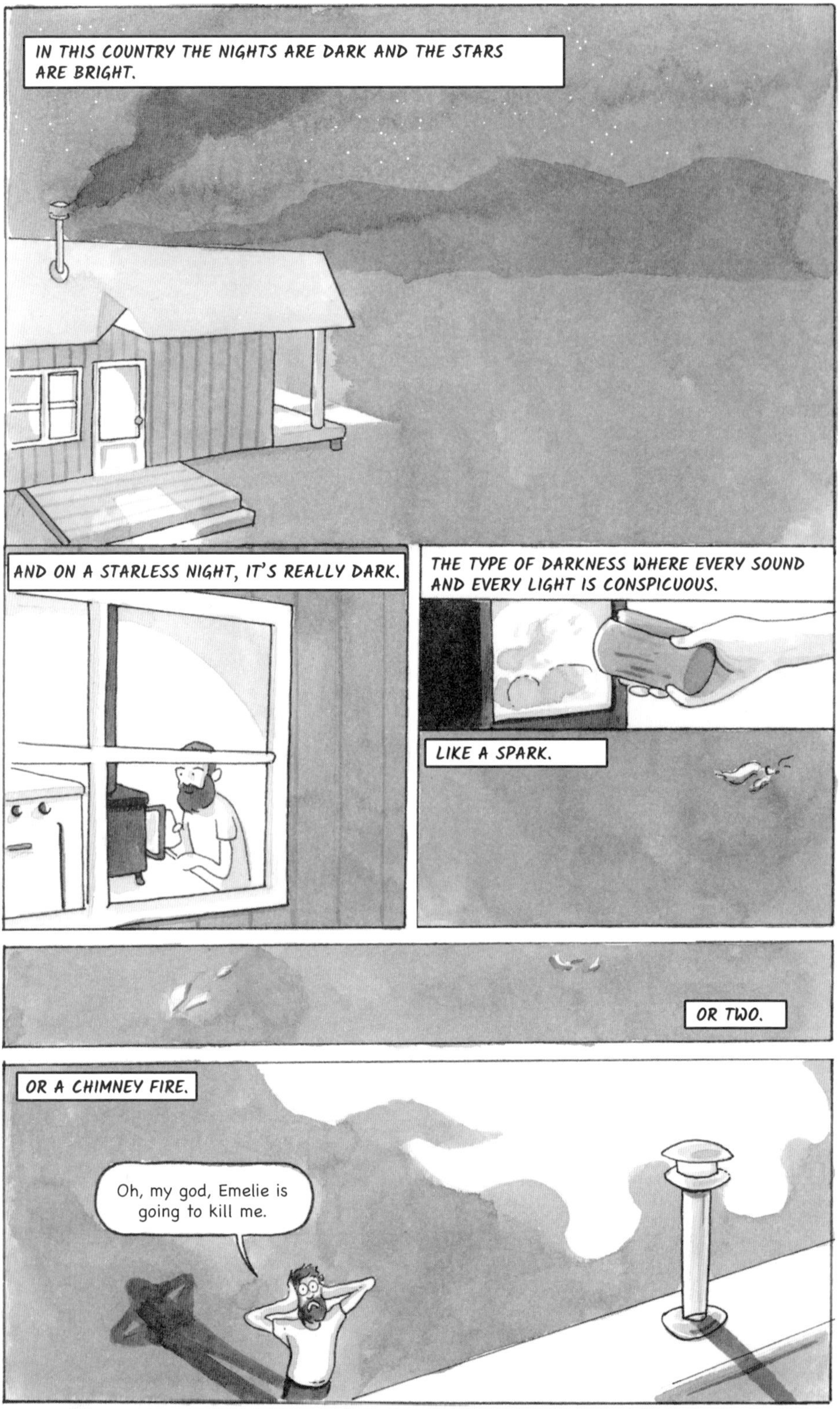
IN THIS COUNTRY THE NIGHTS ARE DARK AND THE STARS ARE BRIGHT.
AND ON A STARLESS NIGHT, IT'S REALLY DARK.
THE TYPE OF DARKNESS WHERE EVERY SOUND AND EVERY LIGHT IS CONSPICUOUS.
LIKE A SPARK.
OR TWO.
OR A CHIMNEY FIRE.
Oh, my god, Emelie is going to kill me.

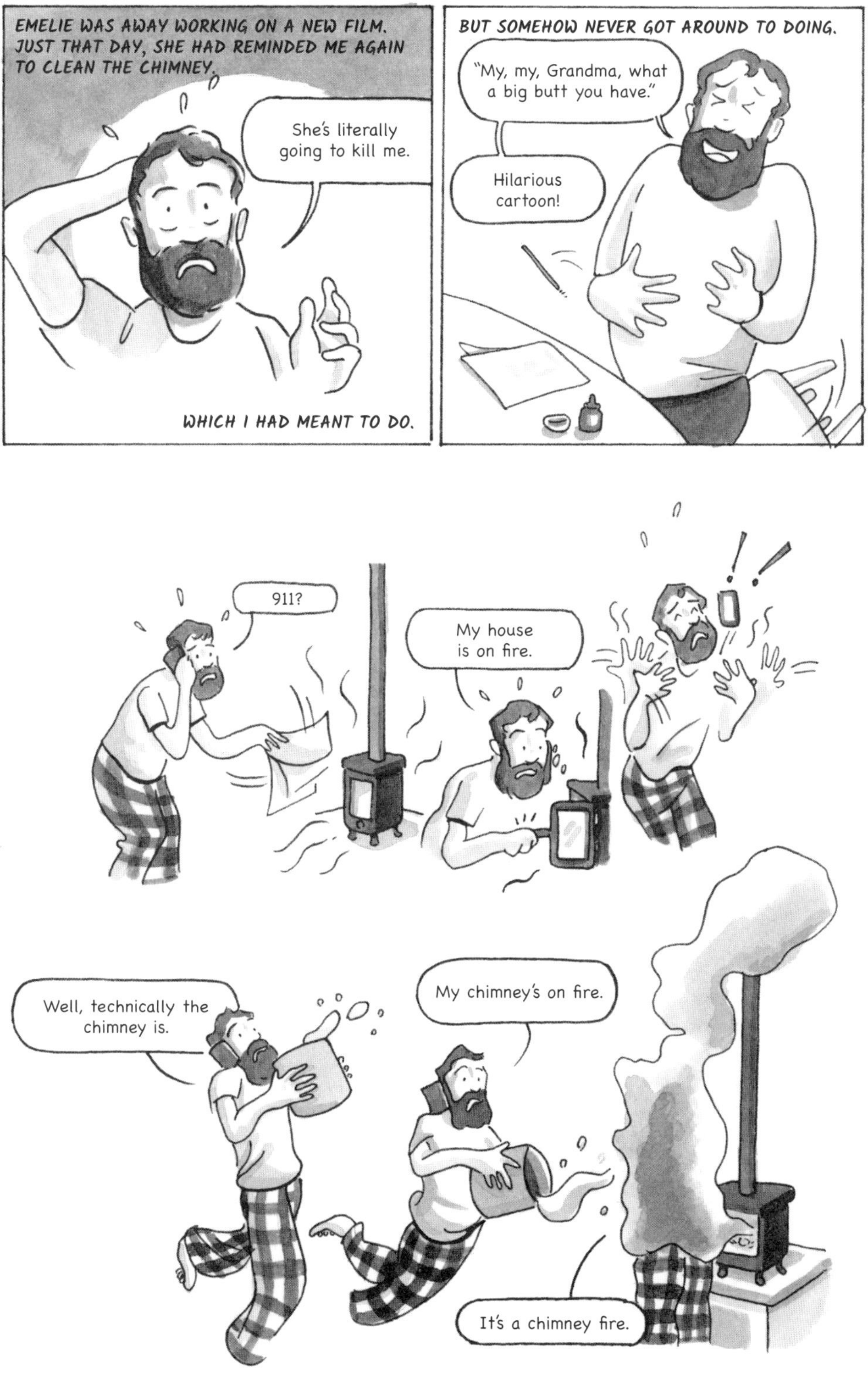
EMELIE WAS AWAY WORKING ON A NEW FILM. JUST THAT DAY, SHE HAD REMINDED ME AGAIN TO CLEAN THE CHIMNEY.
She's literally going to kill me.
WHICH I HAD MEANT TO DO.
BUT SOMEHOW NEVER GOT AROUND TO DOING.
"My, my, Grandma, what a big butt you have."
Hilarious cartoon!
911?
My house is on fire.
!!
Well, technically the chimney is.
My chimney's on fire.
It's a chimney fire.

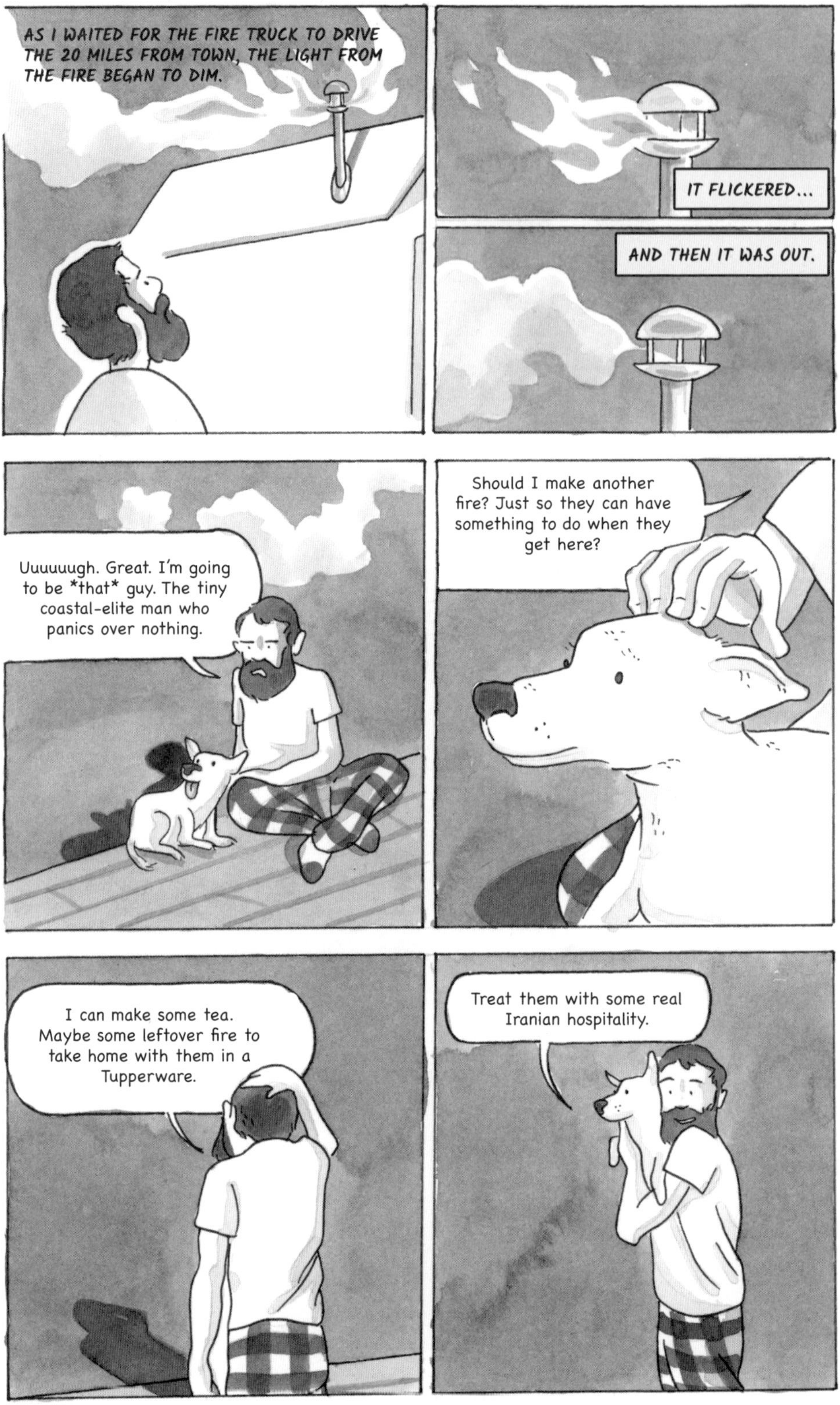
AS I WAITED FOR THE FIRE TRUCK TO DRIVE THE 20 MILES FROM TOWN, THE LIGHT FROM THE FIRE BEGAN TO DIM.
IT FLICKERED...
AND THEN IT WAS OUT.
Uuuuuugh. Great. I'm going to be *that* guy. The tiny coastal-elite man who panics over nothing.
Should I make another fire? Just so they can have something to do when they get here?
I can make some tea. Maybe some leftover fire to take home with them in a Tupperware.
Treat them with some real Iranian hospitality.

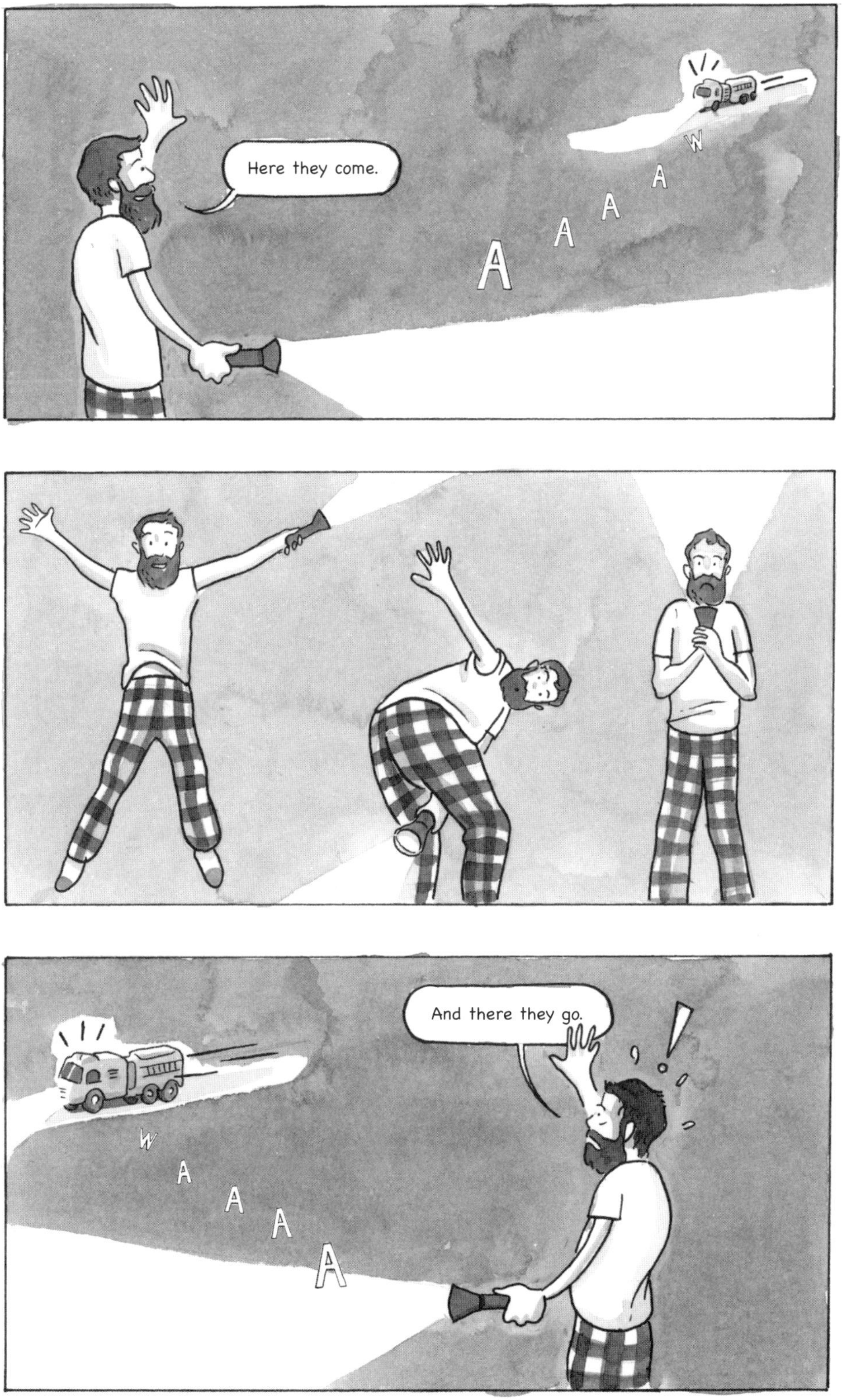
Here they come.
AAAAAW
WAAAAA
And there they go.
!

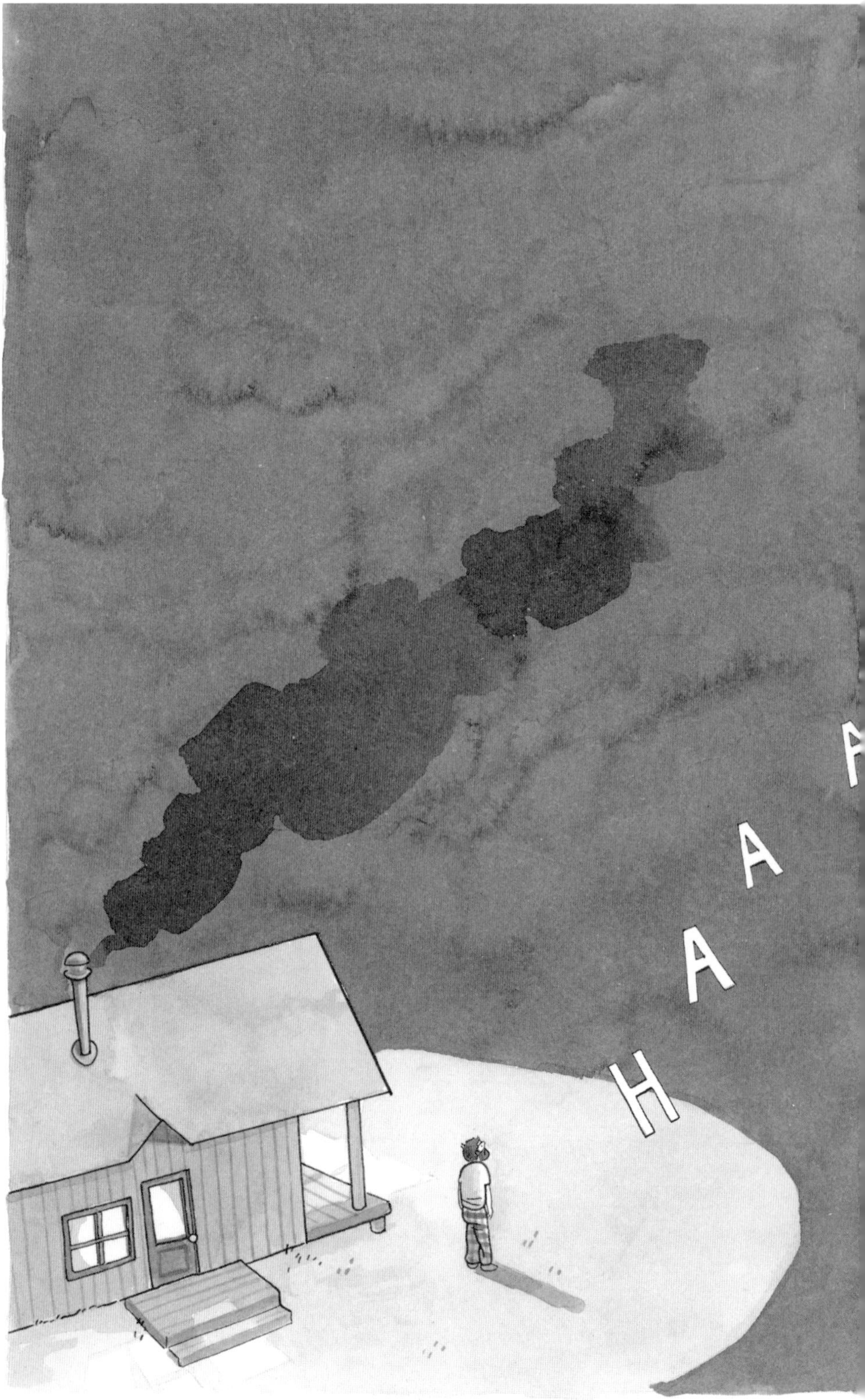

H A A

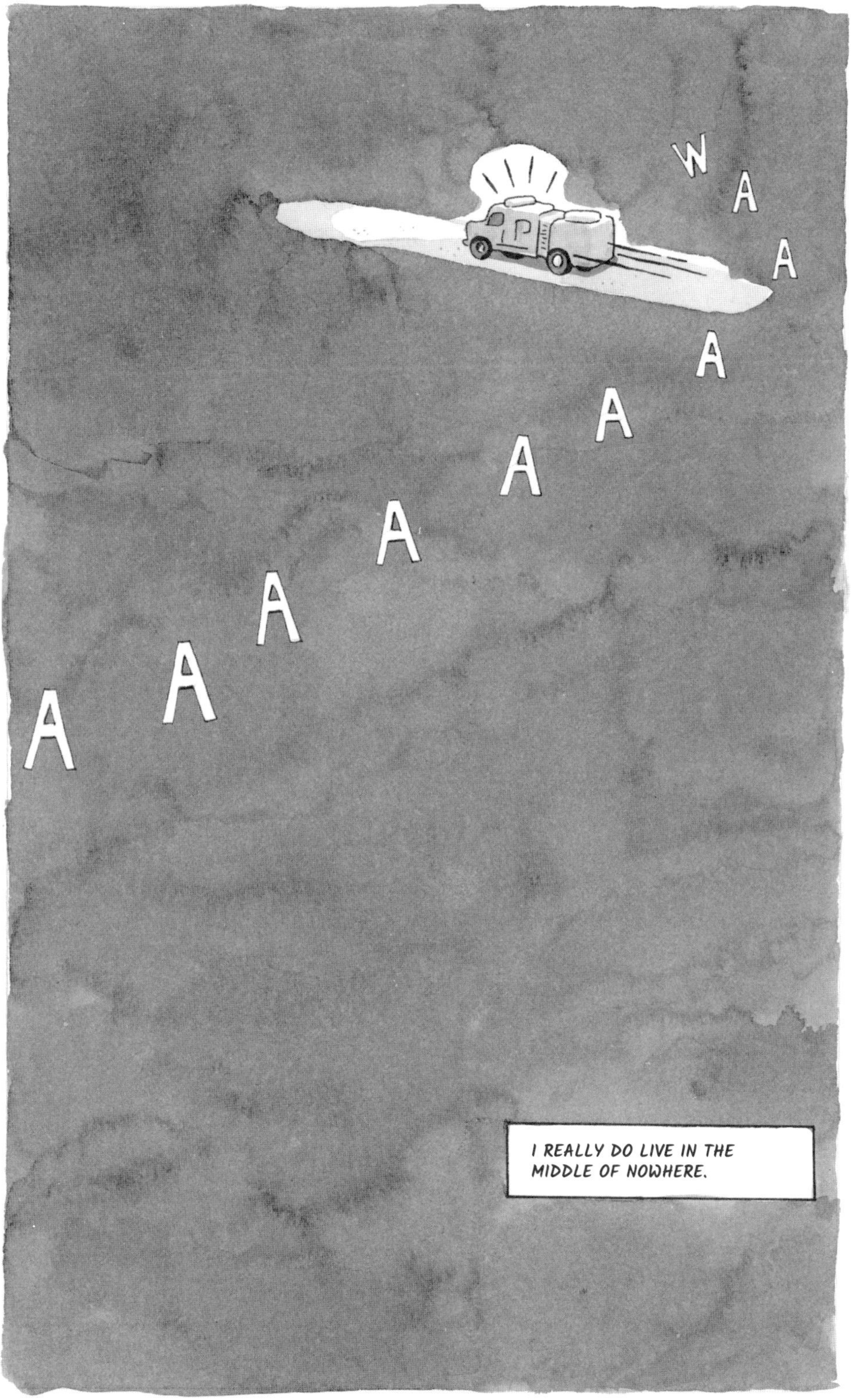
WAAAAAAAAAA
I REALLY DO LIVE IN THE MIDDLE OF NOWHERE.

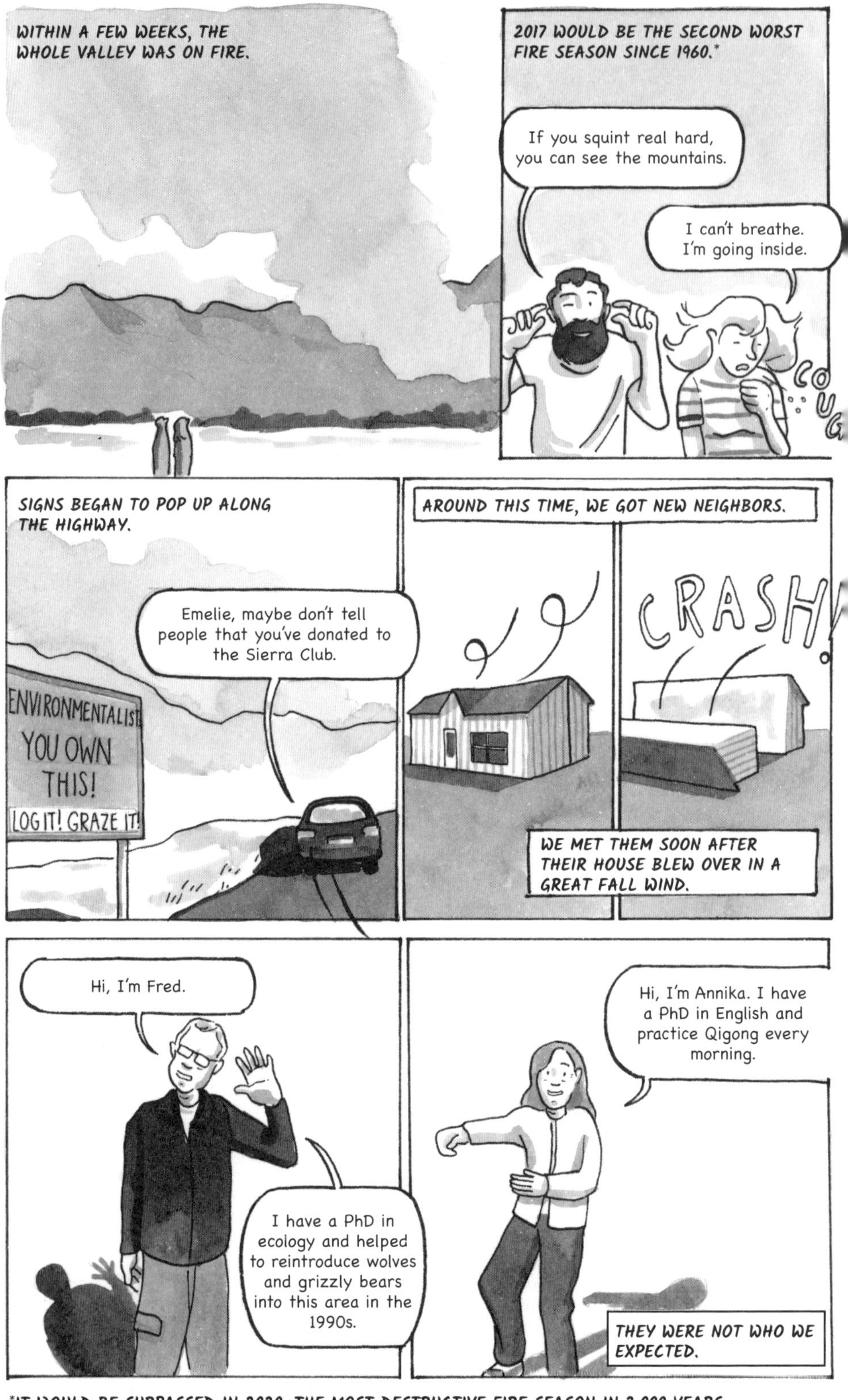

WITHIN A FEW WEEKS, THE WHOLE VALLEY WAS ON FIRE.
2017 WOULD BE THE SECOND WORST FIRE SEASON SINCE 1960.*
If you squint real hard, you can see the mountains.
I can't breathe. I'm going inside.
COUG
SIGNS BEGAN TO POP UP ALONG THE HIGHWAY.
Emelie, maybe don't tell people that you've donated to the Sierra Club.
ENVIRONMENTALIST
YOU OWN THIS!
LOG IT! GRAZE IT!
AROUND THIS TIME, WE GOT NEW NEIGHBORS.
CRASH!
WE MET THEM SOON AFTER THEIR HOUSE BLEW OVER IN A GREAT FALL WIND.
Hi, I'm Fred.
I have a PhD in ecology and helped to reintroduce wolves and grizzly bears into this area in the 1990s.
Hi, I'm Annika. I have a PhD in English and practice Qigong every morning.
THEY WERE NOT WHO WE EXPECTED.

*IT WOULD BE SURPASSED IN 2020, THE MOST DESTRUCTIVE FIRE SEASON IN 2,000 YEARS.

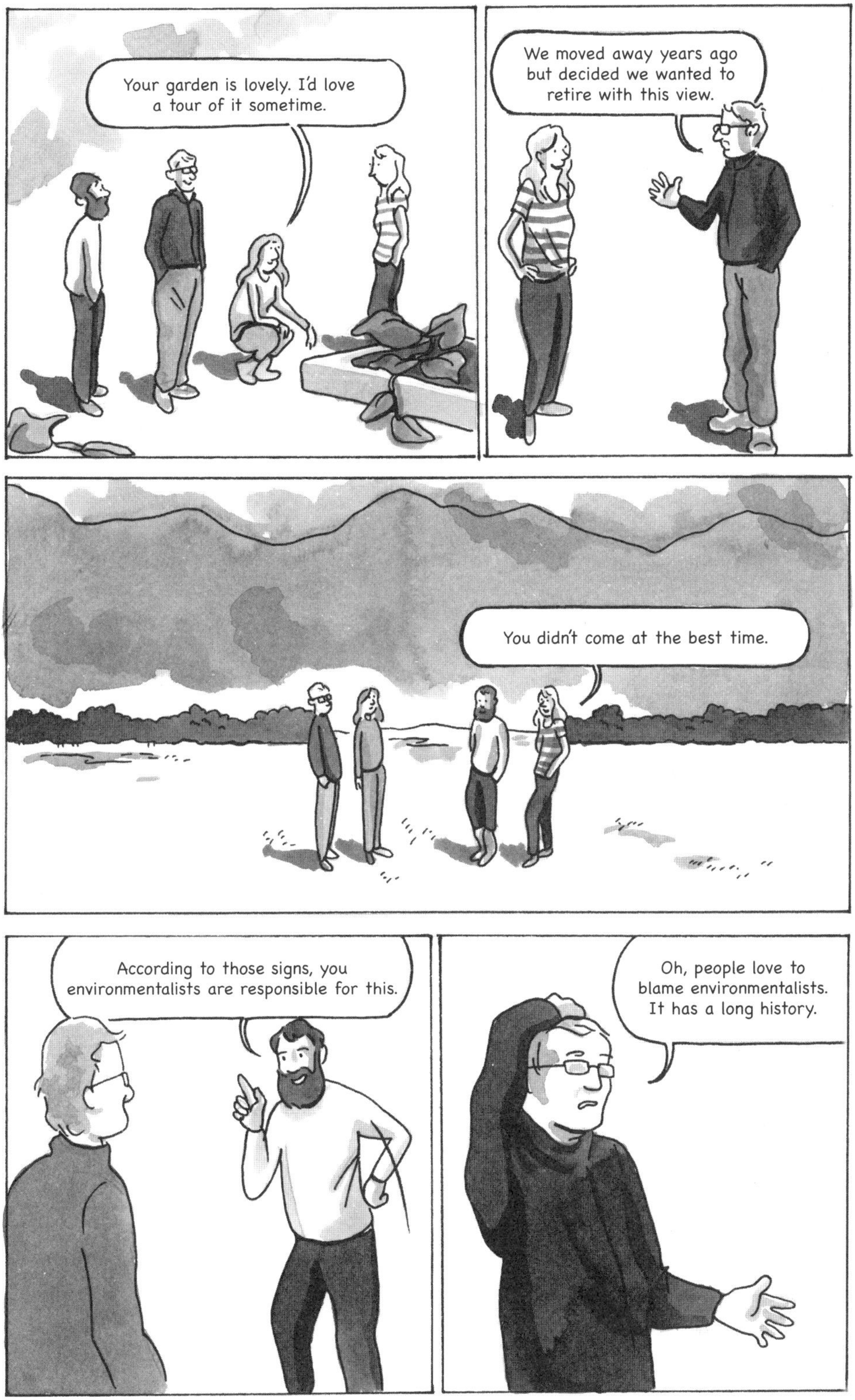
Your garden is lovely. I'd love a tour of it sometime.
We moved away years ago but decided we wanted to retire with this view.
You didn't come at the best time.
According to those signs, you environmentalists are responsible for this.
Oh, people love to blame environmentalists. It has a long history.

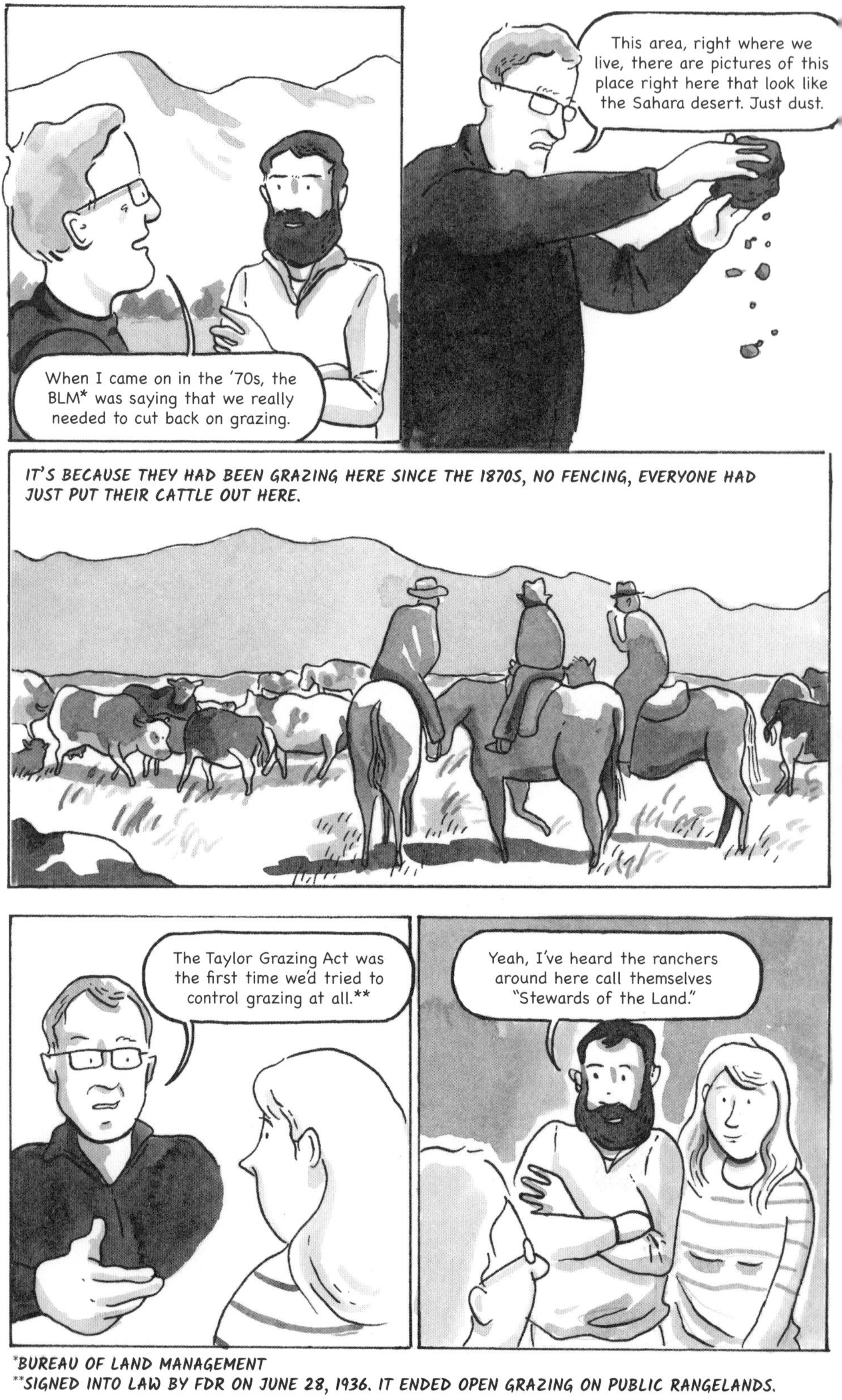
When I came on in the '70s, the BLM* was saying that we really needed to cut back on grazing.
This area, right where we live, there are pictures of this place right here that look like the Sahara desert. Just dust.
IT'S BECAUSE THEY HAD BEEN GRAZING HERE SINCE THE 1870S, NO FENCING, EVERYONE HAD JUST PUT THEIR CATTLE OUT HERE.
The Taylor Grazing Act was the first time we'd tried to control grazing at all.**
Yeah, I've heard the ranchers around here call themselves "Stewards of the Land."

*BUREAU OF LAND MANAGEMENT

**SIGNED INTO LAW BY FDR ON JUNE 28, 1936. IT ENDED OPEN GRAZING ON PUBLIC RANGELANDS.

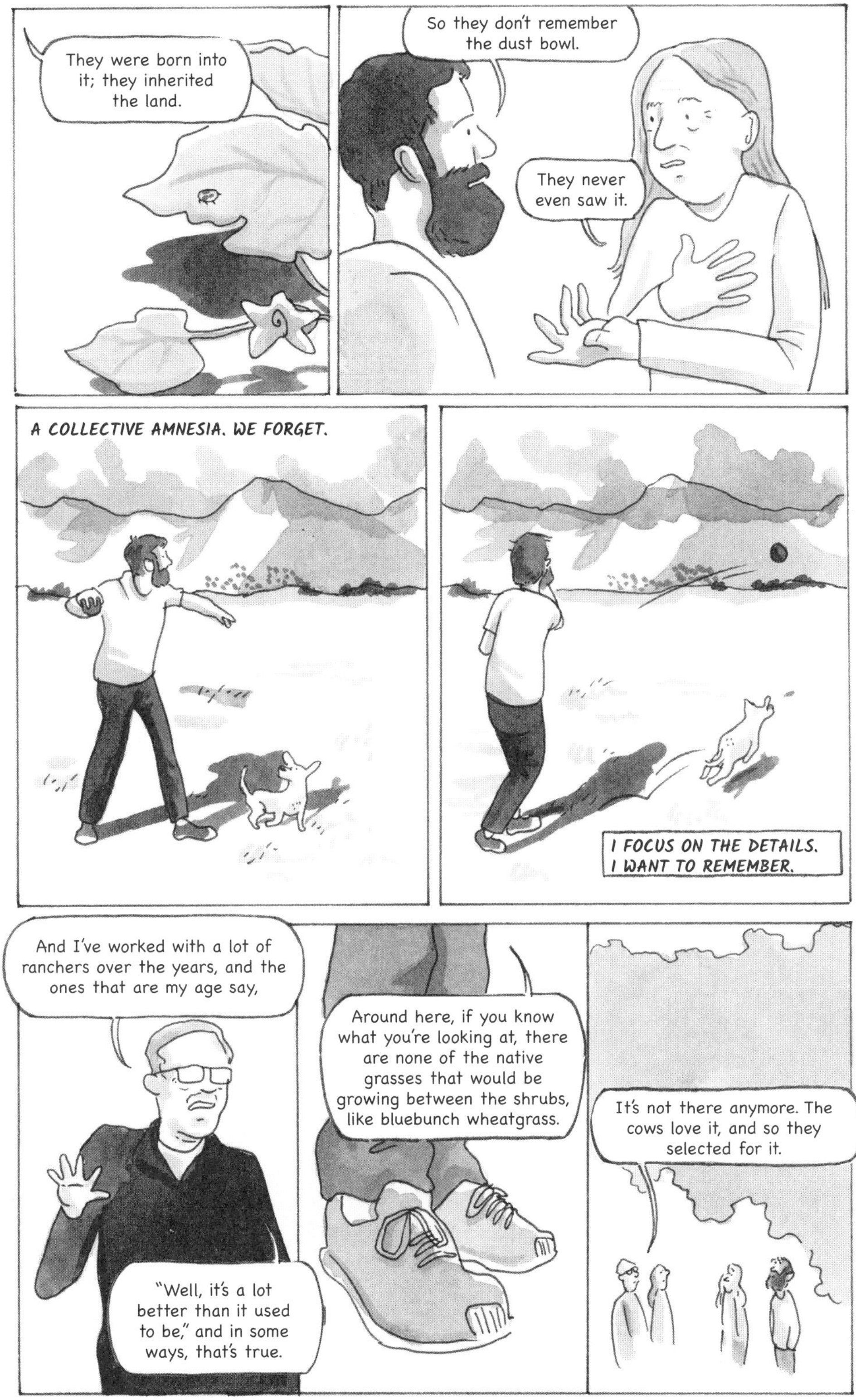
They were born into it; they inherited the land.
So they don't remember the dust bowl.
They never even saw it.
A COLLECTIVE AMNESIA. WE FORGET.
I FOCUS ON THE DETAILS. I WANT TO REMEMBER.
And I've worked with a lot of ranchers over the years, and the ones that are my age say,
"Well, it's a lot better than it used to be," and in some ways, that's true.
Around here, if you know what you're looking at, there are none of the native grasses that would be growing between the shrubs, like bluebunch wheatgrass.
It's not there anymore. The cows love it, and so they selected for it.

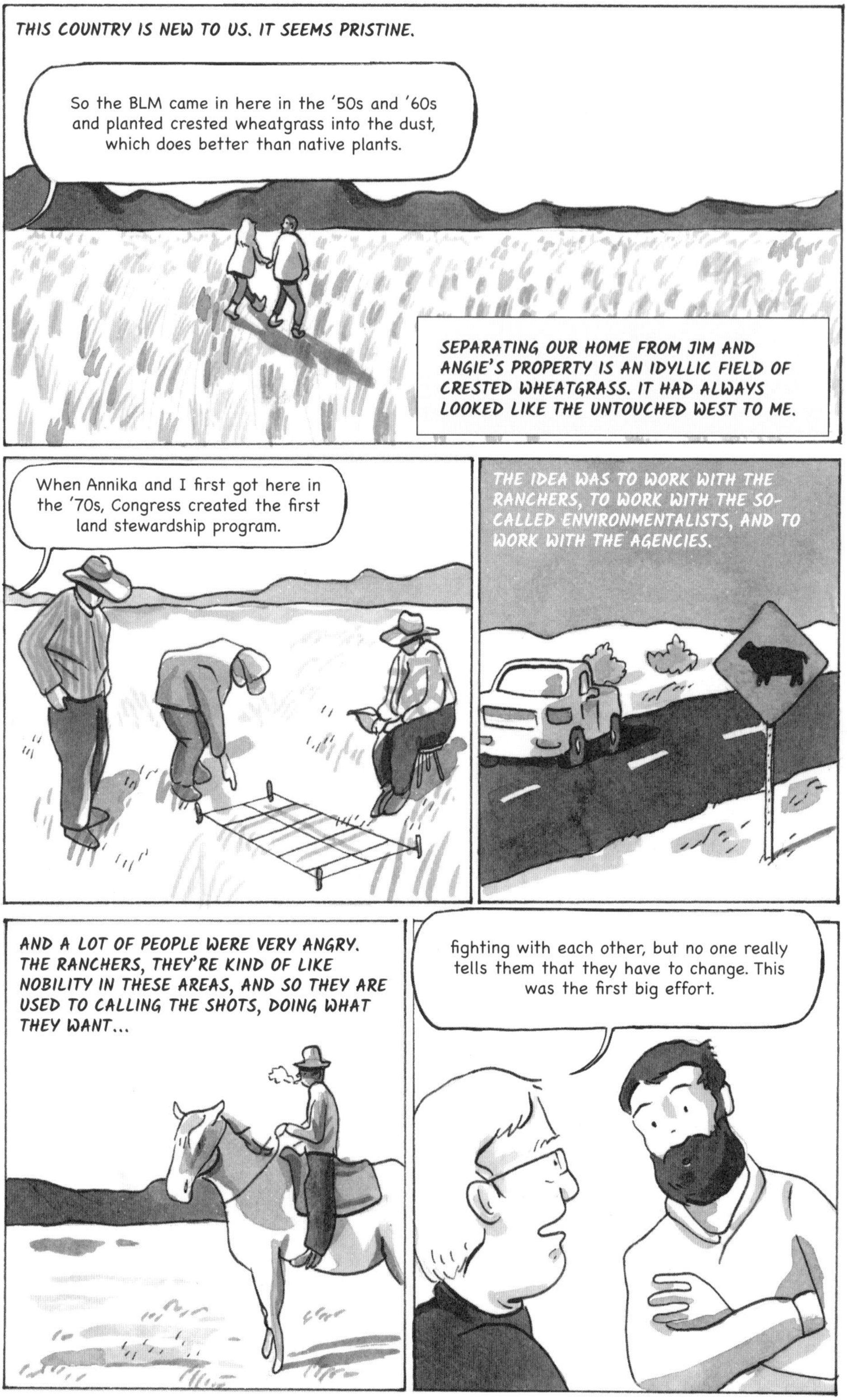
THIS COUNTRY IS NEW TO US. IT SEEMS PRISTINE.
So the BLM came in here in the '50s and '60s and planted crested wheatgrass into the dust, which does better than native plants.
SEPARATING OUR HOME FROM JIM AND ANGIE'S PROPERTY IS AN IDYLLIC FIELD OF CRESTED WHEATGRASS. IT HAD ALWAYS LOOKED LIKE THE UNTOUCHED WEST TO ME.
When Annika and I first got here in the '70s, Congress created the first land stewardship program.
THE IDEA WAS TO WORK WITH THE RANCHERS, TO WORK WITH THE SO-CALLED ENVIRONMENTALISTS, AND TO WORK WITH THE AGENCIES.
AND A LOT OF PEOPLE WERE VERY ANGRY. THE RANCHERS, THEY'RE KIND OF LIKE NOBILITY IN THESE AREAS, AND SO THEY ARE USED TO CALLING THE SHOTS, DOING WHAT THEY WANT...
fighting with each other, but no one really tells them that they have to change. This was the first big effort.

I CAN'T IMAGINE TELLING THE PEOPLE HERE TODAY THAT THEY HAVE TO CHANGE, LET ALONE TELLING THEM 50 YEARS AGO.

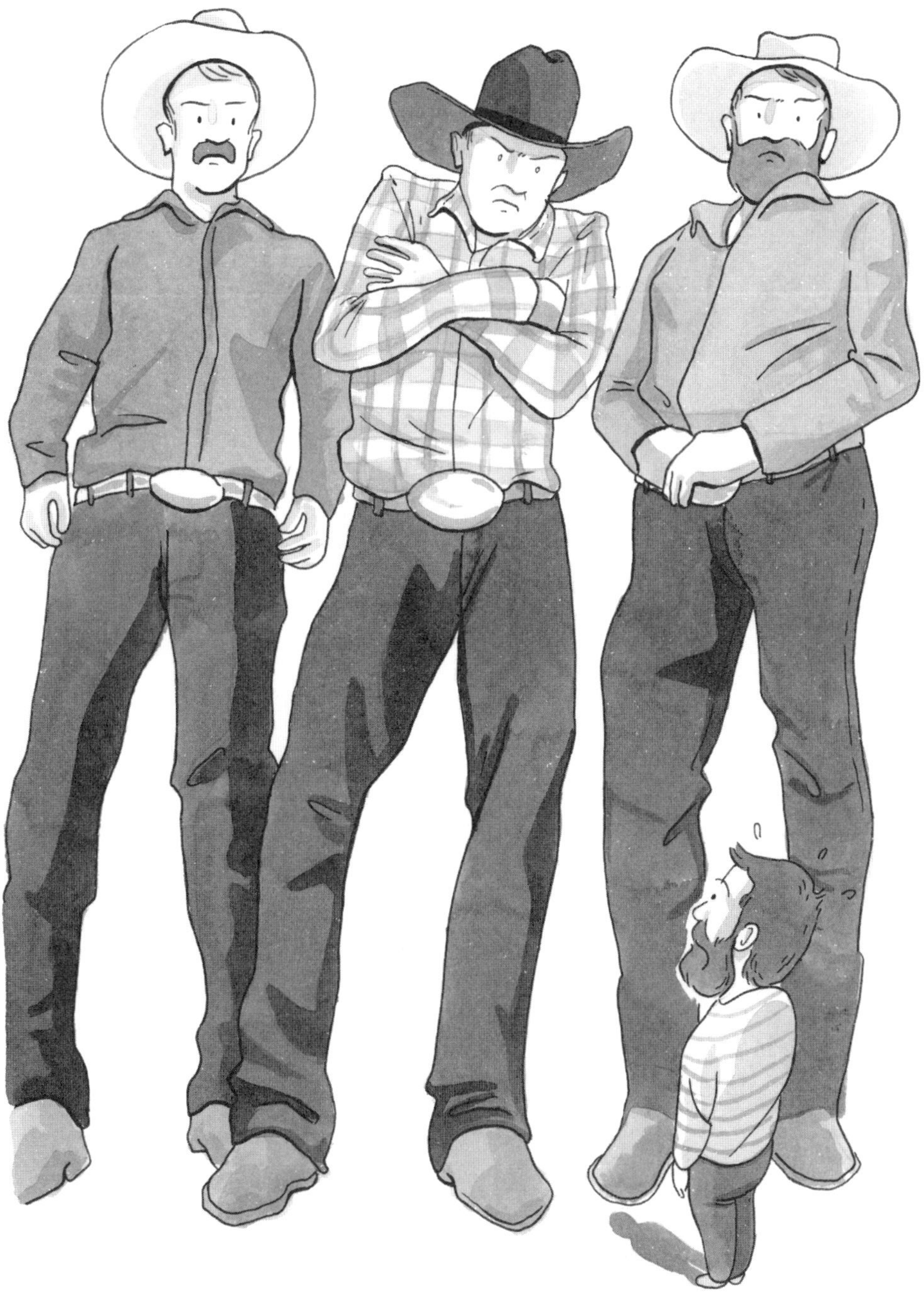

Most of those guys are gone now, but their kids are here, and they've carried on their parents' outlook.

I KNEW THIS ONE GUY WHO WORKED HERE WHO WAS GOING TO GO OUT ON ONE OF THESE "SHOW ME" TOURS, AND THE RANCHERS TOLD HIM, WE'RE GOING TO KILL YOU.

WHEN I WAS HERE WORKING ON MY MASTER'S DEGREE, ONE OF THESE GUYS TOLD ME THAT IF HE SAW ME IN A HELICOPTER AGAIN, HE'D SHOOT ME OUT OF THE AIR.

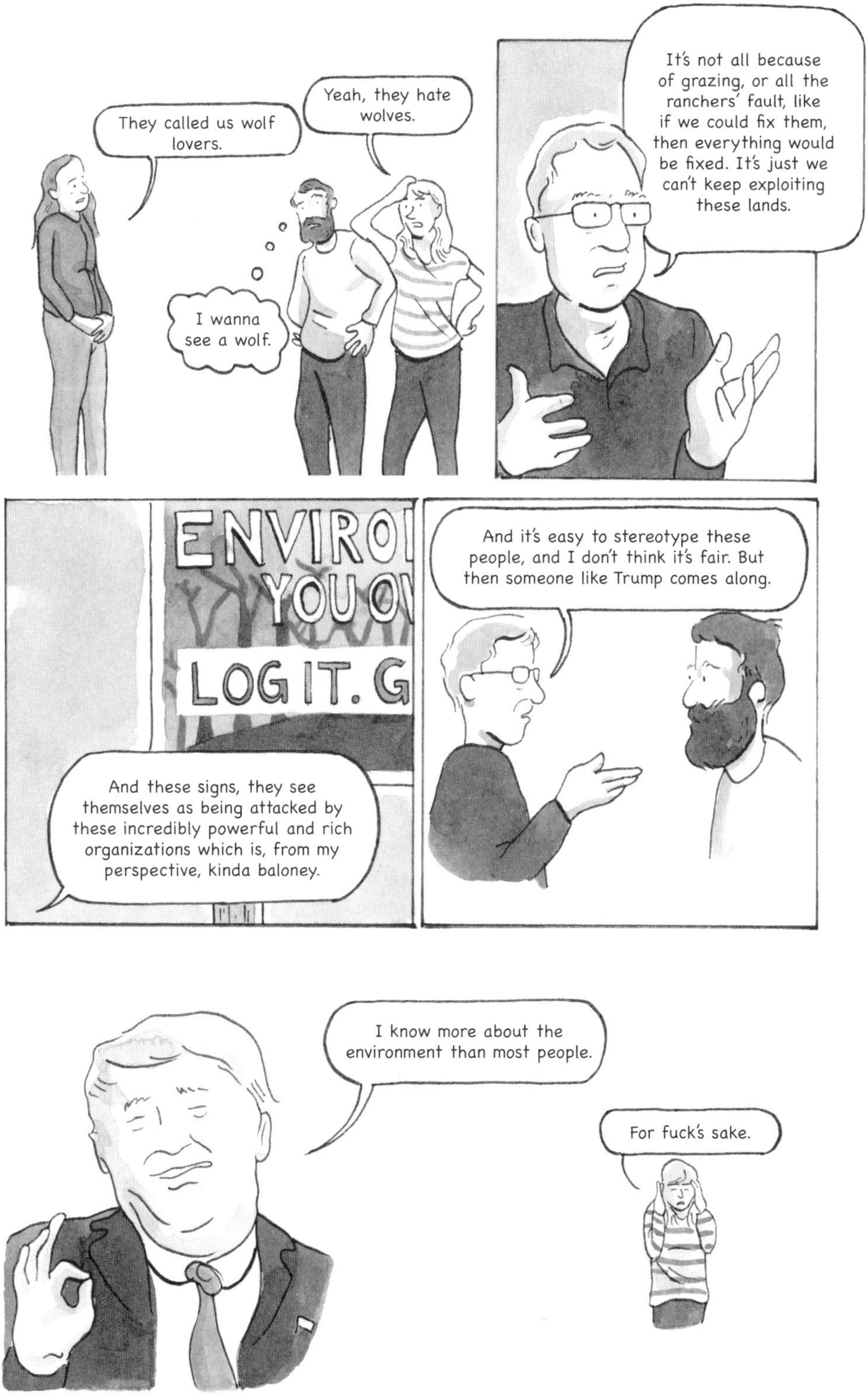

They called us wolf lovers.
Yeah, they hate wolves.
I wanna see a wolf.
It's not all because of grazing, or all the ranchers' fault, like if we could fix them, then everything would be fixed. It's just we can't keep exploiting these lands.
ENVIRO
YOU O
LOG IT. G
And these signs, they see themselves as being attacked by these incredibly powerful and rich organizations which is, from my perspective, kinda baloney.
And it's easy to stereotype these people, and I don't think it's fair. But then someone like Trump comes along.
I know more about the environment than most people.
For fuck's sake.

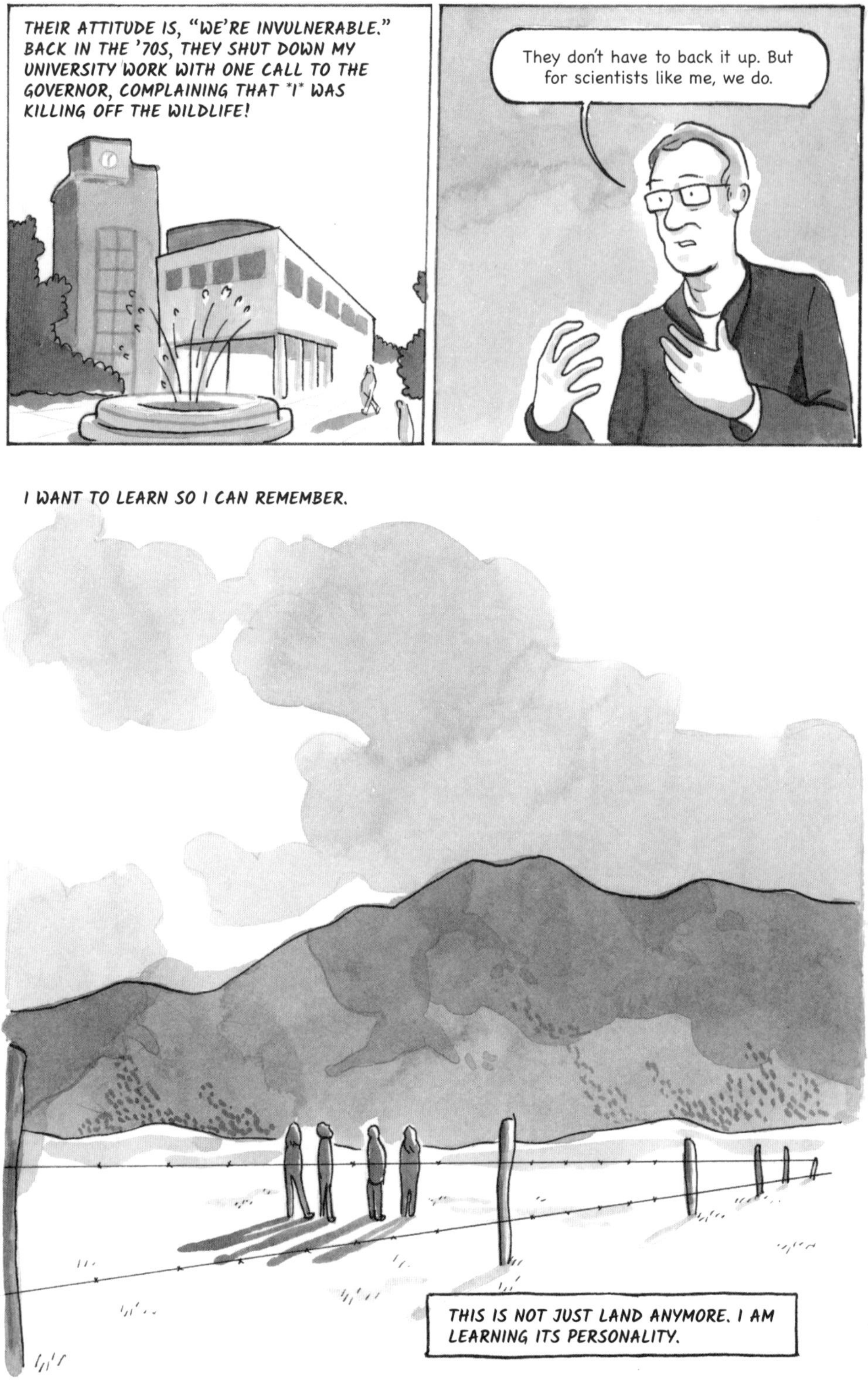
THEIR ATTITUDE IS, "WE'RE INVULNERABLE." BACK IN THE '70S, THEY SHUT DOWN MY UNIVERSITY WORK WITH ONE CALL TO THE GOVERNOR, COMPLAINING THAT *I* WAS KILLING OFF THE WILDLIFE!
They don't have to back it up. But for scientists like me, we do.
I WANT TO LEARN SO I CAN REMEMBER.
THIS IS NOT JUST LAND ANYMORE. I AM LEARNING ITS PERSONALITY.

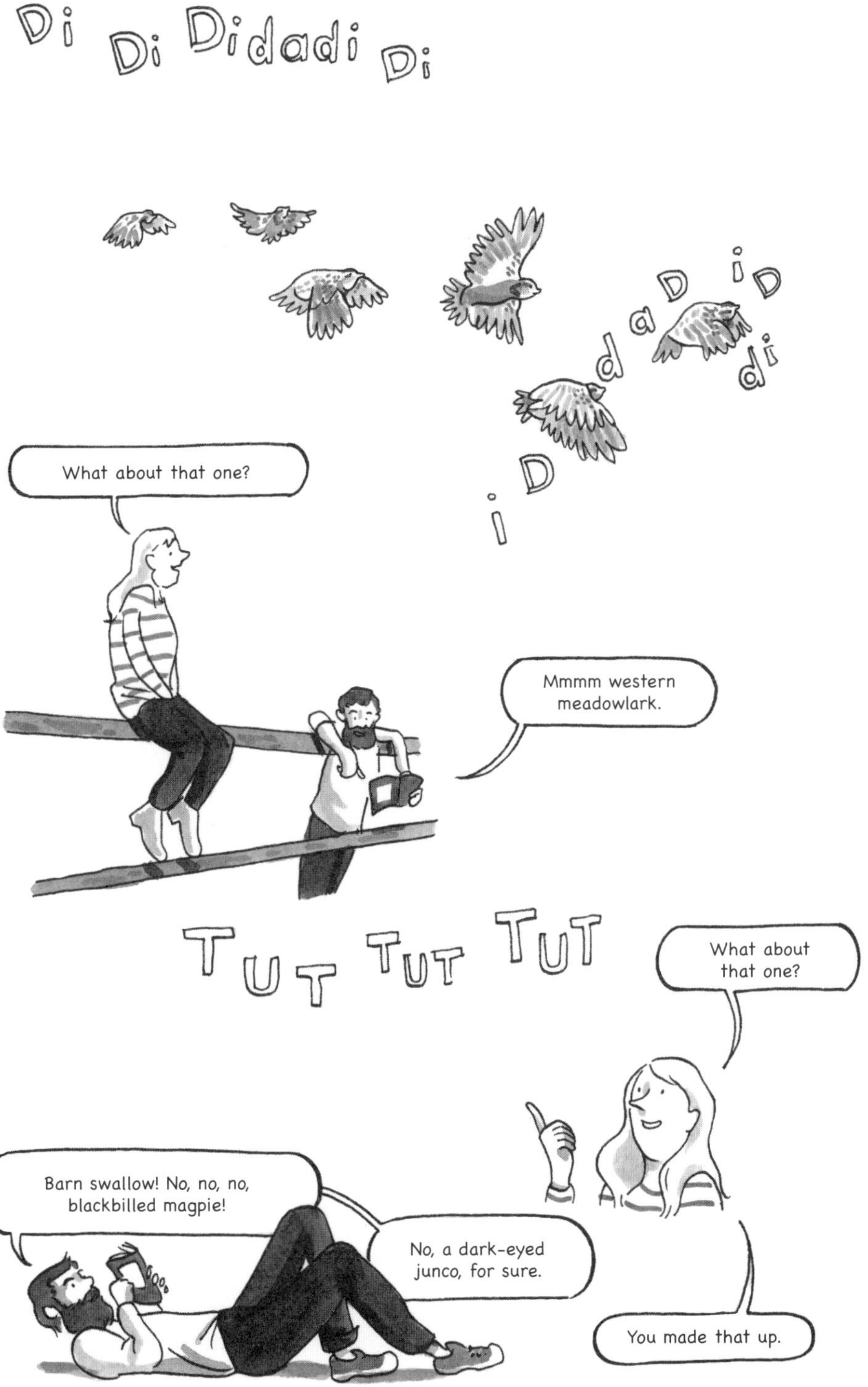

Di Di Didadi Di
iDdadiDdi
What about that one?
Mmmm western meadowlark.
TUT TUT TUT
What about that one?
Barn swallow! No, no, no, blackbilled magpie!
No, a dark-eyed junco, for sure.
You made that up.

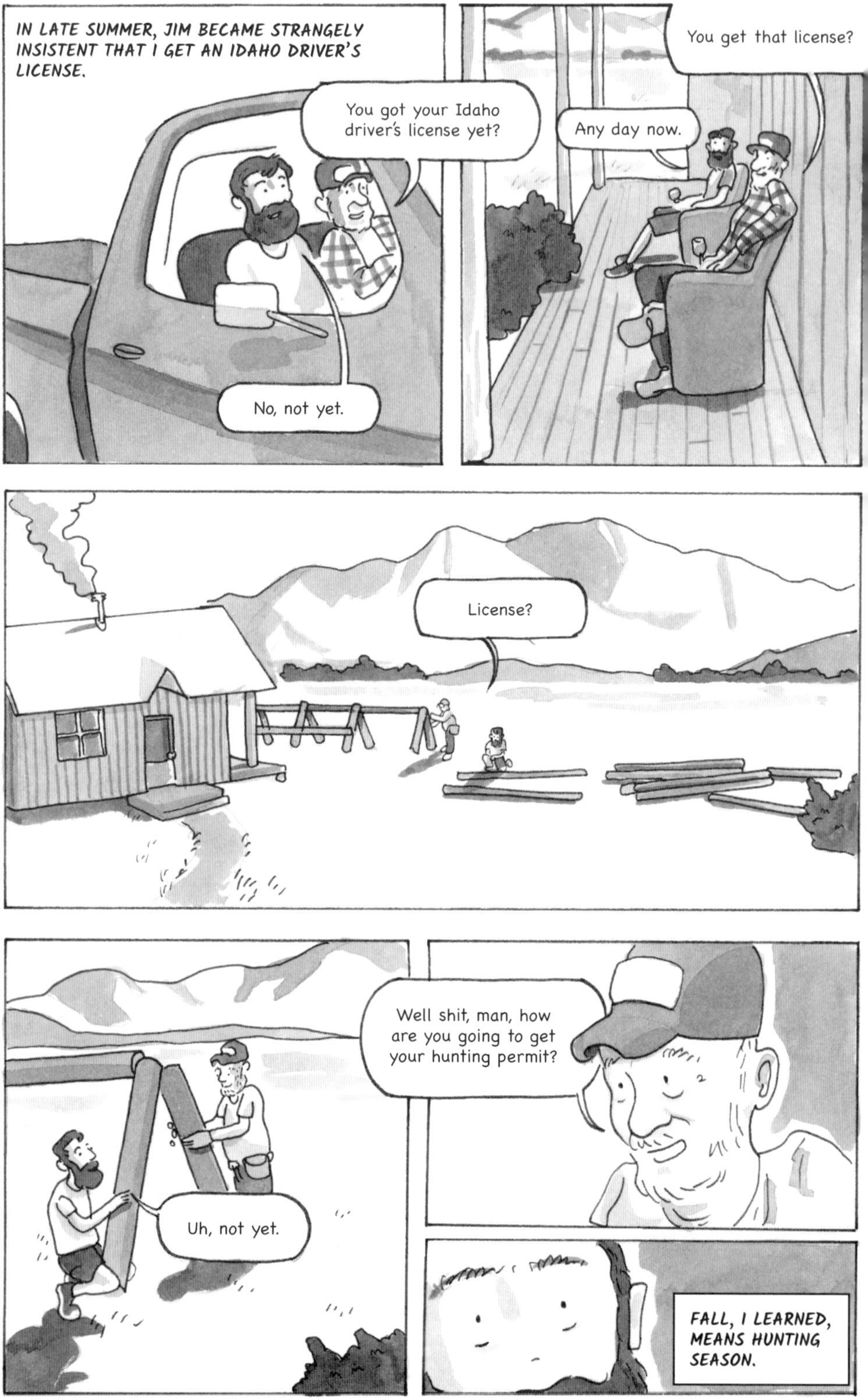

IN LATE SUMMER, JIM BECAME STRANGELY INSISTENT THAT I GET AN IDAHO DRIVER'S LICENSE.
You got your Idaho driver's license yet?
No, not yet.
You get that license?
Any day now.
License?
Uh, not yet.
Well shit, man, how are you going to get your hunting permit?
FALL, I LEARNED, MEANS HUNTING SEASON.

COULD I HUNT?

Bam!

WE DID IN FACT OWN A GUN. EMELIE HAD
INHERITED A SHOTGUN FROM HER FATHER.

The case has
his initials.

It's still got its
blueing.

You don't use
this much,
do you?

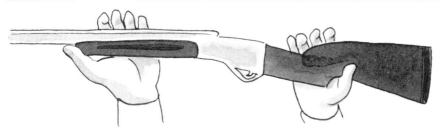

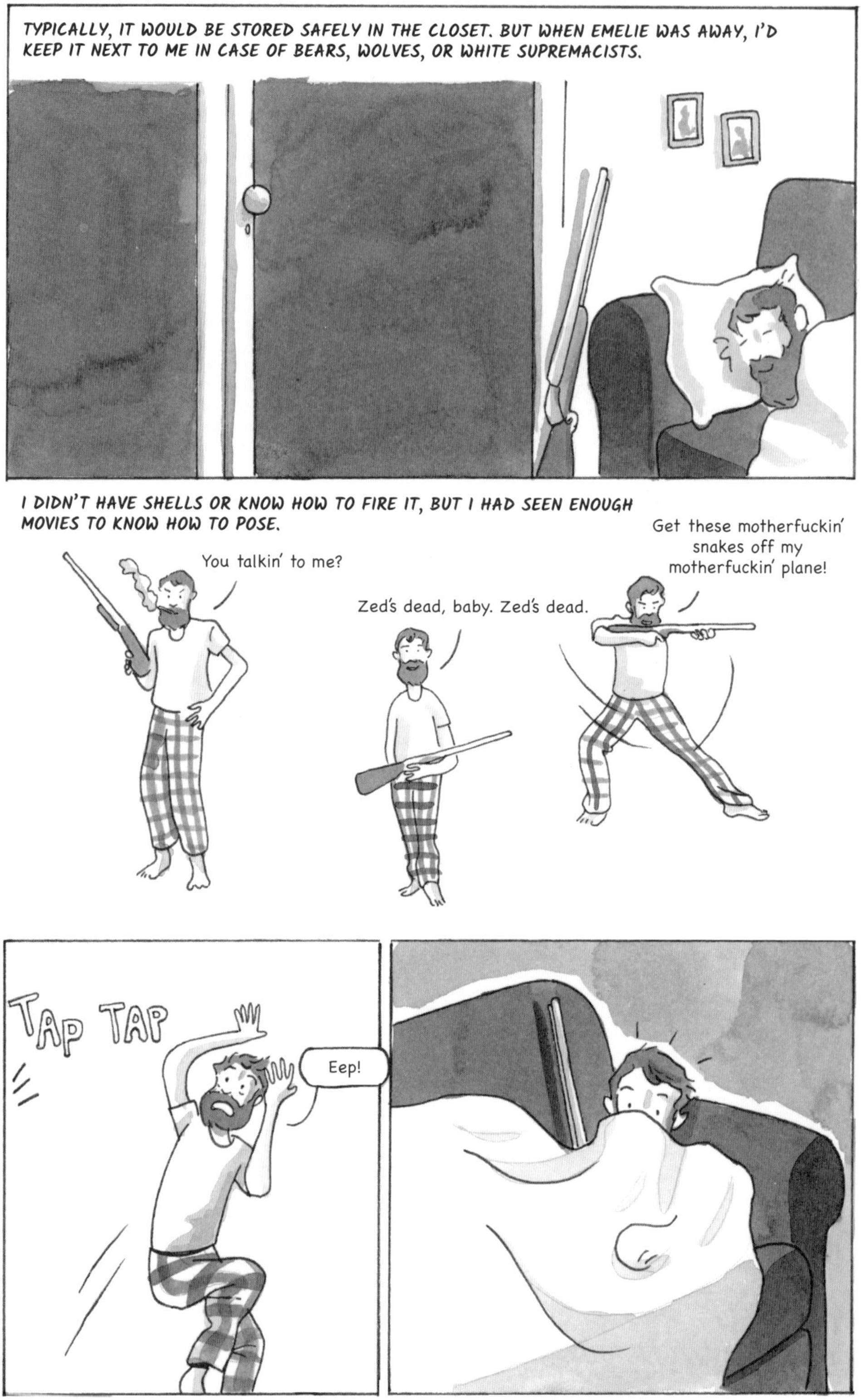
TYPICALLY, IT WOULD BE STORED SAFELY IN THE CLOSET. BUT WHEN EMELIE WAS AWAY, I'D KEEP IT NEXT TO ME IN CASE OF BEARS, WOLVES, OR WHITE SUPREMACISTS.
I DIDN'T HAVE SHELLS OR KNOW HOW TO FIRE IT, BUT I HAD SEEN ENOUGH MOVIES TO KNOW HOW TO POSE.
You talkin' to me?
Zed's dead, baby. Zed's dead.
Get these motherfuckin' snakes off my motherfuckin' plane!
TAP TAP
Eep!

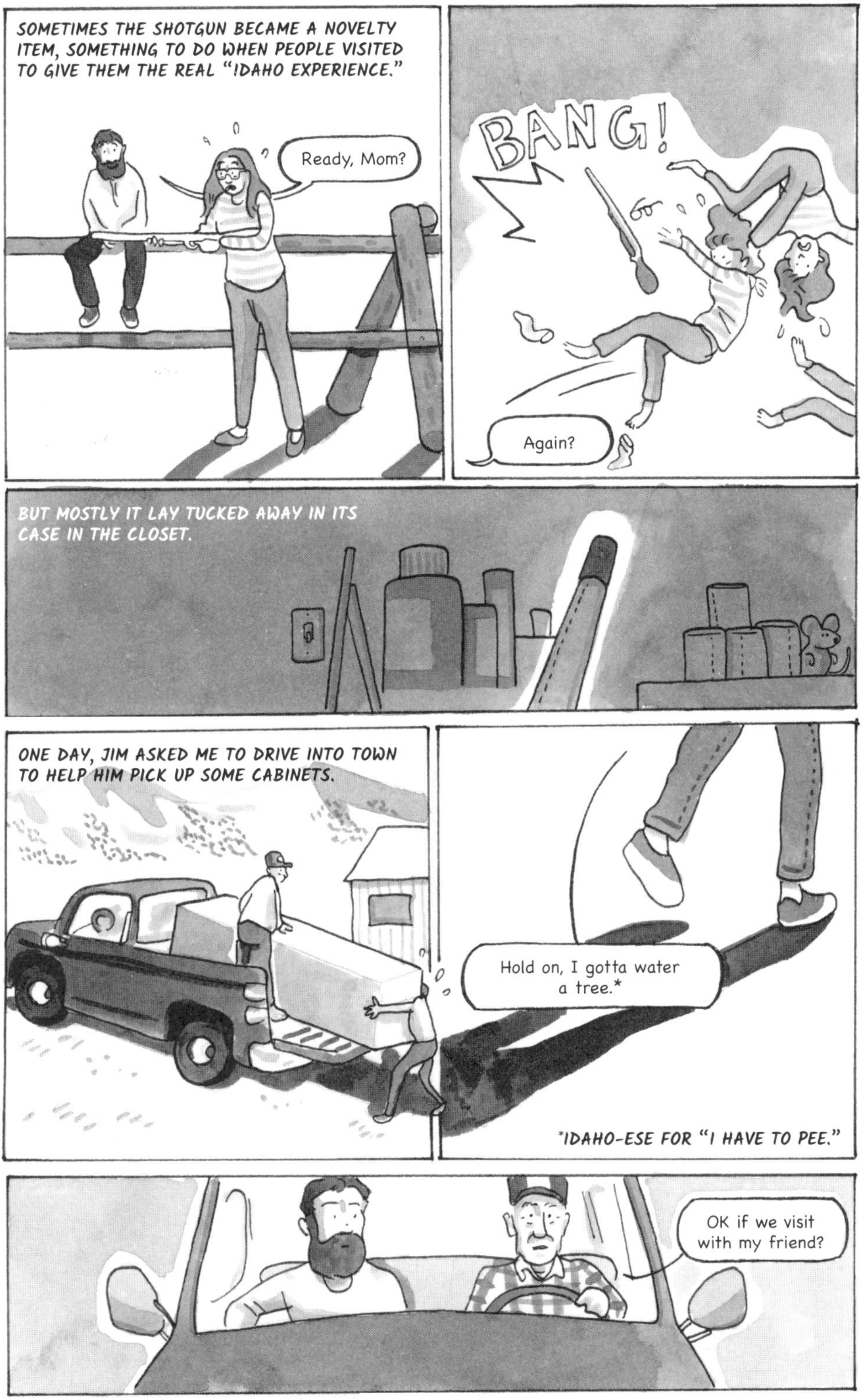

SOMETIMES THE SHOTGUN BECAME A NOVELTY ITEM, SOMETHING TO DO WHEN PEOPLE VISITED TO GIVE THEM THE REAL "IDAHO EXPERIENCE."
Ready, Mom?
BANG!
Again?
BUT MOSTLY IT LAY TUCKED AWAY IN ITS CASE IN THE CLOSET.
ONE DAY, JIM ASKED ME TO DRIVE INTO TOWN TO HELP HIM PICK UP SOME CABINETS.
Hold on, I gotta water a tree.*
*IDAHO-ESE FOR "I HAVE TO PEE."
OK if we visit with my friend?

LIKE JIM, JON WAS OBSESSED WITH GUNS.

And I says "Goddamn it, Imma beat the shit out of whoever didn't put the chain back."

HE EVEN WORE A TINY DERRINGER PISTOL IN A HOLSTER ON HIS SUSPENDERS.

Pleased to meet you.

I got about a hundred or so guns in here. 'Bout a quarter of all my guns and rifles.

"A well regulated militia being necessary to the security of a free state, the right of the people to keep and bear arms shall not be infringed."

ON THE WALL, THERE IS A FRAMED EMBROIDERY OF THE SECOND AMENDMENT.

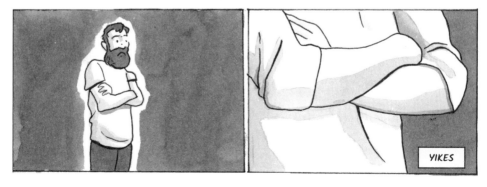

YIKES

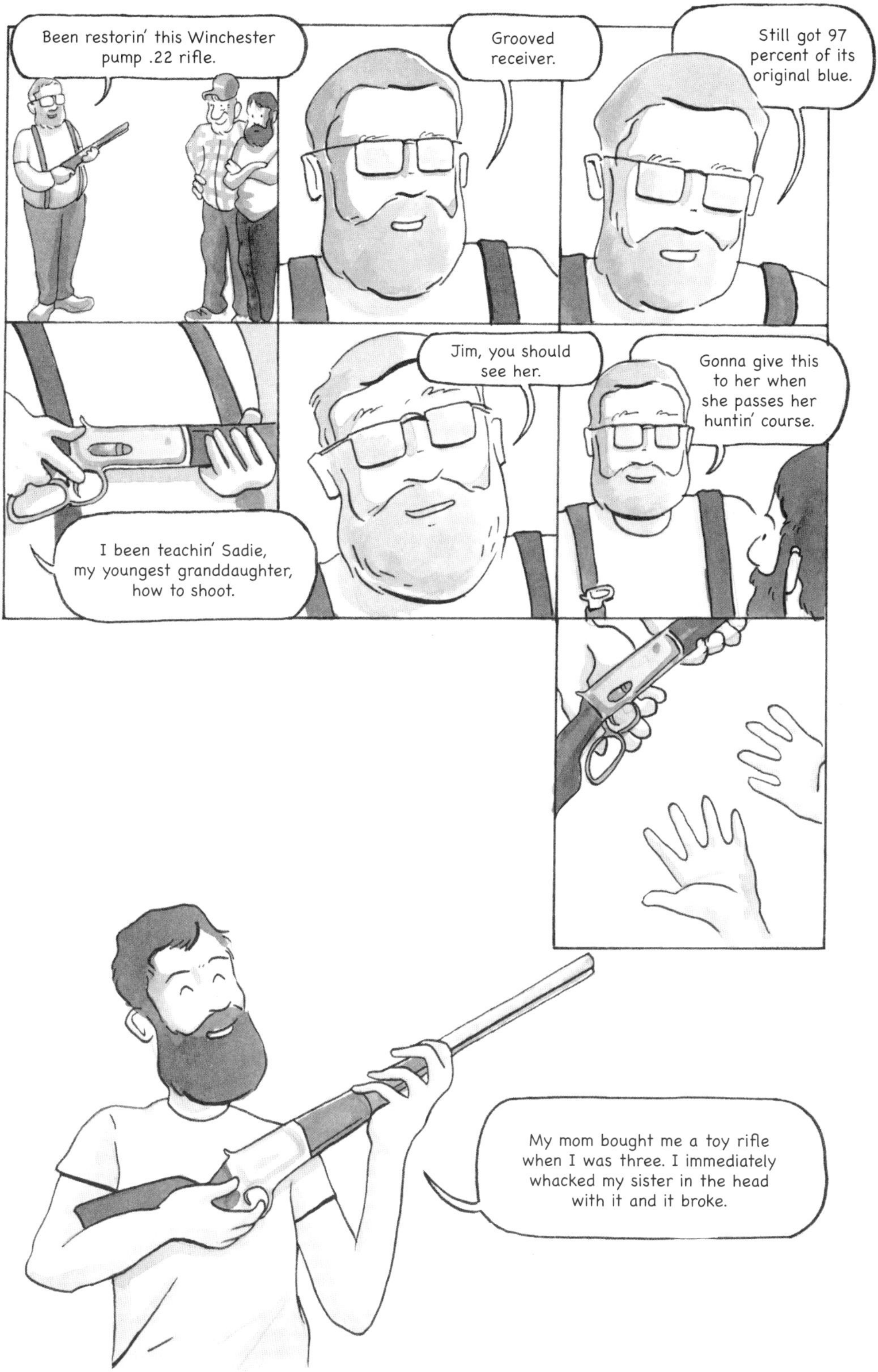
Been restorin' this Winchester pump .22 rifle.
Grooved receiver.
Still got 97 percent of its original blue.
I been teachin' Sadie, my youngest granddaughter, how to shoot.
Jim, you should see her.
Gonna give this to her when she passes her huntin' course.
My mom bought me a toy rifle when I was three. I immediately whacked my sister in the head with it and it broke.

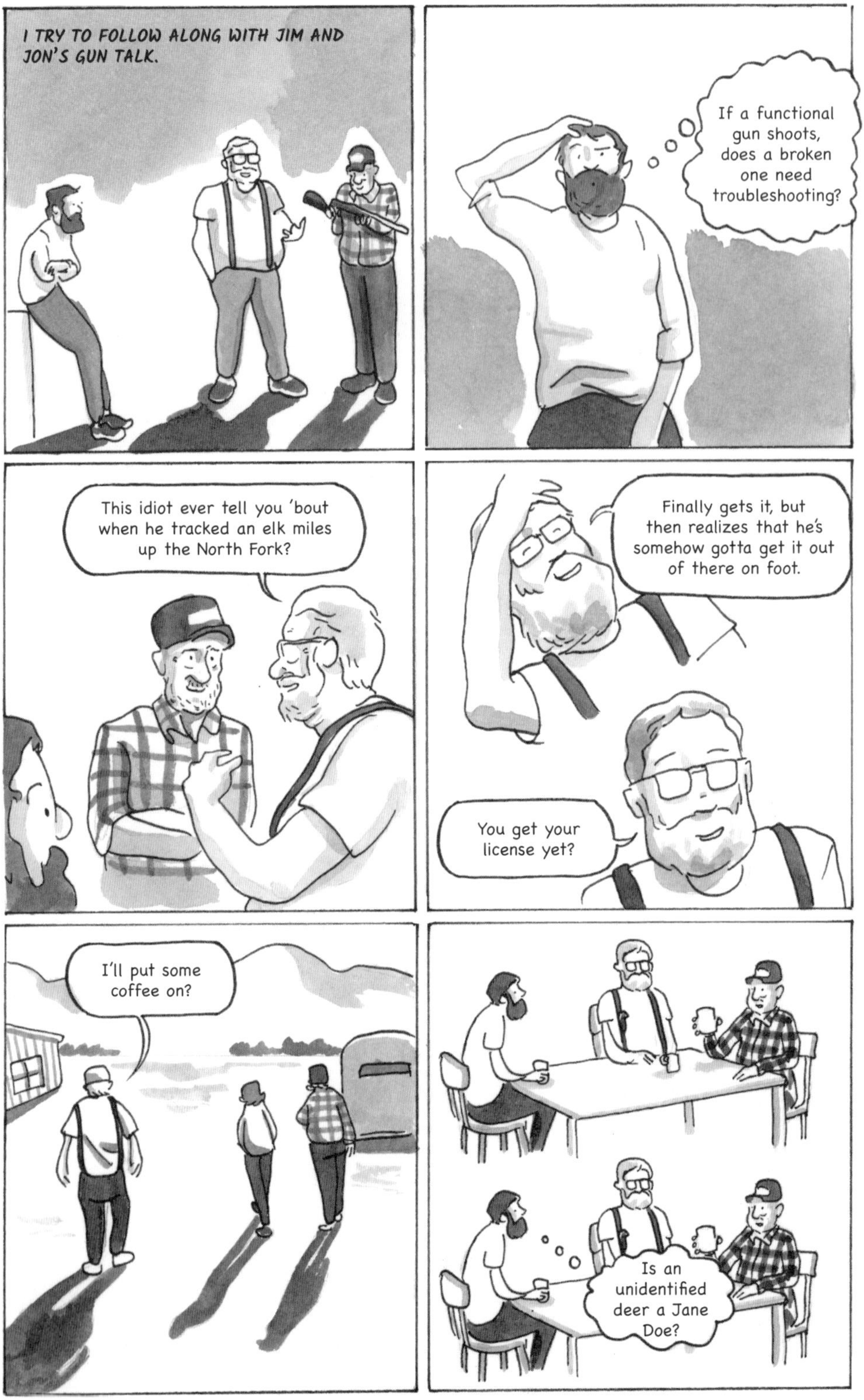
I TRY TO FOLLOW ALONG WITH JIM AND JON'S GUN TALK.
If a functional gun shoots, does a broken one need troubleshooting?
This idiot ever tell you 'bout when he tracked an elk miles up the North Fork?
Finally gets it, but then realizes that he's somehow gotta get it out of there on foot.
You get your license yet?
I'll put some coffee on?
Is an unidentified deer a Jane Doe?

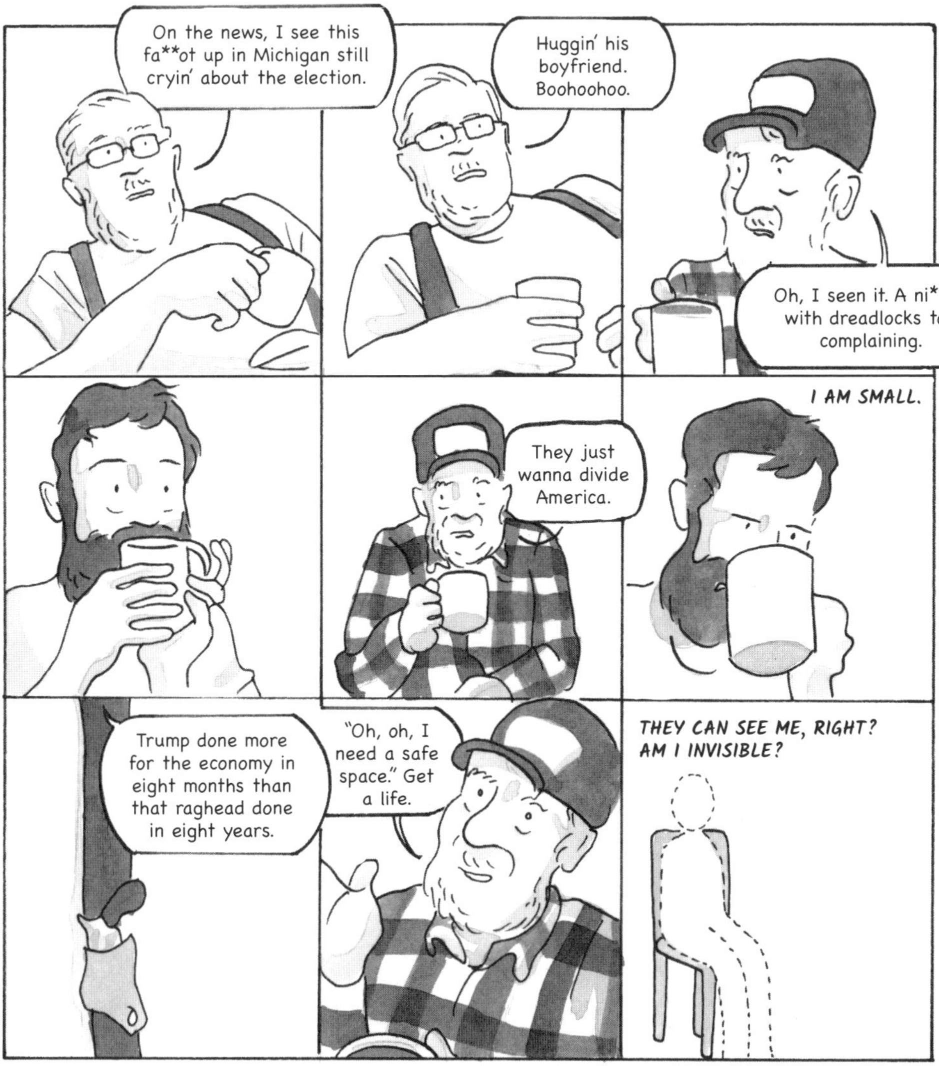
On the news, I see this fa**ot up in Michigan still cryin' about the election.
Huggin' his boyfriend. Boohoohoo.
Oh, I seen it. A ni**er with dreadlocks too complaining.
They just wanna divide America.
I AM SMALL.
Trump done more for the economy in eight months than that raghead done in eight years.
"Oh, oh, I need a safe space." Get a life.
THEY CAN SEE ME, RIGHT? AM I INVISIBLE?

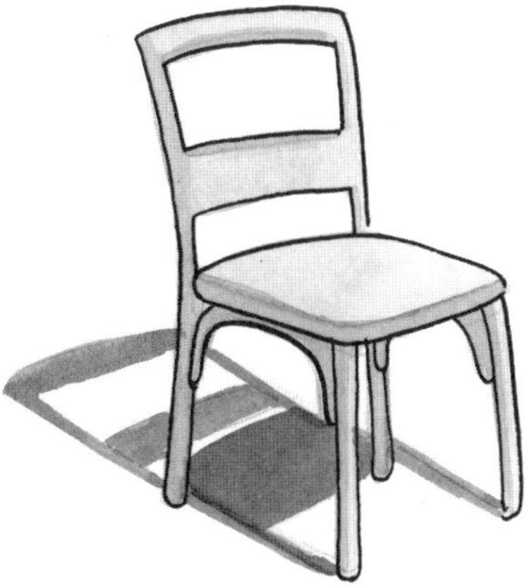

I RECEDE INTO NOTHINGNESS.

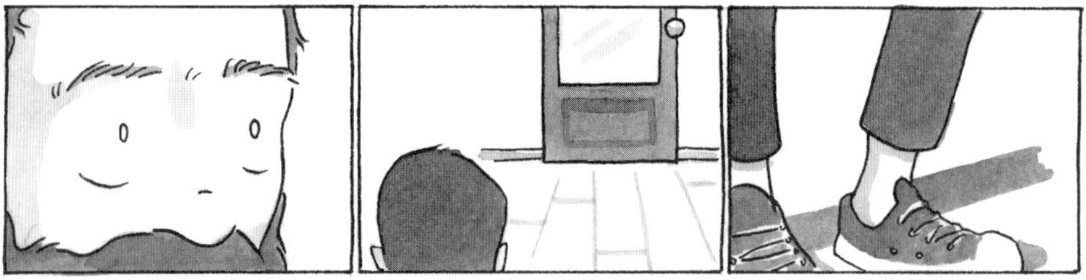

THE WORD MINORITY COMES FROM THE LATIN MINOR, MEANING "LESS, LESSER, SMALLER, JUNIOR." THE MEANING "GROUP OF PEOPLE SEPARATED FROM THE REST OF A COMMUNITY BY RACE, RELIGION, LANGUAGE, ETC." IS FROM 1919. ITS ORIGINAL MEANING, FROM 1530 AND NOW OBSOLETE, WAS THE "STATE OR CONDITION OF BEING SMALLER."

IN THIS MOMENT, I AM ACUTELY AWARE THAT I AM PHYSICALLY SMALLER THAN JIM AND JON.

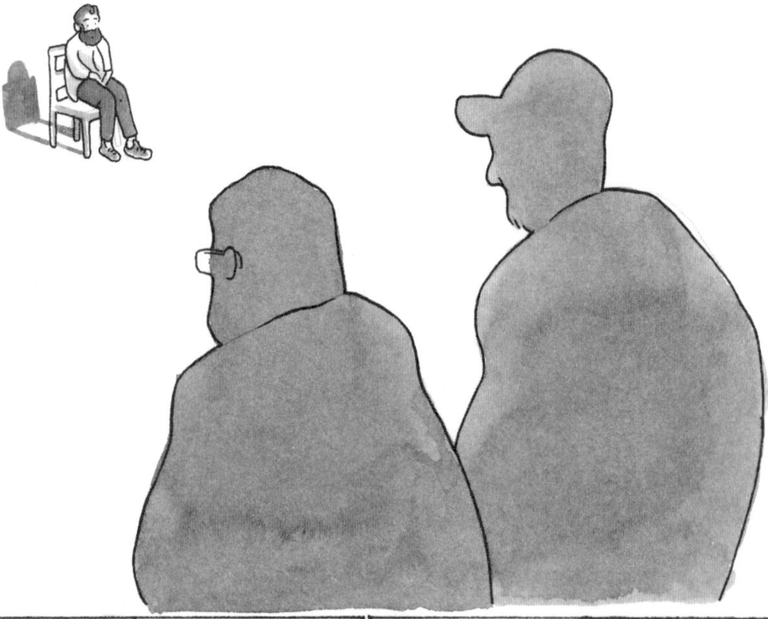

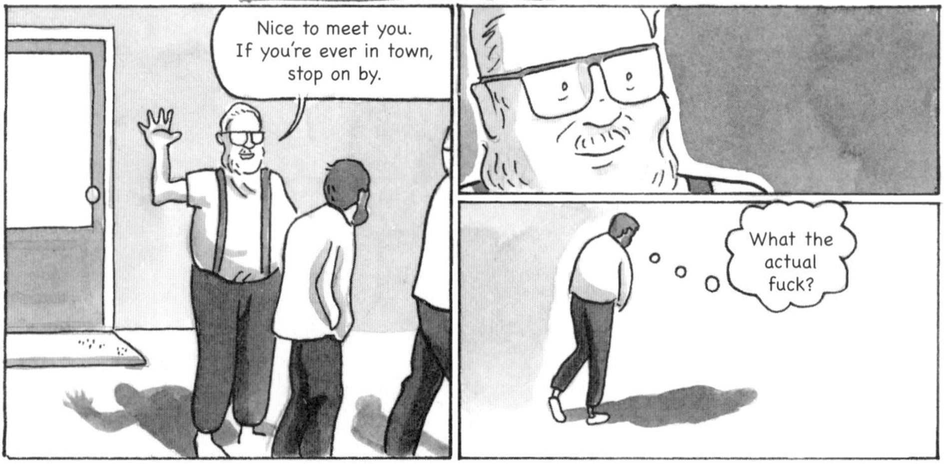
Nice to meet you. If you're ever in town, stop on by.
What the actual fuck?

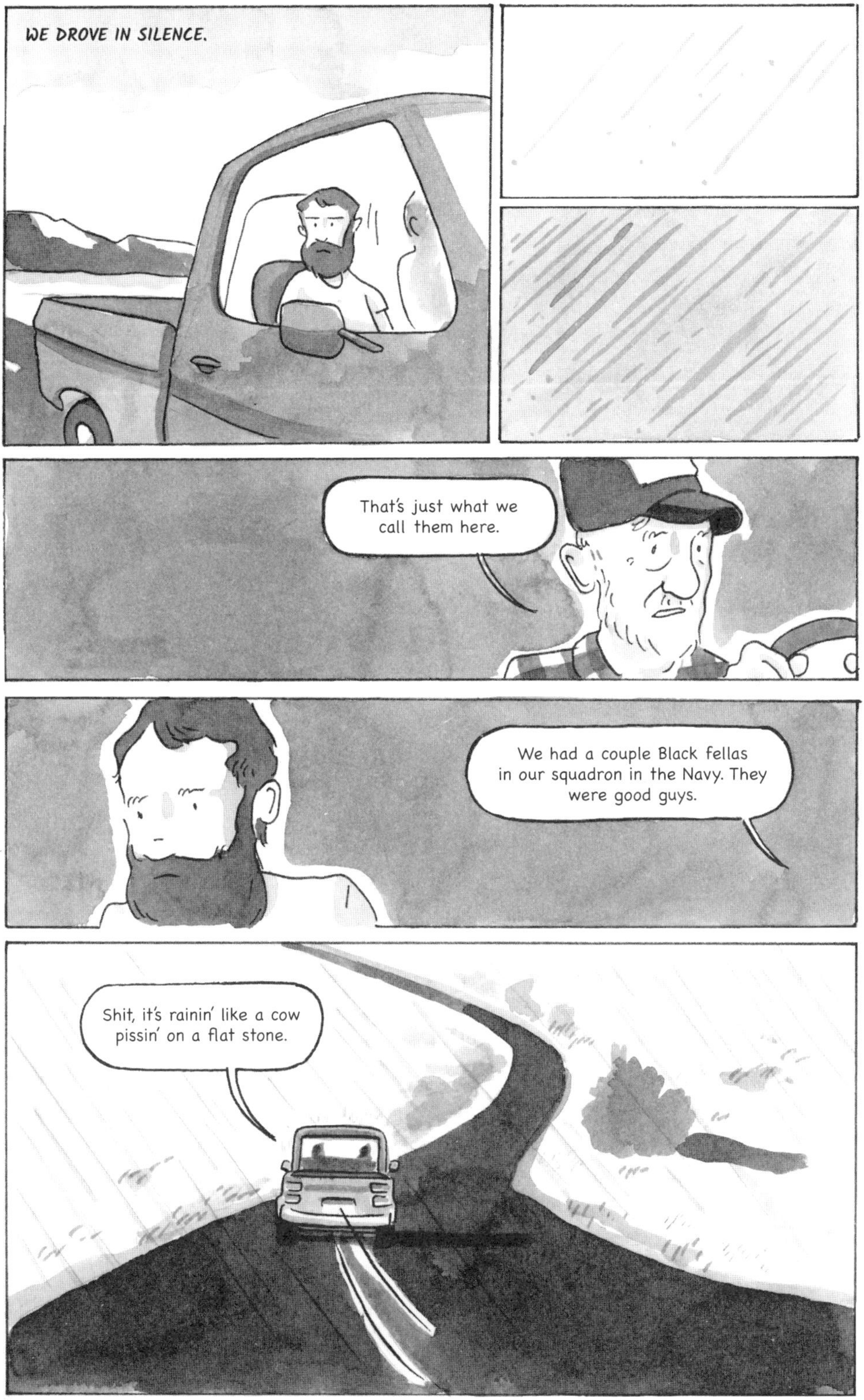
WE DROVE IN SILENCE.
That's just what we call them here.
We had a couple Black fellas in our squadron in the Navy. They were good guys.
Shit, it's rainin' like a cow pissin' on a flat stone.

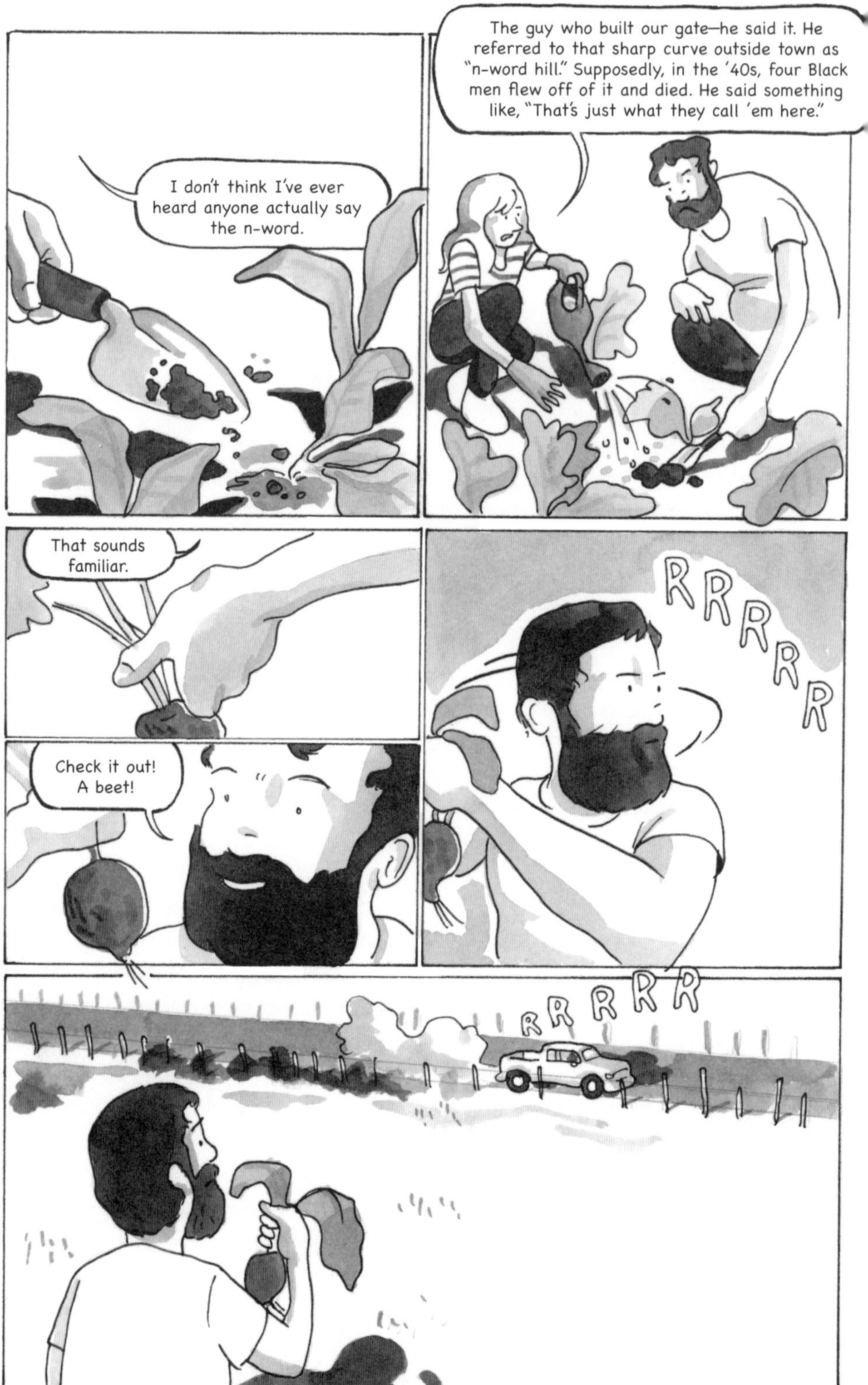
I don't think I've ever heard anyone actually say the n-word.
The guy who built our gate—he said it. He referred to that sharp curve outside town as "n-word hill." Supposedly, in the '40s, four Black men flew off of it and died. He said something like, "That's just what they call 'em here."
That sounds familiar.
Check it out! A beet!
RRRRRR
RRRRRR

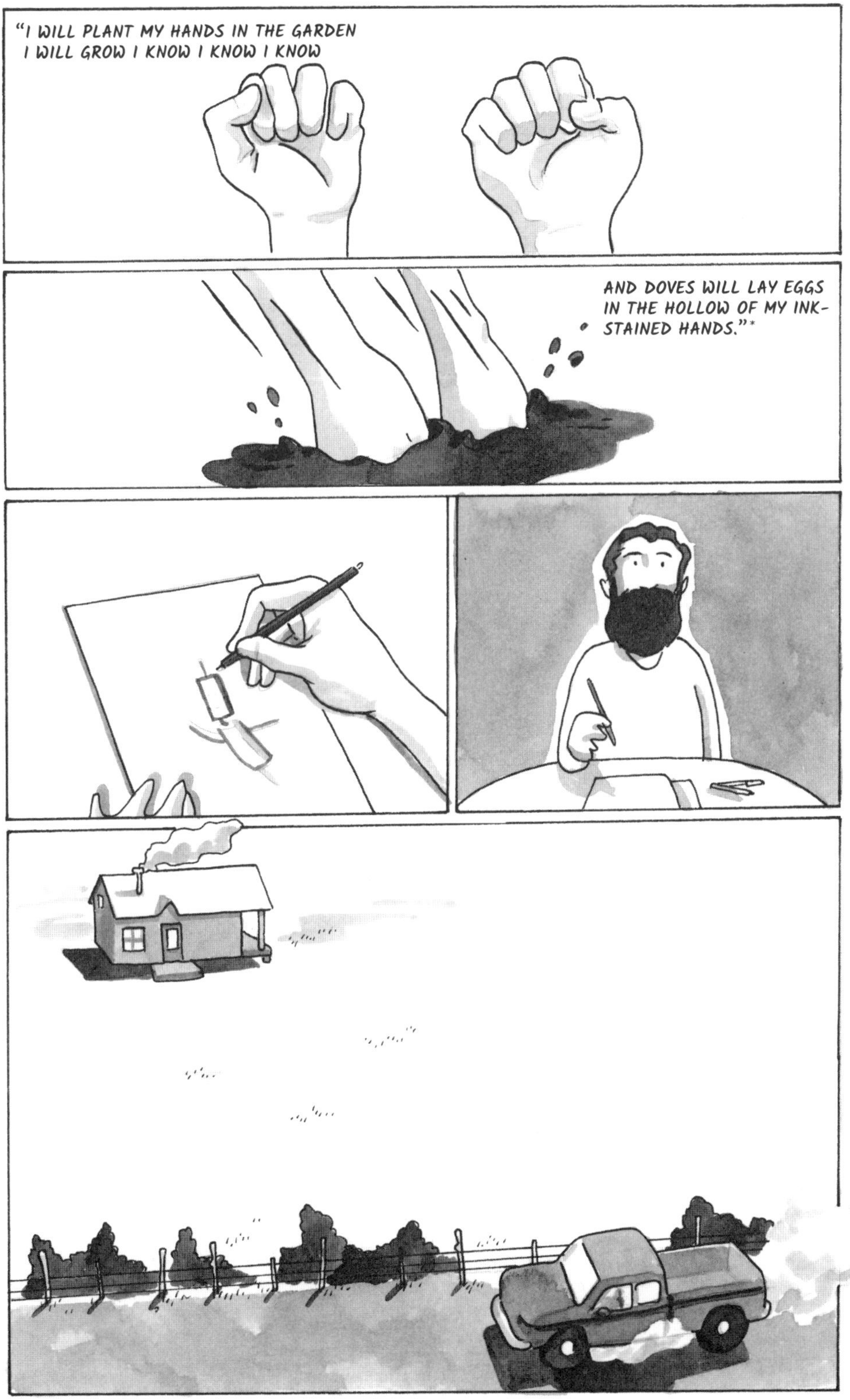
"I WILL PLANT MY HANDS IN THE GARDEN
I WILL GROW I KNOW I KNOW I KNOW
AND DOVES WILL LAY EGGS
IN THE HOLLOW OF MY INK-
STAINED HANDS."*

*FOROUGH FARROKHZAD, "ANOTHER BIRTH"

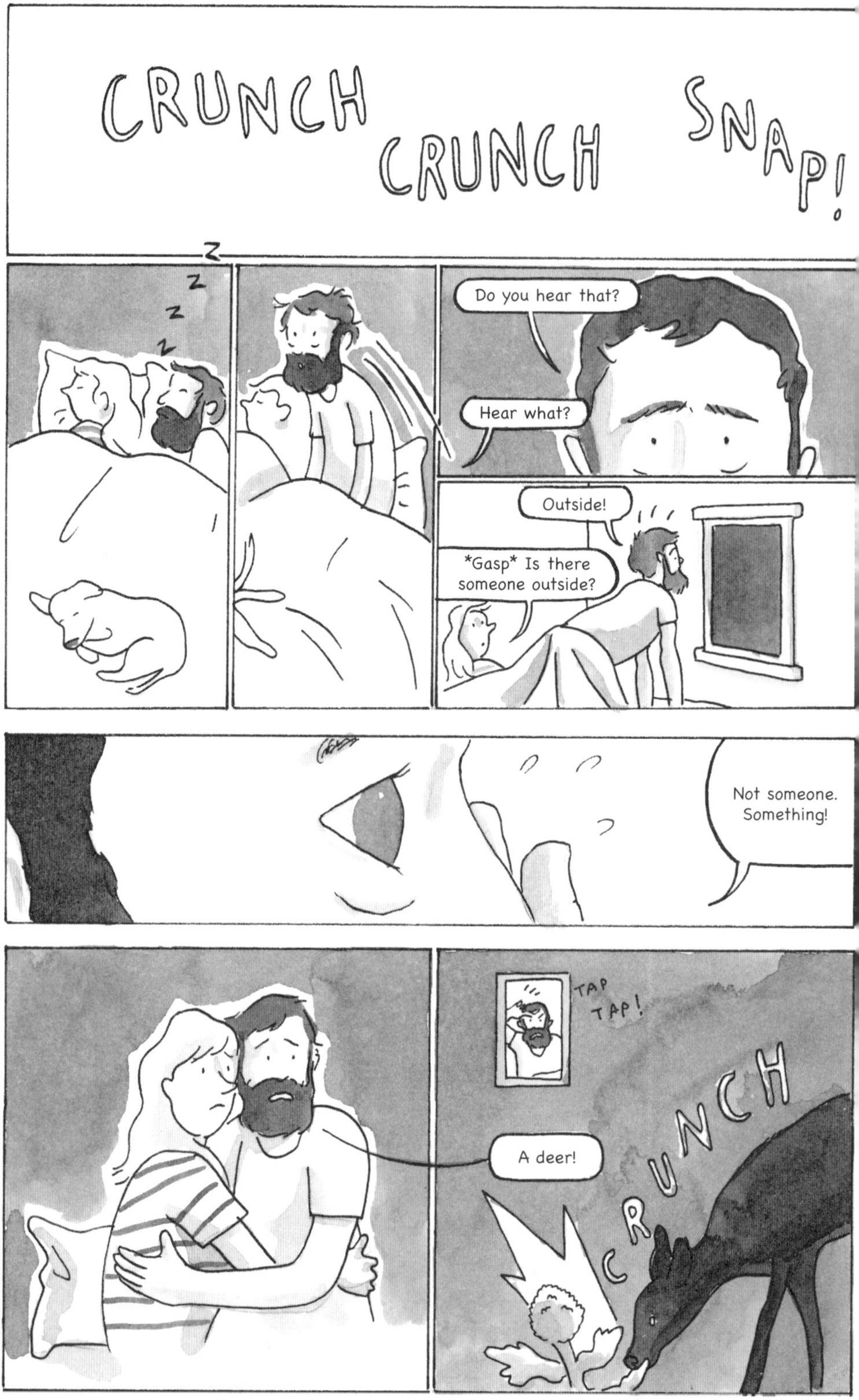
CRUNCH
CRUNCH
SNAP!
Z
Z
Z
Z
Do you hear that?
Hear what?
Outside!
Gasp Is there someone outside?
Not someone. Something!
TAP
TAP!
A deer!
CRUNCH

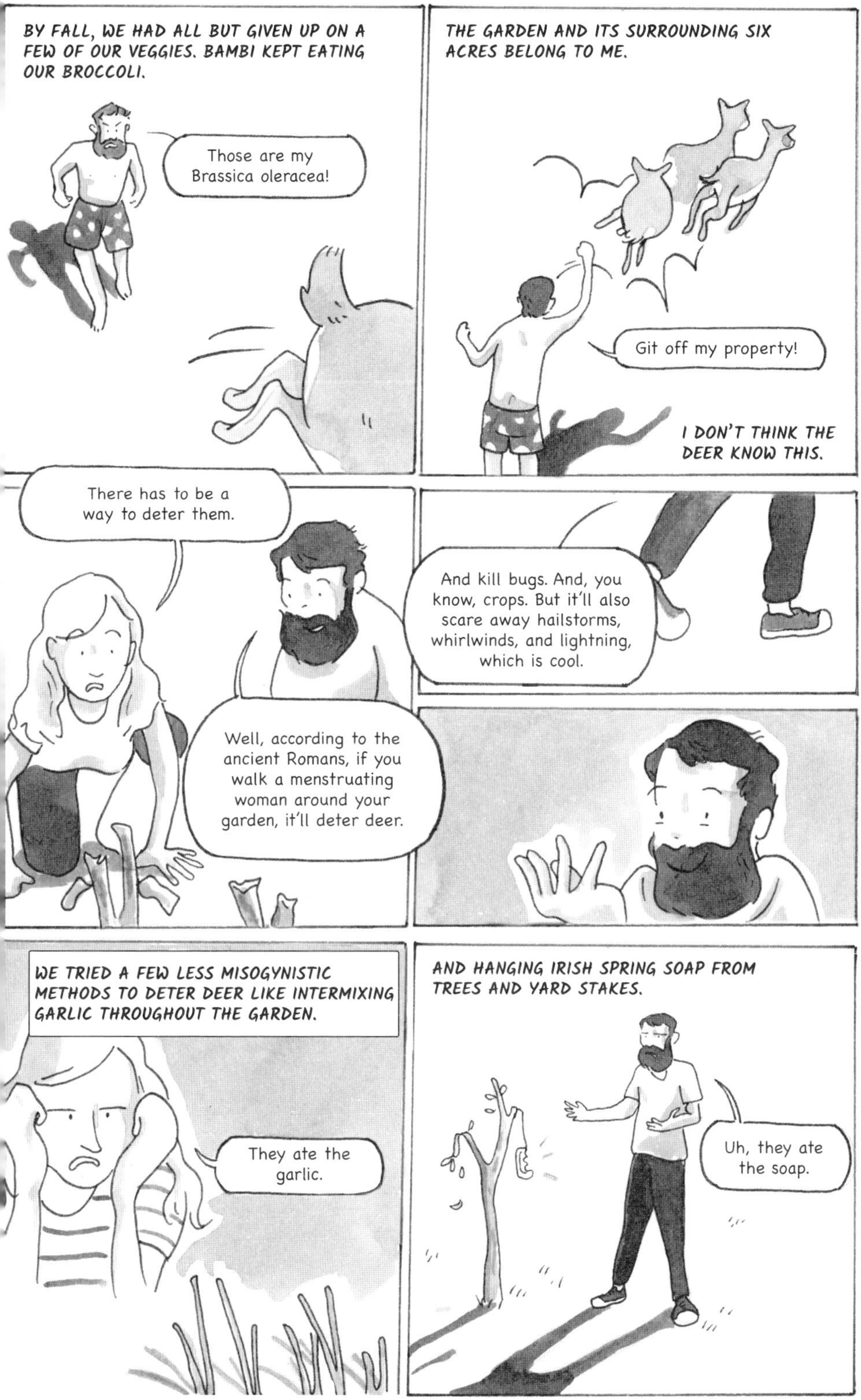
BY FALL, WE HAD ALL BUT GIVEN UP ON A FEW OF OUR VEGGIES. BAMBI KEPT EATING OUR BROCCOLI.
Those are my Brassica oleracea!
THE GARDEN AND ITS SURROUNDING SIX ACRES BELONG TO ME.
Git off my property!
I DON'T THINK THE DEER KNOW THIS.
There has to be a way to deter them.
Well, according to the ancient Romans, if you walk a menstruating woman around your garden, it'll deter deer.
And kill bugs. And, you know, crops. But it'll also scare away hailstorms, whirlwinds, and lightning, which is cool.
WE TRIED A FEW LESS MISOGYNISTIC METHODS TO DETER DEER LIKE INTERMIXING GARLIC THROUGHOUT THE GARDEN.
They ate the garlic.
AND HANGING IRISH SPRING SOAP FROM TREES AND YARD STAKES.
Uh, they ate the soap.

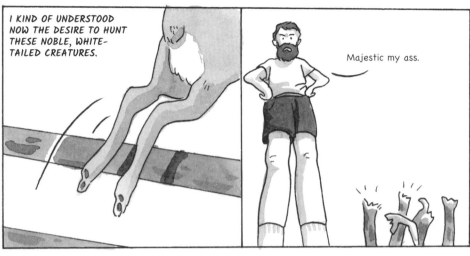

I KIND OF UNDERSTOOD NOW THE DESIRE TO HUNT THESE NOBLE, WHITE-TAILED CREATURES.

Majestic my ass.

ONE NIGHT I HEARD THE TELLTALE SOUNDS OF A RUMINANT ROGUE.

Yeah, motherfucker. I'm eating ALL your kohlrabi.

Scat, you reprobate.

TAP TAP!

BARK! BARK!

STARTLED, IT RUNS HEADFIRST INTO THE MESH SHEEP FENCING, TRAPPING ITSELF.

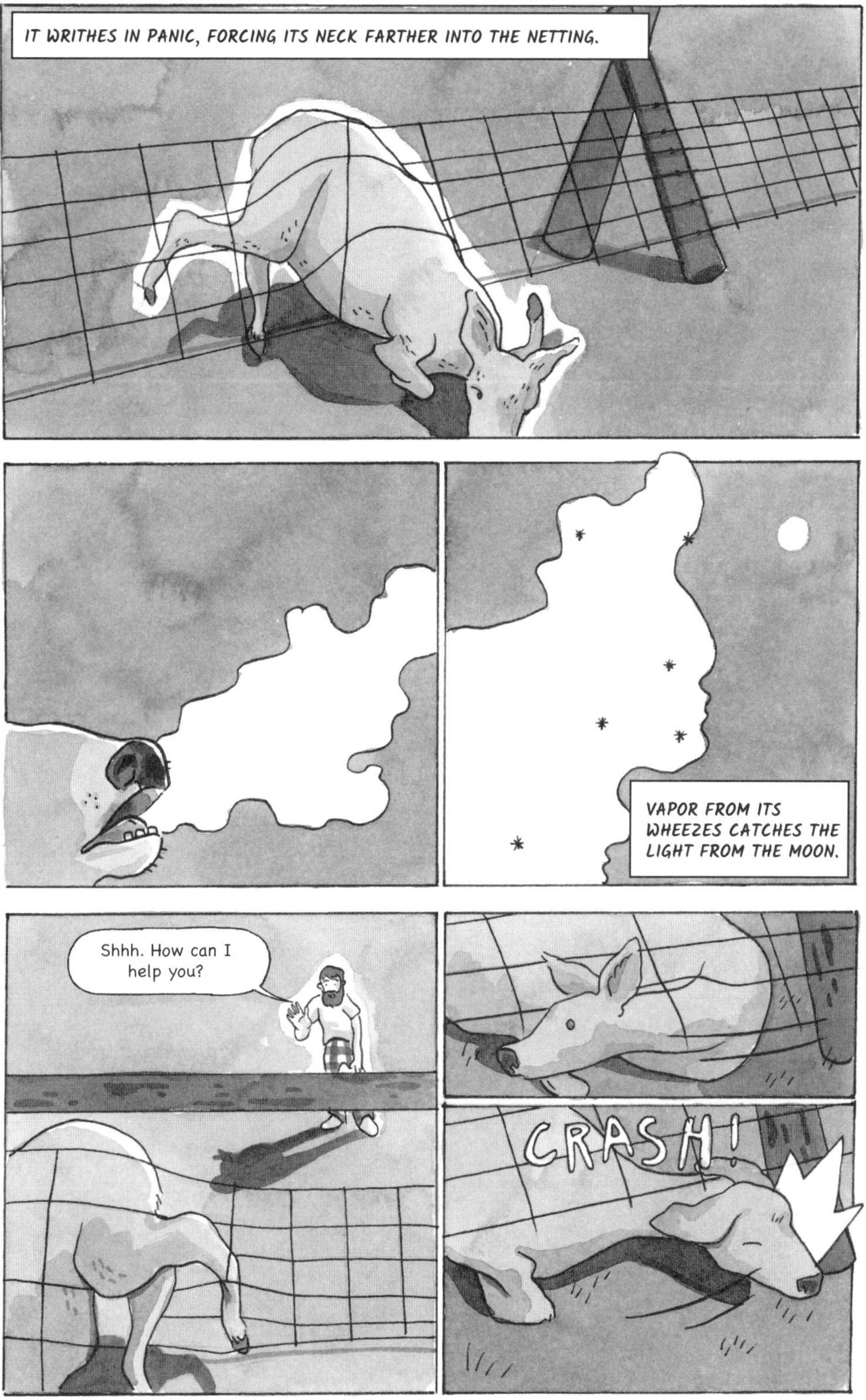
IT WRITHES IN PANIC, FORCING ITS NECK FARTHER INTO THE NETTING.
VAPOR FROM ITS WHEEZES CATCHES THE LIGHT FROM THE MOON.
Shhh. How can I help you?
CRASH!

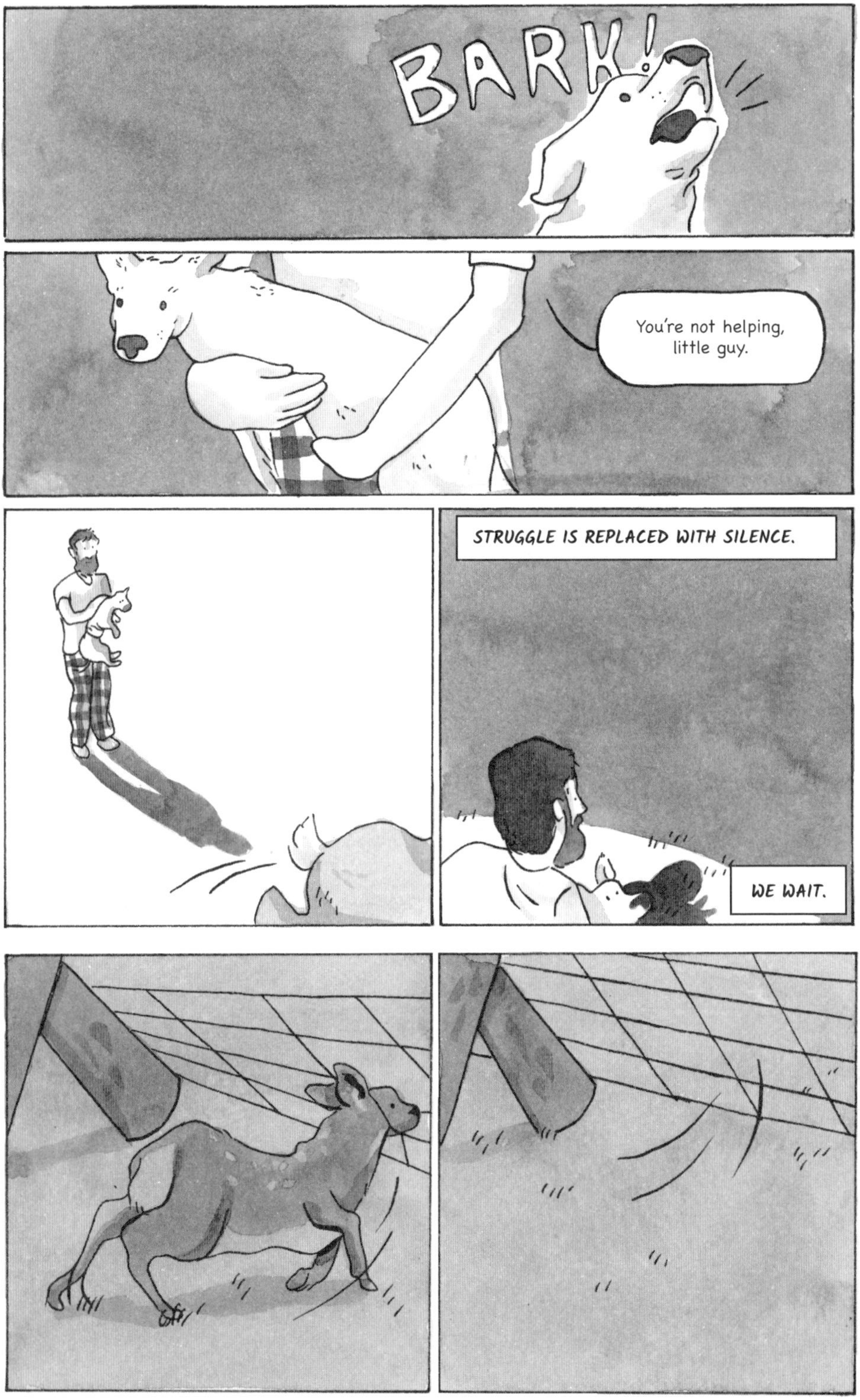
BARK!
You're not helping, little guy.
STRUGGLE IS REPLACED WITH SILENCE.
WE WAIT.

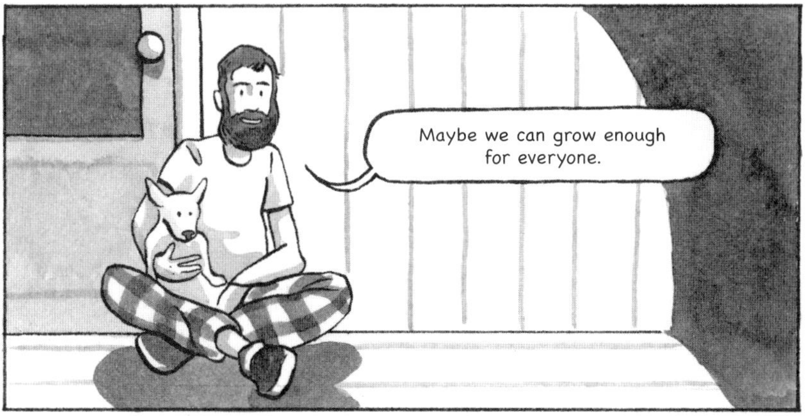
Maybe we can grow enough for everyone.

SUDDENLY, MY SUGGESTED FRIENDS ON FACEBOOK BEGAN TO CHANGE.
Friends
Suggestions
People You May Know
Add Friend
Add Friend
That's Mason and that's his brother... Dixon.
THEIR PROFILE PICTURES ALL LOOKED THE SAME.

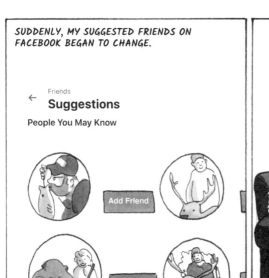

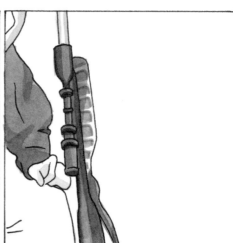

EVEN JOSIAH UPDATED HIS PROFILE PICTURE TO FEATURE A PHOTO OF HIMSELF WITH A DEAD BUCK.

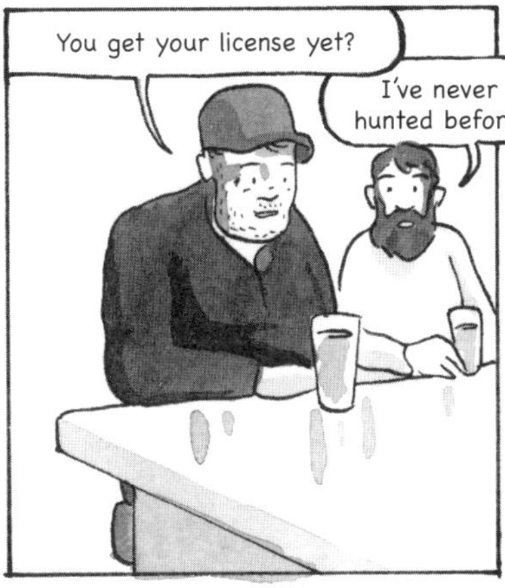

You get your license yet?
I've never hunted before.

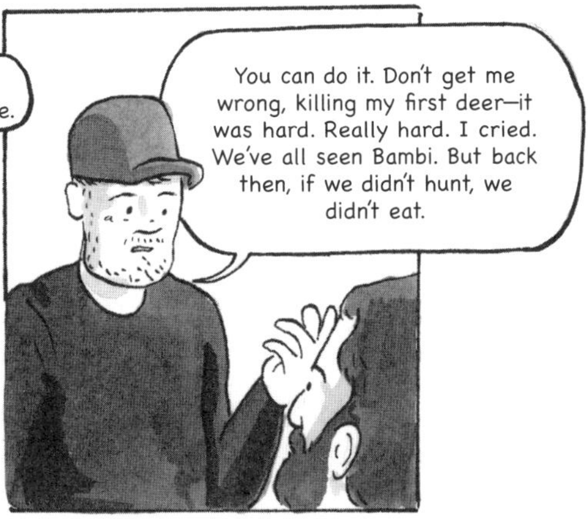

You can do it. Don't get me wrong, killing my first deer—it was hard. Really hard. I cried. We've all seen Bambi. But back then, if we didn't hunt, we didn't eat.

IT'S A STORY I HEARD OFTEN.

I HAD NEVER CONSIDERED THE GUN DEBATE FROM AN ECONOMICS OR CLASS PERSPECTIVE.

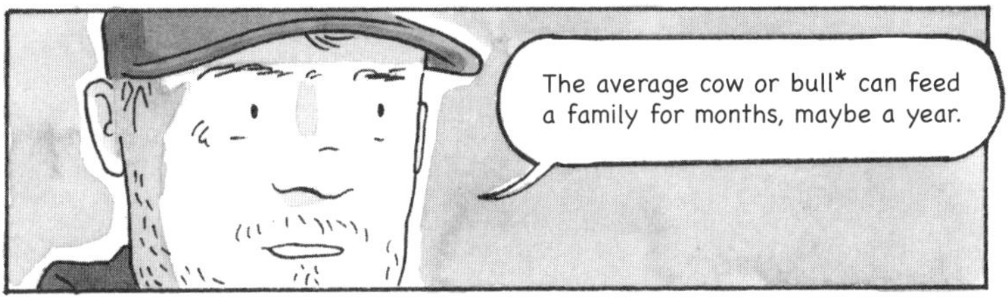

The average cow or bull* can feed a family for months, maybe a year.

AND THERE IS A CERTAIN ENVIRONMENTAL LOGIC TO IT. THE COUNTY, WHICH IS ROUGHLY THE SIZE OF CONNECTICUT, HAS AROUND 4,500 PEOPLE. THE NEAREST CITY IS AN HOUR AND A HALF AWAY. YOU COULD USE YOUR LOCAL RESOURCES, WHICH INCLUDED DEER, ELK, FISH, AND FOWL, OR YOU COULD TRUCK IN FOOD FROM HOURS AWAY.

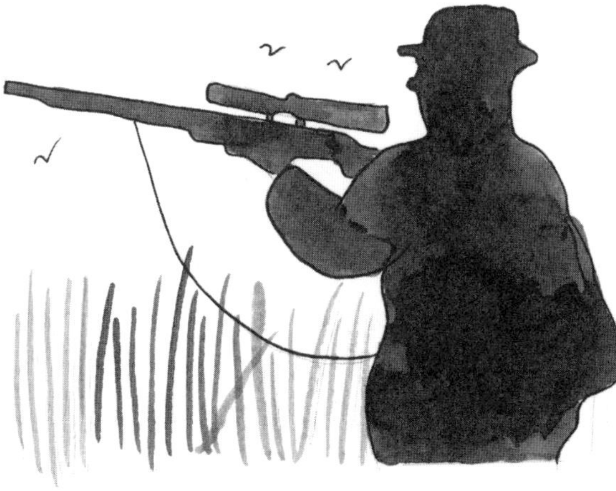

*ELK ARE ALSO REFERRED TO AS COWS AND BULLS.

BUT ALL I WOULD SEE ON SOCIAL MEDIA

AGAIN AND AGAIN

WERE THE SMILING FACES.

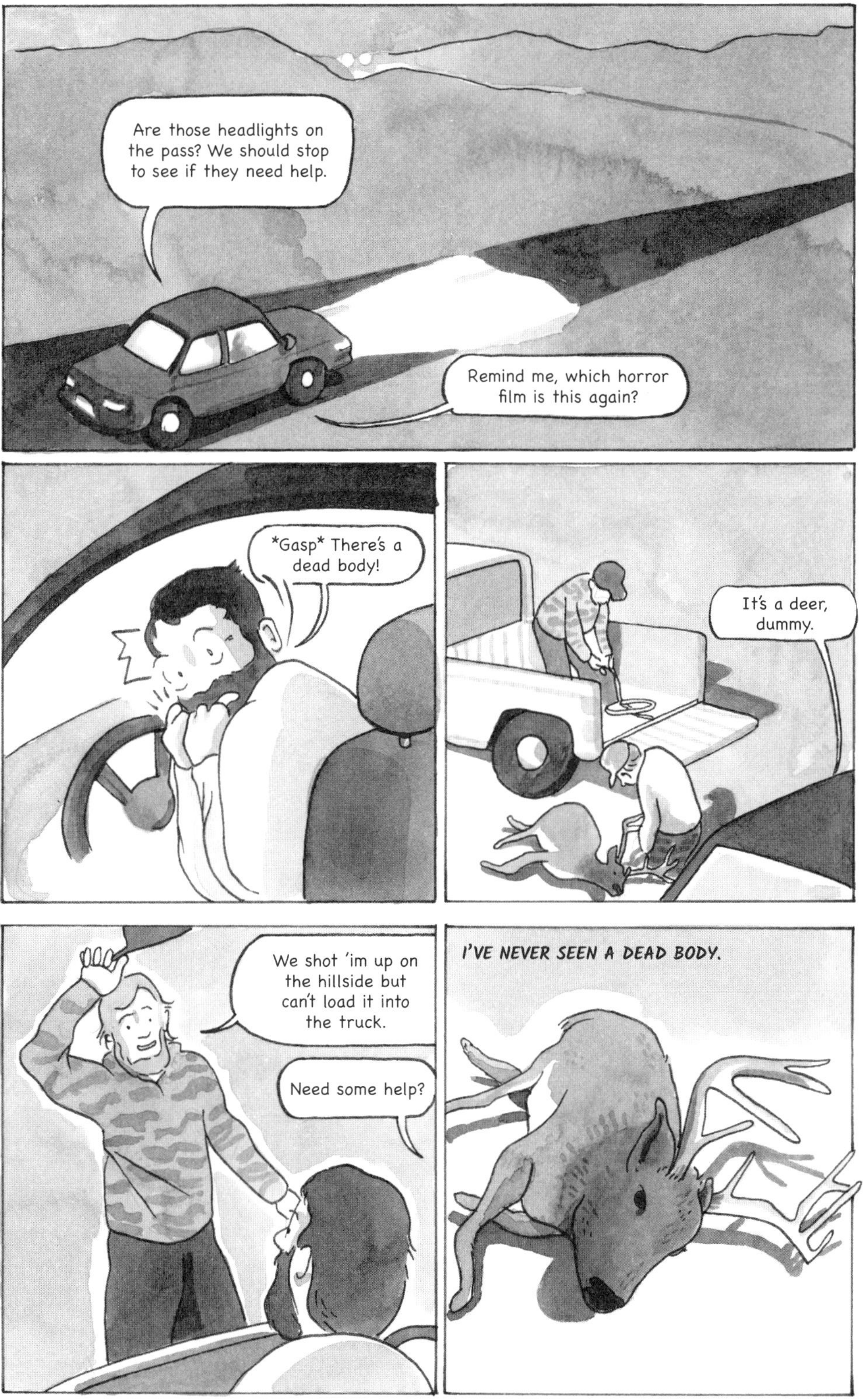
Are those headlights on the pass? We should stop to see if they need help.
Remind me, which horror film is this again?
Gasp There's a dead body!
It's a deer, dummy.
We shot 'im up on the hillside but can't load it into the truck.
Need some help?
I'VE NEVER SEEN A DEAD BODY.

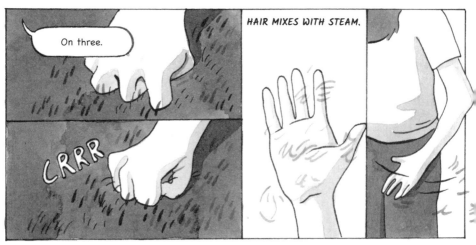

HAIR MIXES WITH STEAM.

On three.

CRRR

Grab there, under the rib. I cut a hole.

How convenient.

One, two, and...

three!

CRACK!

UNDER ITS OWN WEIGHT, RIBS SNAP AGAINST THE SIDEWALL.

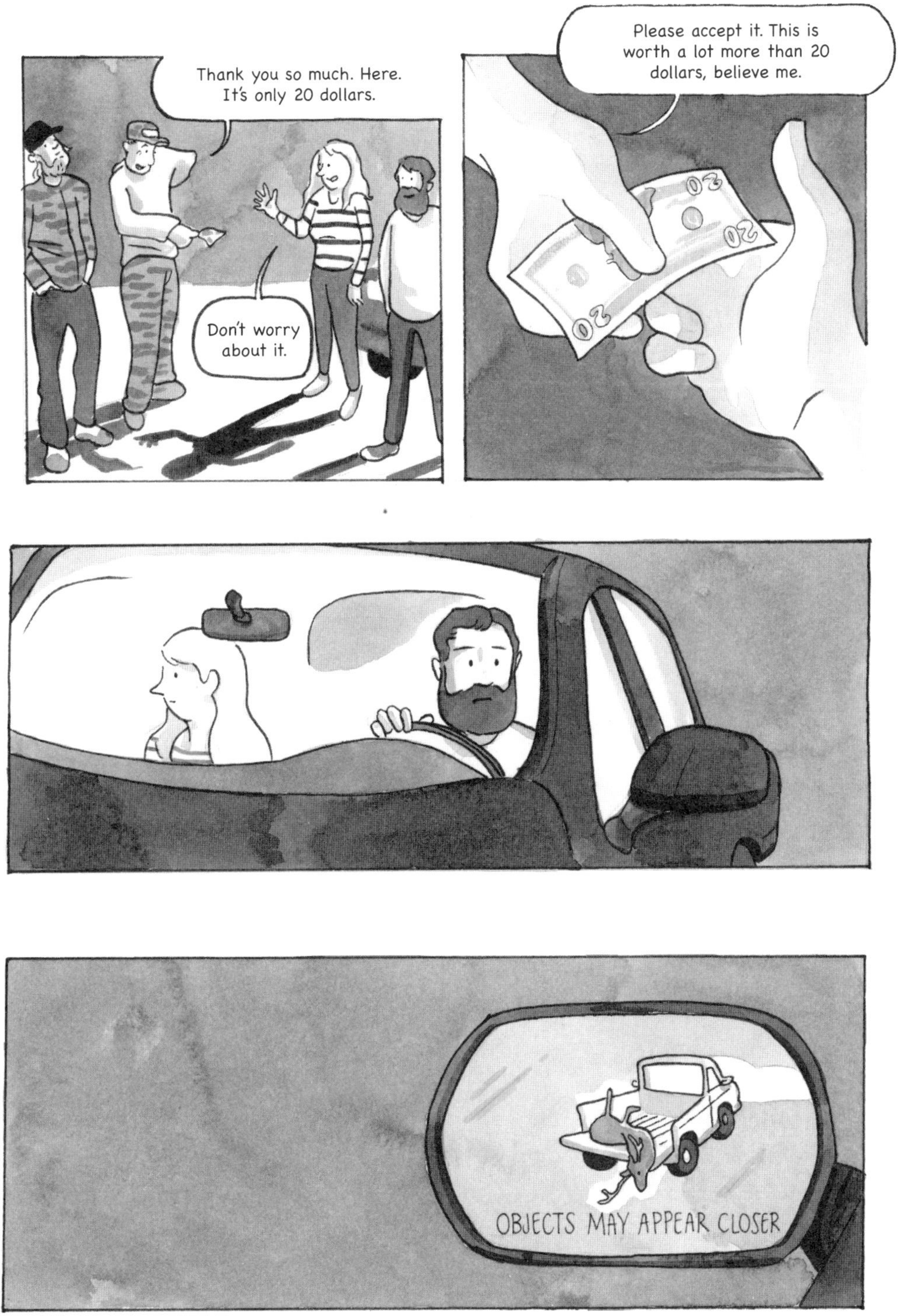

Thank you so much. Here. It's only 20 dollars.
Don't worry about it.
Please accept it. This is worth a lot more than 20 dollars, believe me.
20
OBJECTS MAY APPEAR CLOSER

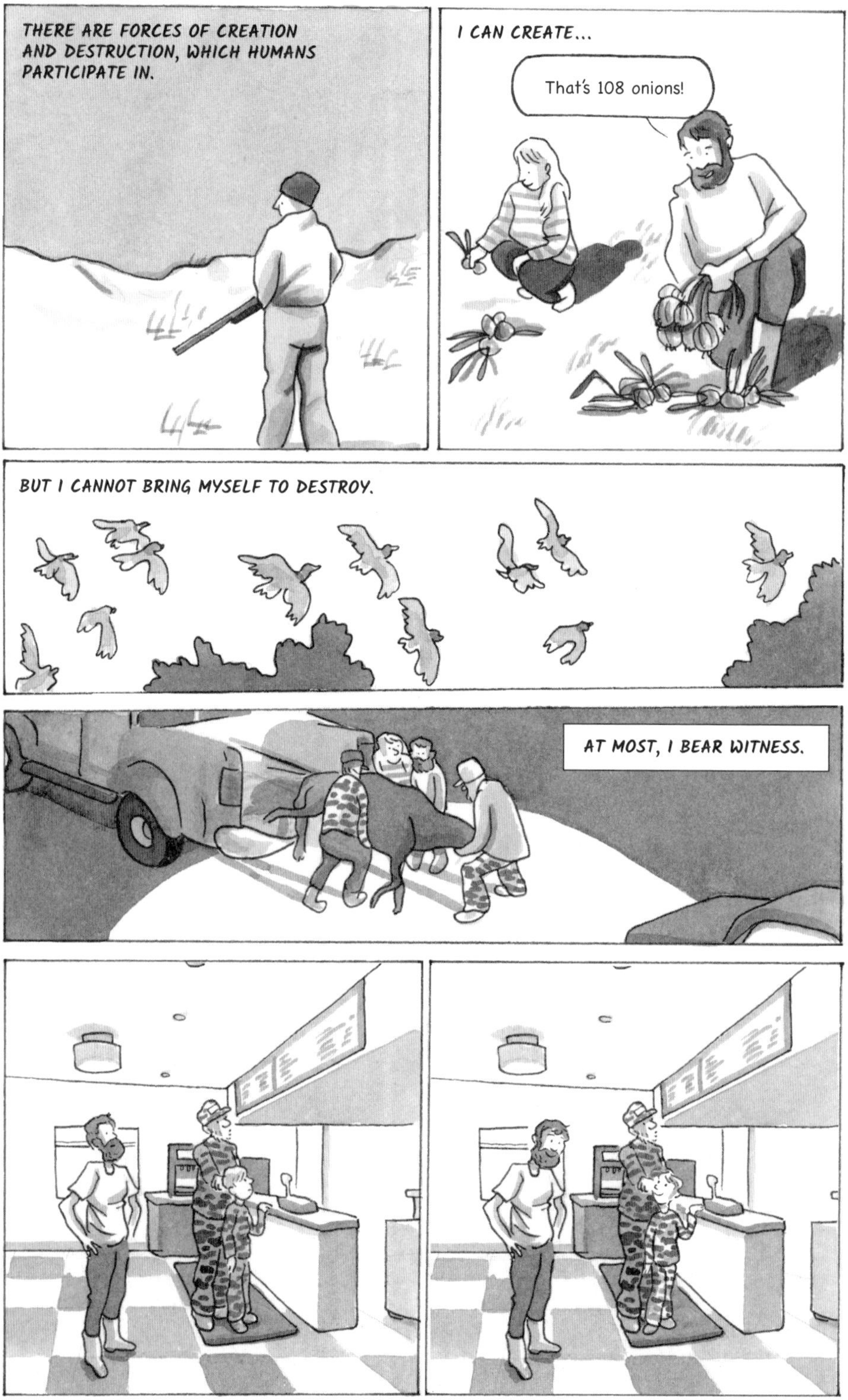

THERE ARE FORCES OF CREATION AND DESTRUCTION, WHICH HUMANS PARTICIPATE IN.
I CAN CREATE...
That's 108 onions!
BUT I CANNOT BRING MYSELF TO DESTROY.
AT MOST, I BEAR WITNESS.

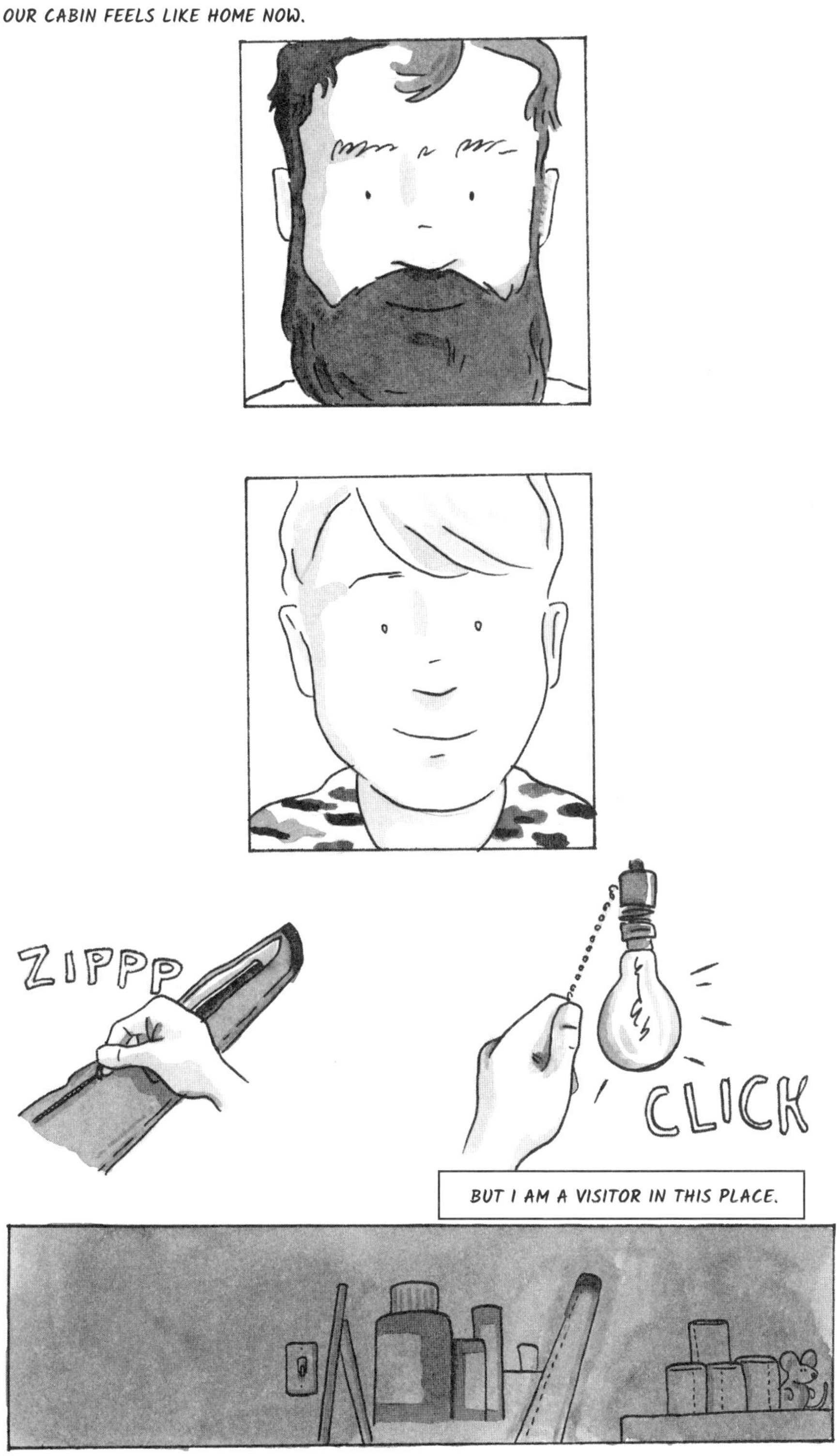
OUR CABIN FEELS LIKE HOME NOW.
ZIPPP
CLICK
BUT I AM A VISITOR IN THIS PLACE.

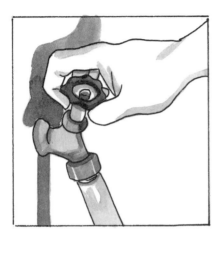

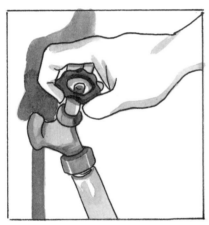

BY FALL, THE GARDEN HAD BECOME A FULL-TIME JOB.

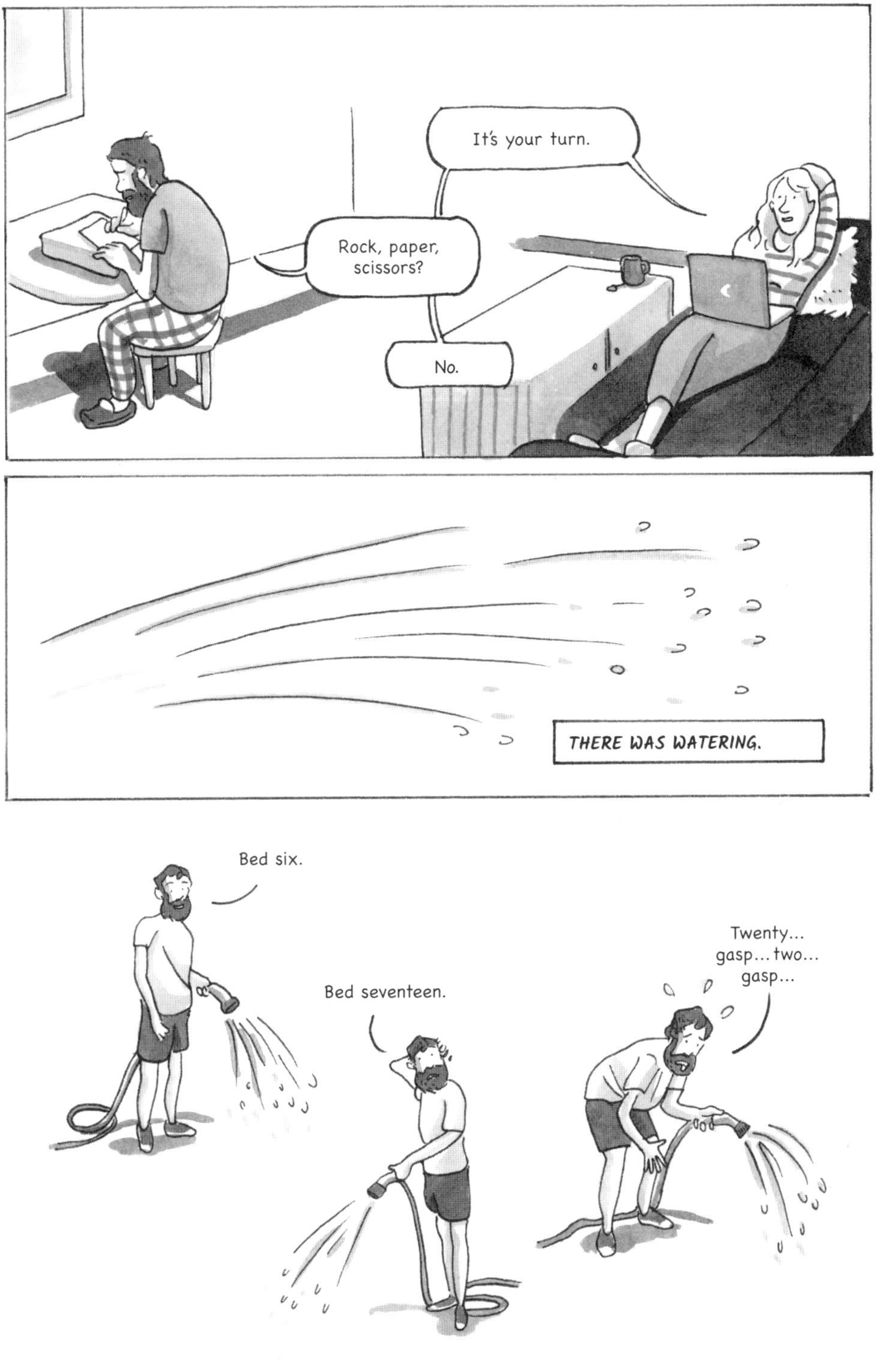

It's your turn.
Rock, paper, scissors?
No.
THERE WAS WATERING.
Bed six.
Bed seventeen.
Twenty... gasp... two... gasp...

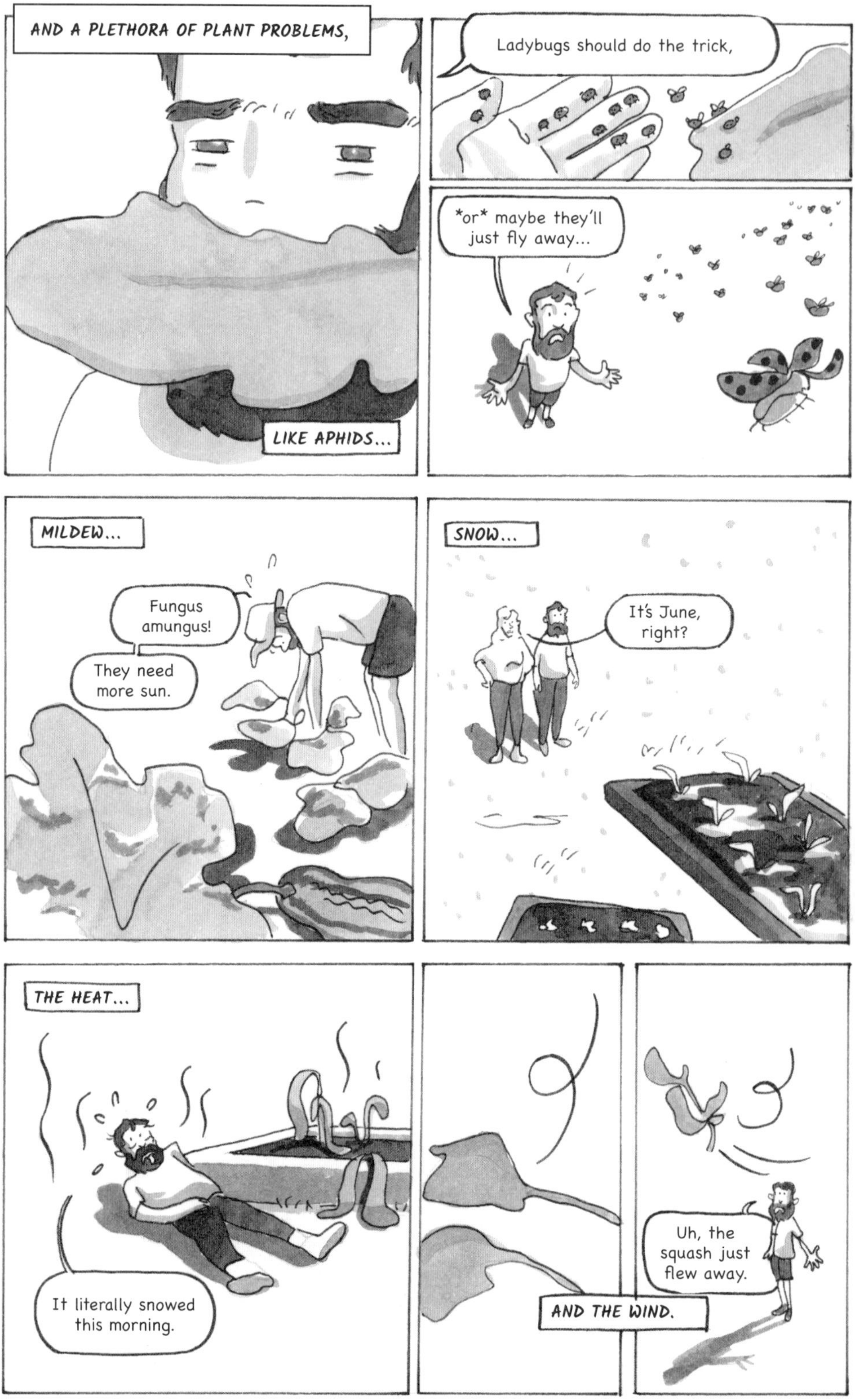
AND A PLETHORA OF PLANT PROBLEMS,
LIKE APHIDS...
Ladybugs should do the trick,
or maybe they'll just fly away...
MILDEW...
Fungus amungus!
They need more sun.
SNOW...
It's June, right?
THE HEAT...
It literally snowed this morning.
AND THE WIND.
Uh, the squash just flew away.

SOMETIMES I FELT LIKE A DETECTIVE IN SOME OLD NOIR.

It's a classic case of overwatering, or is it underwatering?

THE VICTIM

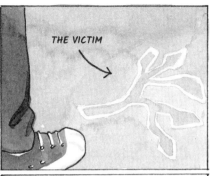

Forget it, Emelie. It's Idahotown.

ROLLING HER EYES OFF-SCREEN.

Five potatoes...in Idaho. The license plates literally say "Famous Potatoes."

I don't think we can live just off the garden yet.

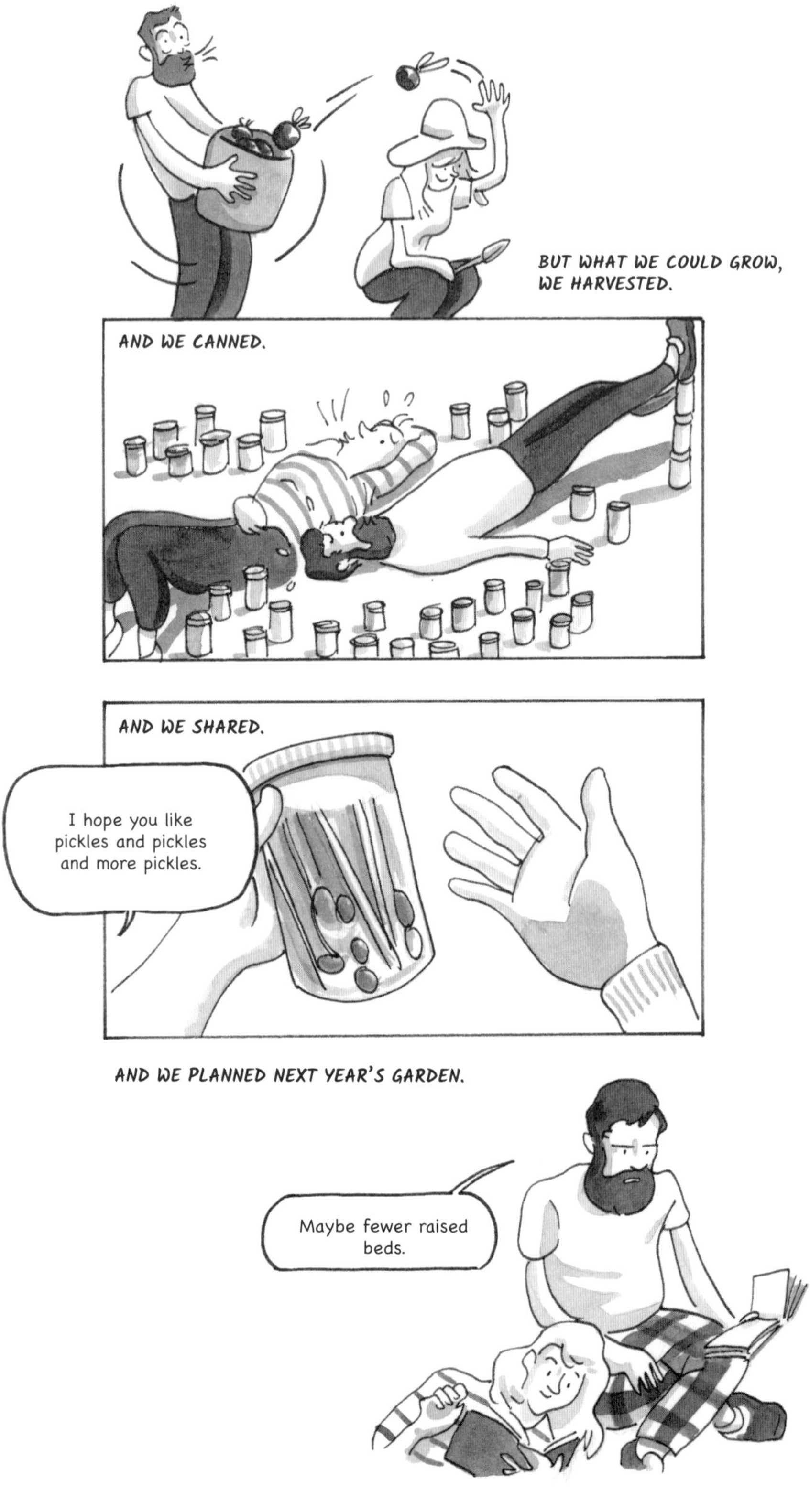
BUT WHAT WE COULD GROW,
WE HARVESTED.
AND WE CANNED.
AND WE SHARED.
I hope you like pickles and pickles and more pickles.
AND WE PLANNED NEXT YEAR'S GARDEN.
Maybe fewer raised beds.

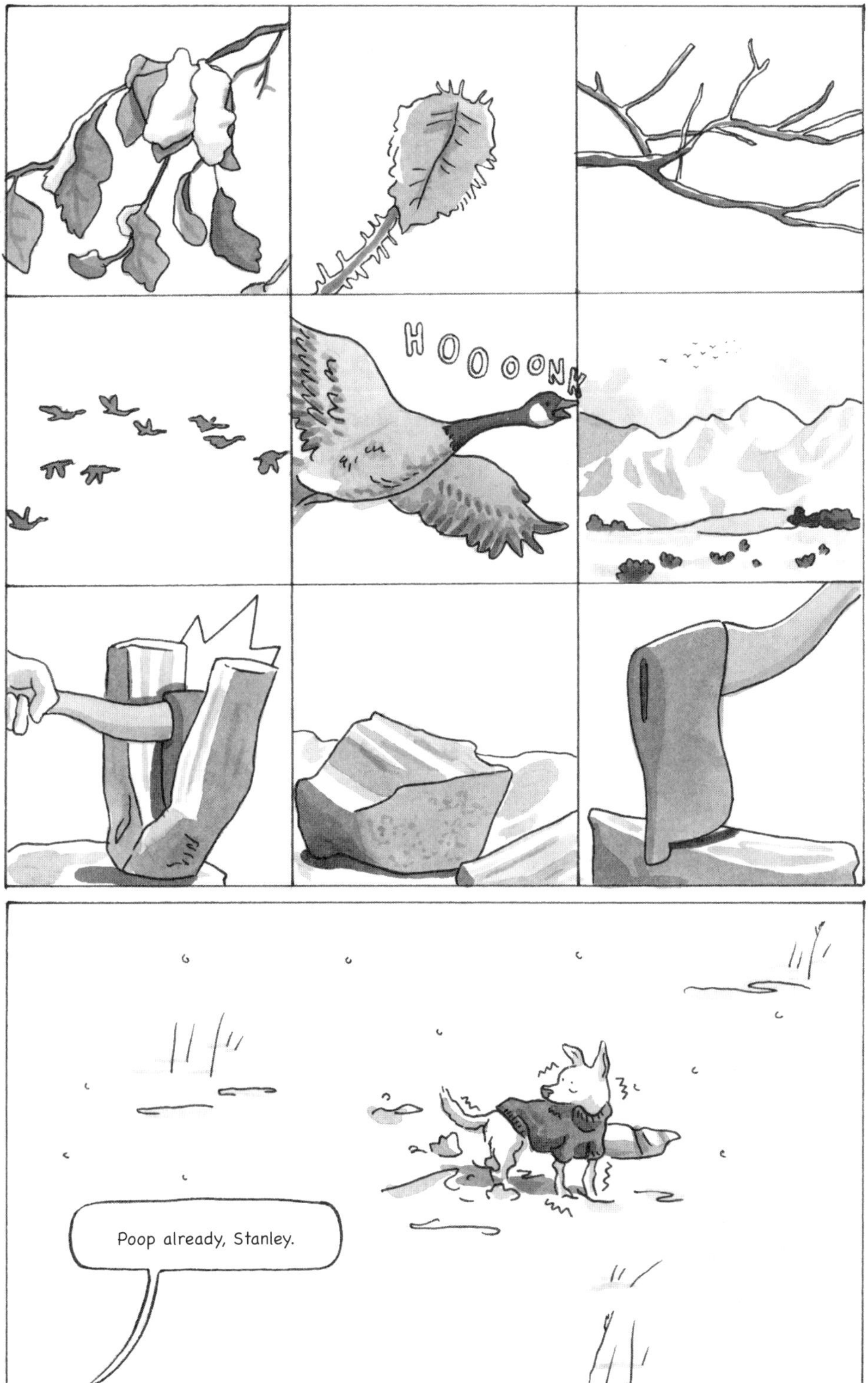
HOOOOONK
Poop already, Stanley.

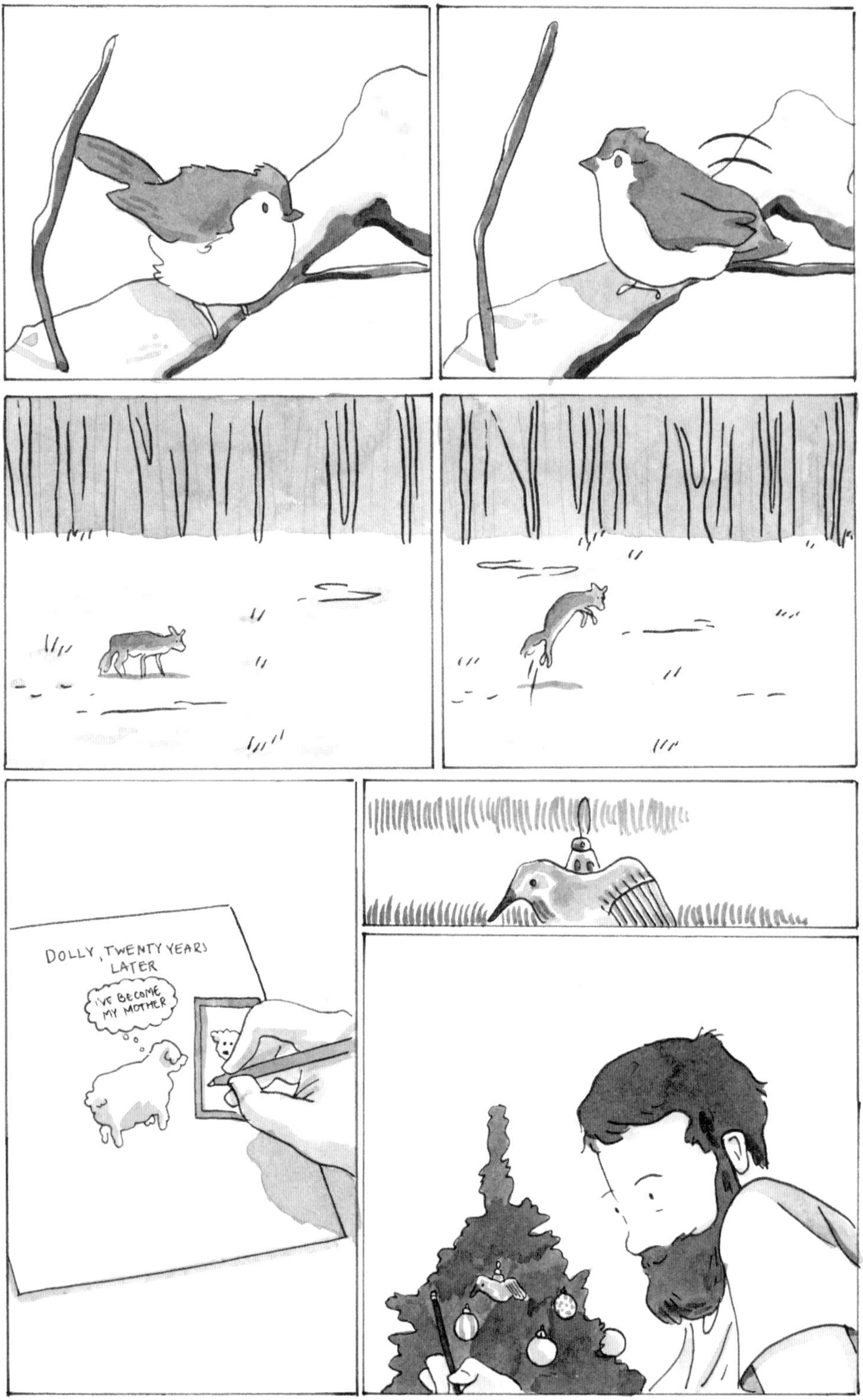
DOLLY, TWENTY YEARS LATER
I'VE BECOME MY MOTHER

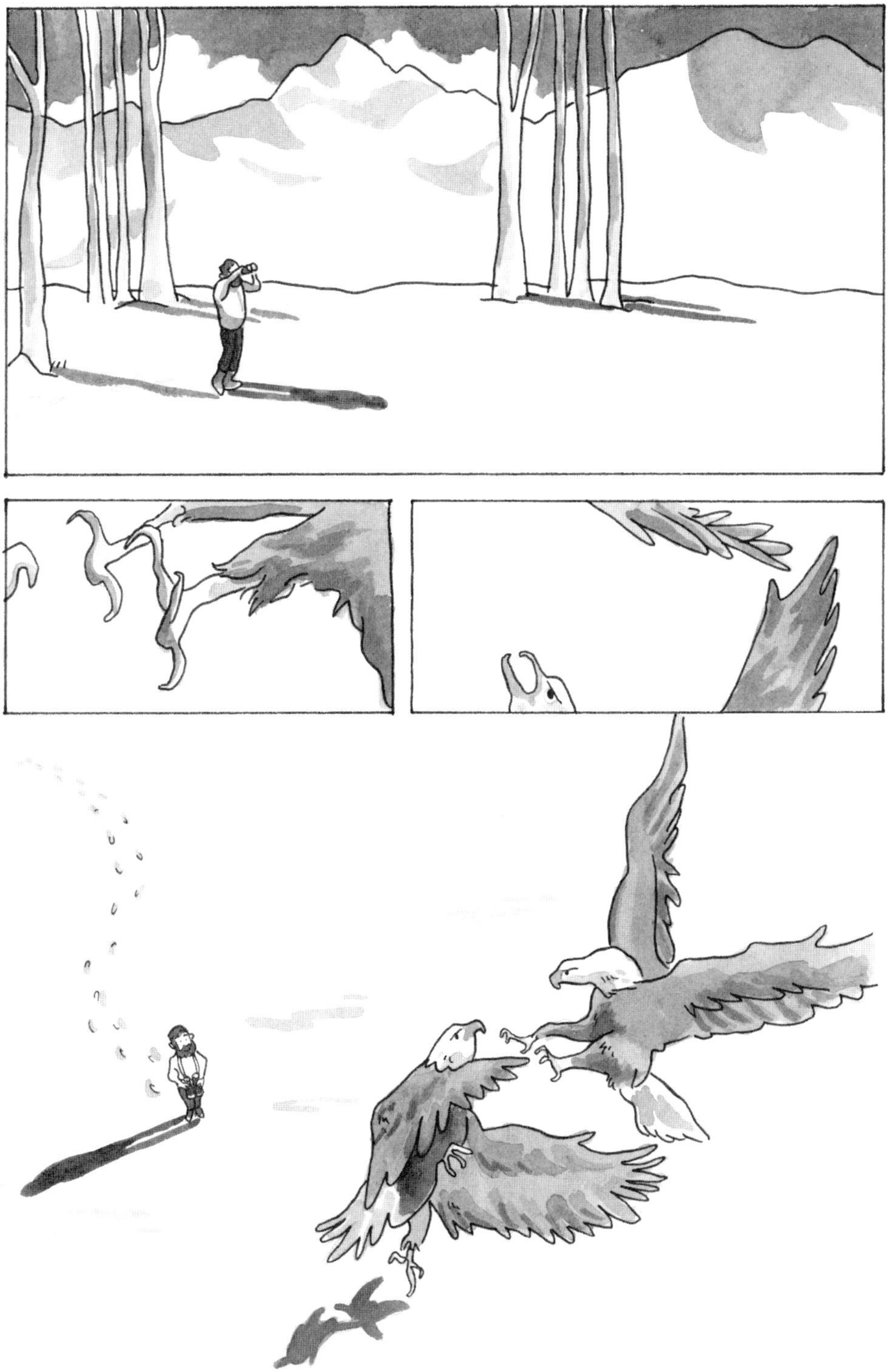

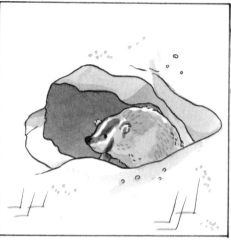

Hello, Mr. Badger.

EEEP!

GROWL

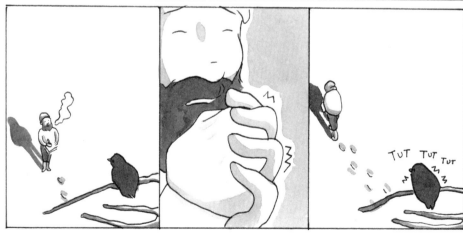

TUT TUT TUT

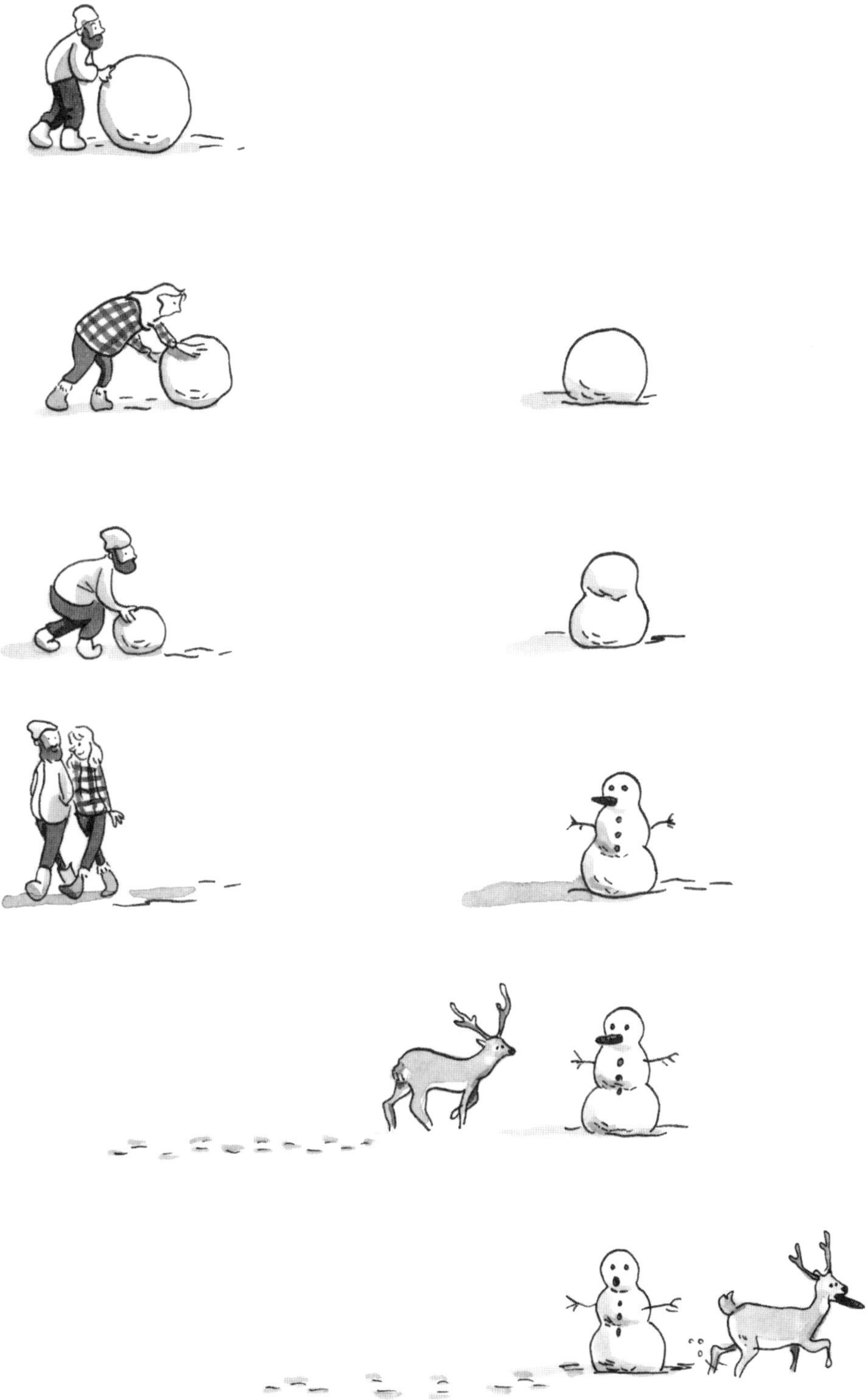

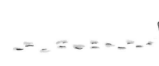

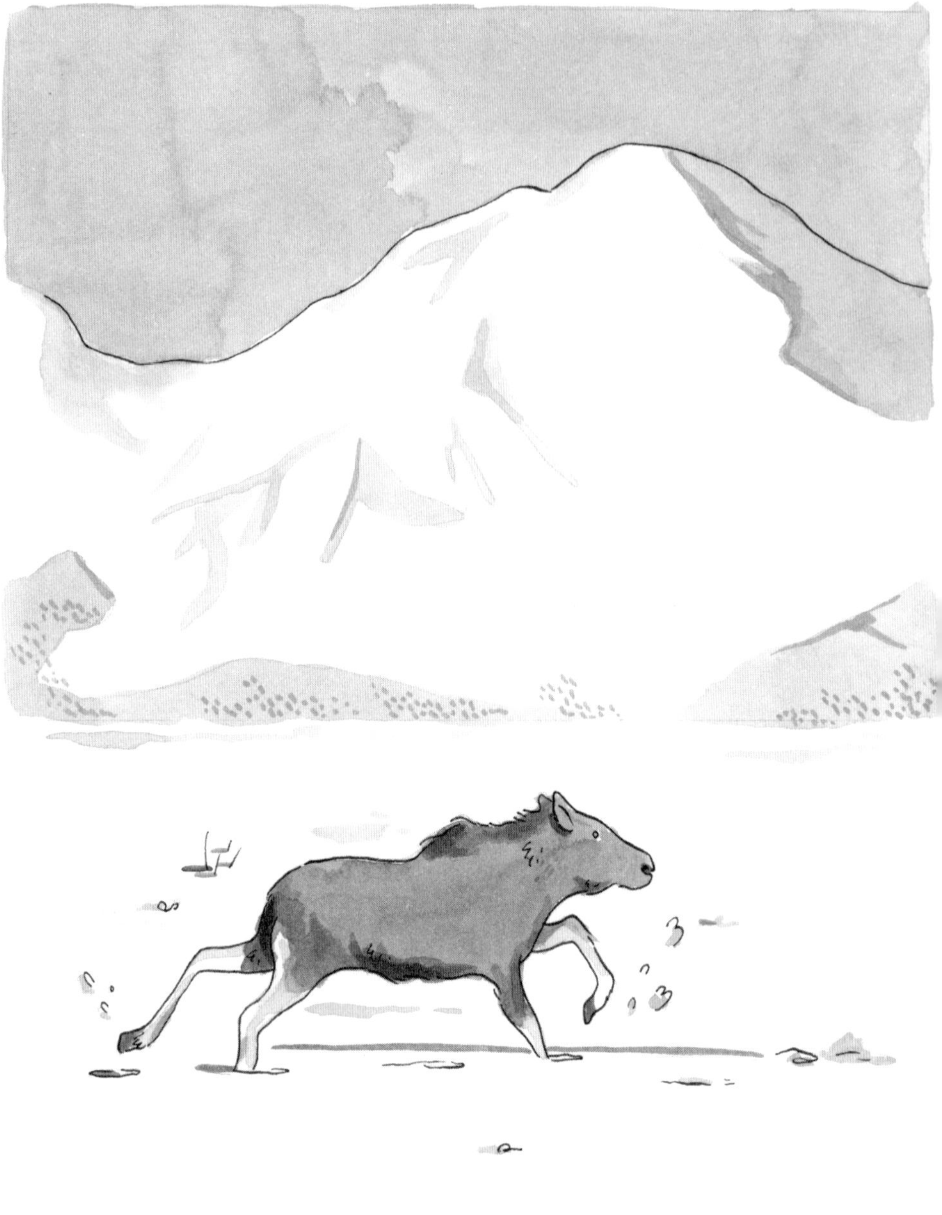

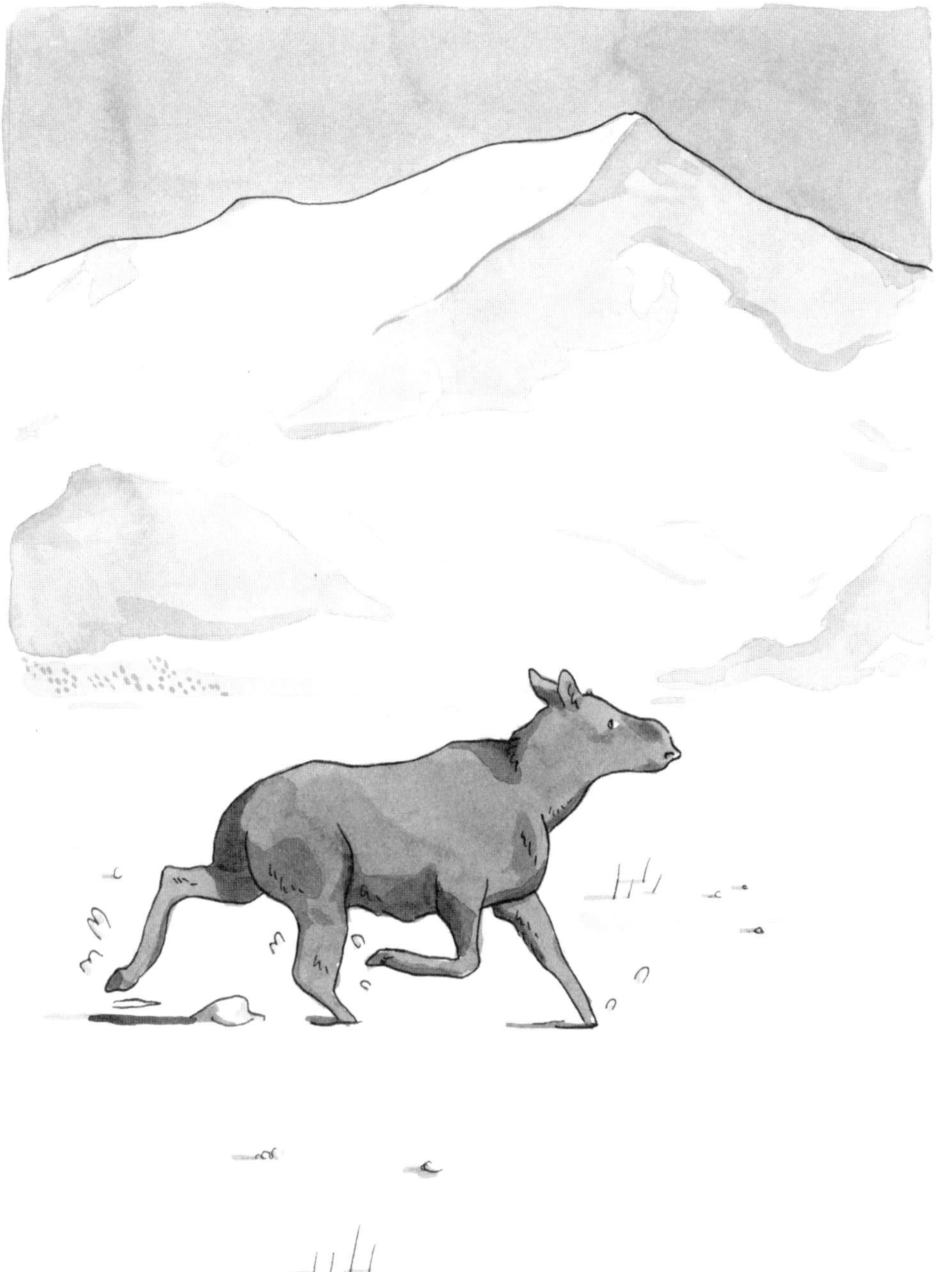

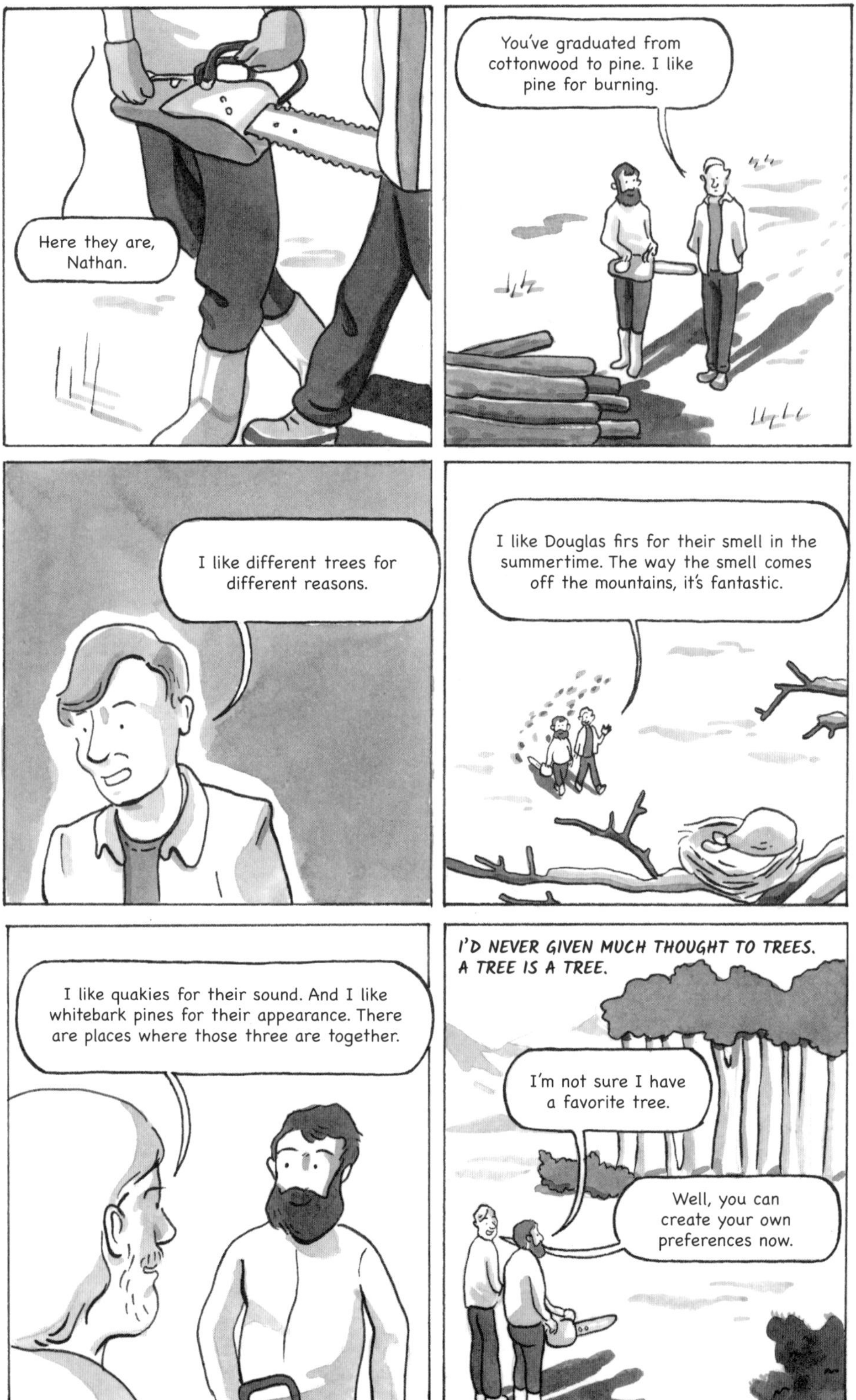
Here they are, Nathan.
You've graduated from cottonwood to pine. I like pine for burning.
I like different trees for different reasons.
I like Douglas firs for their smell in the summertime. The way the smell comes off the mountains, it's fantastic.
I like quakies for their sound. And I like whitebark pines for their appearance. There are places where those three are together.
I'D NEVER GIVEN MUCH THOUGHT TO TREES. A TREE IS A TREE.
I'm not sure I have a favorite tree.
Well, you can create your own preferences now.

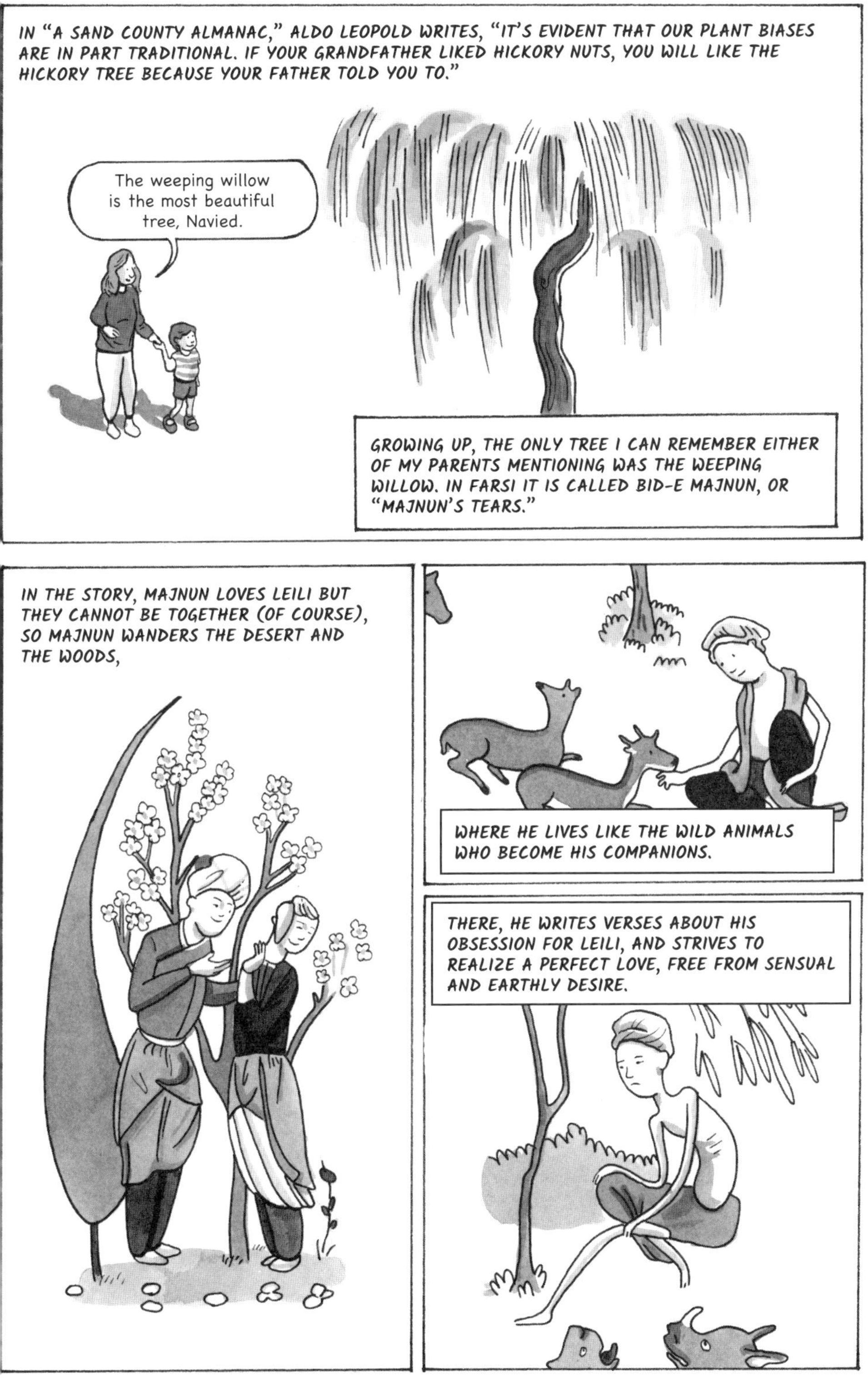
IN "A SAND COUNTY ALMANAC," ALDO LEOPOLD WRITES, "IT'S EVIDENT THAT OUR PLANT BIASES ARE IN PART TRADITIONAL. IF YOUR GRANDFATHER LIKED HICKORY NUTS, YOU WILL LIKE THE HICKORY TREE BECAUSE YOUR FATHER TOLD YOU TO."
The weeping willow is the most beautiful tree, Navied.
GROWING UP, THE ONLY TREE I CAN REMEMBER EITHER OF MY PARENTS MENTIONING WAS THE WEEPING WILLOW. IN FARSI IT IS CALLED BID-E MAJNUN, OR "MAJNUN'S TEARS."
IN THE STORY, MAJNUN LOVES LEILI BUT THEY CANNOT BE TOGETHER (OF COURSE), SO MAJNUN WANDERS THE DESERT AND THE WOODS,
WHERE HE LIVES LIKE THE WILD ANIMALS WHO BECOME HIS COMPANIONS.
THERE, HE WRITES VERSES ABOUT HIS OBSESSION FOR LEILI, AND STRIVES TO REALIZE A PERFECT LOVE, FREE FROM SENSUAL AND EARTHLY DESIRE.

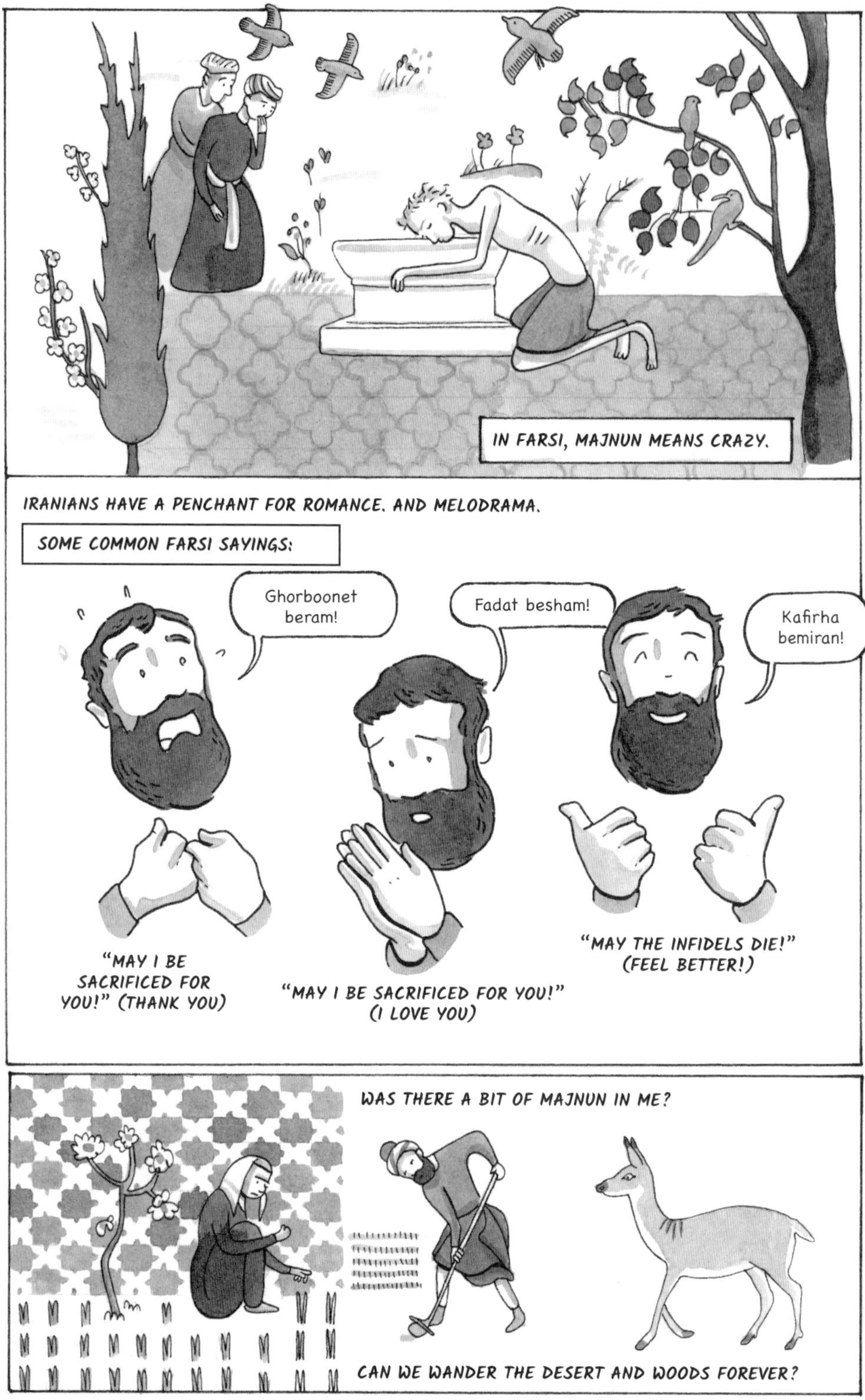
IN FARSI, MAJNUN MEANS CRAZY.
IRANIANS HAVE A PENCHANT FOR ROMANCE. AND MELODRAMA.
SOME COMMON FARSI SAYINGS:
Ghorboonet beram!
Fadat besham!
Kafirha bemiran!
"MAY I BE SACRIFICED FOR YOU!" (THANK YOU)
"MAY I BE SACRIFICED FOR YOU!" (I LOVE YOU)
"MAY THE INFIDELS DIE!" (FEEL BETTER!)
WAS THERE A BIT OF MAJNUN IN ME?
CAN WE WANDER THE DESERT AND WOODS FOREVER?

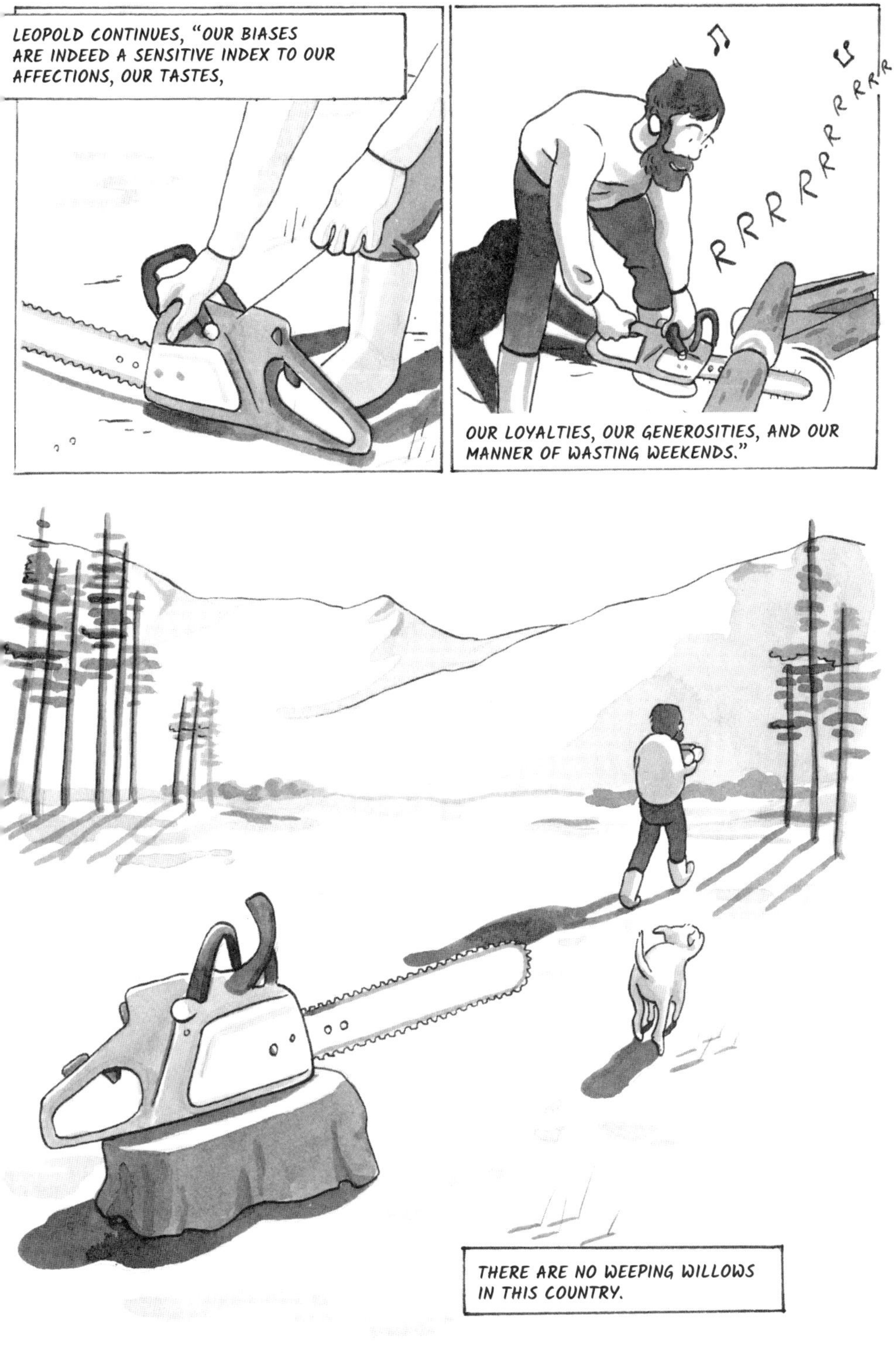
LEOPOLD CONTINUES, "OUR BIASES ARE INDEED A SENSITIVE INDEX TO OUR AFFECTIONS, OUR TASTES,
RRRRRRRRRRR
OUR LOYALTIES, OUR GENEROSITIES, AND OUR MANNER OF WASTING WEEKENDS."
THERE ARE NO WEEPING WILLOWS IN THIS COUNTRY.

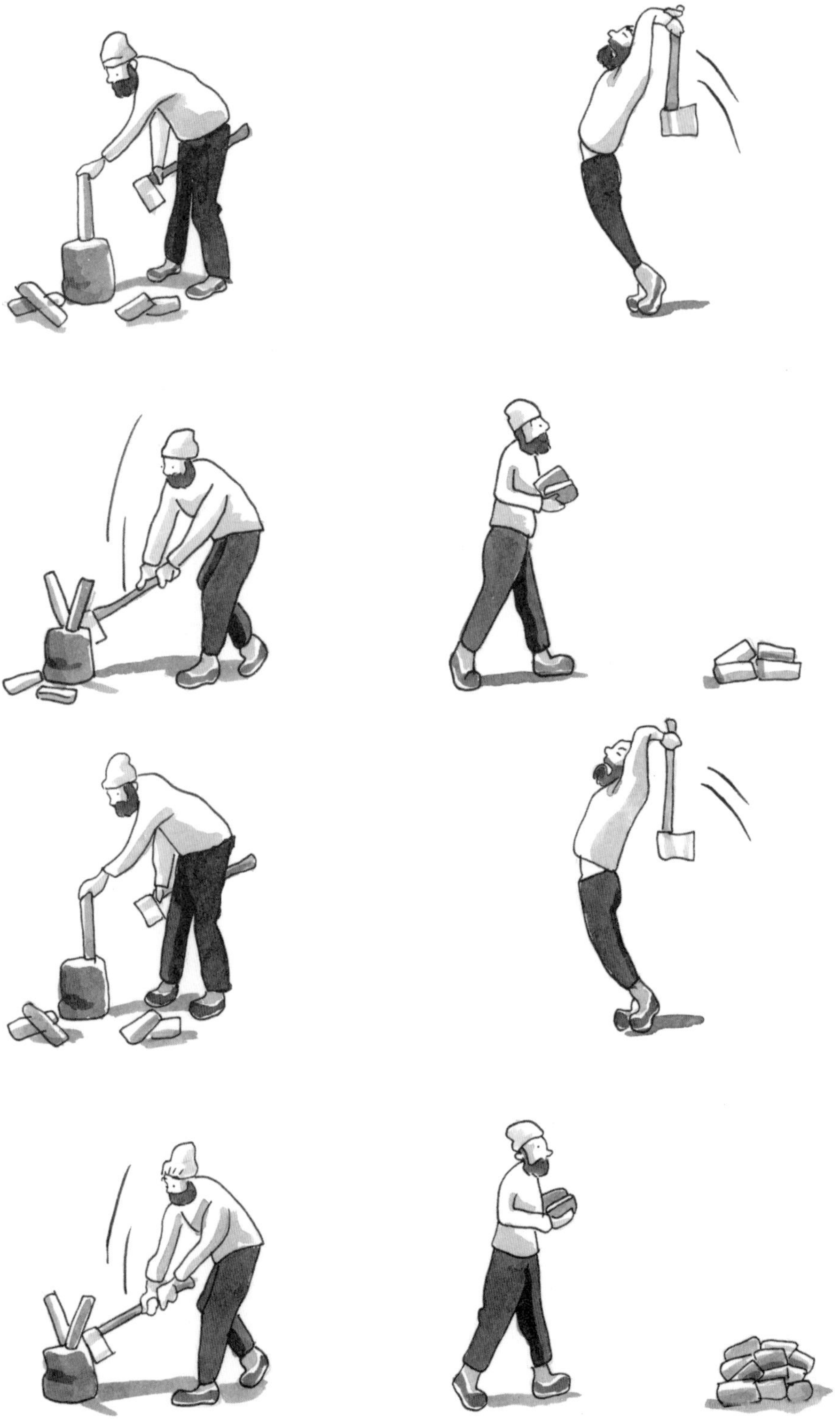

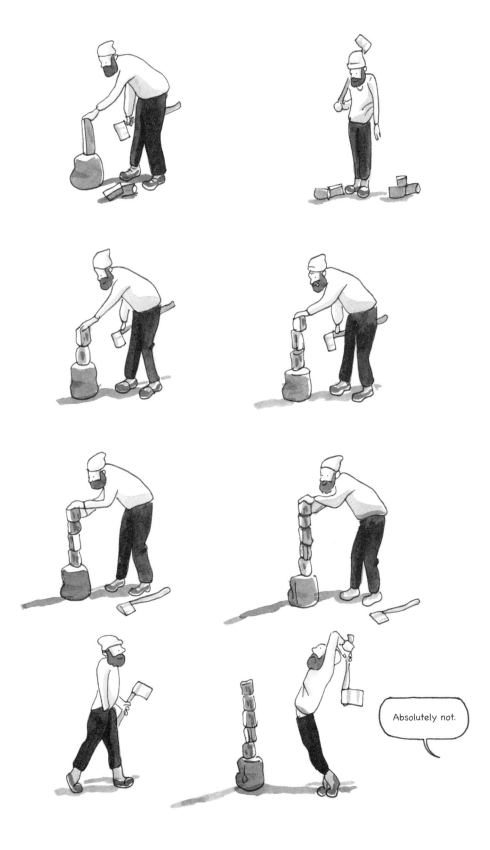

Absolutely not.

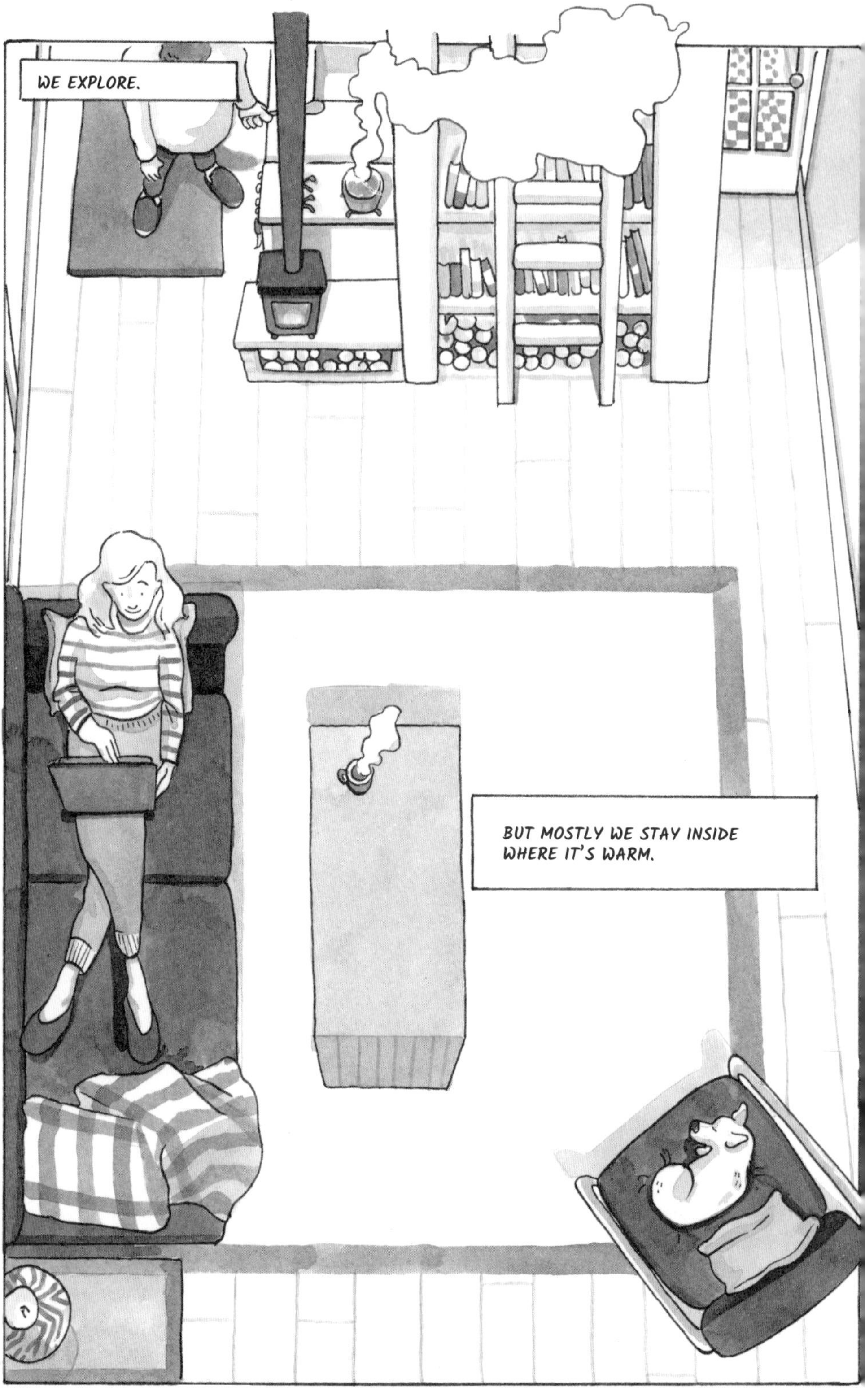
WE EXPLORE.
BUT MOSTLY WE STAY INSIDE WHERE IT'S WARM.

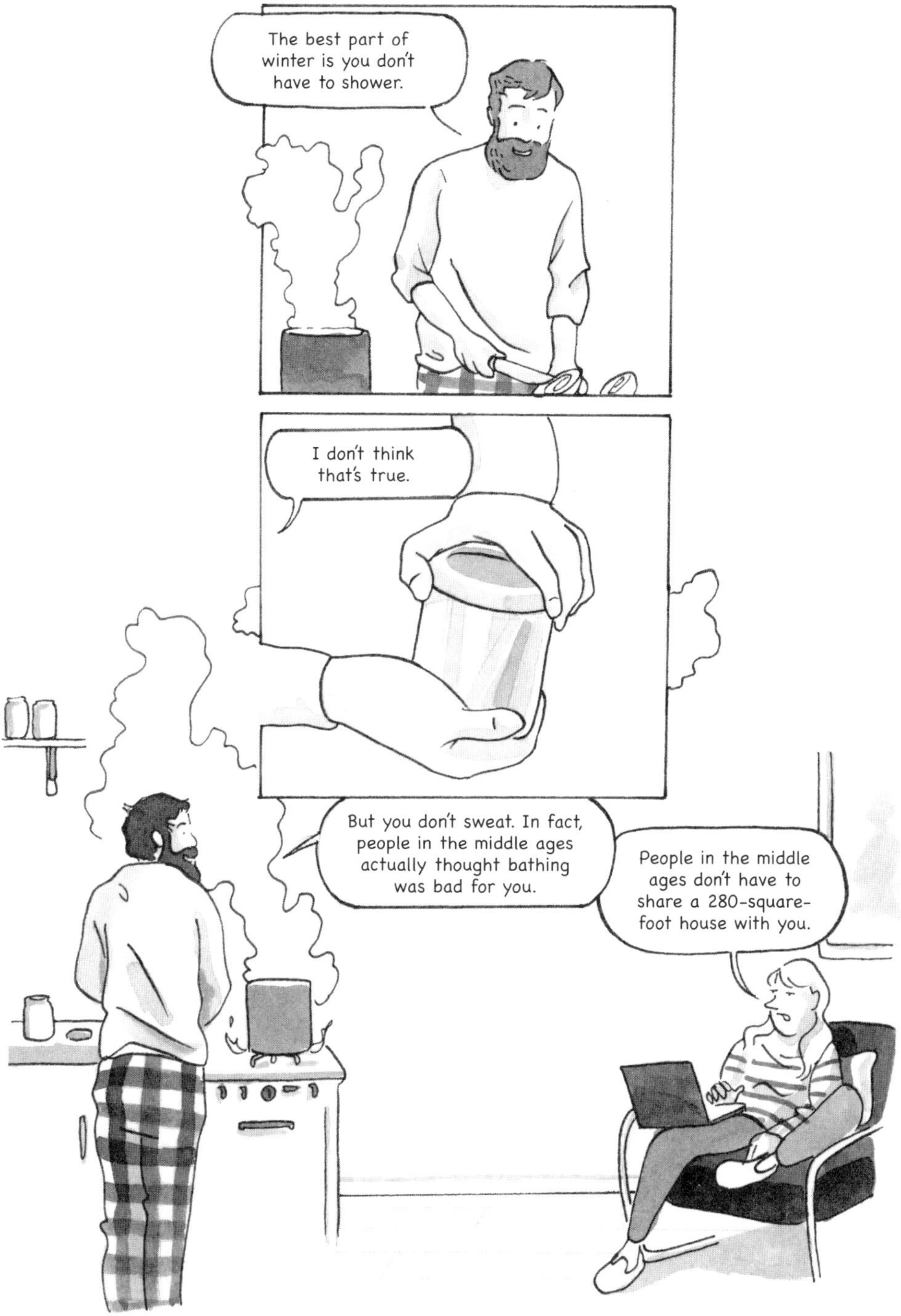
The best part of winter is you don't have to shower.
I don't think that's true.
But you don't sweat. In fact, people in the middle ages actually thought bathing was bad for you.
People in the middle ages don't have to share a 280-square-foot house with you.

PART 3

Spring 2018–Winter 2019

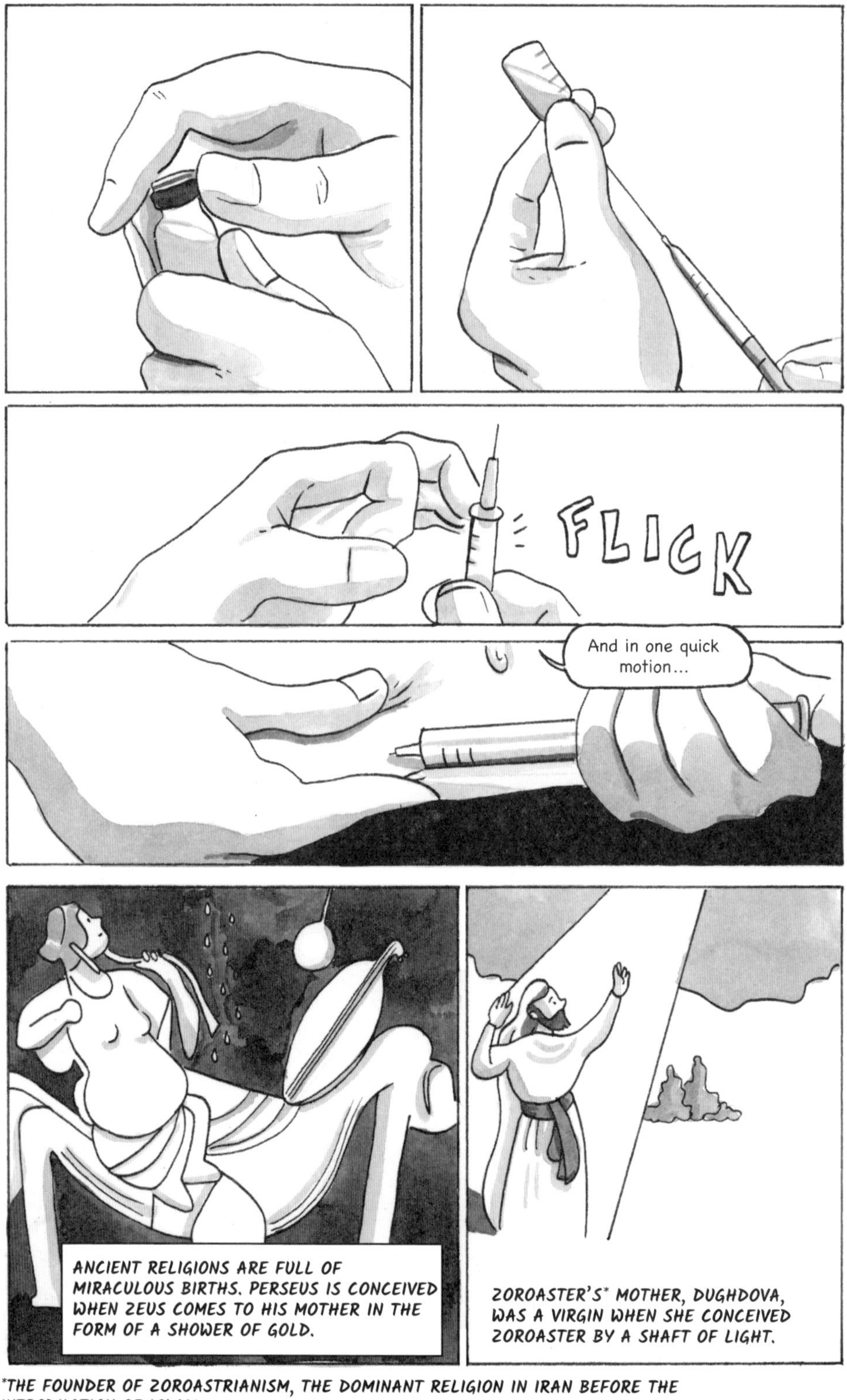
FLICK
And in one quick motion...
ANCIENT RELIGIONS ARE FULL OF MIRACULOUS BIRTHS. PERSEUS IS CONCEIVED WHEN ZEUS COMES TO HIS MOTHER IN THE FORM OF A SHOWER OF GOLD.
ZOROASTER'S* MOTHER, DUGHDOVA, WAS A VIRGIN WHEN SHE CONCEIVED ZOROASTER BY A SHAFT OF LIGHT.

*THE FOUNDER OF ZOROASTRIANISM, THE DOMINANT RELIGION IN IRAN BEFORE THE INTRODUCTION OF ISLAM.

THE WORD MIRACLE DERIVES FROM SMEIROS, "TO SMILE."

CLICK

ONE SMILES AT A MIRACLE. BUT AFTER TWO YEARS, OUR MIRACLE DOES NOT COME.

WE MUST COAX OUR CHILD INTO THE WORLD.

WE MEASURE TIME IN SIX-HOUR INTERVALS.

BEEP!

BEEP!

4:00 AM

BEEP!

These lumps from the injections can last weeks.

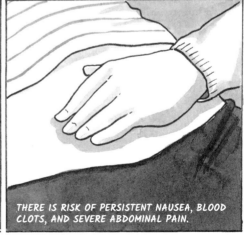
THERE IS RISK OF PERSISTENT NAUSEA, BLOOD CLOTS, AND SEVERE ABDOMINAL PAIN.

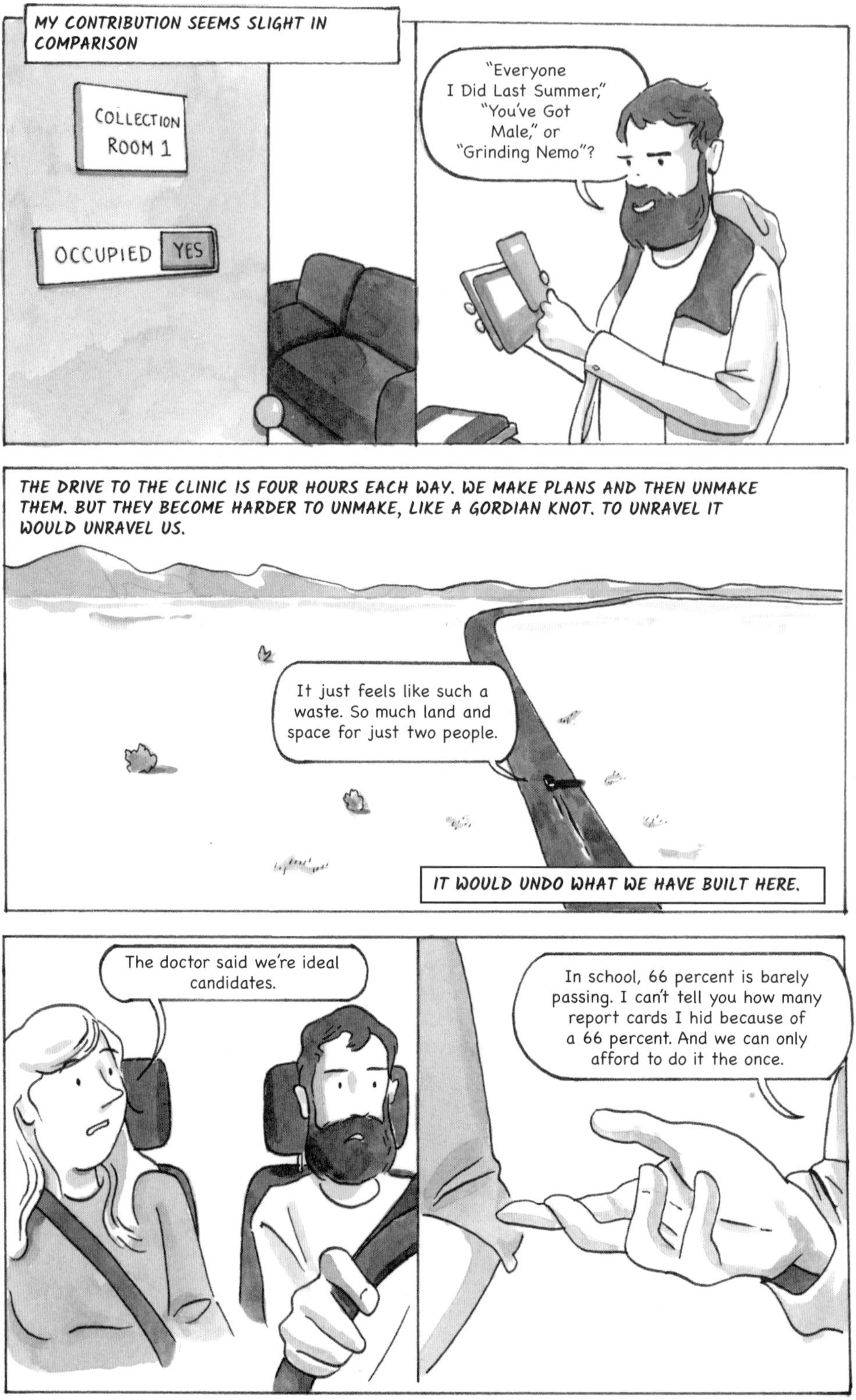
MY CONTRIBUTION SEEMS SLIGHT IN COMPARISON
COLLECTION ROOM 1
OCCUPIED YES
"Everyone I Did Last Summer," "You've Got Male," or "Grinding Nemo"?
THE DRIVE TO THE CLINIC IS FOUR HOURS EACH WAY. WE MAKE PLANS AND THEN UNMAKE THEM. BUT THEY BECOME HARDER TO UNMAKE, LIKE A GORDIAN KNOT. TO UNRAVEL IT WOULD UNRAVEL US.
It just feels like such a waste. So much land and space for just two people.
IT WOULD UNDO WHAT WE HAVE BUILT HERE.
The doctor said we're ideal candidates.
In school, 66 percent is barely passing. I can't tell you how many report cards I hid because of a 66 percent. And we can only afford to do it the once.

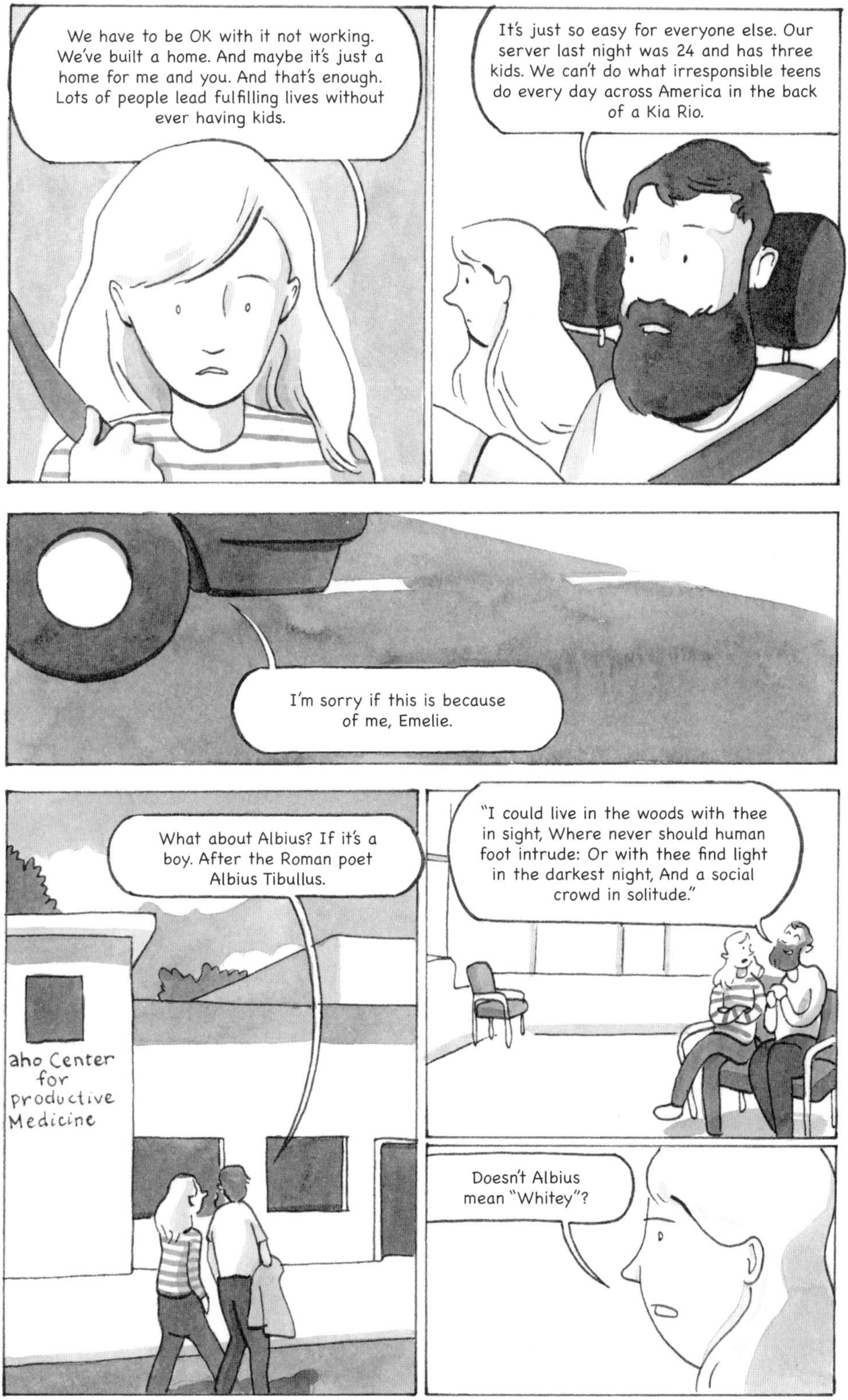
We have to be OK with it not working. We've built a home. And maybe it's just a home for me and you. And that's enough. Lots of people lead fulfilling lives without ever having kids.
It's just so easy for everyone else. Our server last night was 24 and has three kids. We can't do what irresponsible teens do every day across America in the back of a Kia Rio.
I'm sorry if this is because of me, Emelie.
What about Albius? If it's a boy. After the Roman poet Albius Tibullus.
aho Center for productive Medicine
"I could live in the woods with thee in sight, Where never should human foot intrude: Or with thee find light in the darkest night, And a social crowd in solitude."
Doesn't Albius mean "Whitey"?

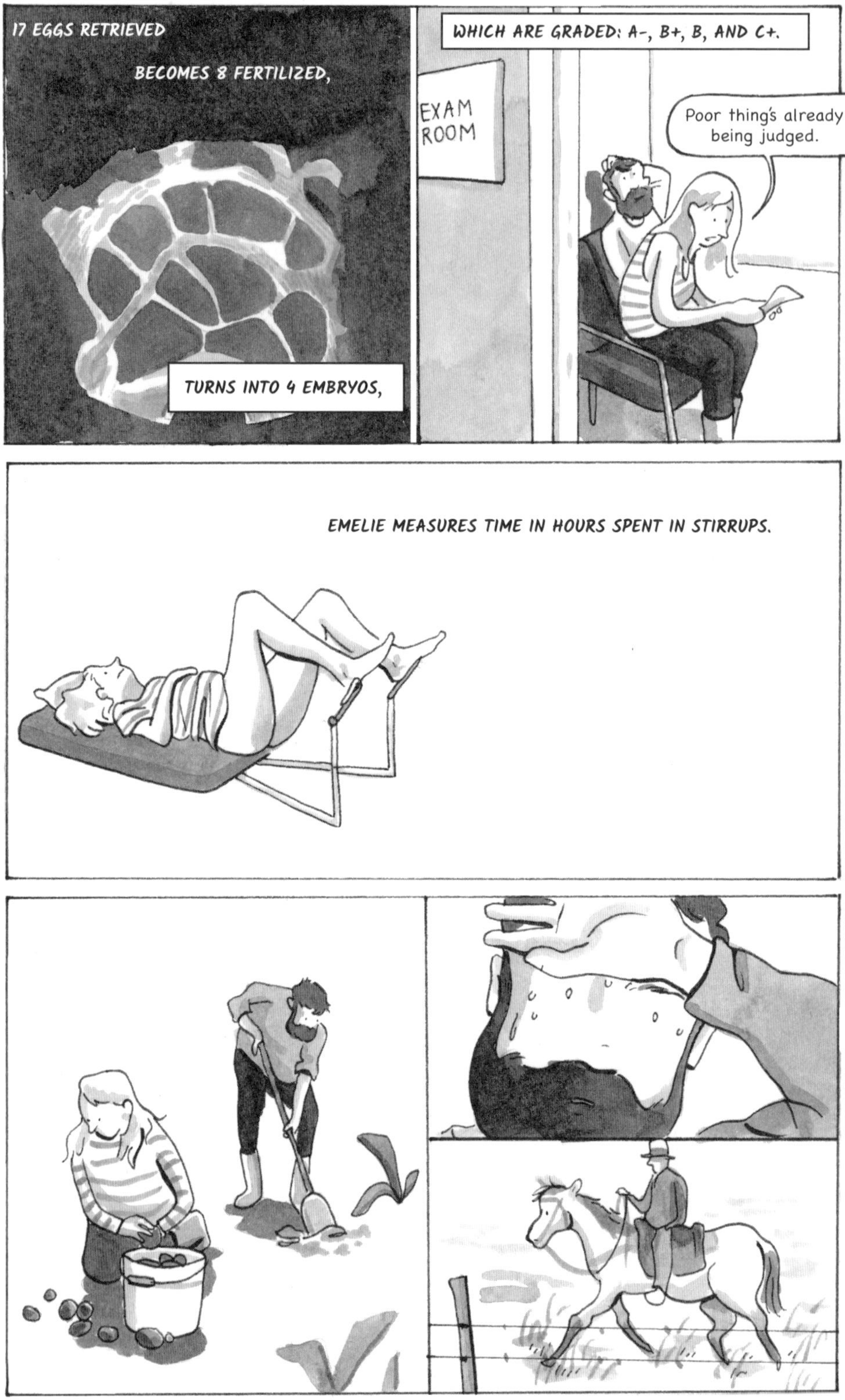
17 EGGS RETRIEVED
BECOMES 8 FERTILIZED,
TURNS INTO 4 EMBRYOS,
WHICH ARE GRADED: A-, B+, B, AND C+.
EXAM ROOM
Poor thing's already being judged.
EMELIE MEASURES TIME IN HOURS SPENT IN STIRRUPS.

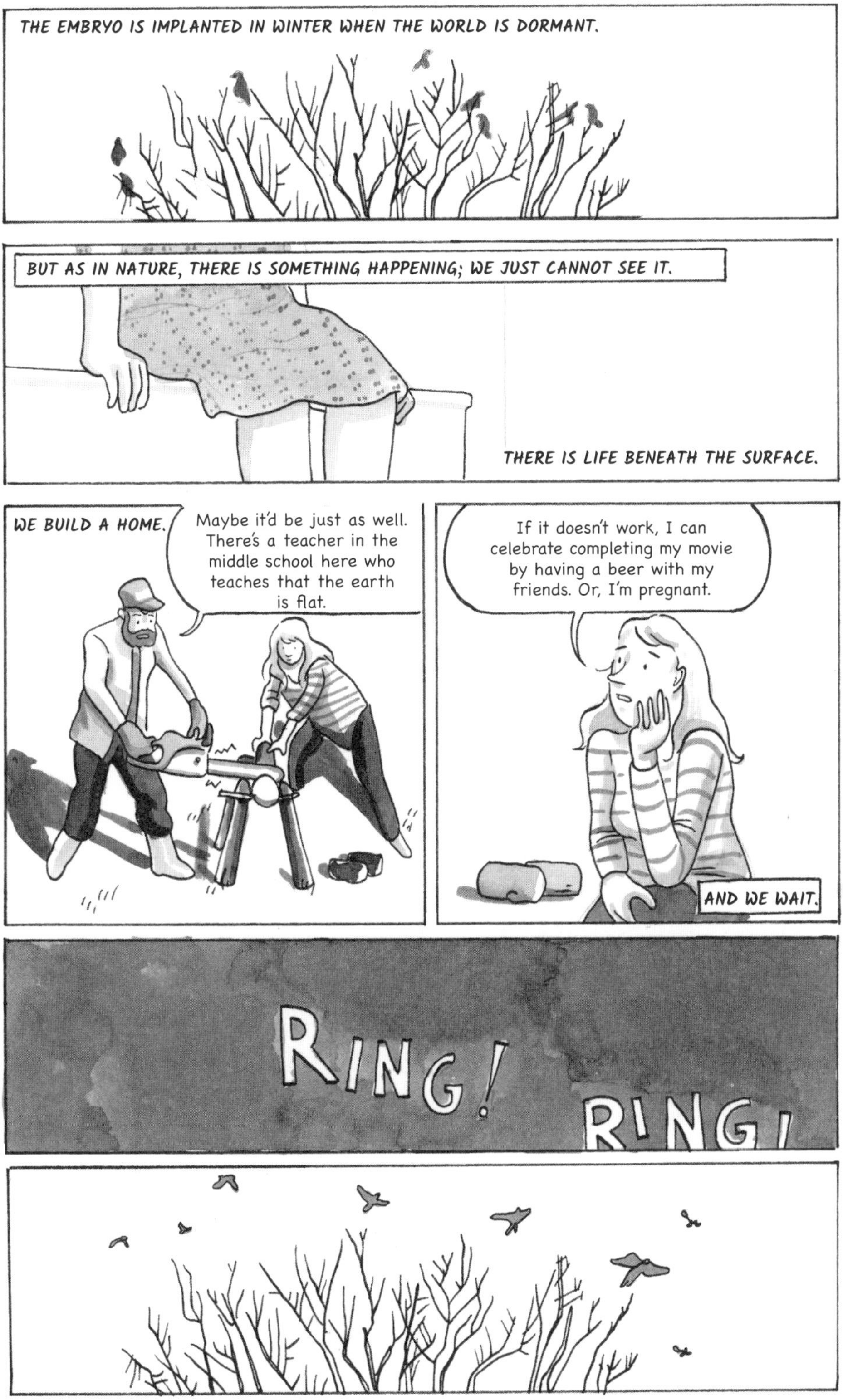
THE EMBRYO IS IMPLANTED IN WINTER WHEN THE WORLD IS DORMANT.
BUT AS IN NATURE, THERE IS SOMETHING HAPPENING; WE JUST CANNOT SEE IT.
THERE IS LIFE BENEATH THE SURFACE.
WE BUILD A HOME.
Maybe it'd be just as well. There's a teacher in the middle school here who teaches that the earth is flat.
If it doesn't work, I can celebrate completing my movie by having a beer with my friends. Or, I'm pregnant.
AND WE WAIT.
RING!
RING!

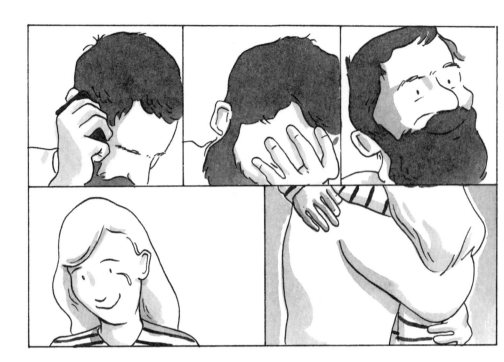

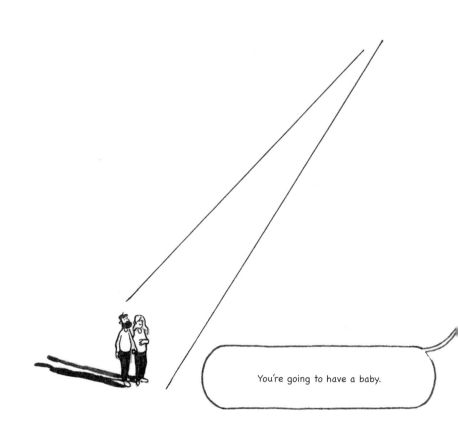

You're going to have a baby.

A SINGLE FLOWER, WHITE TO DEEP PINK OR LAVENDER. IT HUGS THE GROUND, NO DOUBT TO GET AWAY FROM THE CONSTANT WINDS THAT BLOW ACROSS THE HIGH DESERT STEPPE.

IN MAY, SCATTERED AMONG SAGEBRUSH ARE SMALL, SLIGHT SPROUTS.

THEY LOOK LIKE THEY HAVE FALLEN FROM THE SKY.

EX NIHILO. FROM NOTHING.

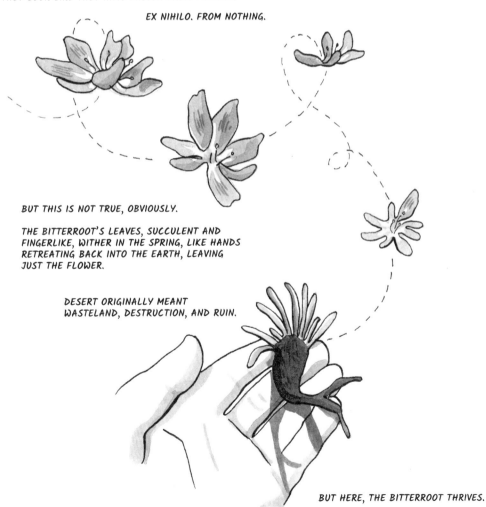

BUT THIS IS NOT TRUE, OBVIOUSLY.

THE BITTERROOT'S LEAVES, SUCCULENT AND FINGERLIKE, WITHER IN THE SPRING, LIKE HANDS RETREATING BACK INTO THE EARTH, LEAVING JUST THE FLOWER.

DESERT ORIGINALLY MEANT WASTELAND, DESTRUCTION, AND RUIN.

BUT HERE, THE BITTERROOT THRIVES.

This is so weird.

THE BITTERROOT IS NAMED AFTER MERIWETHER LEWIS, WHO BROUGHT IT BACK ON HIS 1805 EXPEDITION.

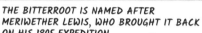

THE SPECIMEN, THOUGH DEPRIVED OF WATER AND SOIL FOR YEARS, WAS PLANTED AND TOOK ROOT AND GREW BACK ANYWAY.

LEWISIA REDIVIVA. ("REDIVIVA" MEANS REVIVED OR REBORN.)

IN 1862, THE ENGLISH BOTANIST JOSEPH HOOKER BOILED ITS ROOTS TO PREVENT IT FROM REGENERATING. A YEAR AND A HALF LATER, IT SHOWED SIGNS OF LIFE.

A PHOENIX REBORN FROM DIRT AND GRAVEL.

They say it's good to sing to the baby. That they can hear you.

Fuck the police!

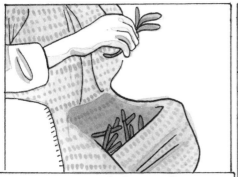

THE SALISH PEOPLE BELIEVE THAT THE BITTERROOT WAS CREATED BY THE SUN IN ORDER TO CONSOLE A DOLEFUL MOTHER, CRYING FROM LACK OF FOOD.

OF COURSE, LEWIS DIDN'T "DISCOVER" THE BITTERROOT. IT HAD LONG BEEN CULTURALLY SIGNIFICANT FOR MANY NATIVE AMERICAN TRIBES. TRADITIONALLY, THE ROOTS WERE GATHERED, DRIED FOR STORAGE, AND USED FOR FOOD OR TRADE.

THE SUN TURNED HER TEARS INTO THE BITTERROOT.

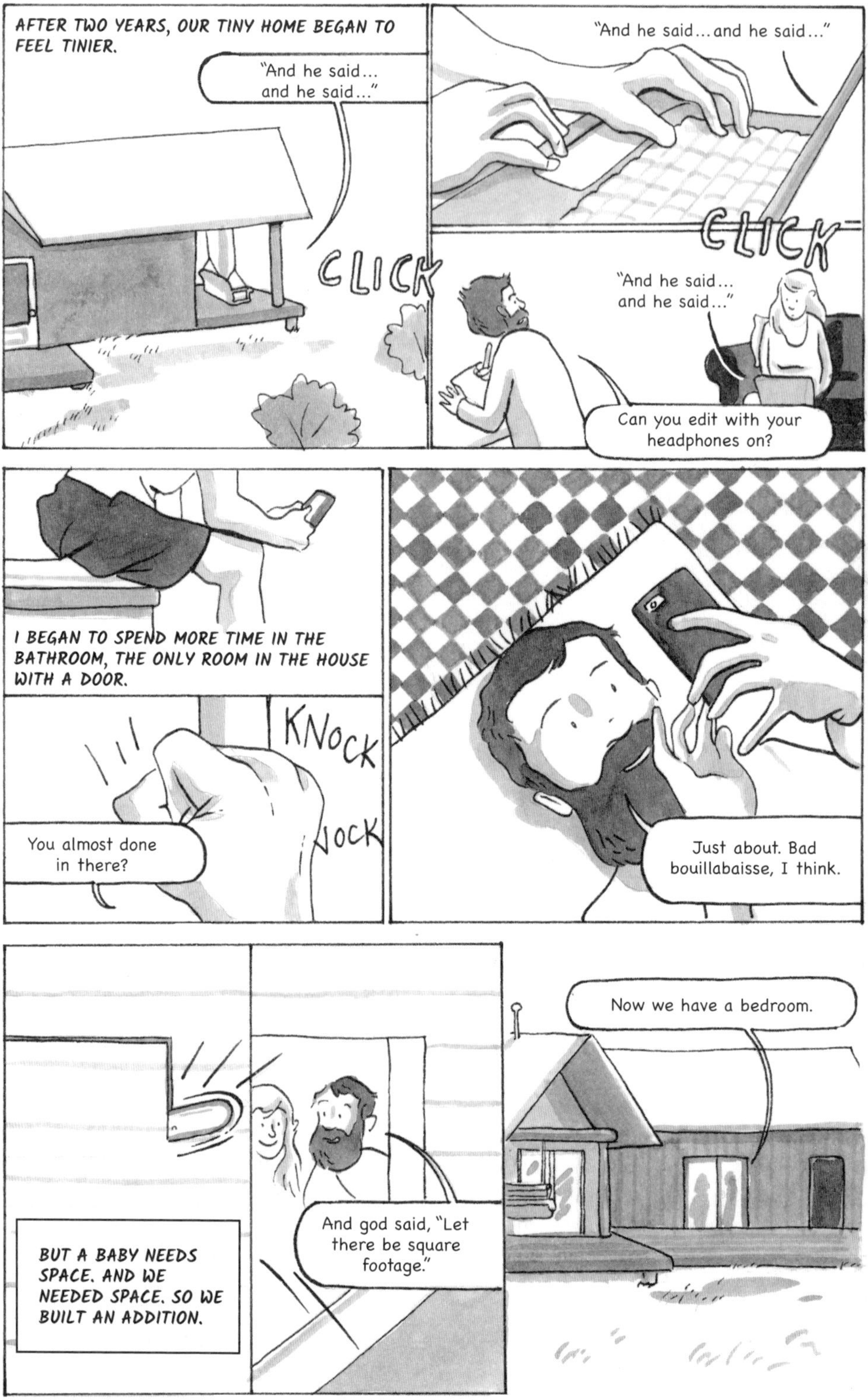
AFTER TWO YEARS, OUR TINY HOME BEGAN TO FEEL TINIER.
"And he said... and he said..."
CLICK
"And he said... and he said..."
CLICK
"And he said... and he said..."
Can you edit with your headphones on?
I BEGAN TO SPEND MORE TIME IN THE BATHROOM, THE ONLY ROOM IN THE HOUSE WITH A DOOR.
KNOCK
KNOCK
You almost done in there?
Just about. Bad bouillabaisse, I think.
BUT A BABY NEEDS SPACE. AND WE NEEDED SPACE. SO WE BUILT AN ADDITION.
And god said, "Let there be square footage."
Now we have a bedroom.

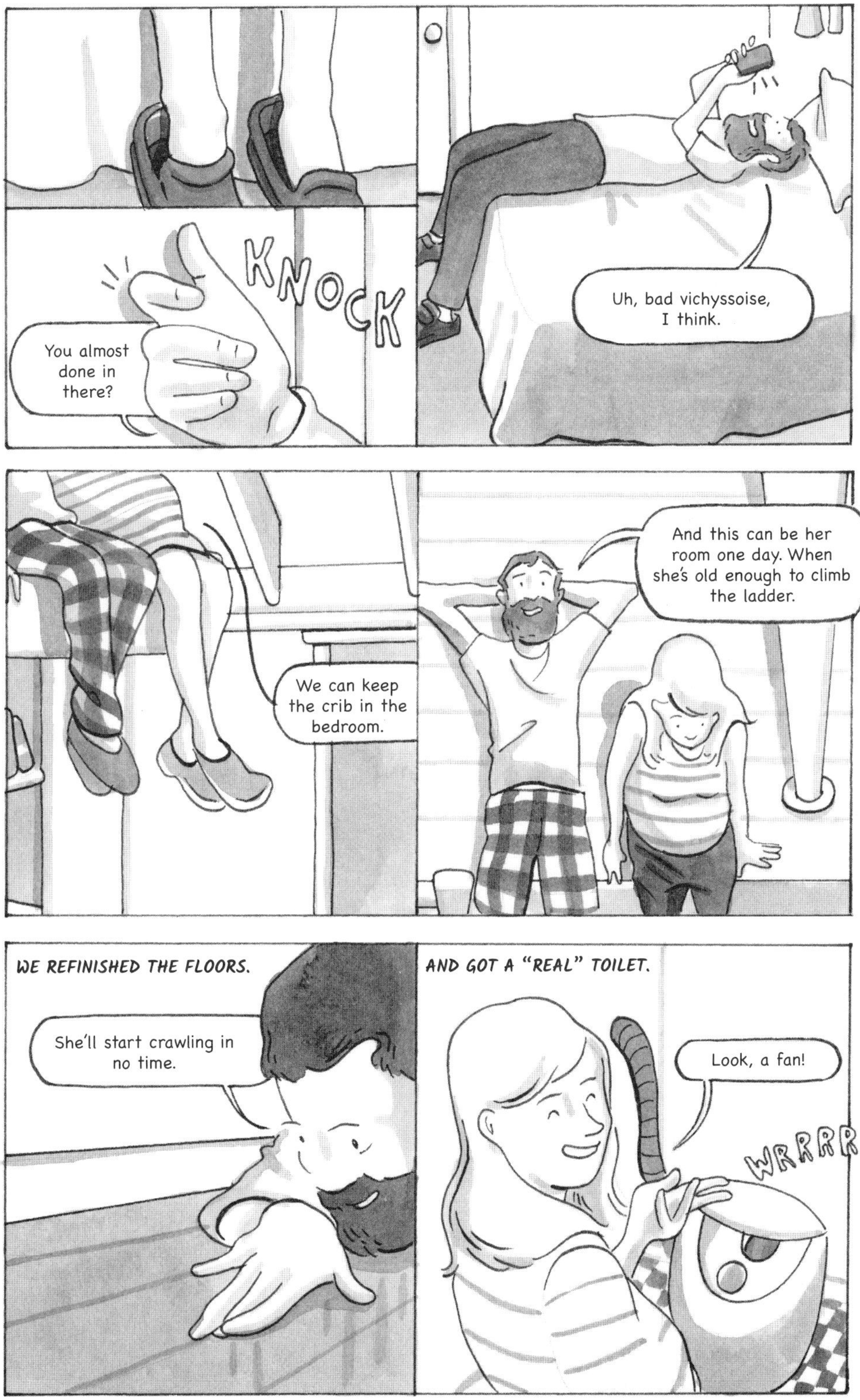

KNOCK
You almost done in there?
Uh, bad vichyssoise, I think.
We can keep the crib in the bedroom.
And this can be her room one day. When she's old enough to climb the ladder.
WE REFINISHED THE FLOORS.
She'll start crawling in no time.
AND GOT A "REAL" TOILET.
Look, a fan!
WRRRR

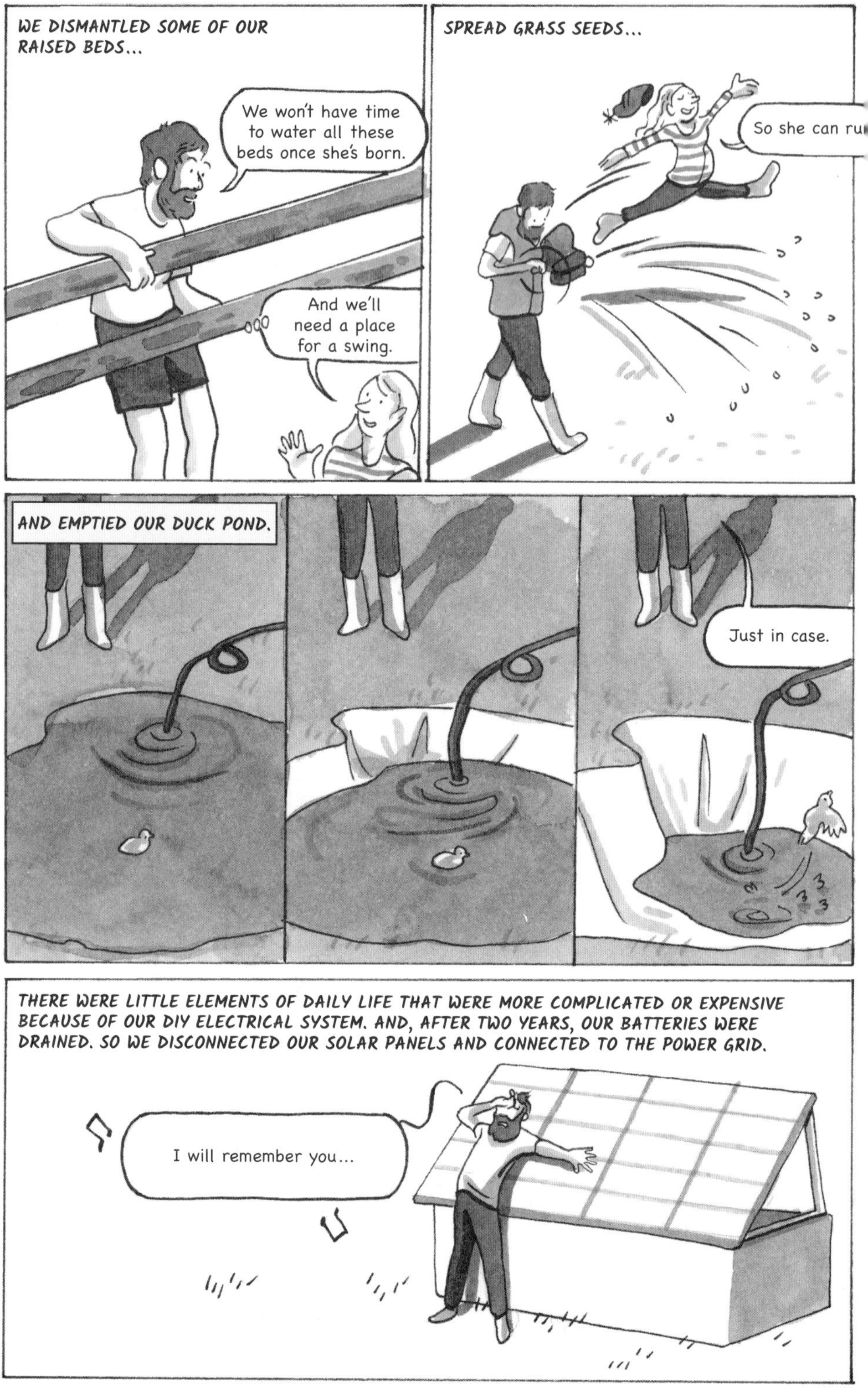
WE DISMANTLED SOME OF OUR RAISED BEDS...
We won't have time to water all these beds once she's born.
And we'll need a place for a swing.
SPREAD GRASS SEEDS...
So she can ru
AND EMPTIED OUR DUCK POND.
Just in case.
THERE WERE LITTLE ELEMENTS OF DAILY LIFE THAT WERE MORE COMPLICATED OR EXPENSIVE BECAUSE OF OUR DIY ELECTRICAL SYSTEM. AND, AFTER TWO YEARS, OUR BATTERIES WERE DRAINED. SO WE DISCONNECTED OUR SOLAR PANELS AND CONNECTED TO THE POWER GRID.
I will remember you...

WE ARE NOW "GRID TIED," OUR HOME PHYSICALLY TETHERED TO THIS PLACE, TO THIS TOWN. BABIES MEAN COMMUNITY, REAL ROOTS. WE LAY POWER LINES THAT WILL CARRY ELECTRONS THE TWENTY MILES TO TOWN AND BACK.

WE BURY OUR ROOTS SIX INCHES BELOW THE SURFACE.

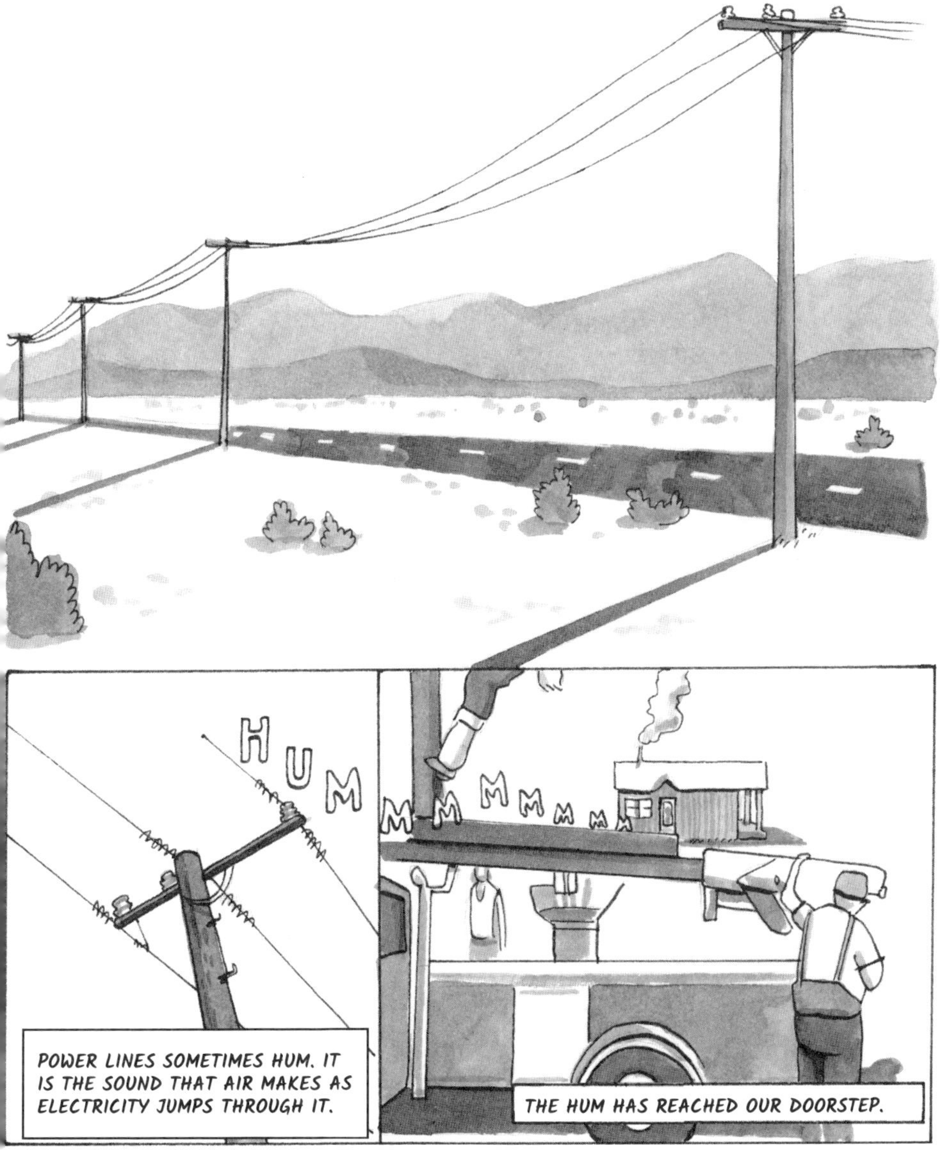
HUM
POWER LINES SOMETIMES HUM. IT IS THE SOUND THAT AIR MAKES AS ELECTRICITY JUMPS THROUGH IT.
MMMMMMMMM
THE HUM HAS REACHED OUR DOORSTEP.

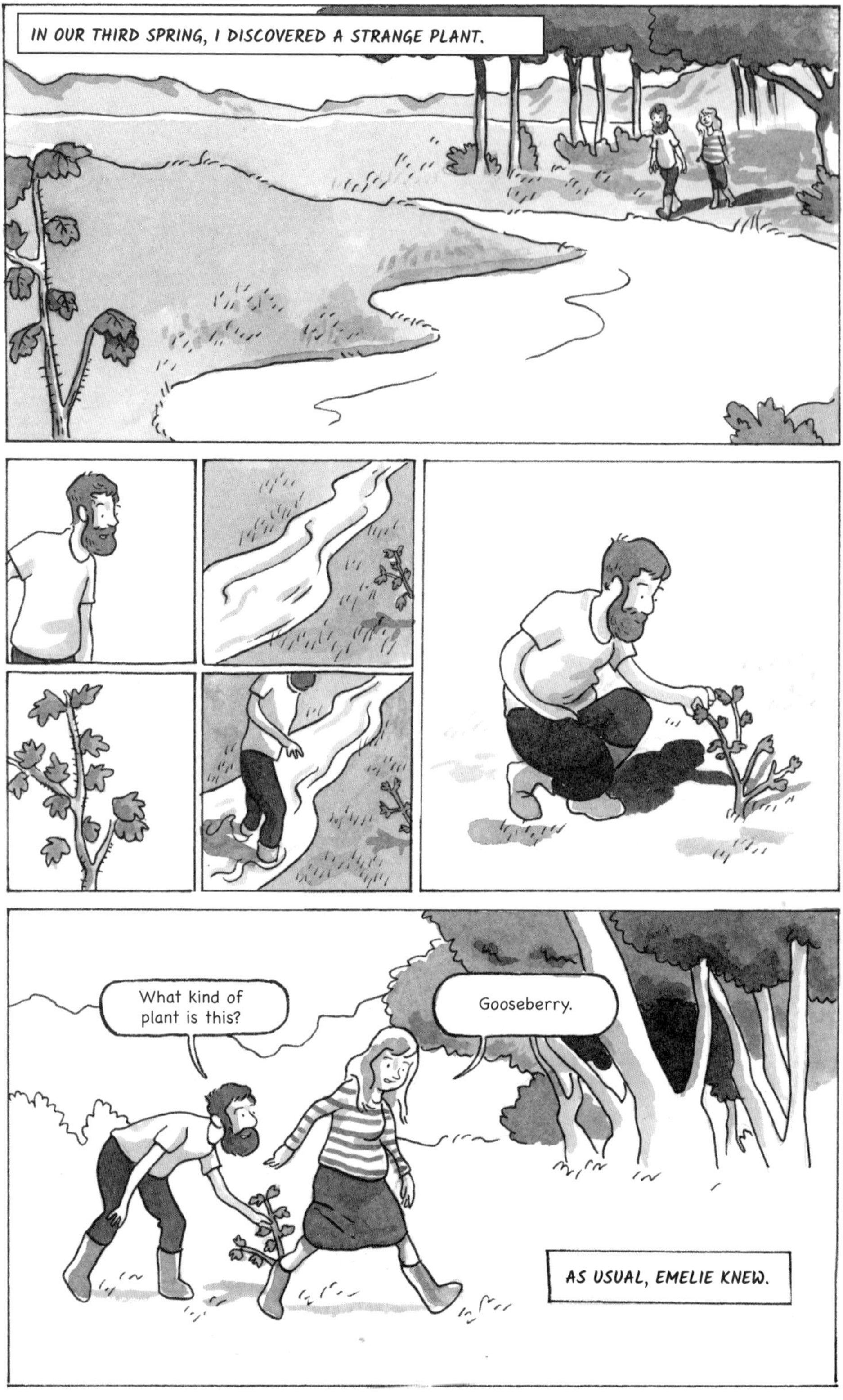
IN OUR THIRD SPRING, I DISCOVERED A STRANGE PLANT.
What kind of plant is this?
Gooseberry.
AS USUAL, EMELIE KNEW.

AFTER DISCOVERING THEM, I SAW THEM EVERYWHERE.

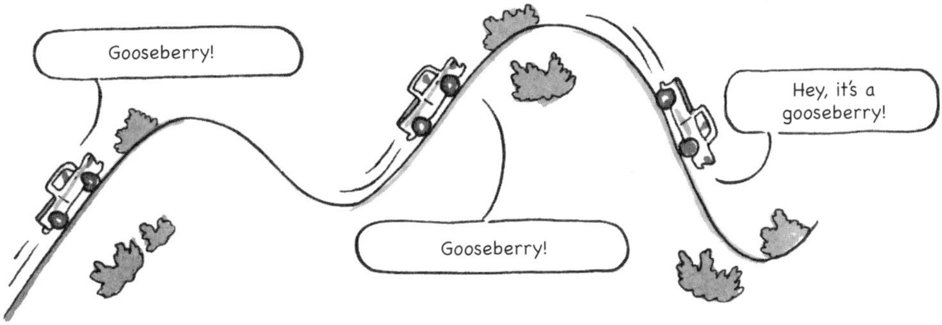
Gooseberry!
Gooseberry!
Hey, it's a gooseberry!

THEY HAD BEEN THERE ALL ALONG. I JUST HADN'T KNOWN TO LOOK.

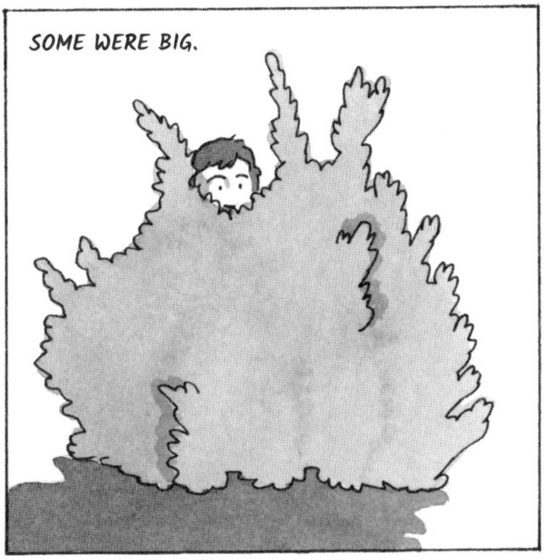
SOME WERE BIG.

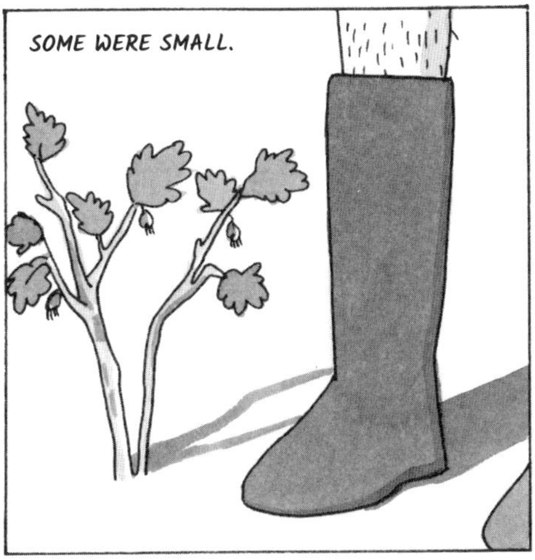
SOME WERE SMALL.

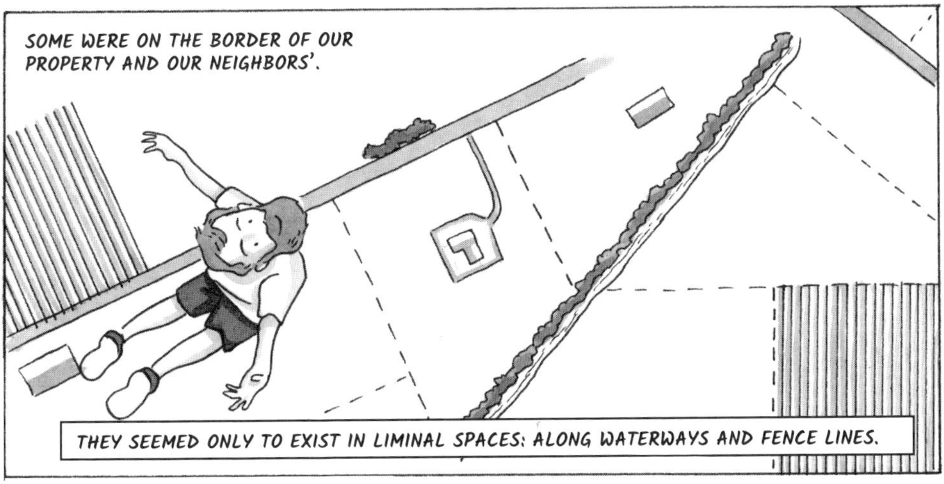
SOME WERE ON THE BORDER OF OUR PROPERTY AND OUR NEIGHBORS'.
THEY SEEMED ONLY TO EXIST IN LIMINAL SPACES: ALONG WATERWAYS AND FENCE LINES.

EVERY DAY I WOULD WALK ALONG THE CANAL AND COUNT THEM.
Salutations, #5.
No berries yet, #2?
Beautiful day, #12.
These are my secret gooseberries.
THERE WERE SEVENTEEN IN TOTAL.

ALONG SOME ROADSIDE DITCHES, THICKETS OF GOOSEBERRIES FED MY IMAGINATION.

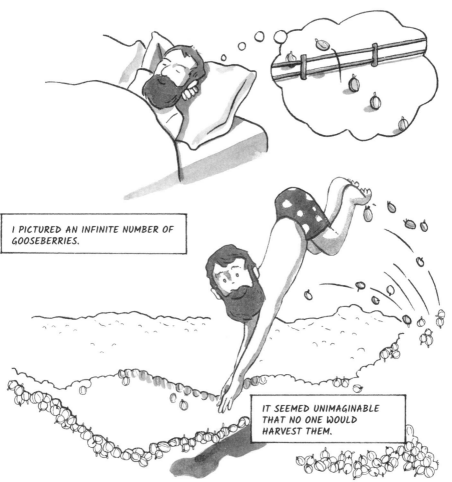

I PICTURED AN INFINITE NUMBER OF GOOSEBERRIES.

IT SEEMED UNIMAGINABLE THAT NO ONE WOULD HARVEST THEM.

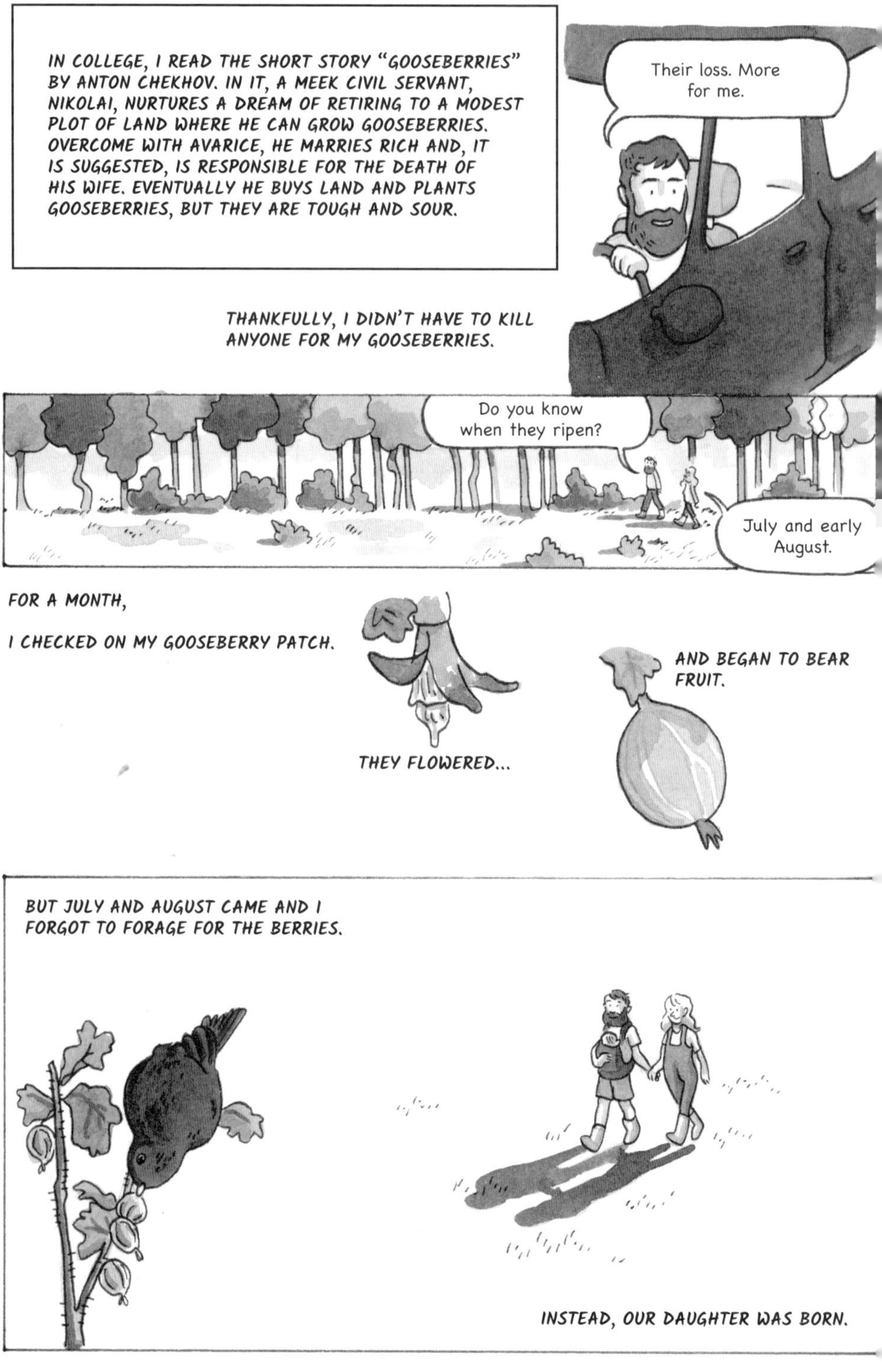
IN COLLEGE, I READ THE SHORT STORY "GOOSEBERRIES" BY ANTON CHEKHOV. IN IT, A MEEK CIVIL SERVANT, NIKOLAI, NURTURES A DREAM OF RETIRING TO A MODEST PLOT OF LAND WHERE HE CAN GROW GOOSEBERRIES. OVERCOME WITH AVARICE, HE MARRIES RICH AND, IT IS SUGGESTED, IS RESPONSIBLE FOR THE DEATH OF HIS WIFE. EVENTUALLY HE BUYS LAND AND PLANTS GOOSEBERRIES, BUT THEY ARE TOUGH AND SOUR.
Their loss. More for me.
THANKFULLY, I DIDN'T HAVE TO KILL ANYONE FOR MY GOOSEBERRIES.
Do you know when they ripen?
July and early August.
FOR A MONTH,
I CHECKED ON MY GOOSEBERRY PATCH.
THEY FLOWERED...
AND BEGAN TO BEAR FRUIT.
BUT JULY AND AUGUST CAME AND I FORGOT TO FORAGE FOR THE BERRIES.
INSTEAD, OUR DAUGHTER WAS BORN.

OUR DAUGHTER WAS BORN THAT AUGUST. WE
PLANTED A FRUIT TREE AND NAMED IT AFTER HER.

WE ALSO NAMED HER AFTER A FRUIT TREE.

ELIKA. BLOSSOMING FRUIT TREE.

ONE DOESN'T PLANT A FOUR-FOOT-TALL FRUIT TREE
WHEN ONE IS IN A RUSH TO GET APPLES.

WE IMAGINED THE TREE IN TWENTY YEARS, WHEN
OUR DAUGHTER IS GROWN AND WE ARE AGING.

ITS BRANCHES WILL SHADE HER CHILDHOOD
SUMMERS, ITS FRUITS FEED HER TEENAGE AUTUMNS.

WE PLANTED A FRUIT TREE NEXT TO THE KITCHEN
WINDOW.

WE NAMED IT FOR OUR DAUGHTER.

AND WE NAMED HER FOR IT.

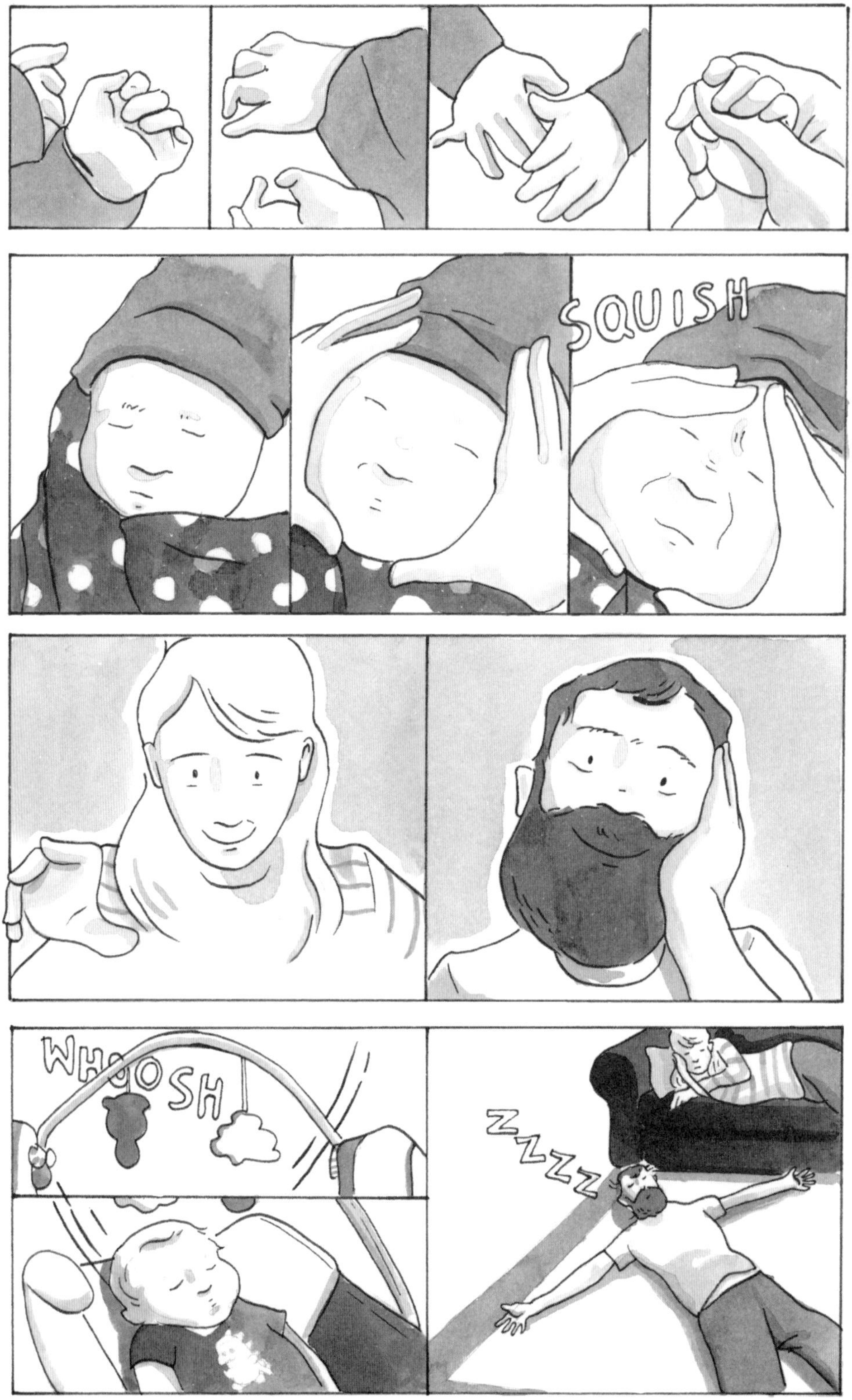
SQUISH
WHOOSH
ZZZZZ

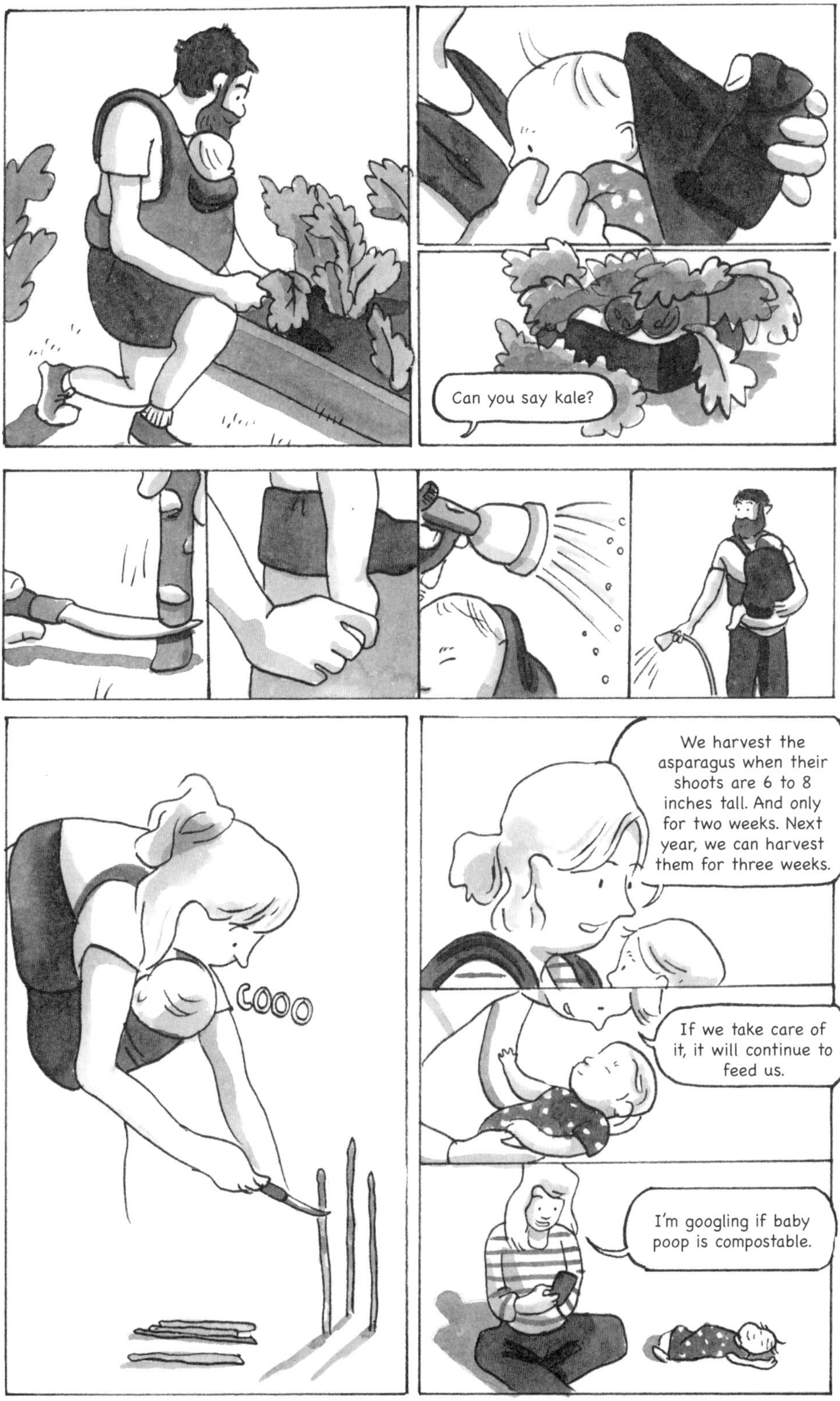

Can you say kale?
We harvest the asparagus when their shoots are 6 to 8 inches tall. And only for two weeks. Next year, we can harvest them for three weeks.
COOO
If we take care of it, it will continue to feed us.
I'm googling if baby poop is compostable.

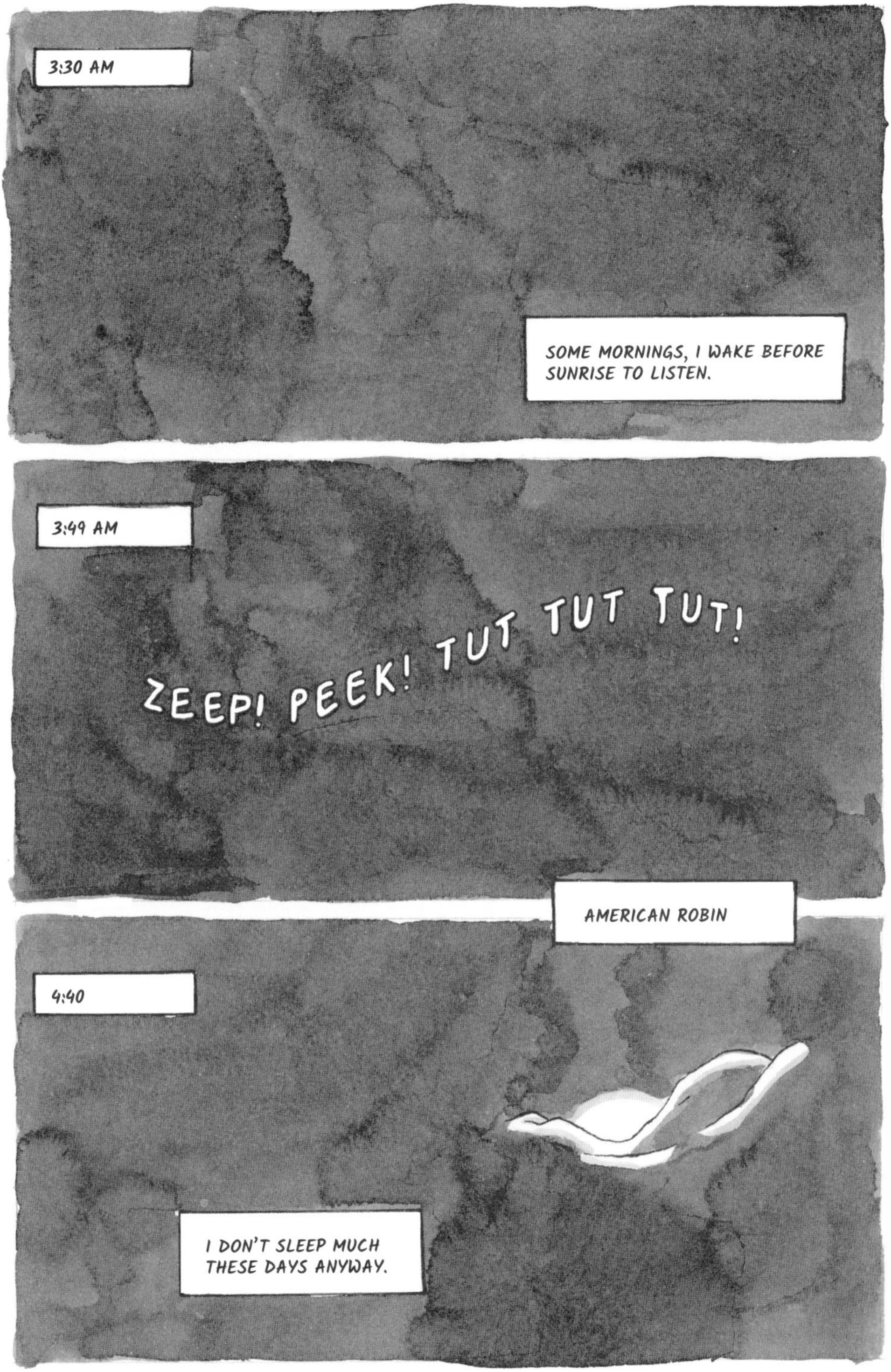

3:30 AM
SOME MORNINGS, I WAKE BEFORE SUNRISE TO LISTEN.
3:49 AM
ZEEP! PEEK! TUT TUT TUT!
AMERICAN ROBIN
4:40
I DON'T SLEEP MUCH THESE DAYS ANYWAY.

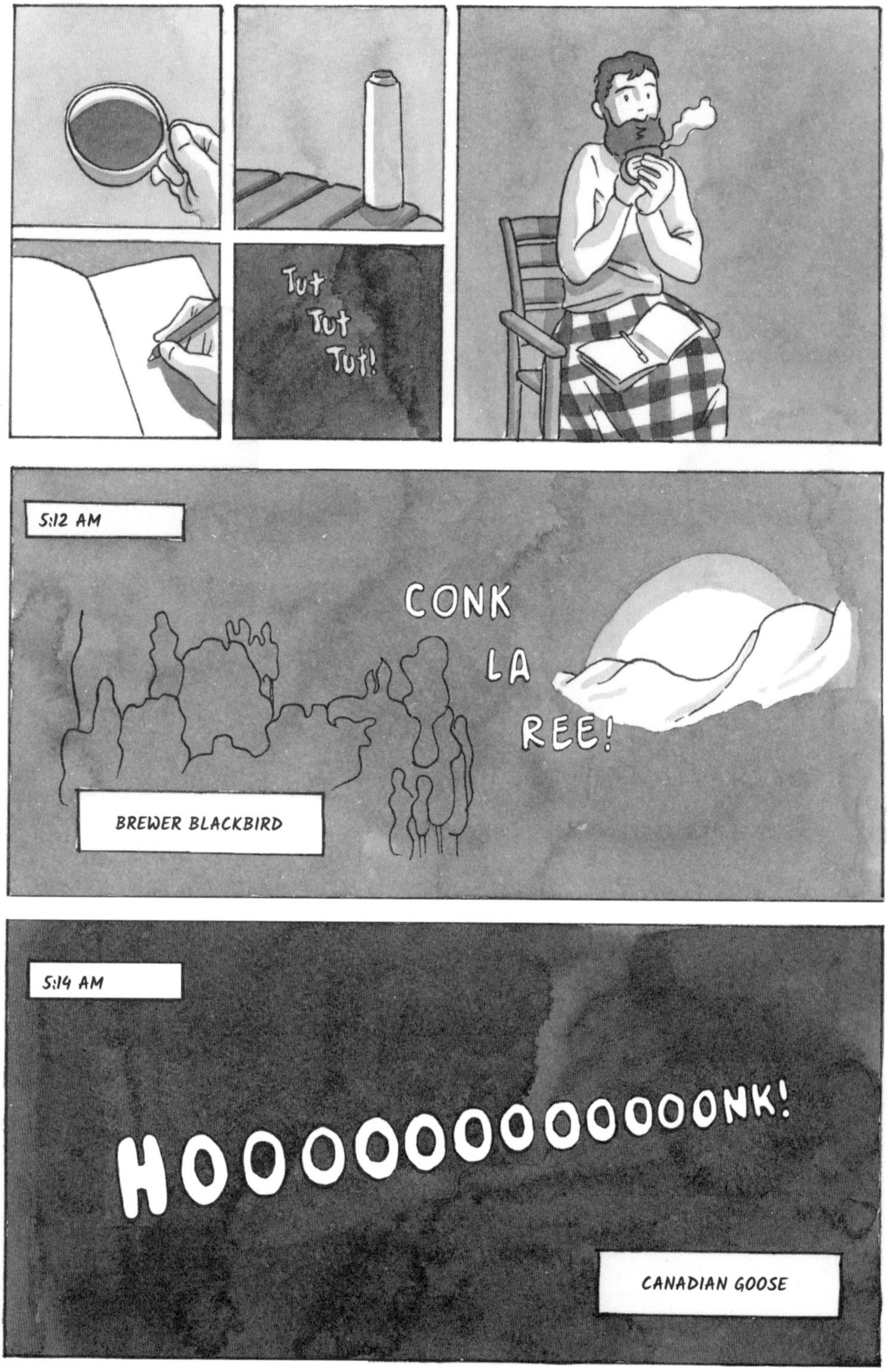
Tut
Tut
Tut!
5:12 AM
CONK
LA
REE!
BREWER BLACKBIRD
5:14 AM
HOOOOOOOOOOOONK!
CANADIAN GOOSE

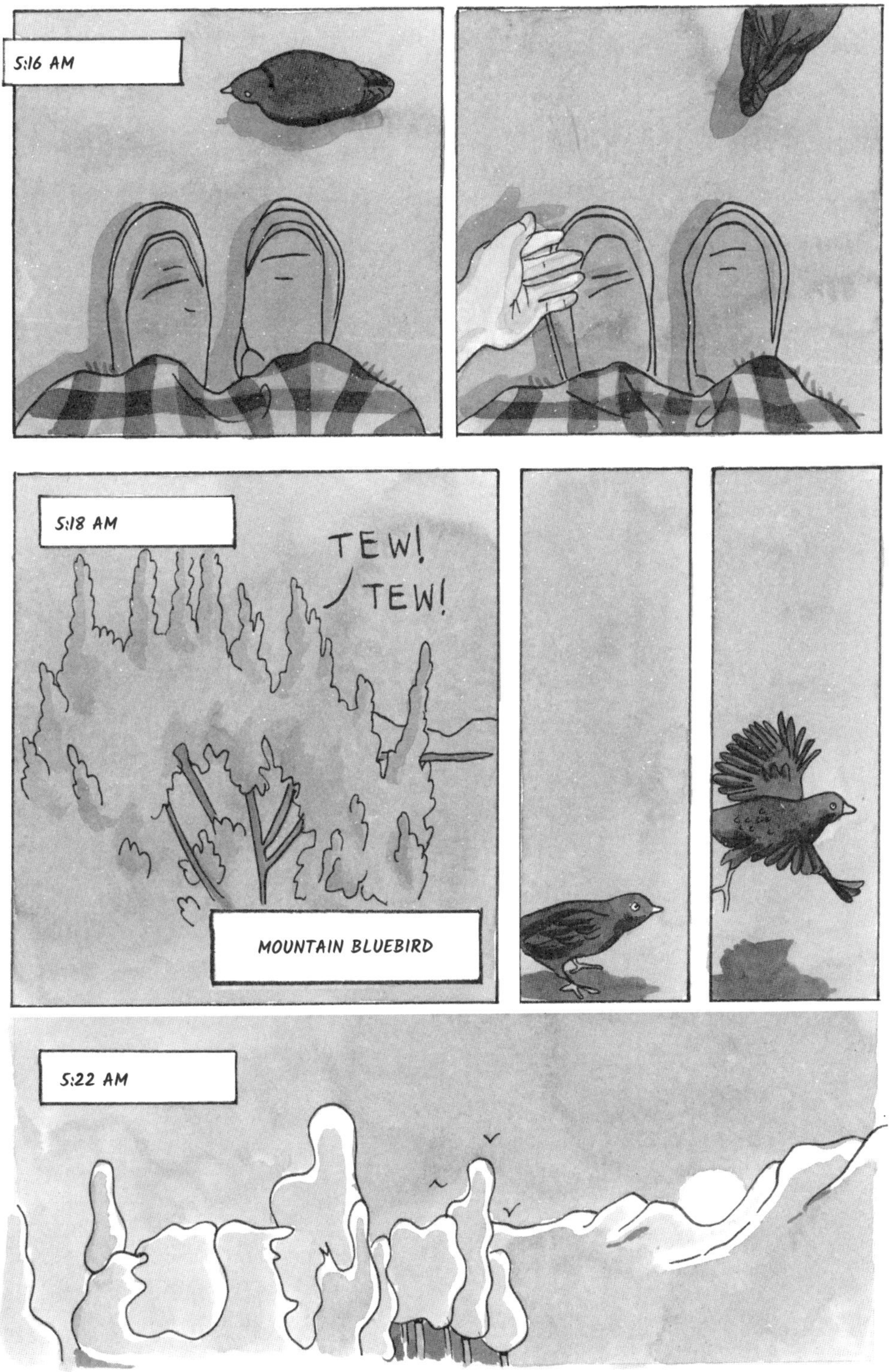
5:16 AM
5:18 AM
TEW!
TEW!
MOUNTAIN BLUEBIRD
5:22 AM

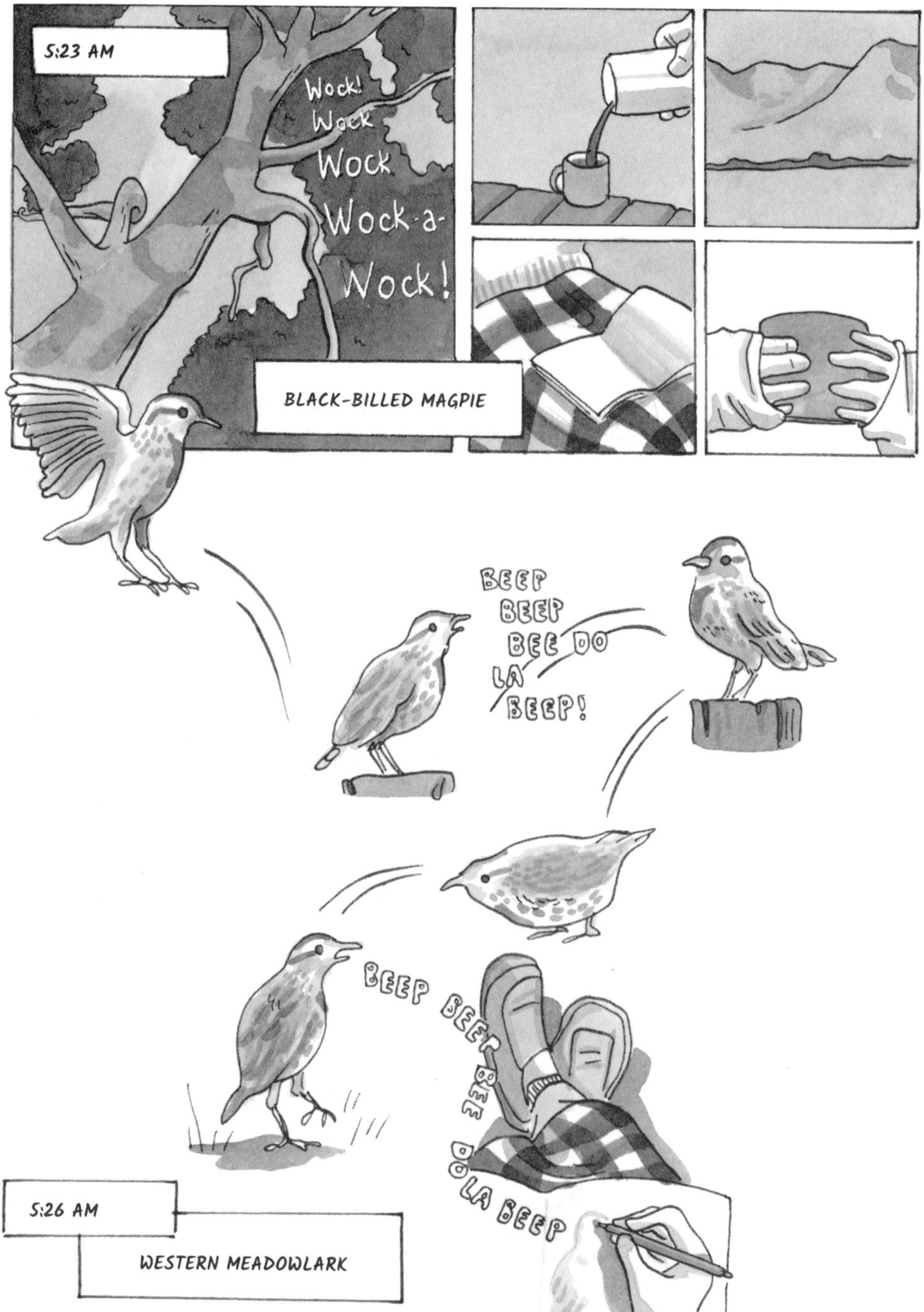
5:23 AM
Wock! Wock Wock Wock-a-Wock!
BLACK-BILLED MAGPIE
BEEP BEEP BEE DO LA BEEP!
BEEP BEEP BEE DO LA BEEP
5:26 AM
WESTERN MEADOWLARK

6:30 AM

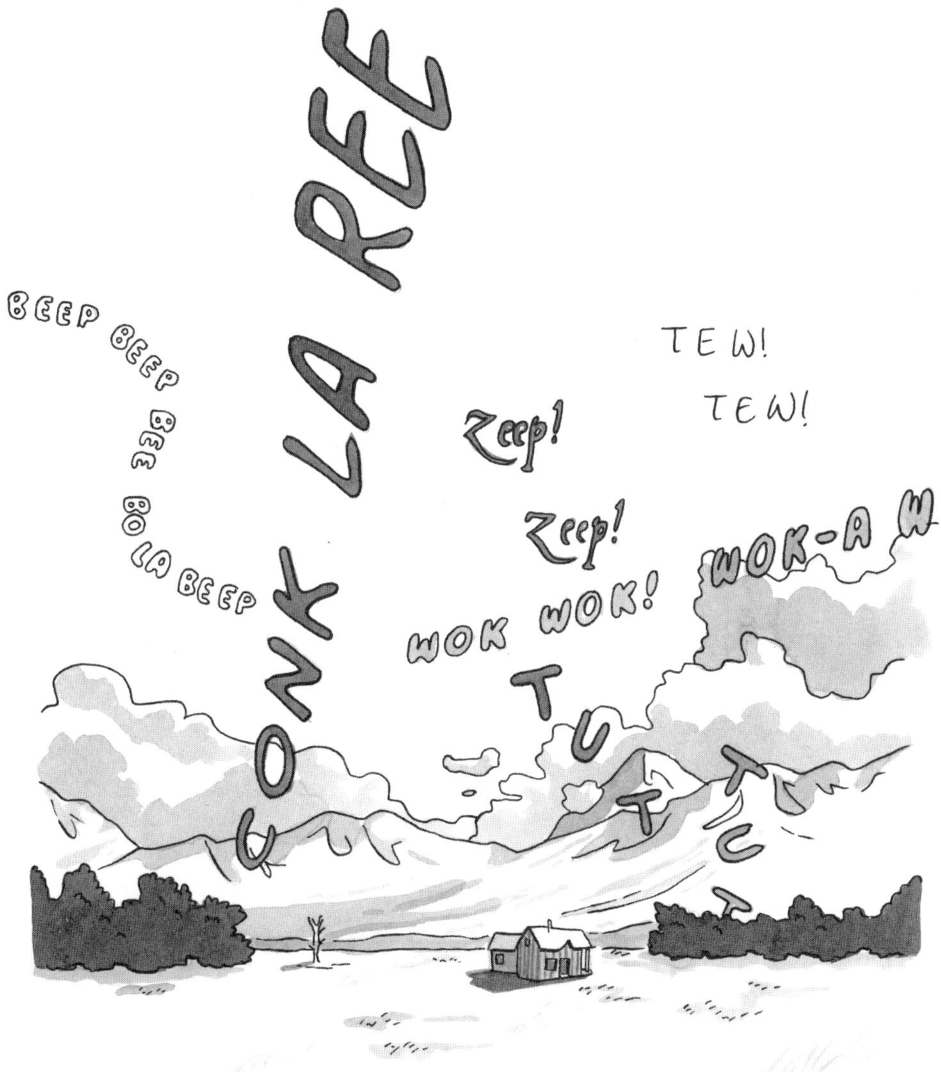
CONK LA REE
BEEP BEEP BEEP BEE BO LA BEEP
TEW! TEW!
Zeep! Zeep!
WOK WOK!
WOK-A W
TUTTUT

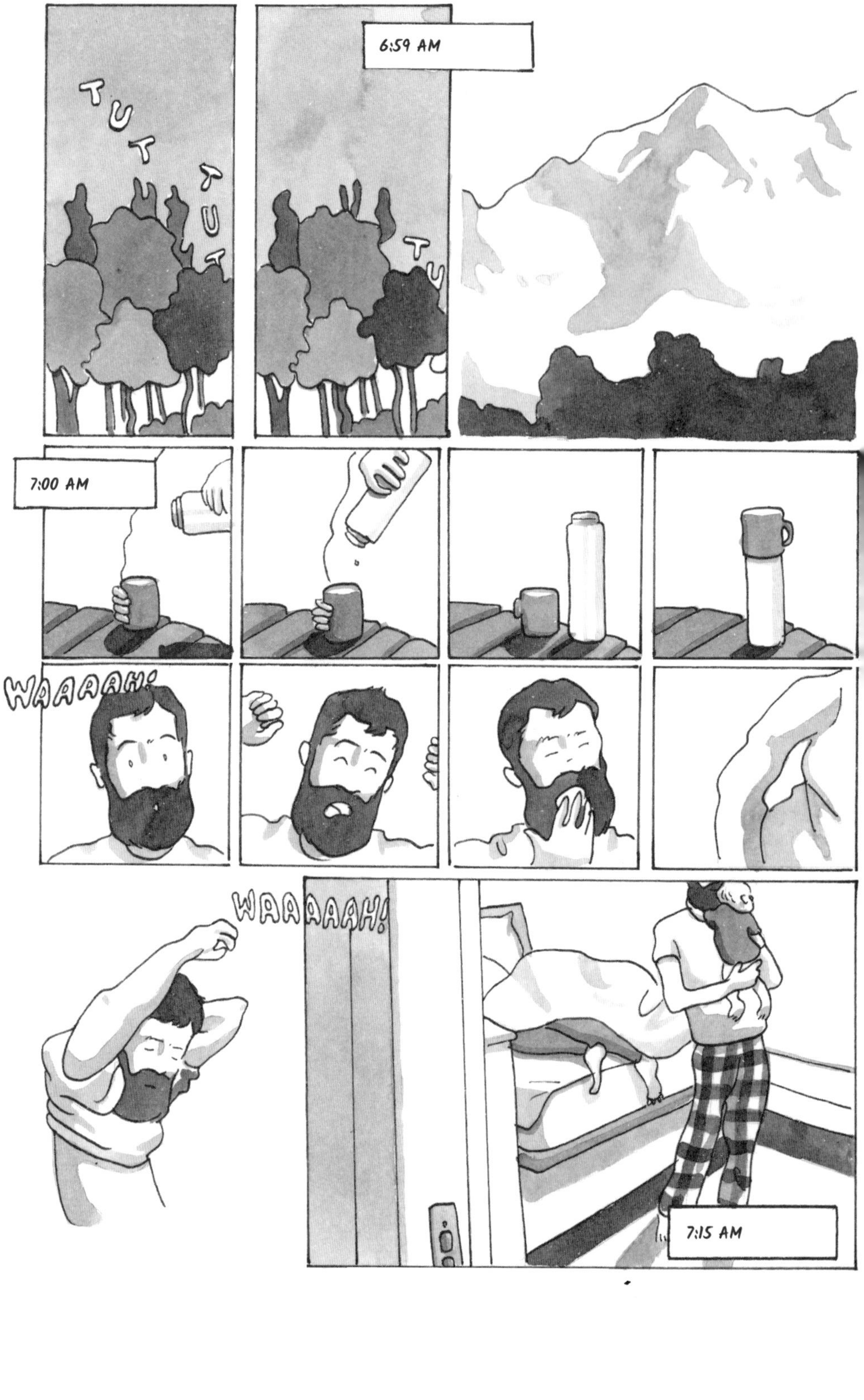
TUT TUT
TU
6:59 AM
7:00 AM
WAAAAH!
WAAAAAH!
7:15 AM

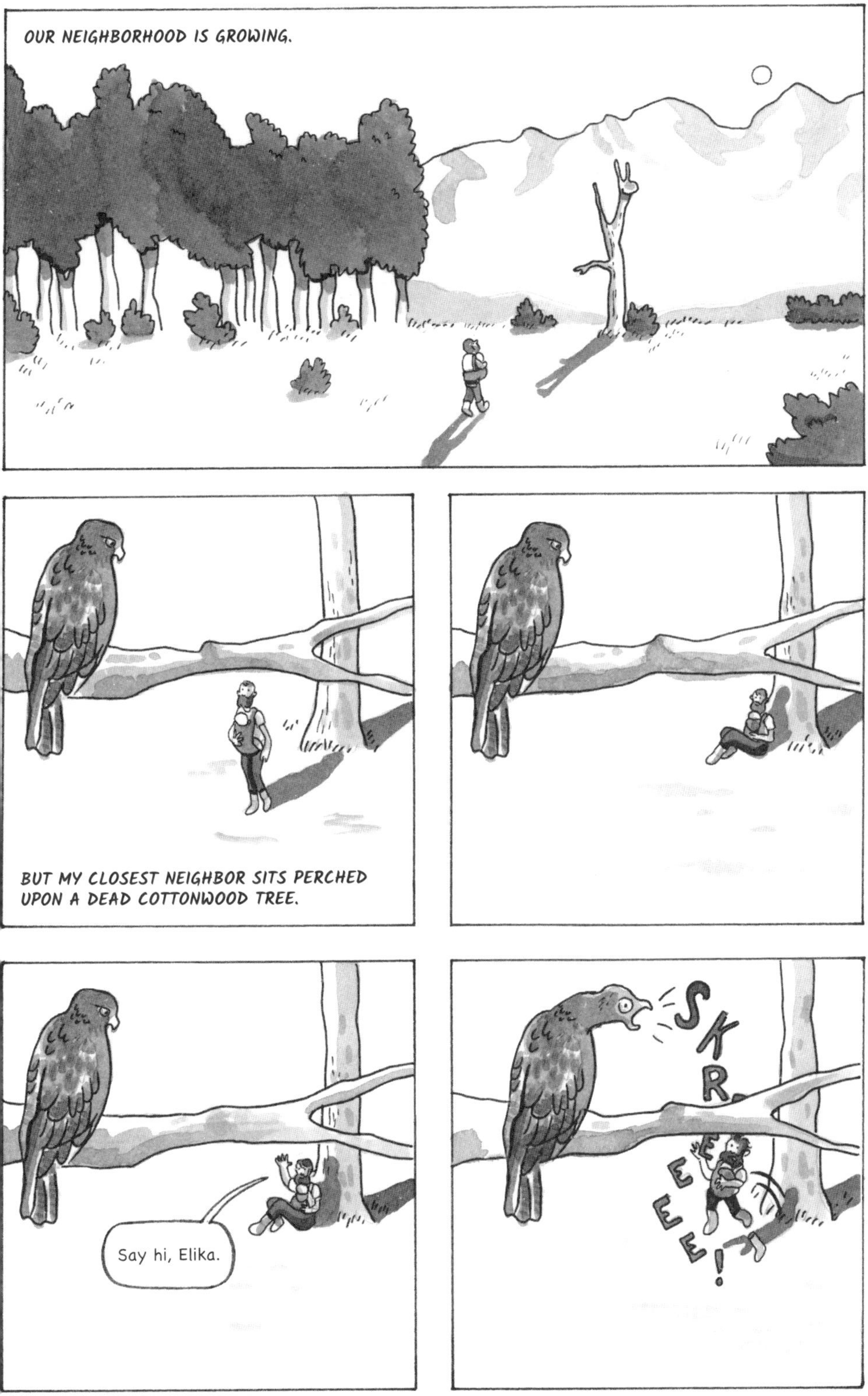
OUR NEIGHBORHOOD IS GROWING.
BUT MY CLOSEST NEIGHBOR SITS PERCHED UPON A DEAD COTTONWOOD TREE.
Say hi, Elika.
SKREEEE!

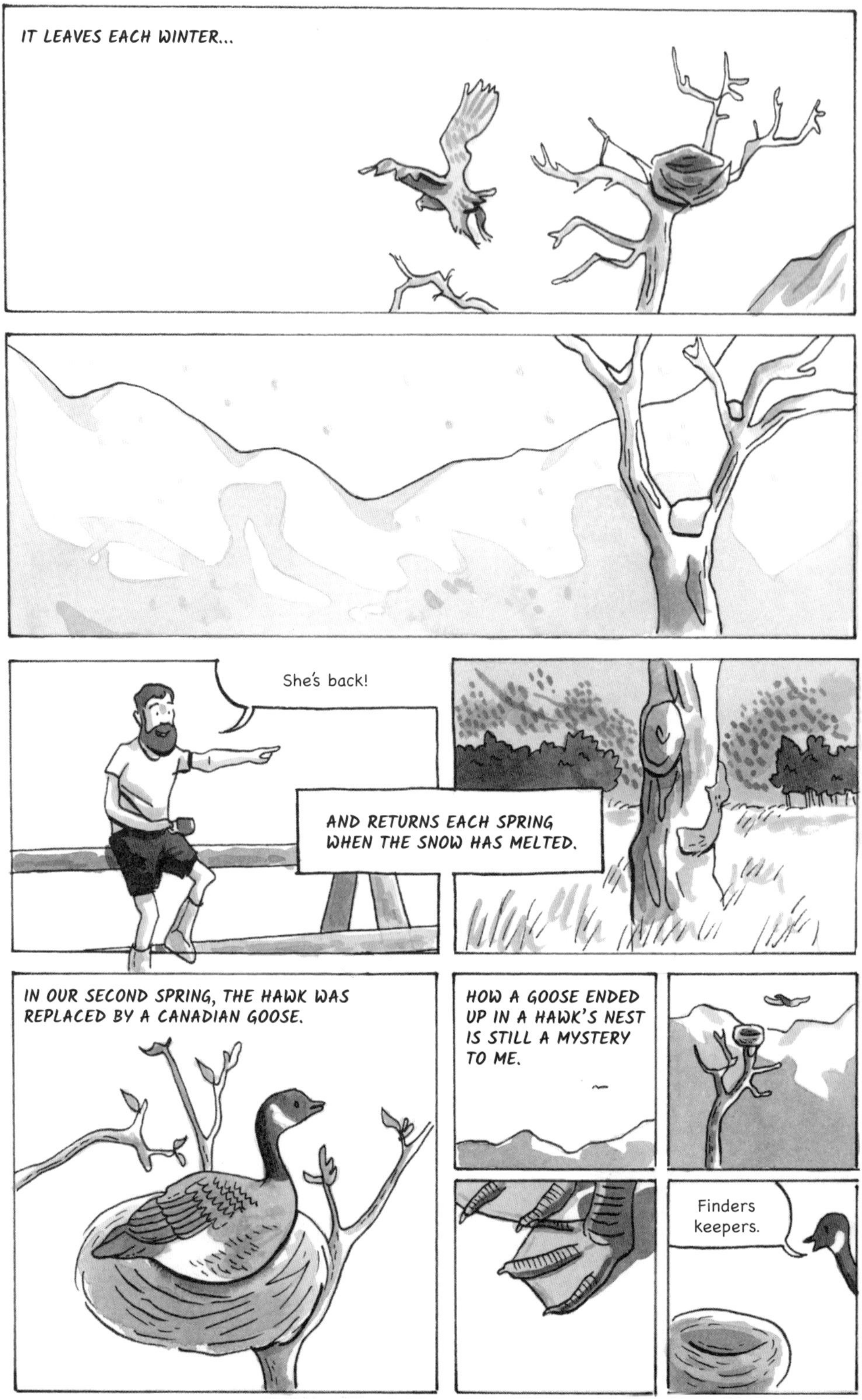
IT LEAVES EACH WINTER...
She's back!
AND RETURNS EACH SPRING WHEN THE SNOW HAS MELTED.
IN OUR SECOND SPRING, THE HAWK WAS REPLACED BY A CANADIAN GOOSE.
HOW A GOOSE ENDED UP IN A HAWK'S NEST IS STILL A MYSTERY TO ME.
Finders keepers.

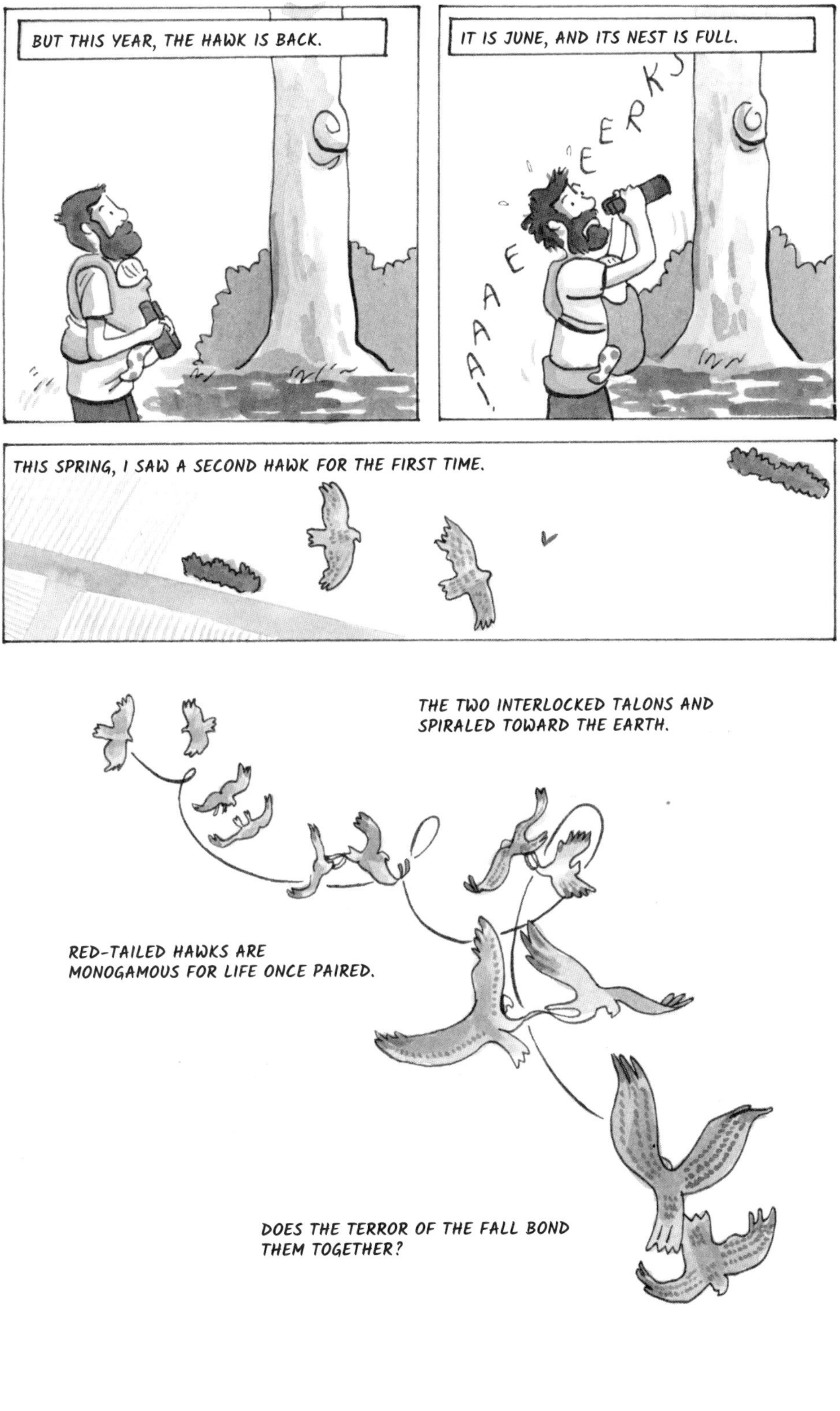
BUT THIS YEAR, THE HAWK IS BACK.
IT IS JUNE, AND ITS NEST IS FULL.
SKREEEAAA!
THIS SPRING, I SAW A SECOND HAWK FOR THE FIRST TIME.
THE TWO INTERLOCKED TALONS AND SPIRALED TOWARD THE EARTH.
RED-TAILED HAWKS ARE MONOGAMOUS FOR LIFE ONCE PAIRED.
DOES THE TERROR OF THE FALL BOND THEM TOGETHER?

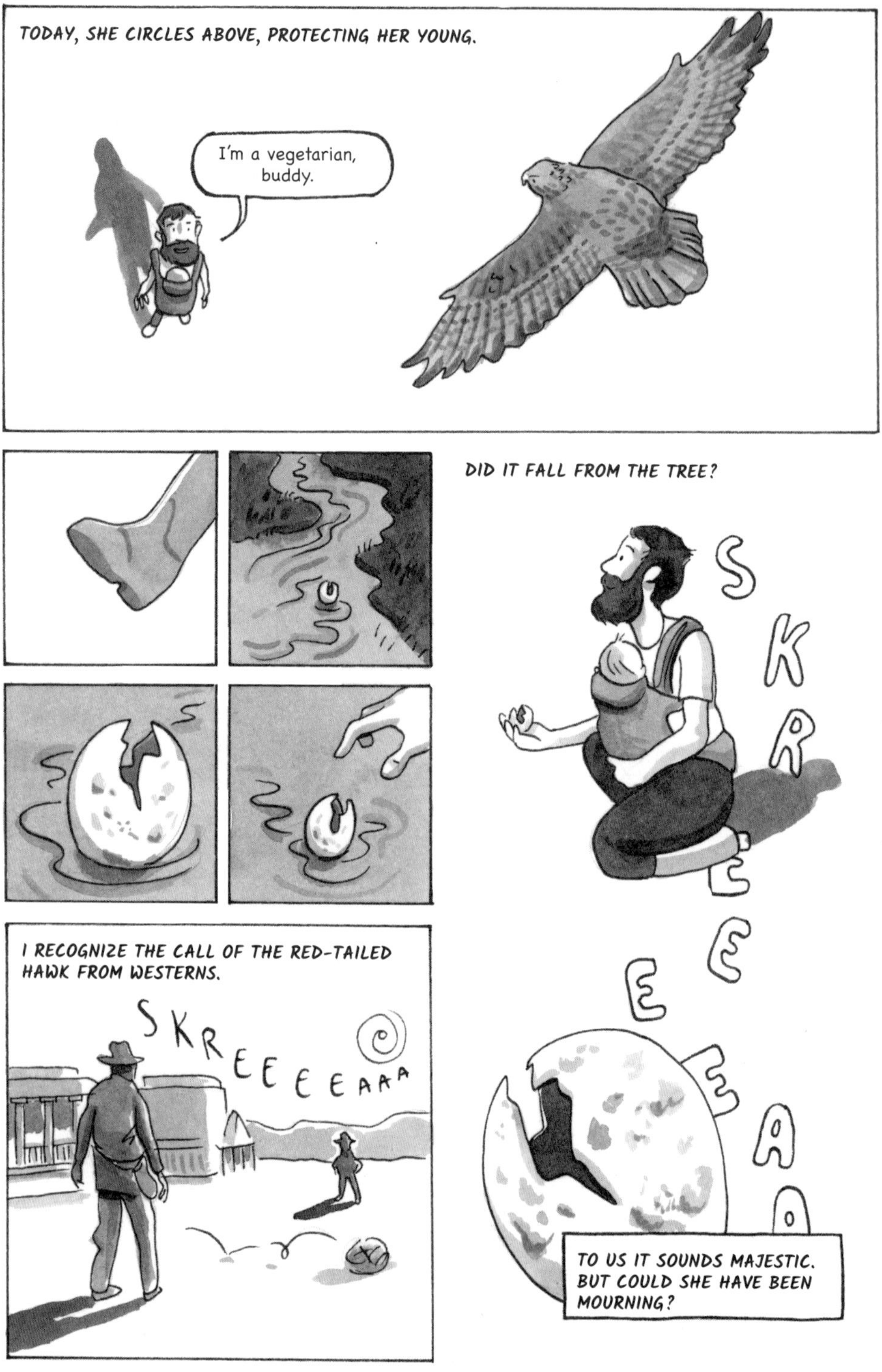
TODAY, SHE CIRCLES ABOVE, PROTECTING HER YOUNG.
I'm a vegetarian, buddy.
DID IT FALL FROM THE TREE?
SKREEEEEAAO
I RECOGNIZE THE CALL OF THE RED-TAILED HAWK FROM WESTERNS.
SKREEEEEAAA
TO US IT SOUNDS MAJESTIC. BUT COULD SHE HAVE BEEN MOURNING?

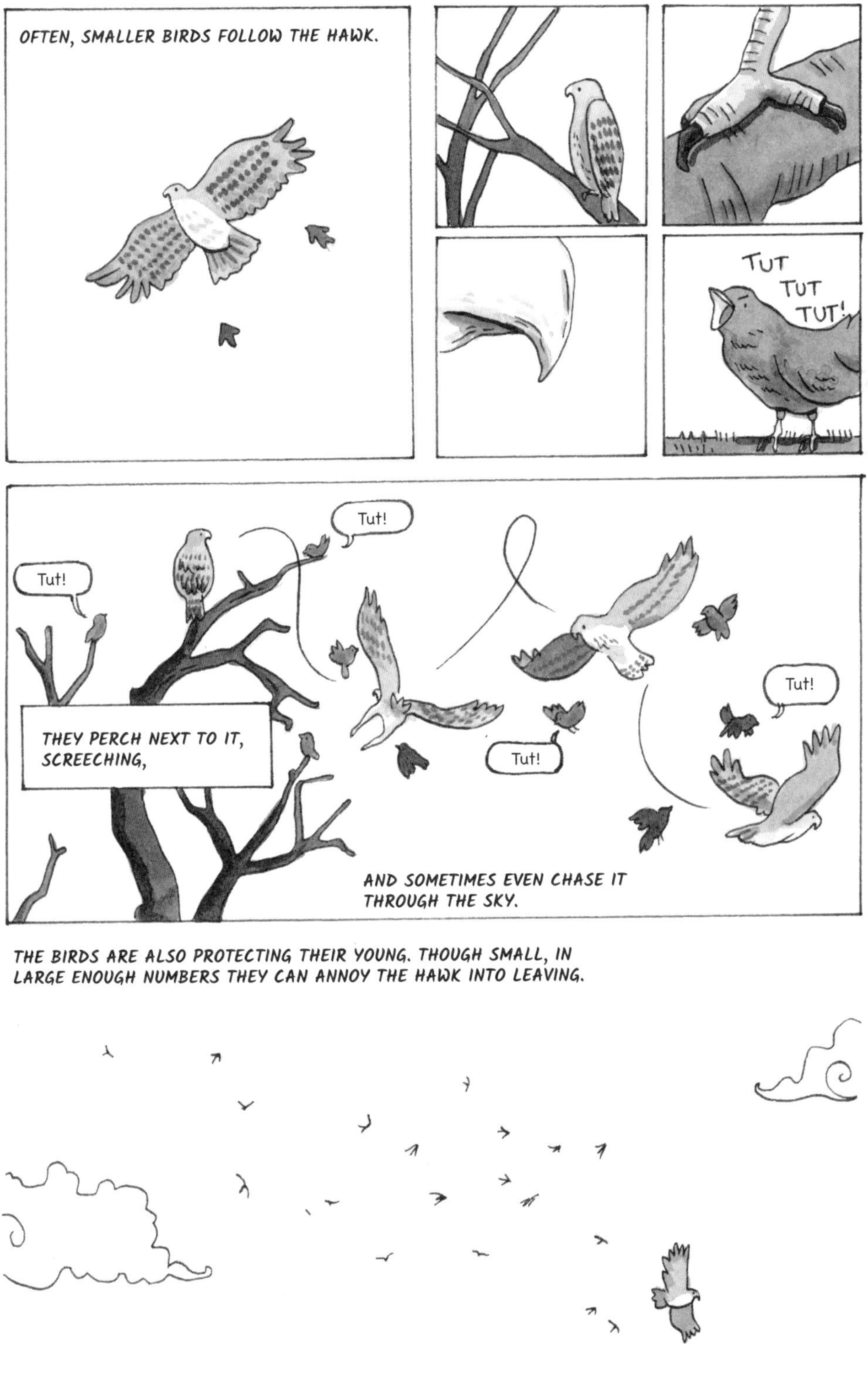
OFTEN, SMALLER BIRDS FOLLOW THE HAWK.
TUT TUT TUT!
Tut!
Tut!
THEY PERCH NEXT TO IT, SCREECHING,
Tut!
Tut!
AND SOMETIMES EVEN CHASE IT THROUGH THE SKY.
THE BIRDS ARE ALSO PROTECTING THEIR YOUNG. THOUGH SMALL, IN LARGE ENOUGH NUMBERS THEY CAN ANNOY THE HAWK INTO LEAVING.

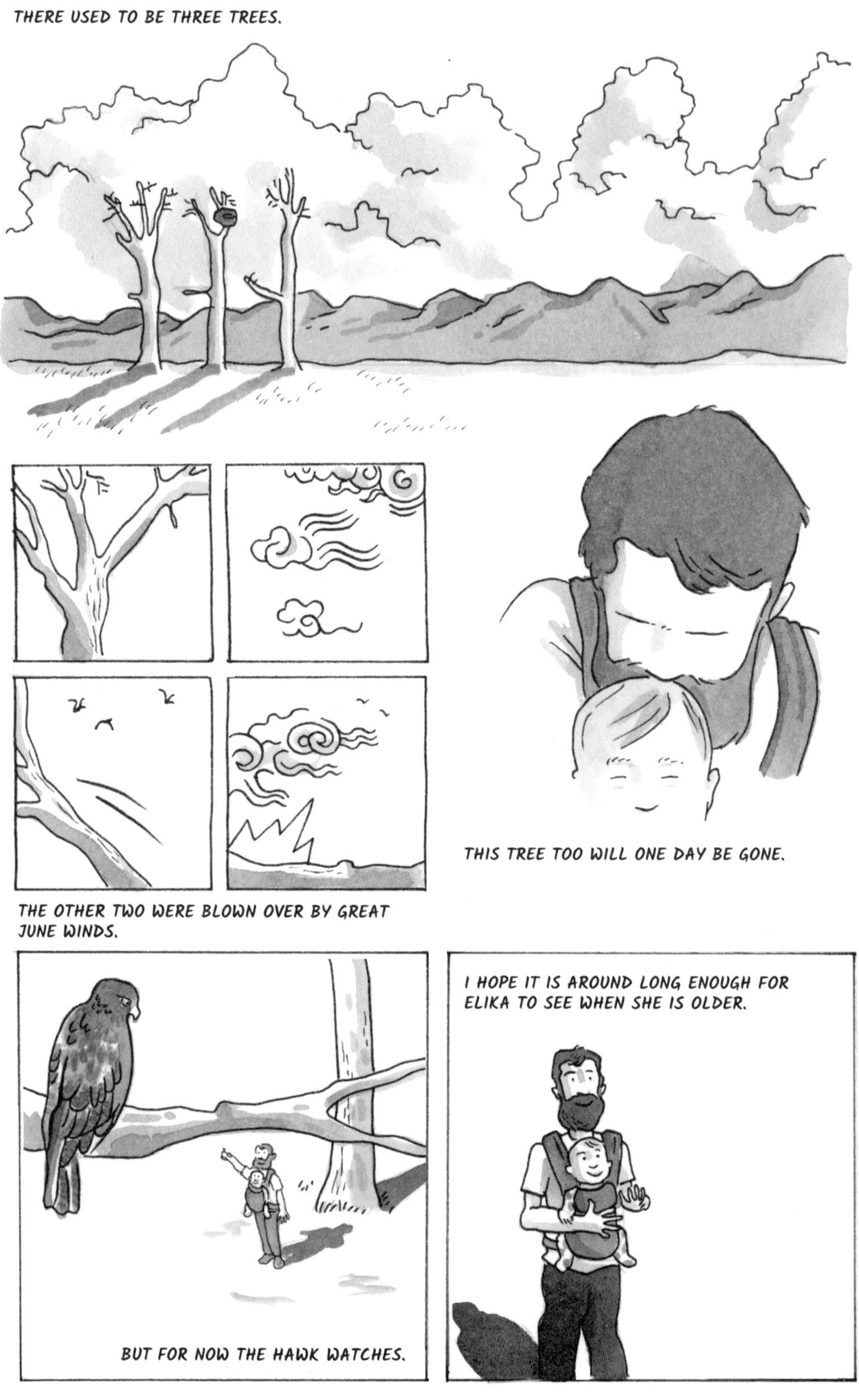
THERE USED TO BE THREE TREES.
THE OTHER TWO WERE BLOWN OVER BY GREAT JUNE WINDS.
THIS TREE TOO WILL ONE DAY BE GONE.
BUT FOR NOW THE HAWK WATCHES.
I HOPE IT IS AROUND LONG ENOUGH FOR ELIKA TO SEE WHEN SHE IS OLDER.

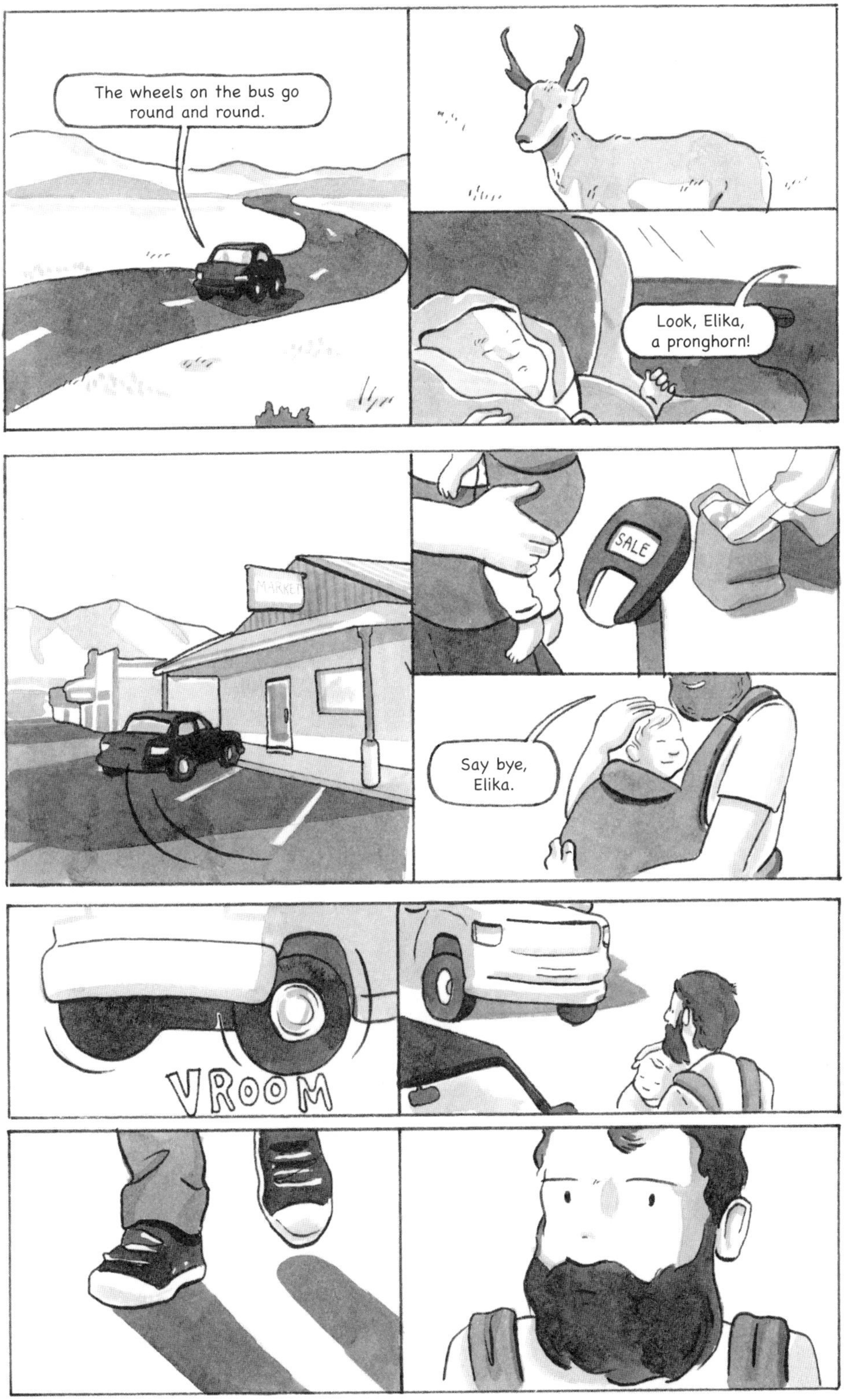
The wheels on the bus go round and round.
Look, Elika, a pronghorn!
MARKET
SALE
Say bye, Elika.
VROOM

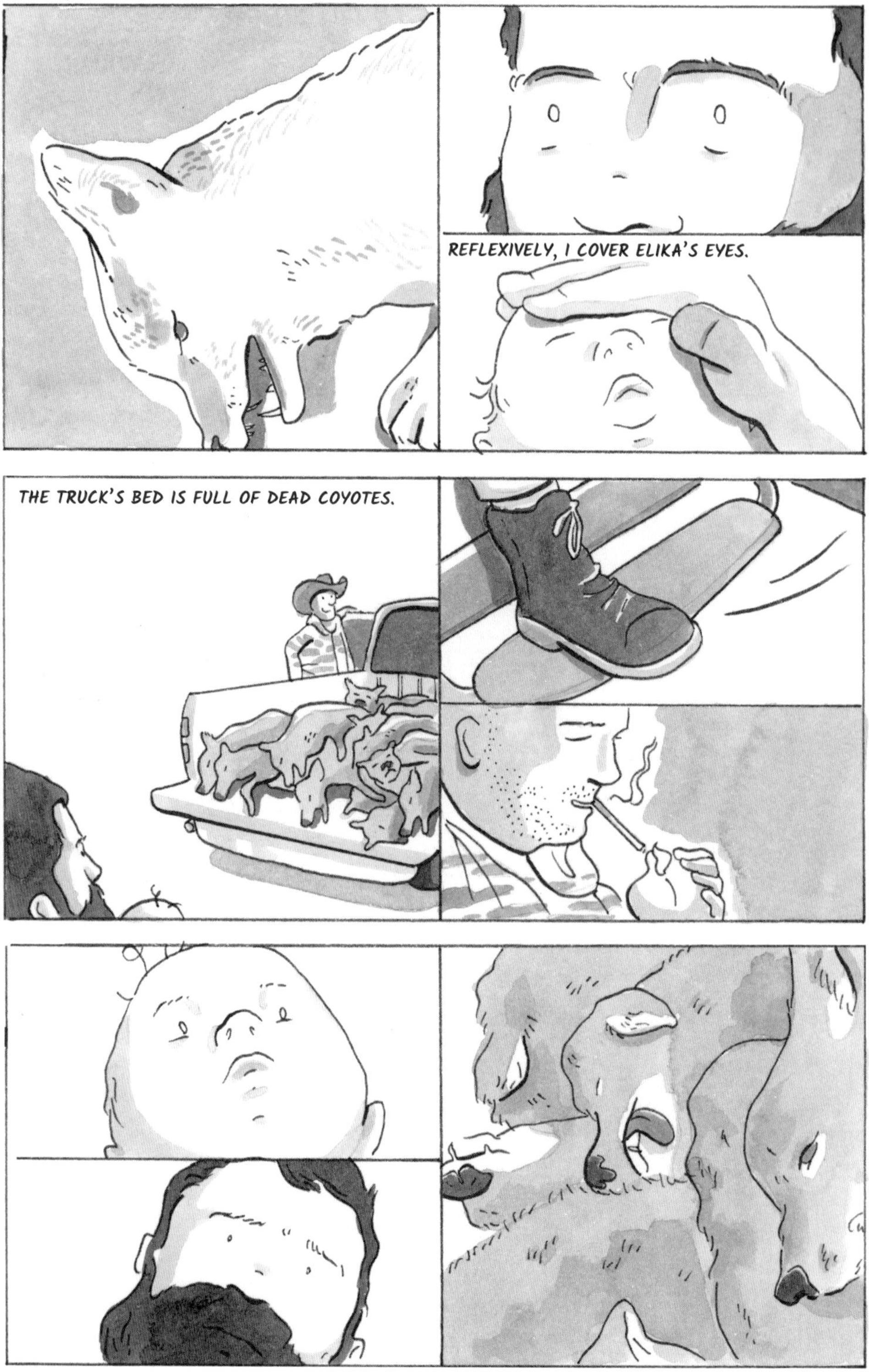
REFLEXIVELY, I COVER ELIKA'S EYES.
THE TRUCK'S BED IS FULL OF DEAD COYOTES.

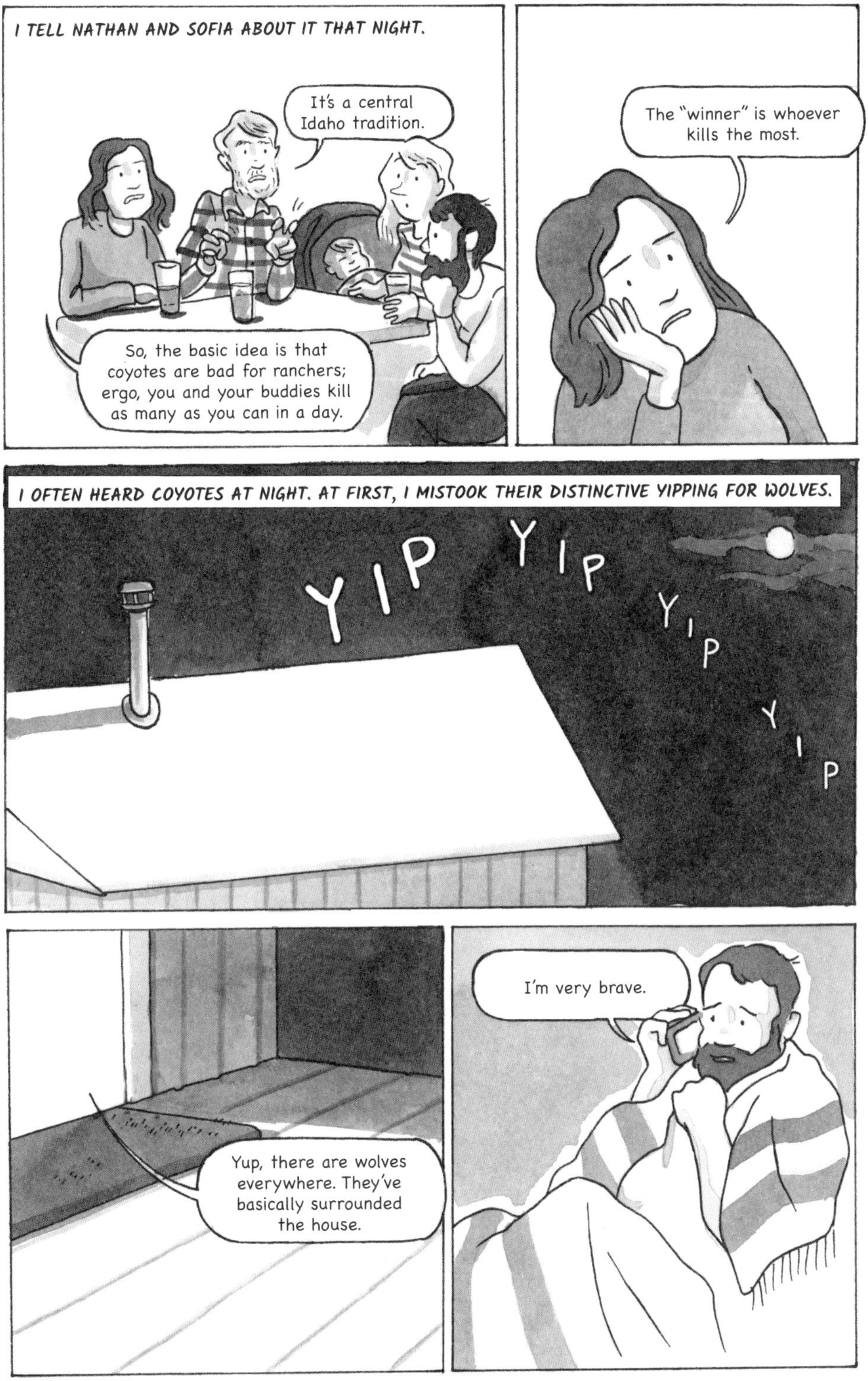
I TELL NATHAN AND SOFIA ABOUT IT THAT NIGHT.
So, the basic idea is that coyotes are bad for ranchers; ergo, you and your buddies kill as many as you can in a day.
It's a central Idaho tradition.
The "winner" is whoever kills the most.
I OFTEN HEARD COYOTES AT NIGHT. AT FIRST, I MISTOOK THEIR DISTINCTIVE YIPPING FOR WOLVES.
YIP YIP YIP YIP
Yup, there are wolves everywhere. They've basically surrounded the house.
I'm very brave.

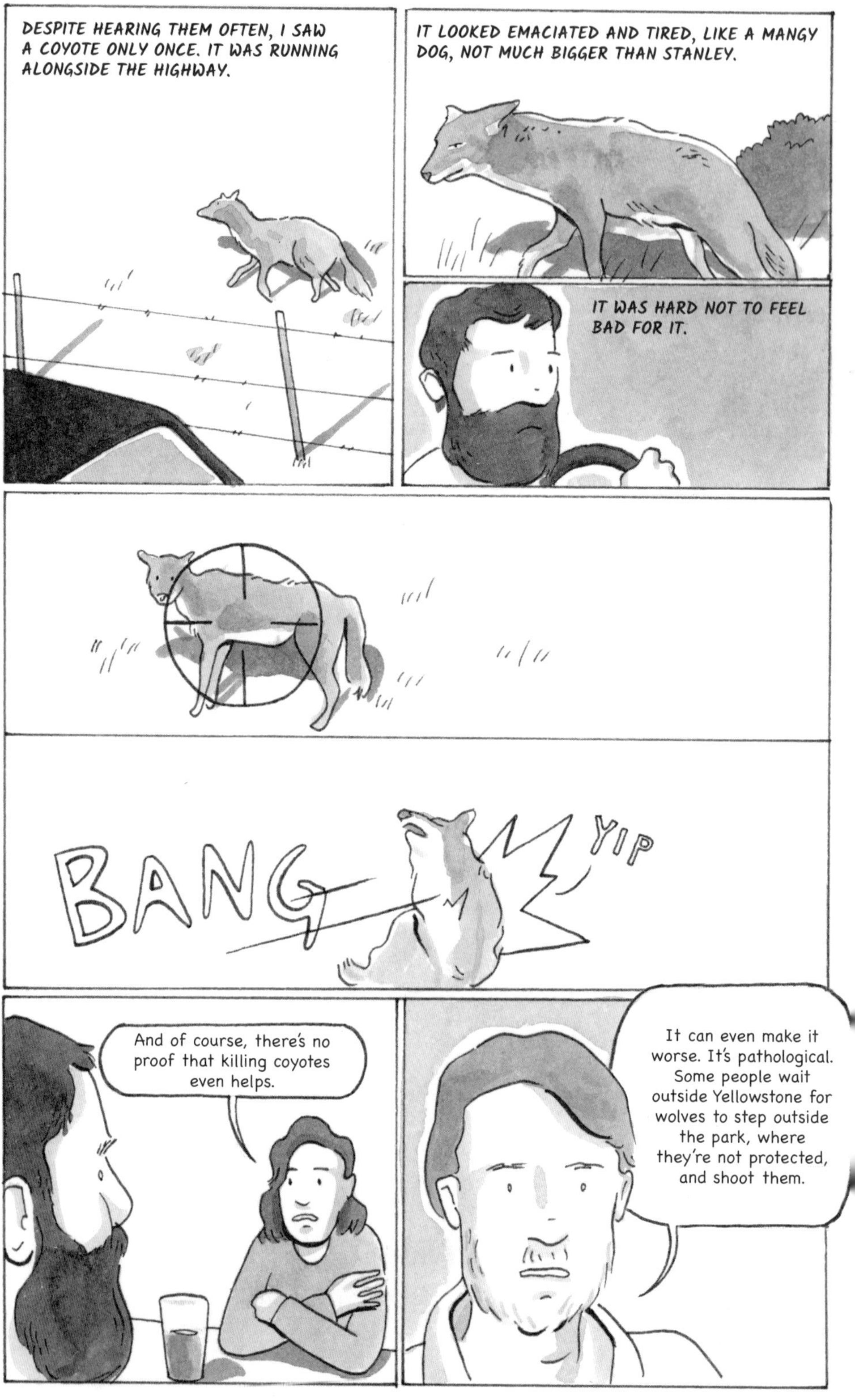
DESPITE HEARING THEM OFTEN, I SAW A COYOTE ONLY ONCE. IT WAS RUNNING ALONGSIDE THE HIGHWAY.
IT LOOKED EMACIATED AND TIRED, LIKE A MANGY DOG, NOT MUCH BIGGER THAN STANLEY.
IT WAS HARD NOT TO FEEL BAD FOR IT.
BANG
YIP
And of course, there's no proof that killing coyotes even helps.
It can even make it worse. It's pathological. Some people wait outside Yellowstone for wolves to step outside the park, where they're not protected, and shoot them.

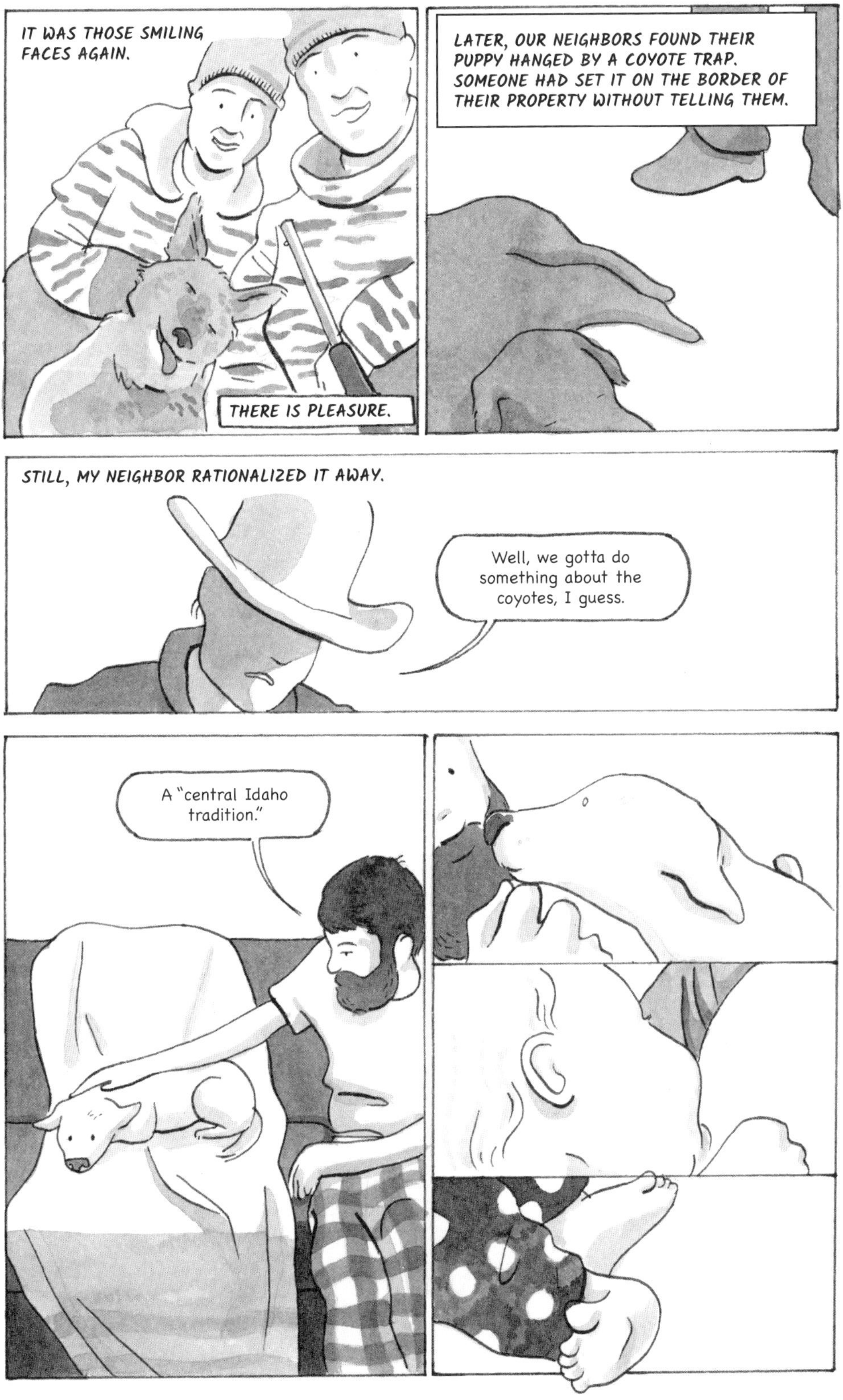
IT WAS THOSE SMILING FACES AGAIN.
THERE IS PLEASURE.
LATER, OUR NEIGHBORS FOUND THEIR PUPPY HANGED BY A COYOTE TRAP. SOMEONE HAD SET IT ON THE BORDER OF THEIR PROPERTY WITHOUT TELLING THEM.
STILL, MY NEIGHBOR RATIONALIZED IT AWAY.
Well, we gotta do something about the coyotes, I guess.
A "central Idaho tradition."

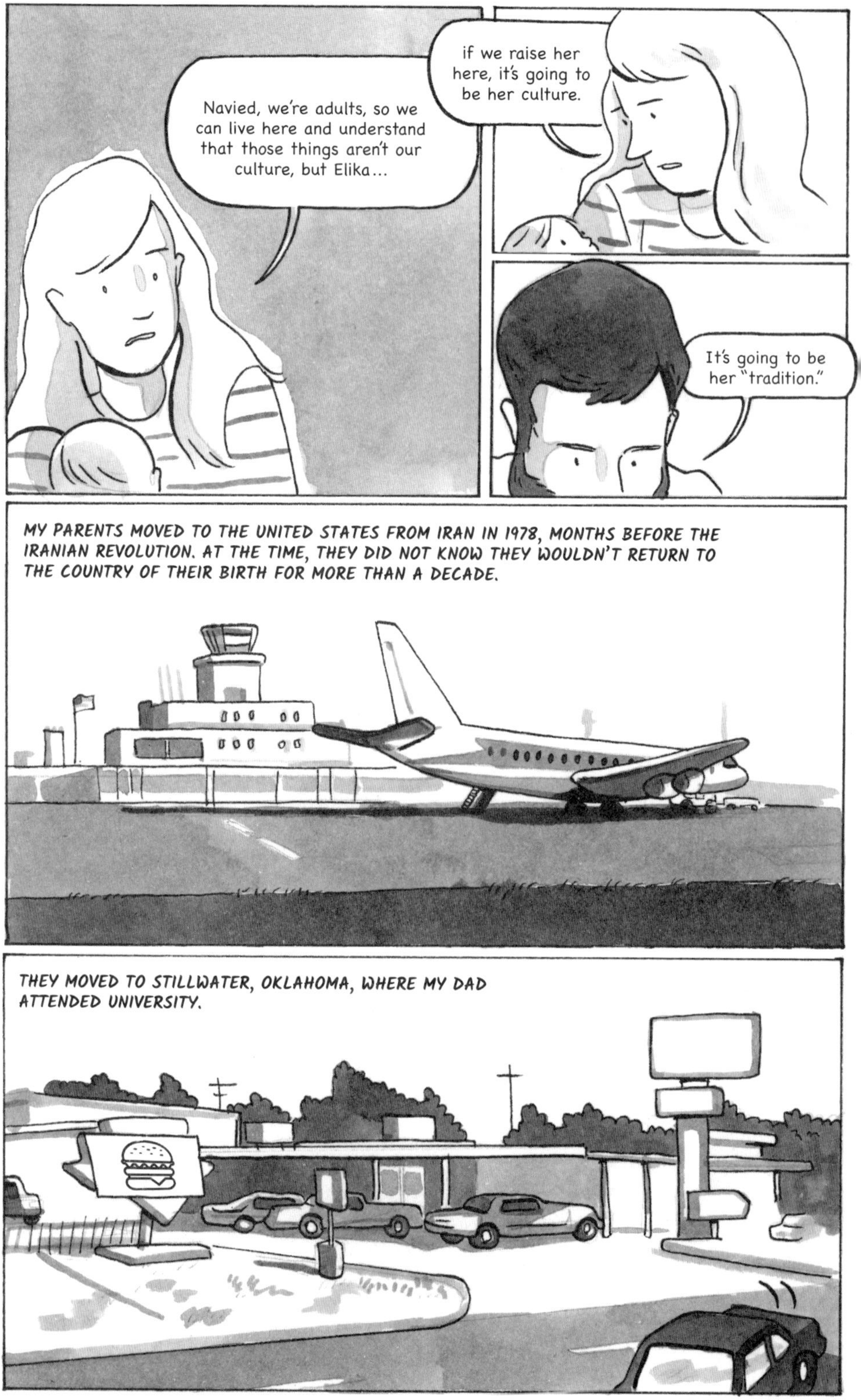
Navied, we're adults, so we can live here and understand that those things aren't our culture, but Elika...
if we raise her here, it's going to be her culture.
It's going to be her "tradition."
MY PARENTS MOVED TO THE UNITED STATES FROM IRAN IN 1978, MONTHS BEFORE THE IRANIAN REVOLUTION. AT THE TIME, THEY DID NOT KNOW THEY WOULDN'T RETURN TO THE COUNTRY OF THEIR BIRTH FOR MORE THAN A DECADE.
THEY MOVED TO STILLWATER, OKLAHOMA, WHERE MY DAD ATTENDED UNIVERSITY.

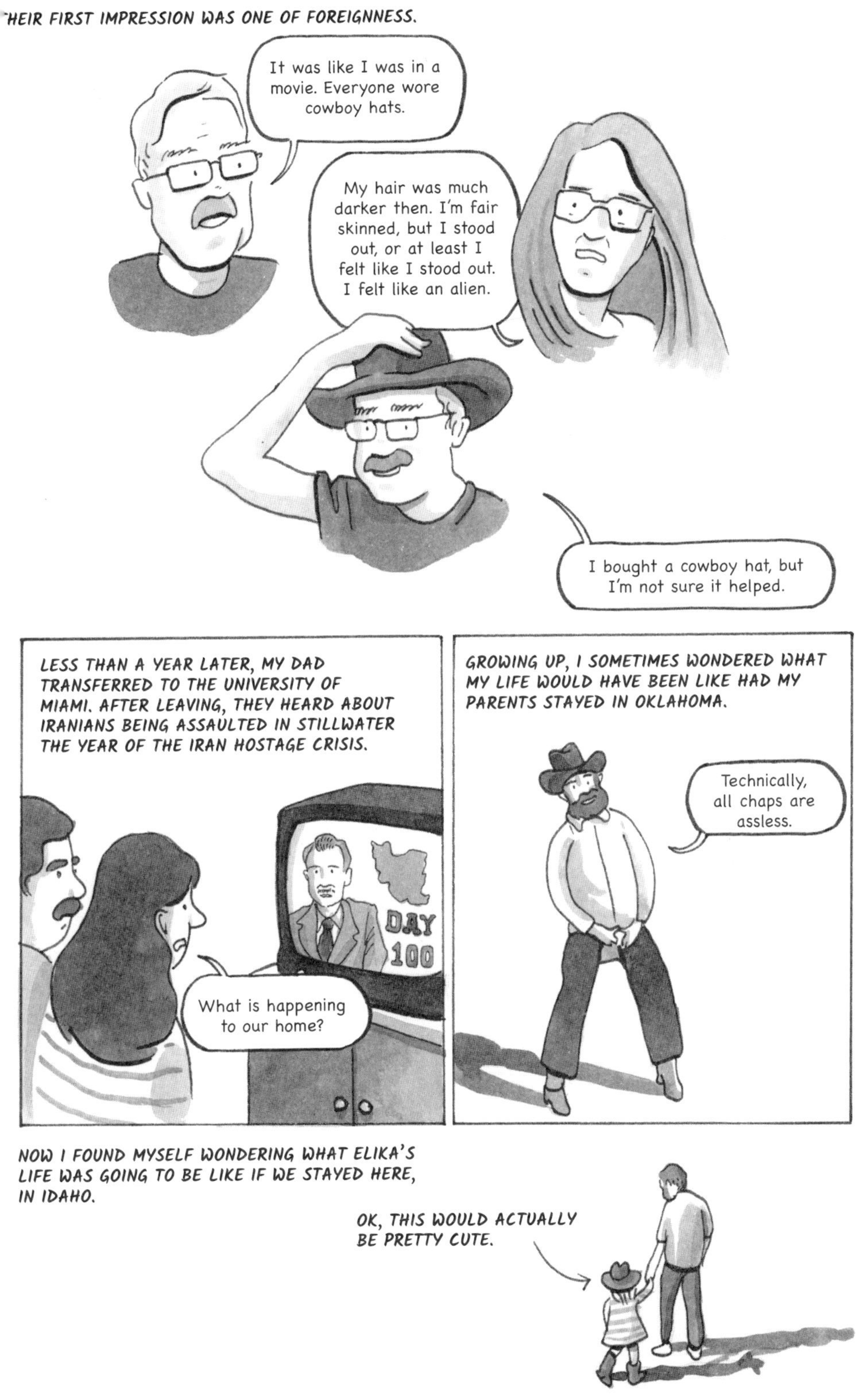
HEIR FIRST IMPRESSION WAS ONE OF FOREIGNNESS.
It was like I was in a movie. Everyone wore cowboy hats.
My hair was much darker then. I'm fair skinned, but I stood out, or at least I felt like I stood out. I felt like an alien.
I bought a cowboy hat, but I'm not sure it helped.
LESS THAN A YEAR LATER, MY DAD TRANSFERRED TO THE UNIVERSITY OF MIAMI. AFTER LEAVING, THEY HEARD ABOUT IRANIANS BEING ASSAULTED IN STILLWATER THE YEAR OF THE IRAN HOSTAGE CRISIS.
DAY 100
What is happening to our home?
GROWING UP, I SOMETIMES WONDERED WHAT MY LIFE WOULD HAVE BEEN LIKE HAD MY PARENTS STAYED IN OKLAHOMA.
Technically, all chaps are assless.
NOW I FOUND MYSELF WONDERING WHAT ELIKA'S LIFE WAS GOING TO BE LIKE IF WE STAYED HERE, IN IDAHO.
OK, THIS WOULD ACTUALLY BE PRETTY CUTE.

I WAS WILLING TO PUT UP WITH THE OCCASIONAL STARE OR POINTED QUESTION.

TO FEEL LIKE AN ALIEN.

I'm from the exotic and strange Far East,

a place called Miami.

BUT WE WERE PARENTS NOW, AND BY STAYING WE WOULDN'T BE GIVING OUR DAUGHTER THAT CHOICE.

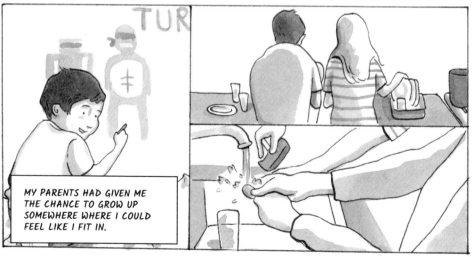

MY PARENTS HAD GIVEN ME THE CHANCE TO GROW UP SOMEWHERE WHERE I COULD FEEL LIKE I FIT IN.

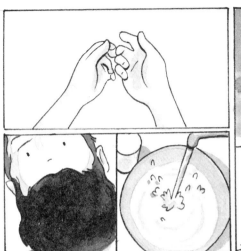

There's a university position in Salt Lake City.

I DECIDED TO DO THE SAME FOR MY DAUGHTER.

I think you should apply.

SO WE MOVED.

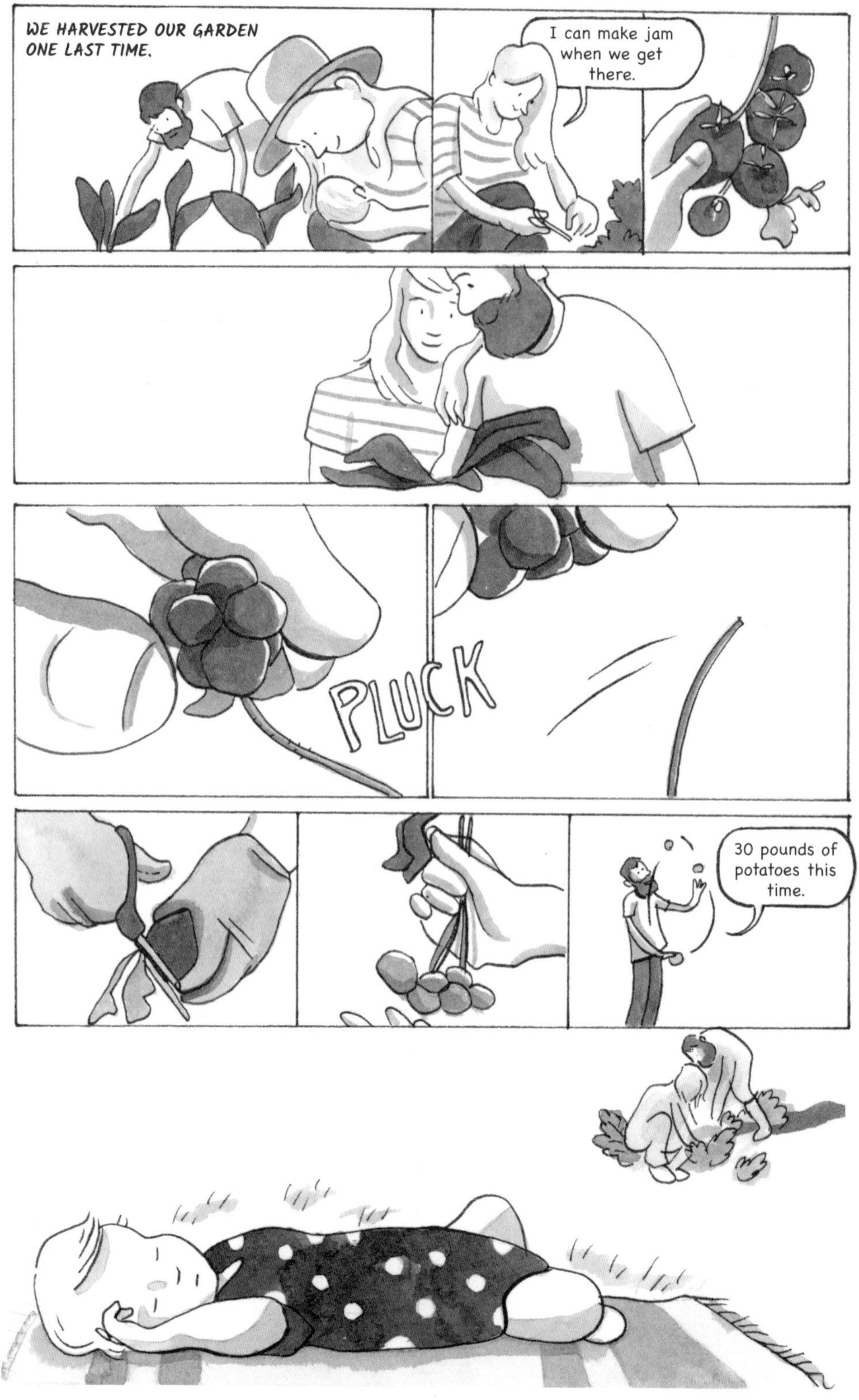
WE HARVESTED OUR GARDEN ONE LAST TIME.
I can make jam when we get there.
PLUCK
30 pounds of potatoes this time.

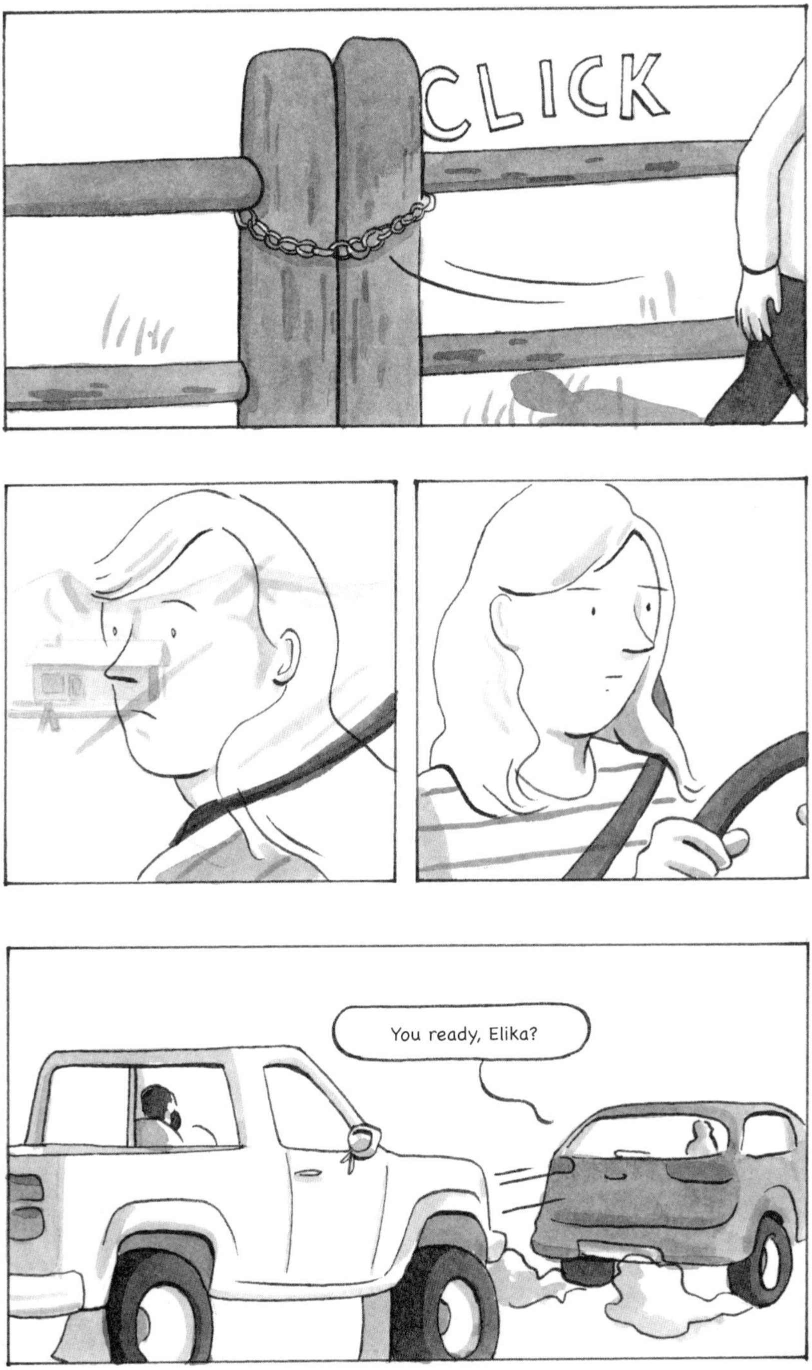
CLICK
You ready, Elika?

AND MOVED INTO AN APARTMENT.

OUR TRUCK DIED FOR GOOD EN ROUTE.

It was your turn to get the oil changed.

Absolutely not.

I'm going to see how many paces our new place is.

3 feet...

5 feet...

9 feet...

THE ONIONS LASTED INTO THE NEW YEAR.

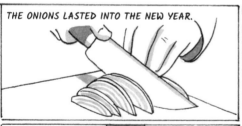

WE FORGOT ABOUT THE SQUASH.

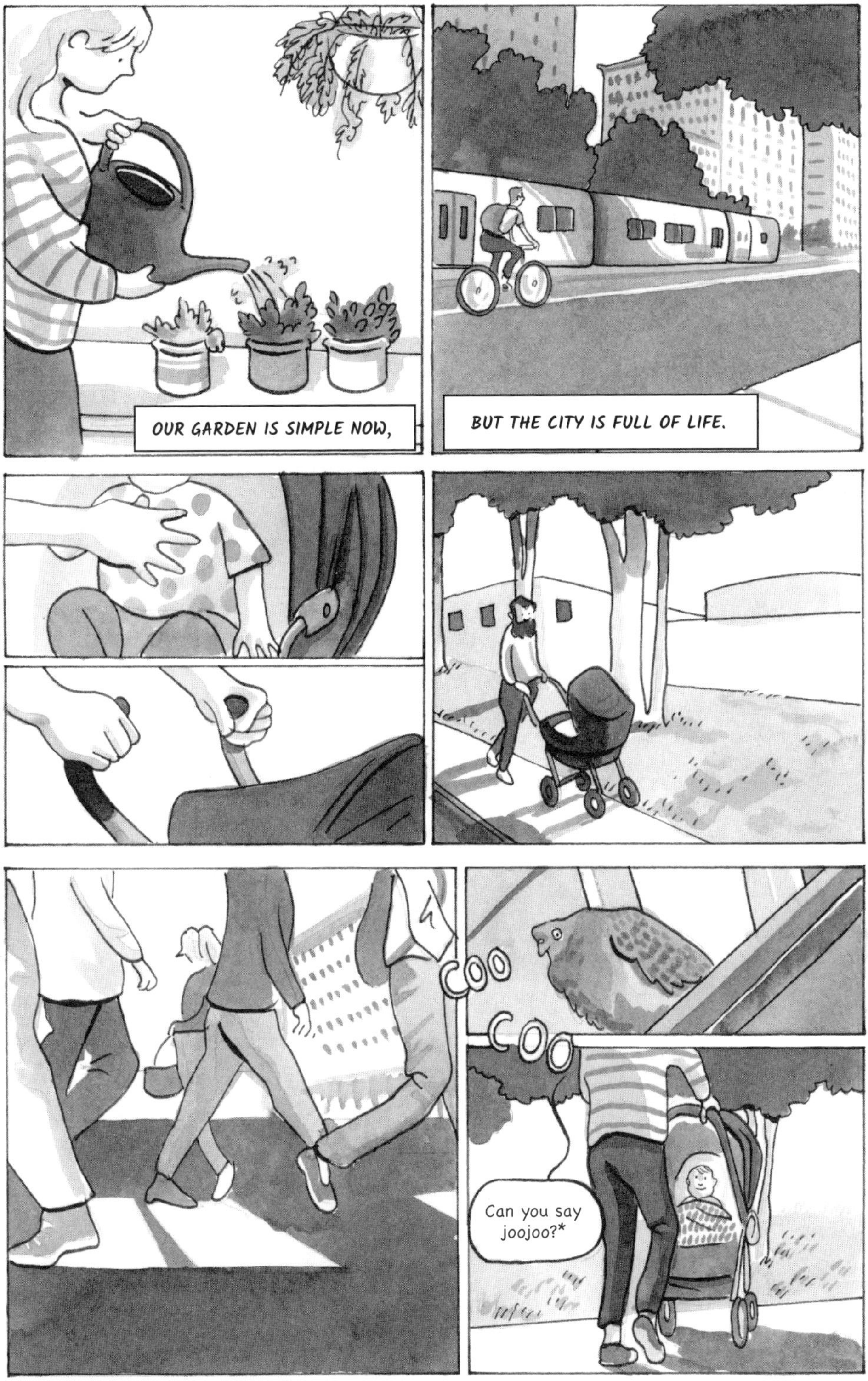
OUR GARDEN IS SIMPLE NOW,
BUT THE CITY IS FULL OF LIFE.
COO
COO
Can you say joojoo?*

*BIRDIE IN FARSI

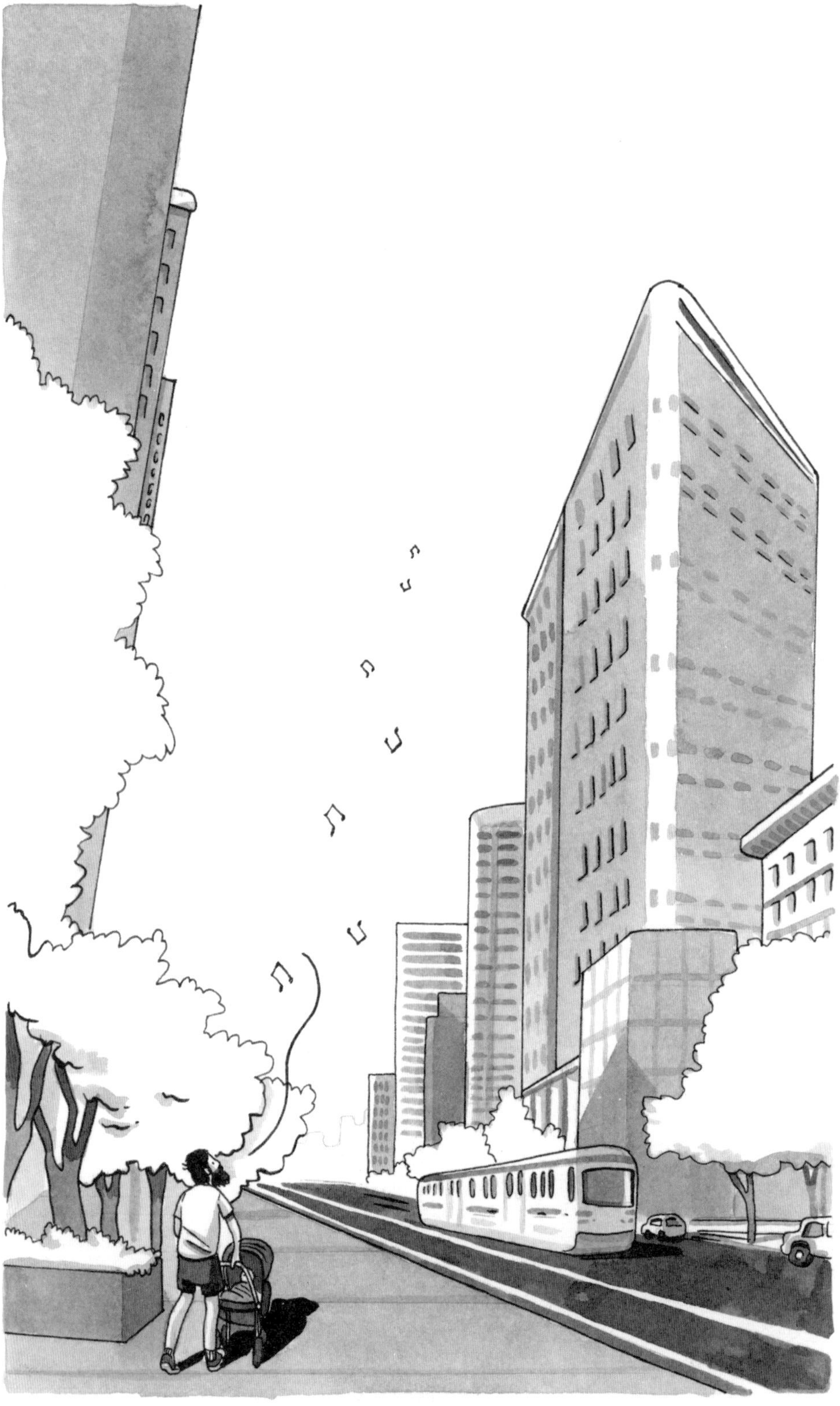

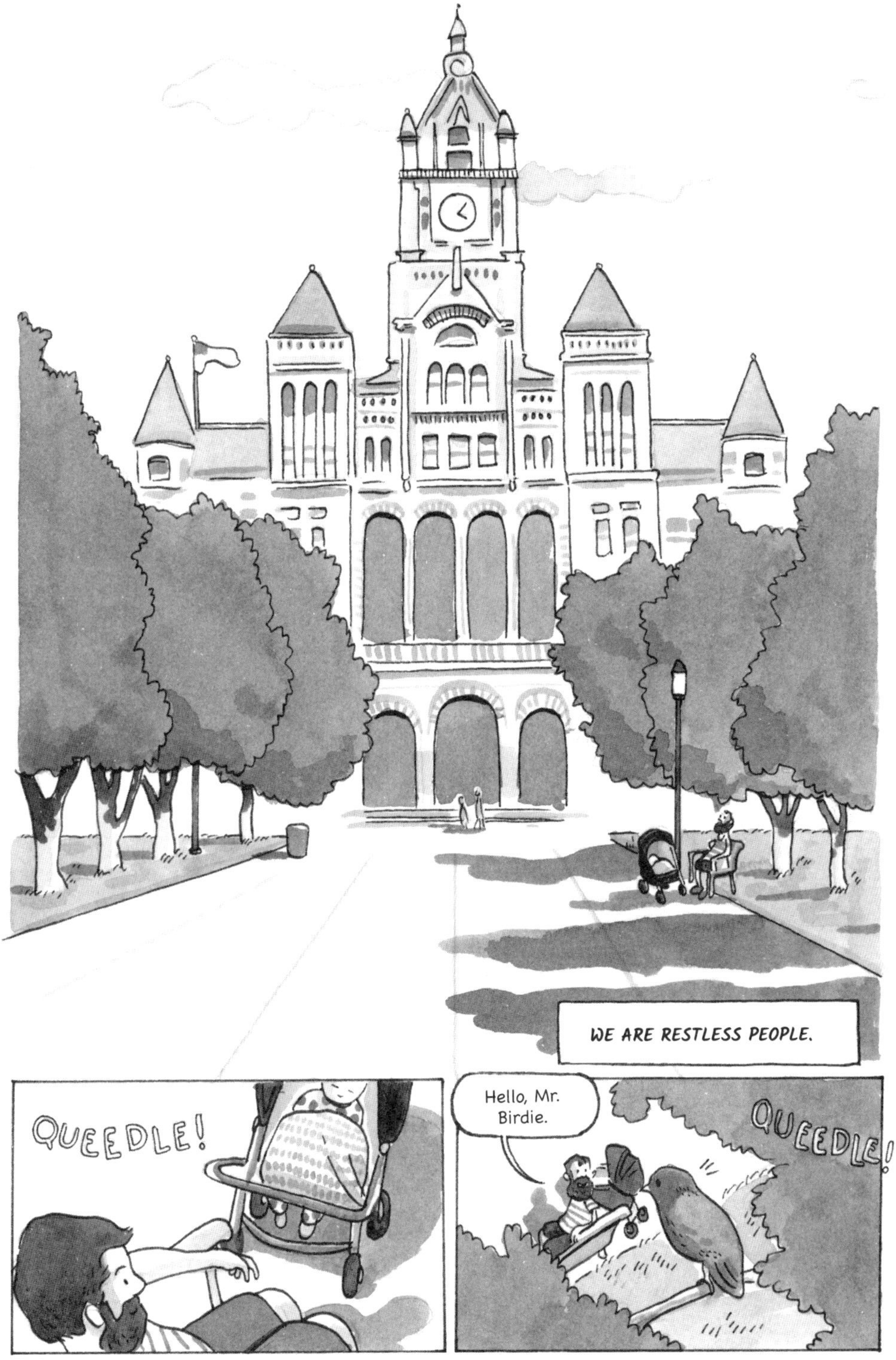
WE ARE RESTLESS PEOPLE.
QUEEDLE!
Hello, Mr. Birdie.
QUEEDLE!

BUT FOR A TIME, IN THE DESERT AND THE WOODS,

WE FOUND QUIET.

WE PLANTED SEEDS THAT GREW INTO
CAREERS AND FRIENDSHIPS,

AND WE BUILT A HOME.

FOR A FEW YEARS, WE HAD TIME.

EPILOGUE

Spring 2022

THE DRIVE FROM SALT LAKE CITY TO OUR CABIN IS FOUR HOURS.

Are we there yet?

WE'RE GOING FOR THE LAST TIME BEFORE WE SELL IT.

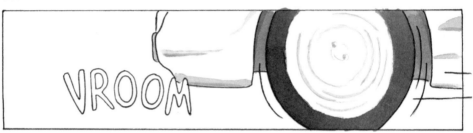

VROOM

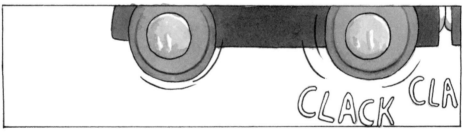

CLACK CLA

ELIKA IS THREE NOW. SHE IS A CITY KID.

CLACK

Can I watch my show?

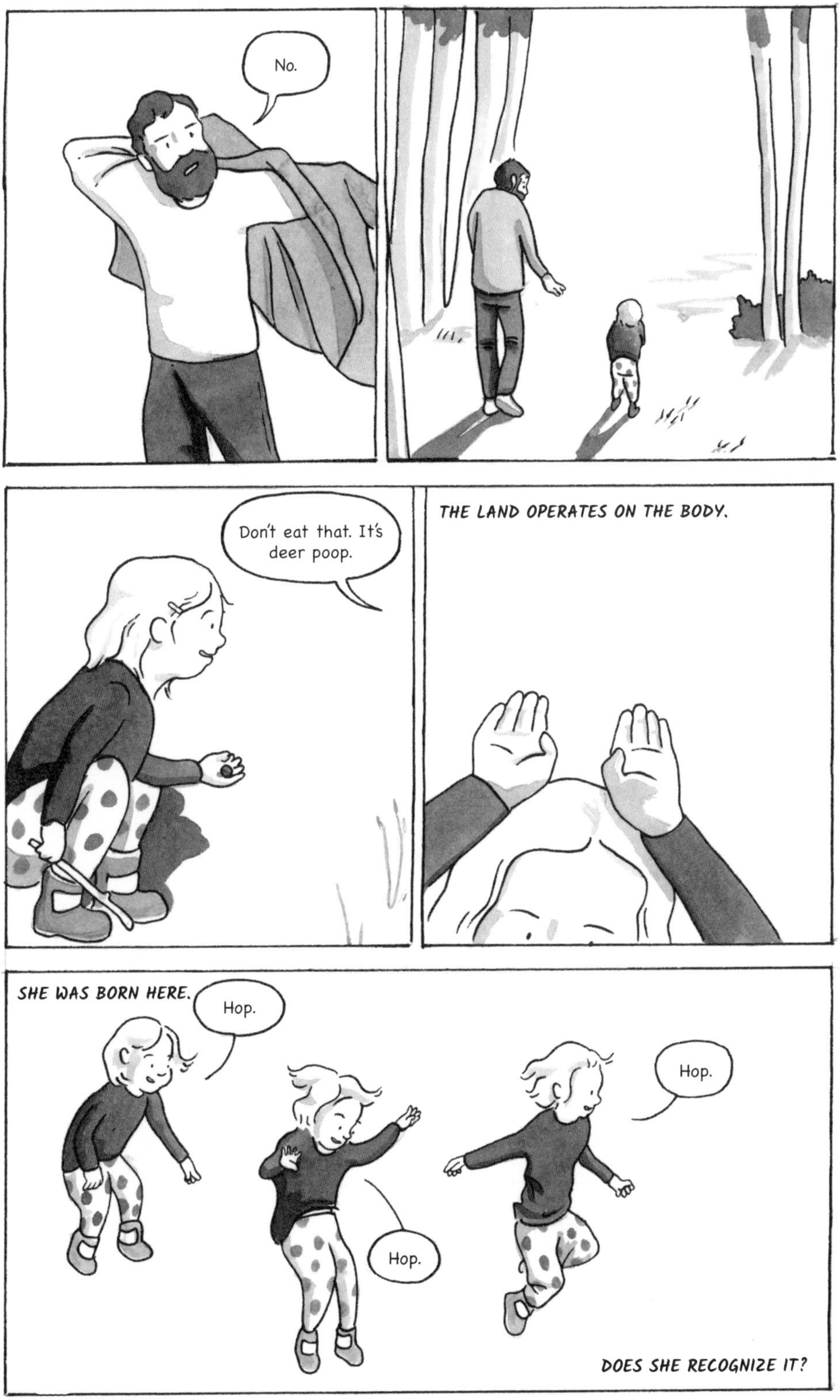
No.
Don't eat that. It's deer poop.
THE LAND OPERATES ON THE BODY.
SHE WAS BORN HERE.
Hop.
Hop.
Hop.
DOES SHE RECOGNIZE IT?

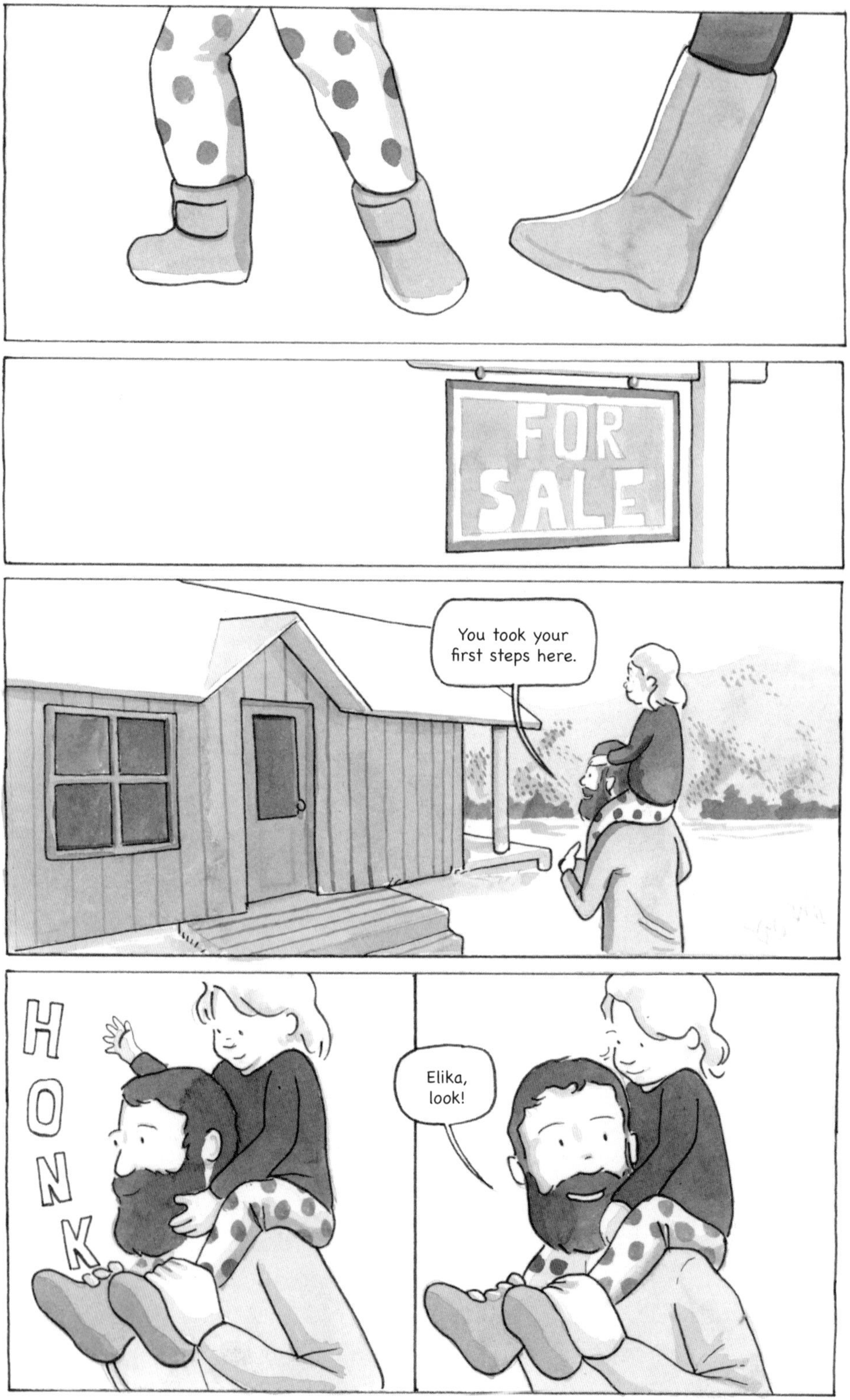
FOR SALE
You took your first steps here.
HONK
Elika, look!

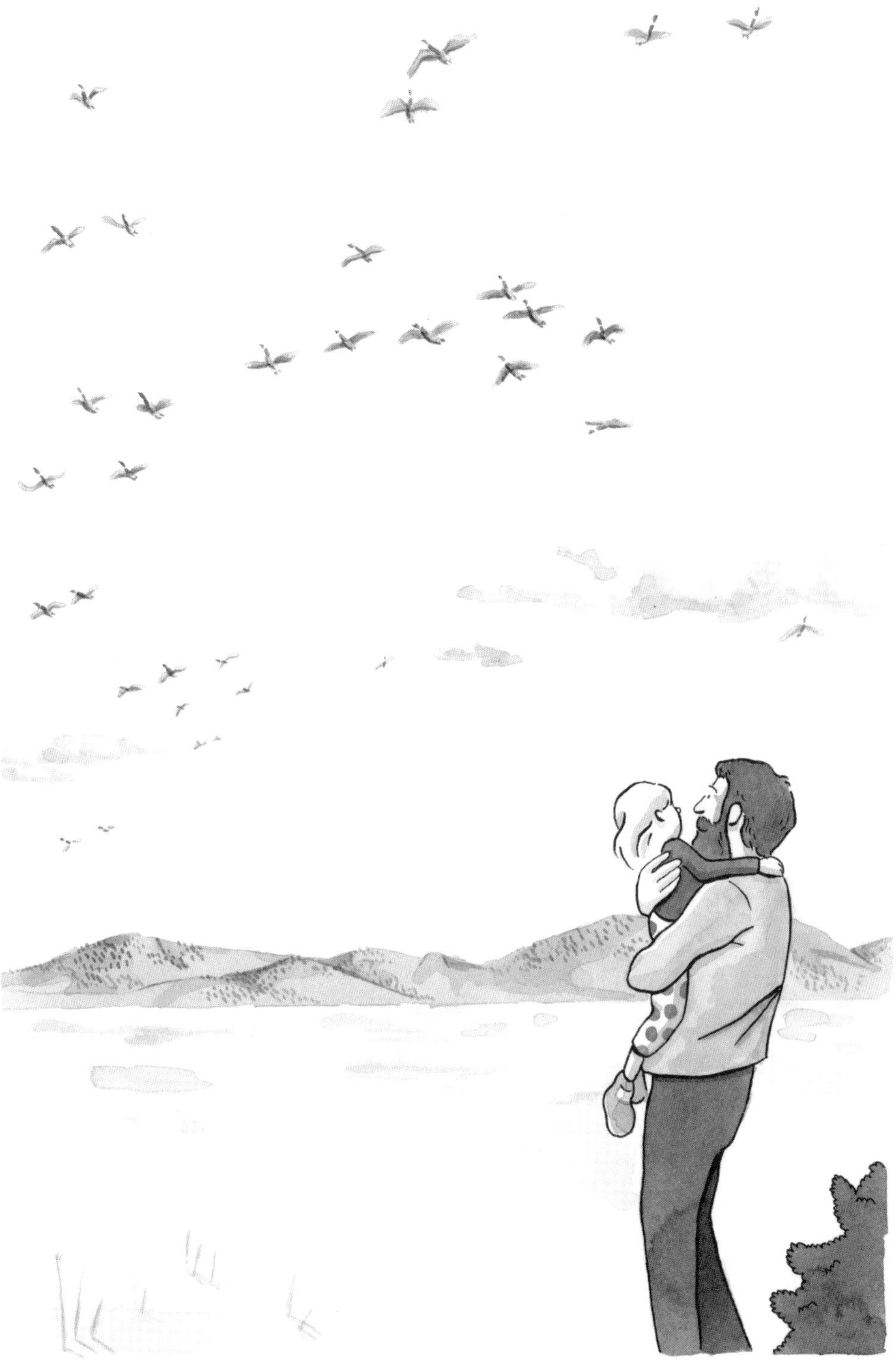

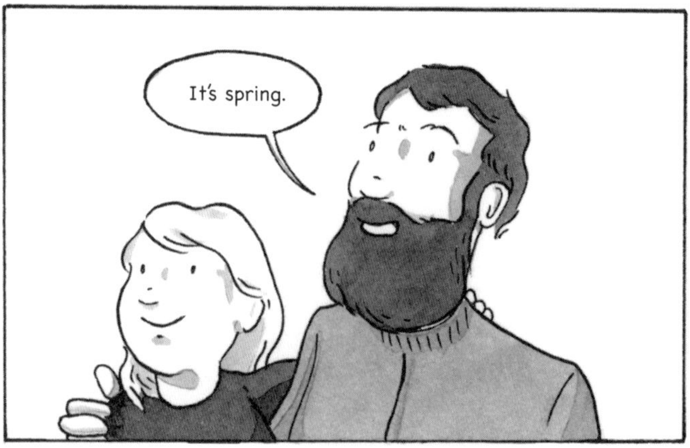
It's spring.

Acknowledgments

Cartooning can be a lonely business. Writing a book filled with cartoons while living in Salt Lake City, Utah, can be the loneliest. Thankfully, cartoonists are also a supportive community (strangely so—what ARE you all after?). Thank you, Ellis Rosen, Brendan Loper, Jared Nangle, Asher Perlman, Kendra Allenby, Zoe Si, Jeremy Nguyen, and Jon Adams for taking the time to read my manuscript and for your indispensable feedback, loving support, and humor. This book was conceived of and its first pages sketched in Amy Kurzweil's graphic memoir course in the summer of 2020. I still don't know what I am doing, but whatever I do know, it is thanks to you, Amy. Sofia Warren, thank you for reading my manuscript not once, not twice, but thrice. You were the first person to read any of my script and the only person to call me out on my pretentious "flexing." To my non-cartooning friends and loved ones who read my book, Bryn, Adriana and Richard, Christian, Jonathan, Ari and Molly, Brian and Betsy, and Tom, thank you and I love you (even though you're not cartoonists). And to the *New Yorker* and Emma Allen in particular, thank you. I became a cartoonist the day you bought a cartoon from me, so, in some sense, this book is your fault.

To my agent, Dan, this book would literally not exist if it weren't for you. Thank you for championing me and my vision, and for helping me realize my dad's lifelong dream of me writing a book. And to Jason Katzenstein, thank you for introducing us.

Thank you to everyone at Princeton Architectural Press for taking a chance on me. To Kristen Hewitt, my editor, thank you for your patience, wisdom, and deadlines. You "got" what I was trying to do and helped me turn memory into story.

Thank you to MacDowell for the residency and for giving me the chance to finish the book in your woods. And to Yellow Bird Artscape and La Napoule Art Foundation for your support.

My mom and dad have each asked that the book be dedicated to one of them. I hope a public apology here for constantly complaining about them sending me to art class in middle school will suffice. You were just two immigrant kids when you became parents, and I am continually amazed at how little you fucked up. Mojdeh, I can't tell you how lucky I feel to be your baby brother and the butt of your many pranks growing up.

Emelie, this book is basically about you. I would still be a teacher in the Bay Area (instead of drawing cartoons about dog butts) if not for you and your sense of wonder and adventure. Thank you for, like, everything.

Finally, to my daughter, Elika: in many ways, I wrote this book for you. I hope it will serve as a record of a period of your life that you will not remember. I love you. (You can read it when you're old enough to see an illustrated penis.)

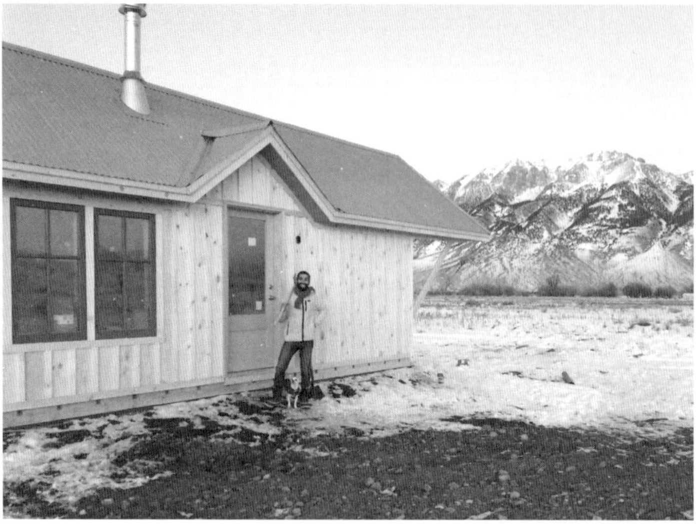

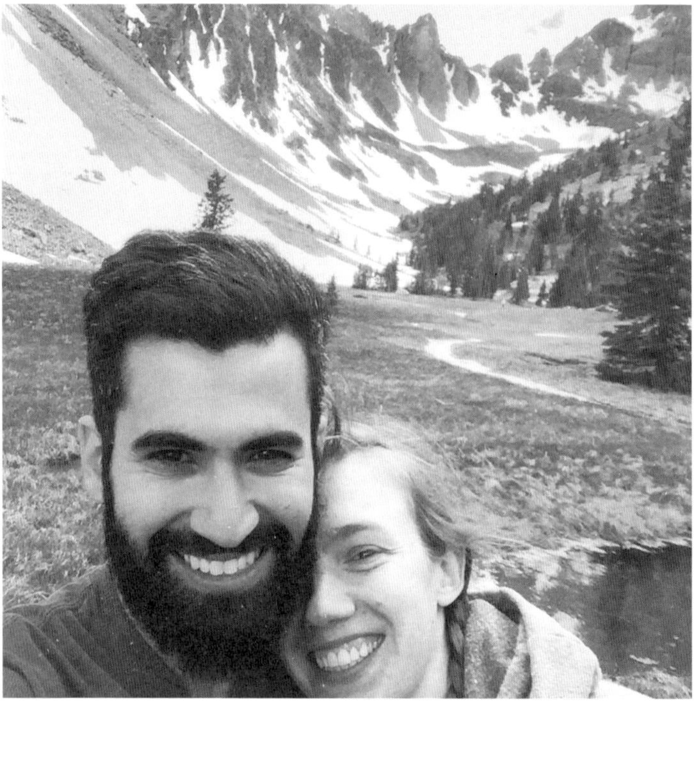

Author Bio

Navied Mahdavian has been a contributing cartoonist at the *New Yorker* since 2018. His work has also been published in *Reader's Digest, Wired,* and *Alta Online* and in the books *The Rejection Collection* and *Send Help!* Before becoming a cartoonist, he taught the fifth grade where he learned most of his jokes. Mahdavian was born in Miami and lives in Salt Lake City, Utah.

While this book is nonfiction, some names of people and places have been changed, some events have been compressed, and some dialogue has been recreated from memory.

Published by
Princeton Architectural Press
A division of Chronicle Books LLC
70 West 36th Street
New York, NY 10018
www.papress.com

Printed and bound in China
26 25 24 23 4 3 2 1 First edition

Editor: Kristen Hewitt
Designer: Natalie Snodgrass

Library of Congress Cataloging-in-Publication Data
Names: Mahdavian, Navied, 1985– author.
Title: This country : searching for home in (very) rural America / Navied Mahdavian.
Description: First edition. | New York : Princeton Architectural Press, [2023] | Summary: "A gorgeously illustrated debut graphic memoir about belonging, identity, and making a home in the remote American West"—Provided by publisher.
Identifiers: LCCN 2022059597 (print) | LCCN 2022059598 (ebook) | ISBN 9781797223674 (paperback) | ISBN 9781797227016 (ebook)
Subjects: LCSH: Mahdavian, Navied, 1985– | Cartoonists—United States—Biography—Comic books, strips, etc. | Identity (Psychology)--Comic books, strips, etc. | National characteristics, American—Comic books, strips, etc. | West (U.S.)—Comic books, strips, etc. | LCGFT: Autobiographical comics.
Classification: LCC PN6727.M23428 Z46 2023 (print) | LCC PN6727.M23428 (ebook) | DDC 741.5/973 [B]--dc23/eng/20221212
LC record available at https://lccn.loc.gov/2022059597
LC ebook record available at https://lccn.loc.gov/2022059598